BLACK AMERICA:
Geographic Perspectives

Robert T. Ernst is a professor in the Department of Geography and Geology at Eastern Michigan University. His research interests include urban social problems in central city situations and philosophy of geography. Lawrence Hugg is in the Geography Department at Michigan State University.

BLACK AMERICA:
Geographic Perspectives

EDITED BY

Robert T. Ernst and Lawrence Hugg

ANCHOR BOOKS
Anchor Press / Doubleday
Garden City, New York
1976

The Anchor Press edition is the first publication of BLACK AMERICA: GEOGRAPHIC PERSPECTIVES
Anchor Books edition: 1976
ISBN: 0-385-05536-6
Library of Congress Catalog Card Number 74-15783
Copyright © 1976 by Doubleday & Company, Inc.
All Rights Reserved
Printed in the United States of America
First Edition

Grateful acknowledgment is made to the following contributors for permission to reprint the material contained within this book:

William Bunge for "Racism in Geography," *The Crisis*, 72 (October 1965). Reprinted with permission of the Crisis Publishing Company.

Richard L. Morrill and O. Fred Donaldson for "Geographical Perspectives on the History of Black America." Reprinted by permission of *Economic Geography*.

Harold M. Rose for "The Origin and Pattern of Development of Urban Black Social Areas." Reprinted by permission from *Journal of Geography*, 68 (September 1969).

John Fraser Hart for "The Changing Distribution of the American Negro," *Annals*, 50 (September 1960). Reproduced by permission from the *Annals* of the Association of American Geographers, Volume 50, 1960.

Mark Lowry II for "Population and Race in Mississippi, 1940–1969," *Annals*, 61 (September 1971). Reproduced by permission from the *Annals* of the Association of American Geographers, Volume 61, 1971.

Harold M. Rose for "Metropolitan Miami's Changing Negro Population, 1950–1960," *Economic Geography*, Volume 40, No. 3, 1964. Reprinted by permission of *Economic Geography*.

Ralph A. Sanders and John S. Adams for "Age Structure in Expanding Ghetto Space: Cleveland, Ohio, 1940–1965," *Southeastern Geographer*, Volume 11, No. 2 (1971). Reprinted by permission of *Southeastern Geographer*.

Louis Seig for "Concepts of 'Ghetto': A Geography of Minority Groups." Reproduced by permission from *The Professional Geographer* of the Association of American Geographers, Volume 23, 1971.

Harold M. Rose for "The Development of an Urban Subsystem: The Case of the Negro Ghetto." Reproduced by permission from the *Annals* of the Association of American Geographers, Volume 60, 1970.

J. Tait Davis for "Sources of Variation in Housing Values in Washington, D.C." Reprinted from *Geographical Analysis*, Volume 3, (January 1971), pp. 63–76. Copyright © 1971 by the Ohio State University Press. All rights reserved.

William H. Brown, Jr., for "Access to Housing: The Role of the Real Estate Industry." Reprinted by permission of *Economic Geography*.

Allan Pred for "Business Thoroughfares as Expressions of Urban Negro Culture." Reprinted by permission from *Economic Geography*.

Harold M. Rose for "The Structure of Retail Trade in a Racially Changing Trade Area." Reprinted from *Geographical Analysis*, Volume 2 (April 1970), pp. 135–48. Copyright © 1970 by the Ohio State University Press. All rights reserved.

James O. Wheeler for "Transportation Problems in Negro Ghettos." Reprinted by permission from *Sociology and Social Research: An International Journal.*

Howard G. Salisbury for "The State Within a State: Some Comparisons Between the Urban Ghetto and the Insurgent State." Reproduced by permission from *The Professional Geographer* of the Association of American Geographers, Volume 23 (April 1971).

Stanley D. Brunn and Wayne L. Hoffman for "The Spatial Response of Negroes and Whites Toward Open Housing: The Flint Referendum." Reproduced by permission from the *Annals* of the Association of American Geographers, Volume 40 (March 1970).

Michael A. Jenkins and John W. Shepherd for "Decentralizing High School Administration in Detroit: An Evaluation of Alternative Strategies of Political Control." Reprinted by permission from *Economic Geography.*

John S. Adams for "The Geography of Riots and Civil Disorders in the 1960s." Reprinted by permission from *Economic Geography.*

Donald I. Warren for "Neighborhood Structure and Riot Behavior in Detroit: Some Exploratory Findings." Reprinted by permission from *Social Problems.* Copyright © 1969 by *Social Problems.*

Paul S. Salter and Robert C. Mings, "A Geographic Aspect of the 1968 Miami Racial Disturbance: A Preliminary Investigation." Reproduced by permission from *The Professional Geographer* of the Association of American Geographers, Volume 21 (March 1969).

Reynolds Farley for map, "The Changing Distribution of Negroes Within Metropolitan Areas: The Emergence of Black Suburbs." Copyright © 1970 by the University of Chicago Press. All rights reserved. Reprinted by permission from the University of Chicago Press.

Harold M. Rose for "The All-Negro Town: Its Evolution and Function." Reprinted by permission from *Geographical Review.*

James O. Wheeler and Stanley D. Brunn for "Negro Migration Into Rural Southwestern Michigan." Reprinted by permission from *Geographical Review.*

Contents

Preface

BLACK AMERICA is a collage of topics, issues and problems which have become important in all the social sciences. With this book, the authors introduce students to the role of geography in research on black America. As this text is introductory in nature, materials from some of the articles have been extracted, particularly maps, tables, and statistical formulae. The decision to exclude these materials was a very difficult one for geographers; nevertheless, cost considerations necessitated it. However, it is the authors' hope that students will become interested enough in many articles to read the unedited originals.

This book is meant to serve as a supplementary text for a variety of geography courses, particularly, urban, economic, political, and cultural. It is also hoped that it will be used in other social science courses on black America.

Introduction

The social geography of ethnic and racial minorities in the United States has become, in recent decades, a topic of much interest and research specialization among American geographers. Reflecting this interest is a growing body of literature concerning the spatial behavior and characteristics of such minority groups. Much current geographic research on minority groups is focused specifically on black Americans. The majority of these articles deal with three major facets of black locational experience: rural to urban migration, inner city ghetto systems, and changing urban-suburban environments. However, numerous works have appeared which have concentrated on other themes of black America. Unfortunately, despite these many statements on the nature and approaches to the geographic study of race, rarely does one find a chapter or section of a text devoted to the subject; most of the research is published in scattered articles and monographs in the geographic literature.

The principal intention of this book is to collect and assess some significant works concerning areal aspects of black America. It is hoped that this collation will make possible or at least facilitate an understanding of geography's contribution to racial research. Although areal factors of race long have been neglected by geographers, the multiplicity of current publications and research on the subject are worthy of detailed examination and analysis.

It is unfortunate that geography had to wait until the 1960s and 1970s for the seminal contributions of Hart, Rose, and Morrill. One wonders why the monumental studies of John Dollard, Kenneth Clark, and Gunnar Myrdal did not create waves of sympathetic vibration influencing research in geography as they did in sociology, anthropology, psychology, and political science. Perhaps the conservatism of geography in the United States is partially to blame. Possibly geographers were wary of being stung philosophically and intellectually as they were by the environmental determinism of years past.

Whatever the causes or influences, geographers contributed very little to racial literature prior to the 1950s. C. Warren Thornwaithe and Richard Hartshorne did submit articles on the subject in 1934 and 1938 respectively, but their efforts were largely ignored; fertile seed falling on fallow ground.

However, since the late 1940s, geographic interest in racial topics gradually built to a peak in the 1970s. From 1949 to 1970, a total of two hundred eighty-three articles on the geography of race appeared. One hundred eighty-four articles (or 65 per cent of the total) were published between 1968 and 1970, and of these forty-four (or almost 35 per cent) were theses and dissertations. Thus, research in the geography of black America is being emphasized strongly at the graduate level, indicating that many young geographers are developing research interests in locational aspects of race. An interest which, if sustained, should result in the continuation of the current trend in the publication of numerous articles of significance to all geographers.

The articles in this book are structured into chapters dealing with singular aspects of areal organization of black American society. Emphasis is placed upon geographic phenomena resulting from man's occupance of the earth. These human-social geographic features include population, settlement, politics, and economics. Many of the works compiled here are concerned with various locational aspects of the urban environment. This focus on the geography of cities becomes more and more important as the number of urban residents and resulting problems increase.

The articles included in this anthology were chosen for two primary reasons. First, individual articles were selected for pertinence and quality of their research contributions to the literature on racial geography. Second, special emphasis was placed on articles utilizing divergent techniques in geographic research investigating spatial patterns and processes of black America. A combination of descriptive, statistical, and theoretical work allows this book to present to introductory students many aspects of current geographic methodology.

BLACK AMERICA:
Geographic Perspectives

CHAPTER I

Geography of Black America:
An Overview

INTRODUCTORY NOTE

The first chapter is designed as a microcosm of the geographic study of black America. The several research themes which are introduced are intended to orient the reader to the nature, extent, and applicability of geographic research to black America. Many students of geography and social science in general are not aware of contributions geographers have made to racial research. Consequently, the first chapter is a general overview consisting of three articles concerned with specific aspects of black environment in the United States.

William Bunge's article deals with racism in geography and attempts to reveal both subtle and blatant white ethnocentrism in the discipline. This inherent attitude of superiority of the Caucasian race, accompanied by a lack of concern for other racial and ethnic groups, has long pervaded the minds and works of Western geographers.

Bunge presents a reasoned and grimly humorous exposé of the often subconscious attitudes in geography that are falsely enshrined as knowledge. The most dangerous form of ethnocentrism in geography is not overt bigotry, which can be identified or refuted easily; rather, concealed or subconscious racism is one of geography's most serious problems; as these attitudes are so inbred and disguised they are very difficult to counteract.

Particularly distasteful is arrogance attached to the concept of "discovery." Bunge states that "For us to maintain that Marco Polo 'discovered' China is a bit like Sitting Bull claiming he 'discovered' Washington, D.C., on his trip there." Other terms described as equally ethnocentric are: Darkest Africa, natives and settlers, and barbarism and civilization.

Emotion-laden pseudo-intellectual racism in geography is brought to full view by Bunge and excoriated mercilessly. What Bunge wishes geographers to do is to admit that in a country where racism is institutionalized individuals seldom if ever escape its tenacles unaffected. But even more important it is necessary first to understand and counter racism within oneself before it can be defeated elsewhere.

William Bunge, providing a different perspective on geographers and their attitudes, poses several very difficult questions that geographers must resolve before turning their attention to utilizing spatial analysis in contributing to solution of racial problems in contemporary society. Unfortunately, most geographers would rather discuss and analyze the distribution of race than patterns of bigotry and racism. Hopefully, ignorance and prejudice that foster racism and ethnocentrism are waning and future geographic thought will be free from these anti-intellectual problems.

The article by Morrill and Donaldson is concerned with the historical geography of blacks in the United States. The authors view the United States as a dual society of a white majority that regards itself as superior to a black minority that has experienced centuries of subjugation, discrimination, and weakness.

> The inferiority-superiority relationship has been manifested spatially by separate institutions and facilities for blacks and whites, and by segregation of living space enforced either by law or by community pressure and custom.

Morrill and Donaldson examine pertinent geographic aspects of black America through time, and identify as particularly important changing black population distributions, regional variation in the social environment of blacks, and development of segregation and black ghettos.

The article's analysis begins in colonial America and continues to the 1970s, documenting initial black resistance to slavery, the plantation oligopoly that made slavery a profitable institution, internal slave breeding and migration, slave rebellions, sociopolitical conditions in post-Civil War South, economic slavery of tenancy and sharecropping, the great rural South to urban North and West migrations, relative deprivation of blacks after World War II, and failure of recent federal government legislation initiating programs meant to alleviate urban poverty and segregation.

Morrill and Donaldson present a general but well-structured article that does justice to one of the most important topics in geography today: analysis of black America from a historical-areal perspective. And, although the article is somewhat brief in developing the racial topics it examines, it serves two useful purposes. It is a well-documented introduction to the historical geography of black America. And it contains a substantial non-geographic but spatially oriented bibliography on black America that can be used by students for more detailed research into specific questions.

In the past, urban geographers largely have ignored studying roles and problems of black urban residents and the territorial space they occupy. Recent wide-scale population redistributions occurring in the United States, with blacks moving into central cities and whites escaping to suburbs, and many and varied interracial conflicts have roused geographers to analyzing the resulting multifaceted urban racial environment.

Harold Rose has long illustrated geographic problems of blacks in the city in many publications. In "The Origin and Pattern of Development of Urban Black Social Areas," Rose presents an areal view of existing racial patterns in the urban social milieu in order to further comprehension of the nature and extent of recent conflicts which have evolved within the metropolitan complex. Rose visualizes black ghettos as extensions and evolutions of territorially based ethnic communities that have been a common phenomenon in American society. To facilitate this analysis, Rose examines in detail the evolution of the ghetto, its persistence, continuous expansion, geographic pattern in the United States, and spatial-social conditions found in urban black social areas.

In the article's conclusion, Rose states that although the long-range future of black ghettos is highly speculative, these areas are likely to become increasingly territorially based at a time when such social communities are declining in numbers and importance. Rose further concludes: "If this is the case, one can only expect a widening of the drift that has led to the social ferment in the cities."

RACISM IN GEOGRAPHY

William Bunge

Racism has a long history in geography. Even such an outstanding geographer as Mackinder was infected with it. Today, with the knowledge of many tropical empires in mind, the professional geographer can hardly help but guffaw at claims that the Tropics produce lower intelligence. In fact, civilization has never been this far North before and considering the way we blond, Nordic, super-duper types are conducting ourselves in this world, this might be as far North as anyone takes it. The myth of innate inferiority of the Slavs has been hard to sustain in the face of the Teutonic defeat of World War II and the recent space feats. The Jews are obviously great. This evidence is so overwhelming that some racists now claim the Jews are racially superior in order to reinforce the Principle of Racism and, besides, these same racists might feel that in the last generation they burned up enough Jews to reduce their "threat" to insignificance compared to, say, the Negroes.

Unfortunately, blatant Hitlerian theories are not the only forms of racist expression that find their way into geography. Subtler and more difficult forms exist. It is these hidden trends, so deeply imbued in our culture that they are often subconscious, to which I wish to draw the attention of my colleagues.

Robert Alexander, then a fellow graduate student at the University of Washington, used to tell the story of a Negro member of an expedition in southwestern United States. This man was so infected with white chauvinism that he claimed that he was the "first white man" to climb a certain mountain on route of march. Not only does racism infect Negroes; it infects Caucasians even more deeply. Alexander would then paint a picture of the Royal Ethiopian Explorers Society becoming fascinated with the "Problem of the Rhine." It seems no Ethiopian had ever navigated that river past the first cataract. The Ethiopians therefore mounted an expedition to discover the source of the Rhine by paddling up stream, claiming all lands adjacent thereto, bestowing trinkets on the natives and so forth. Hilarious versions of Alexander's turnabout have a serious side.

Consider the arrogance of the old globe that used to decorate my grandfather's library in La Crosse, Wisconsin. As a child I was fascinated by it and twirled it slowly, looking intently and letting my imagination carry me to the places under my finger. On this old globe rather large areas in the Arctic, Antarctic and Africa were in white color and marked with a mysterious "unexplored." I dreamed of exploring there. In retrospect this harmless fantasy has its less innocent side. "Unexplored" by whom? Surely the people that live there were not lost. Somehow through my childhood culture it seemed that it was the shame of the people in those areas, Eskimos and Africans, to have not been discovered. How backward of them for us not to have found them. The entire concept of the "Known World" comes into doubt. Every tribe, including those to whom our ancestors belonged, had a "Known World." Some of these "Known Worlds" were larger than others. It is doubtful that the Europeans had the largest "Known World" over most of history. The Chinese, the Incas, the Arabs and the Hausa had enormous "Known Worlds." In the end, the Europeans, with the help of local guides, completed the job of conventional exploration, but even here there are tremendous distortions of geography.

Not only are the great explorers of other countries ignored, such as the various Chinese expeditions, but certain out-and-out falsification dominates the education system up to and including some graduate schools. For instance, did the Europeans, especially Portuguese, Dutch, and English, really "discover" East Africa, India, and Indonesia? Did not the Arabs have a complete system of trade and colonization? Did not Mohammedanism reach Jakarta before Christianity? In fact, is there not evidence that the Portuguese were not the first to travel around Africa, rather the Arabs and perhaps the Phoenicians, traveling from East to West.

Who did "round the Horn?" You might argue that many mature geographers question grade school certificates. I would counterargue that only partly is the grade school damage undone and I would further argue that as the highest guardian of geographic standards in the country, we have responsibility, even a mission, to these younger minds. After all, there are millions and millions being misled in their youth and only a handful partly corrected later.

The entire idea of "discovering" someone smacks of arrogance. Discovery is always mutual. For us to maintain that Marco Polo "discovered" China is a bit like Sitting Bull claiming he "discovered" Washington, D.C., on his trip there. Italy was a poor and relatively backward place. It was not just the splendor of the Chinese court that made China the Land of Opportunity compared to Italy. China had a higher standard of living. Its farmers were better off. Italy with its tiny squabbling states and the even tinier state of Venice, a pipsqueak place no bigger than a minor subprovince of China, hardly discovered China.

Somehow the white explorers of the Americas "discovered" quinine, rubber, and so forth. Ridiculous! The culturally-deprived white men were patiently instructed by knowledgeable American Indians in the areas of European ignorance. Gratefully and humbly, a sixteenth-century Marshall Plan, the Europeans took their knowledge home with them praising the savants of the New World as fellow Learned Men. The racism and arrogance of the term "Darkest Africa." Dark to whom? The great empires of Western Africa? Timbuctoo had a higher form of government, law, and some claim ethical religion in 1400, than Paris.

What about Darkest America? Have we adequately mapped our poverty, lynchings . . . need I go on? Has exploration ended? Does the mapping of the mountains, rivers and coastlines end the job? Notice how, when Caucasians give diseases to native peoples with low resistances, it seems the Natives are weak compared to the Settlers; a sort of Caucasian Darwinian satisfaction is somehow conveyed to the child. "It's too bad those Eskimos, Indians, or whoever, just couldn't stand the disease we white men so easily handle such as smallpox and TB." Survival of the fittest. But when the shoe is on the other foot, when the Natives give the Settler the disease, such as the decimation that syphilis, evidently a gift from the American Indians, caused in Europe before immunities developed, such decimations are because the dirty people gave us a dirty disease.

In some cases we simply revert to an out-and-out environmentalism and dub our white biological collapse a "tropical disease." This is similar to the German explanation that the Cold Russian Winters were defeating them. Was it warmer on the Russian side? "Inferior Whites are overcome by mild diseases here in the Congo since Darwin and God bestowed powers of resistance on we Chosen Black People." How's that for turnabout? The "Yellow Menace" indeed. It is the whites who have exploded their population from 15 per cent to 30 per cent. It is the whites who have conquered and ravaged much of the earth's surface. The human race faces the "White Menace."

The entire matter of Settlers and Natives needs exposure. Natives are the people who were called the Settlers by the people who were there before them. In South Africa the situation is confused. The whites and the Bantu both were migrating into the area at the same time. This made the Bushmen the natives. The American Indian is obviously a Native of Asia

and a Settler in the New World. Americans seem to attach great importance to the length of their families' time in this country, very similar to
the whites in the Union of South Africa, provided their ancestry does not
go back too far! The whole subject of human migration is only partially
taught. America is not a white country. With the new diffusion techniques
in geography why not map the races of the future? When and where will
the last blond or black man live, with appropriate probabilities attached,
of course?

It is a geographical fact that the blood types from Europe to Africa
shade off imperceptibly. Why indeed are Italians swarthy? We almost all
refute Hitler's pure race theory. This means that we accept an impure race
theory. If all our ancestors could come to life in a place would all of them
be white? If 85 per cent of Americans of African ancestry have white
blood, do not whites have African? After three hundred years of cohabitation have no Negroes passed as white? Why has geography been so
negligent in producing a map of race mixing in this country? Intrepid explorers, off to Alabama with you and your blood kits!

Why is it that almost every child knows where the English Americans
got off the boat? Plymouth Rock. Yet almost none of us is much English
and no one seems to know where anyone else got off the boat. Sophisticated geographers can tell you the Germans disembarked in Baltimore,
but what of the bulk of the American people? Where did the Poles get on
and off? The Africans? Are not the Africans our forefathers? Perhaps
teaching the geography of America's settlers, both voluntary and involuntary, would open too many questions, such as, should not the African have
a quota on the migration system? (What am I trying to do, make the
problem worse? Just when we were getting "them" sort of lightened up.)
Who did contribute the most to our culture? Would you describe 1965
America as more akin to our Puritan or our Ashanti forefathers? Flow
maps from Africa, Puerto Rico, Ireland and Russia, please.

Somehow, by no seeming design, which is the most convincing way, we
obtain the childhood impression that historic geography has always shone
on our personal biological ancestors. Unless we are Italian, and even then
hardly for sure, we were not at the Pope's side defending the Holy from
the Barbarians. Our ancestors were the Barbarians! Our naked and savage
ancestors sacked and raped the Civilized World. Somehow we gain this
strange historic-geographic dream that "our" people were in Western
Europe starting with the Renaissance. Before that "our" people were in
Rome building great roads. Before that "our" people were in Greece, not
as the dominant group of slaves, of course, but sitting around the temples
calculating the shape and size of the earth. The Torch of Civilization just
followed us about the map, didn't it? How incredibly naive, yet I insist

this is the emotional-intellectual impression that "somehow" our American culture passes to its young.

This is a polemic with a purpose. If any readers share, even in part, these misgivings or have others they wish to raise, please write to me so that we can consider further action. For instance, if enough support develops, we can petition our Association to commission a study group leading to missionary work among the nation's school systems. Perhaps the International Geographical Union or the appropriate agencies of the United Nations could be enlisted. Whatever you suggest.

GEOGRAPHICAL PERSPECTIVES ON THE HISTORY
OF BLACK AMERICA

Richard L. Morrill and O. Fred Donaldson

Before it became wealthy, before it became powerful, before it became the United States, America was black and white. The first non-Indian permanent settlers in America may have been blacks, slaves who fled from a Spanish colony near the Pedee (now Peedee) River, South Carolina, in 1526 [1, p. 163]. As the British began to dominate the profitable trade established by the Spanish and Portuguese—the purchase of black from black—more and more slaves were imported, mainly into the Southern colonies and states. And as the number of slaves increased, so of course did the number of rebellions, some culminating in arson, violence, or death. The Thirteenth, Fourteenth, and Fifteenth Amendments, passed after the Civil War, acknowledged the American black as a free human being, an enfranchised citizen of the country he had helped to shape. The amendments did not suggest to him the way to free himself of ignorance, poverty, and laws created by whites to protect their supremacy, or the irrational fears of human prejudices.

As headlines and newscasts make clear every week, the relationship of black and white in the multi-racial United States is still evolving; so great is the concern that most Americans believe blacks represent much more than 11 per cent of the American population. Still, that 11 per cent, twenty-three million citizens, most inescapably distinguished by color, is a very significant and obvious minority, particularly when it is highly concentrated in specific cities and in certain areas of the country (Table 1).

America has a dual society—a white majority which regards itself as superior and which traditionally has enjoyed almost total economic, social, and political power, and a black minority which was early proclaimed inferior and which has suffered centuries of subjugation, discrimination, and weakness. The inferiority-superiority relationship has been manifested

TABLE 1
Regional Summary of the Development of the Black Population

Date	South	Northeast	North Central*	West	U.S.
Proportion of Black Population by Region					
1790	91	9			
1850	97	2	1		
1910	89	5	6		
1940	77	11	11	1	
1960	60	16	18	6	
1970	53	19	20	8	
Percent of Regional Population Black					
1790	32	6			19
1850	39	2	1		16
1910	30	2	2	1	11
1940	24	4	4	1	10
1960	21	7	7	4	11
1970	19	9	8	5	11
Percent of Black Population Urban					
1910	21	85	72	80	27
1940	35	90	87	85	48
1960	59	95	96	93	73
Total Black Population (000s)					
1790	700	67			767
1850	3534	149	44	11	3639
1910	8749	489	543	51	9828
1940	9905	1370	1420	171	12866
1960	11308	3029	3445	1071	18850
1970	12064	4342	4572	1695	22673

Source: United States Censuses, 1790 to 1970.

*Excludes Missouri 1790 and 1850.

spatially by separate institutions and facilities for blacks and whites, and by segregation of living space enforced either by law or by community pressure and custom. Competition for jobs and for living space leads to overt conflict and to violence. Since the mid-1950s, the Civil Rights movement has not only heightened the amount and intensity of conflict, but also moved black and white closer to equality than anything else in the previous three centuries. For a time the ideal of integration led to attempts to desegregate housing as well as schools, jobs, and public accommodations; but white resistance, and the black's realistic fear of diluting his culture and power, have produced a countermovement, spatial separatism as one basis for black power.

A distinction of color need not, in theory, be of such overwhelming concern, but the realities of history and of human prejudice and behavior have made it so. The American dilemma, which Myrdal [28] explored so well, is how to ensure to black Americans the full fruits of citizenship. But inequality has so long been an institution, first in the extreme of legal slavery and later in a complex of discriminatory laws and customs, that a deep-seated fear and distrust continues to exist between black and white.

The purpose of this paper is to examine a number of geographic aspects of black America as they have developed through time; these include: the changing distribution of the black population from the period of slavery on southern plantations, to the recent period of migration to the cities and concentration in the ghettos; regional variations in the conditions, treatment, and revolts of black people; and finally the development of ghettos and other forms of segregation.

THE COLONIAL PERIOD, 1500 TO 1790

The Slave Trade. During the sixteenth century, many Portuguese, Spanish, and later British plantations in the New World became short of labor. Disease, enslavement, and overwork had so decimated the Amerindian population that the importing of slaves from Africa to the colonies came rather early (they had been imported earlier to Portugal and Spain) [23, p. 25]. From European trading posts in Senegal, Gold Coast, Ivory Coast, and Slave Coast (mainly Nigeria), Portuguese, and in the seventeenth century, British and Dutch companies began to purchase slaves from local rulers, generally in exchange for European manufactured goods (especially clothing, metal goods, spirits, and weapons). These slaves were sometimes criminals or debtors but usually captives taken during conflicts among the West African states. Most went to Cuba and Brazil, but some were taken to Florida in the late sixteenth century.

Under Portuguese and Spanish rule, slaves were treated according to Roman law, with the right to purchase their freedom, and to own property [23, p. 26]. Black men often were on the Portuguese and Spanish trips of exploration, and traveled to many areas on the North American continent before 1619 [3, p. 360]. The first non-Indian permanent settlers in America may have been blacks, slaves who revolted and fled from a Spanish colony near the Pedee River, South Carolina, in 1526. Blacks helped build the city of St. Augustine, in 1565, and Cortes brought three hundred blacks with him to the California coast in 1737. In the sixteenth century, Estevanico, an African explorer with the Spanish expeditions, explored parts of Florida, New Mexico, and Arizona. The purpose of his last journey was to find "Cibola, or the Seven Cities of Gold."

Black Settlement. Continuous black settlement in America began with the landing of nineteen indentured black servants in Jamestown, Virginia, in 1619. At first, restrictive laws were few, and some purchased their freedom. By the end of the century, however, the traffic in slaves had increased. The number entering New York, New Jersey, and New England was small in comparison with the number entering Virginia to work on tobacco plantations, and the Carolinas to work on tobacco, indigo, and rice plantations [23, pp. 36–40]. Most of the plantations were very close to tidewater. Particularly productive were the Sea Islands along the Carolina coast. As more slaves were imported, the form of slavery soon became more restrictive. Under English law, slaves were mere property and had no human rights themselves.

After 1700 the demand for plantation products increased rapidly, as did the opening of new lands, and consequently the rate of slave importation. But the largest numbers of black slaves were still being taken to Brazil and Cuba and other islands of the Caribbean. In Senegal and particularly the Slave Coast and Guinea, the increasing demand for slaves soon led to cruel and destructive intertribal and interkingdom warfare, by which whole villages were sold into slavery and the countryside depopulated.

The British soon came to dominate the profitable slave trade. A kind of triangular pattern was common. British goods purchased the slaves, British ships transported them to New World plantations; and the plantation products, including sugar for the rum which became a major commodity in trading for slaves, moved back to Britain.

By 1750 there were at least 236,000 slaves in the American colonies (including French Louisiana), still predominantly in Virginia and Maryland. The proportion of blacks in the total population reached its apex (21 per cent) during this period. Settlement and slavery were moving slowly westward from the coast, but slavery never gained a major foothold in the Piedmont or mountain areas, owing mainly to the small size of farms. The plantation system with its prodigious labor demands slowly spread down the coast into Carolina and Georgia.

Between 1750 and 1800 some 500,000 to 1,000,000 slaves came to this country. New England shippers began to share in the fortunes to be made from the slave trade. Still, in the North slaves were rarely more than 5 per cent of the population. In the South, however, the slave proportion was increasing, owing to the predominantly large-scale plantation agriculture, orientation to growing commercial exports, and only moderate white immigration [23, pp. 39–40].

By 1770 exploitative agriculture in more accessible but marginal lands near the Virginia coast had already worn out the land; new slave shipments were now destined for the Carolinas and Georgia. About 1780, a new and valuable crop, cotton, was introduced, greatly increasing the demand both for land, especially in more southerly, warmer areas, and for slaves to clear the land and farm it. At first, because of its high humidity requirements, cotton was grown mainly along the coast, from Virginia to Georgia; plant disease, land erosion, demand for more cotton varieties, and the invention of the cotton gin in 1793 led to a fairly rapid shift south and west after 1800.

Black Resistance. From the beginning of slavery in the colonies, black resistance occurred. In fact, the first slave revolt took place in the Pedee River colony in South Carolina. Slave revolts were not the only forms of resistance to bondage. There was the day-to-day resistance of destroyed tools and crops, and work slowdowns. Attempts to kill masters and set fires also appear to have been common. In some slave states so many fires were set that some insurance companies refused to insure homes [*18, p. 100*]. Slaves pretended to be lame, sick, blind, or insane in order to interrupt the work of the plantation; running away was common. Thousands escaped to cities, the North, Canada, Mexico, Indian areas, and wilderness areas. Maroon colonies grew up in forested mountains or swampy areas of the Carolinas, Virginia, Louisiana, Florida, Georgia, Mississippi, and Alabama. Evidence of at least fifty such communities in various places and at various times from 1672 to 1864 have been found [*1, p. 167*].

THE ANTE-BELLUM PERIOD: PLANTATION AND SLAVERY,
1790 TO 1865

The Slavery System. By 1790 the economy of the South was based firmly on export agriculture, which in turn depended on slave farm labor for its low cost. The majority of farmers may not have been slaveholders, but their farms usually were small, occupied less desirable land, and were essentially subsistent [*23, p. 56*]. Economic and political powers were a function of the amount of land owned, and rested in the hands of large plantation owners. In the North, however, plantations were never really successful, farming practices being transferred fairly directly from practices in the mother country. Many northern farmers, nevertheless, did employ immigrant indentured servants. Further white immigration was not encouraged by the plantation owners of the South.

In 1820 slavery was as much a part of the few urban places in the South as it was of rural farms and plantations. During the ante-bellum period the residences of blacks and whites in southern cities usually were not spatially segregated; this was, of course, not intended to promote integration but to prevent the growth of a cohesive black community. There were, however, segregated black residential areas; and by 1860 housing segregation was increasing. The segregated black areas were usually near markets, docks, alleys, and the peripheries of the cities and towns. Town slaves, while at times restricted to the owner's compound, tended to be much better off than slaves on the plantations. Many worked at building and other trades. Not much contact or aggregation of slaves was permitted; loyalty was aided by the terrible threat of being sold off to a plantation.

Although commercial export made the South as rich or richer than the North at this time, a comparable system of towns and cities failed to develop. Direct export relations with Europe were often carried out from many small river and estuary ports, of which only a few (Charleston, South Carolina, Mobile, Alabama, New Orleans, Louisiana, and Norfolk) became very large. Based on the slave labor of many, exports permitted the owners of large plantations a relatively aristocratic income and the luxury of importing needed goods from England. So long as profits were high, there was little incentive to consider alternatives to slave labor.

Gradually, however, in the areas of early settlement, mainly coastal Virginia, Maryland, and North Carolina, the land deteriorated from misuse and overuse, and owners found it more and more costly to maintain large slaveholdings. Fortunately for these declining plantation areas, the rapid expansion of settlement into the richer lowlands of Georgia, Alabama, Mississippi, Louisiana, and Tennessee after 1800, and the emergence of cotton as the most profitable export crop created a huge demand for slaves, just as the slave trade was becoming more difficult.

Migration of Slaves. From 1790 to 1810 the slave trade continued high, with the origins shifting east and south to Nigeria, the Congo, and even Angola, where the Portuguese engaged in direct kidnapping raids. Some slaves were brought from Cuba to be sold in the United States. Meanwhile the American market for slaves shifted south and west to Alabama (Mobile) and the Mississippi Delta (through New Orleans). The British Parliament outlawed the slave trade in 1808, and although American ships ran the British blockades, the volume of trade began to fall drastically.

In the older settled areas, especially in Virginia, the black population had grown rather in excess of local needs, simply through years of natural increase. Instead of being feared, the "surplus" was desired, for the owners in declining farming areas found it most profitable to specialize in the breeding and raising of slaves for sale and shipment to the expanding plantation areas of the Southwest [3, pp. 83–84; 23, p. 51]. The local slave markets, such as Alexandria, blatantly advertised the fecundity of female slaves, and owners gave privileges to women who bore many children. Slaves were thought of as a capital investment, earning between 5 and 15 per cent per year.

From 1810 to 1865, then, a large and profitable internal trade in slaves occurred from the "old" to the "new" South. In the early part of the century, before 1830, blacks went mainly from Virginia and Maryland to Kentucky, Tennessee, Georgia, and Alabama; after 1830, the Carolinas, and even Georgia and Kentucky, began to export slaves to Mississippi, Arkansas, Louisiana, and Texas. The trade routes ran along the coast, down the Piedmont, along the Appalachian Corridor, and down the Mississippi and Ohio rivers. Since most slaves had to walk in chains, it is not surprising that many did not make it.

Population Redistribution. As a consequence of the decline of agriculture on the coastal plain, and the rapid expansion in the Southwest, the distribution of slaves changed radically between 1790 and 1860. Although Virginia remained the leading slave state, its slave population had increased rather slowly; Maryland dropped from second to tenth in number of slaves. The proportion of blacks had fallen in both. From 1790 to 1850, Tennessee, Alabama, Mississippi, and Louisiana grew the most. By 1850 South Carolina (59 per cent), Mississippi, and Louisiana (each 51 per cent) had slave majorities. By 1850 the center of the black population had shifted from Virginia to South Carolina, and by 1865 west into Georgia.

Health on the Plantation. The health care of blacks on the plantation must be understood in relation to the general environment, medical practices, and social climate of the time. The frontier conditions, inadequate medical facilities, isolated settlements, undrained lowlands and swamps, coupled with a mild climate, difficulty of preserving food, and ignorance of health practices all contributed to make the population, white and black, vulnerable to epidemic and endemic diseases. But the provision of health care was the responsibility of the dominant white society which, as it often continues to do, treated blacks as "outpatients" at best, or not at all. Under the conditions of plantation society, the food, shelter, clothing, and medical care of the slave were subject to the control and whim of the master.

Black Mortality. It was generally true throughout the South that slaves had higher death rates and shorter life expectancies than whites [*36*, p. 158; *33*, p. 318; *35*, p. 573]. There were two to three times as many black as white deaths in South Carolina from 1853 to 1859. The infant death rate differential between white and black was even greater than that of the general mortality rate. On a sugar plantation in Louisiana

21 per cent of the black babies born from 1834 to 1857 died; on a North Carolina plantation during the 1850s, 67 per cent of the black infants died; in an eleven-year span in Charleston 48 per cent of the black babies died before they were four years old [33, p. 320].

The size, type, and location of the plantation appear to have made a difference in the quality of slave life. In general, it seems that housing, food, clothing, and health care were better on small farms than on large plantations [3, p. 72]. The health problems were most acute in the swampy coastal areas of South Carolina and Georgia and in the river bottom plantations of Alabama, Mississippi, Louisiana, and Arkansas. Most unhealthy of all were the rice plantations [19, p. 141; 33, p. 297].

There was also an abnormally high death rate among blacks in the cities [7, p. 227]. Even though Wade [39, p. 134] has indicated that slaves were treated better in the city than in the countryside, black mortality rates in the ante-bellum city were at least twice those of whites [15, p. 42].

Black Rebellion.   From the beginnings of slavery in America, the strategy of whites was to make the slave forget his African culture and accept the slave identity and permanent inferiority of his status as property.

Blacks from different tribes were mixed, so that communication was difficult; talk was often forbidden and learning to read and write English was proscribed, so that "ignorance" became self-fulfilling. Even "good" masters acted as though slaves had no rights, often selling members of families separately; "good" plantations offered incredibly bad living conditions, and only the economic value of slaves as workers kept the death and maiming rate from alarming levels.

As a result of injustice, cruelty, and inhuman conditions, the slave was naturally discontented and often driven to rebellion. The layout and security measures taken within the plantation and the distance of one plantation from another made successful large-scale revolt impossible. Organization for revolt within the plantation was made difficult by a system of favoritism and informing.

But the difficulties imposed upon black communication and organization did not ensure peace for the whites. Guerrilla raids, carried out by bands of escaped slaves living in the extensive swamps or forests, were common from the seventeenth century until the Civil War. No one is certain how many "revolts" occurred, partly because the definitions of "revolt" do not coincide. Kilson [20], defining "revolt" as an attempt by a group of slaves to achieve freedom, has identified 65 cases. Aptheker [2, p. 16] has recorded approximately 250 revolts and conspiracies, not including those outbreaks and plots that occurred aboard slave traders; he requires a "revolt" to involve at least ten slaves, to have the aim of freedom, and to have contemporary references labeling the event in terms equivalent to revolt. If revolt was defined as it was in Texas in 1858, as a group of three or more slaves with arms who intend to obtain freedom by force, Aptheker asserts that several hundred slave insurrections could be counted.

Slave revolts were not evenly distributed among the states but were concentrated in Virginia, South Carolina, and Louisiana. Within these states, the revolts were clustered in only a few counties. In Virginia, for example, revolts tended to occur in the coastal, tobacco counties. In South Carolina most took place in Charleston County. And in Louisiana most revolts occurred along the Mississippi River north and west of Baton Rouge.

The more successful revolts tended to be where the slaves were better treated, especially near cities such as Richmond and Charleston where the chance to go to black churches made it easier for slaves to organize their revolts. (In the North, too, riots broke out in the cities—in Cincinnati in 1820, Providence in 1824 and 1834, Philadelphia in 1834, and in New York in 1834 and 1836 [23, p. 71, 97].) In the Southwest, where plantations were larger, conditions for the slaves harsher, and discipline more severe, revolts were rarer, although discontent was undoubtedly greater.

The Underground Railroad. Escape of the individual slave to freedom in the North was a more practical alternative to armed rebellion, but his chances of success were not high, considering the great distances and his ignorance of the geography beyond his immediate area. Nevertheless, hundreds of thousands of attempts resulted in some many thousand successful escapes. The underground railroad was the clandestine network of antislavery individuals, including many escaped slaves, by which an escaped slave could be guided into a haven in the North [6, 34]. So perilous was the journey within the South that little is known about the routes or the mechanisms; within the North the "railway" was more organized but still secret, since the national Anti-Fugitive Slave Laws of 1850 required northern states to return escaped slaves and permitted owners' representatives to go north and capture them. There remains a controversy over whether or not the underground railroad was a systemized network or rather a restricted number of blacks and whites organized to move slaves in certain localities [23, p. 112].

Depending on time and place, the black slave had a number of options in terms of places to which to escape. These options included Mexico, Canada, free states, southern cities, maroon colonies, or Indian tribes such as Creeks, Cherokees, and Seminoles. In the early nineteenth century, a movement developed, among white abolitionists and some blacks, for emigration of blacks to colonies in Africa. The Liberian colony was established in 1821, but only about 15,000 emigrated over a fifty-year period [3, p. 131; 23, pp. 121, 128]. At different times certain border cities were seen by blacks as entry points or gateways to freedom. During the 1700s Pittsburgh was used by slaves escaping to the Northwest Territory. By the turn of the century, Cleveland also served this function; it was touted as the "negroe's paradise" [30].

Many sought the relative security of the small, free black communities of northern cities, such as New York, Chicago, Rochester, Philadelphia, and Boston, where many joined the growing abolitionist forces in the North [3, chap. 6]. Their accounts of the hideousness of life in the South were hardly believed at first, and abolitionist white sentiment began largely on ethical and religious grounds among the Quakers and Congregationalists. By 1783 slavery had been abolished in Massachusetts, and by 1805 in most of the North. In the 1850s too, Massachusetts was not zealous in enforcing the Anti-Fugitive Slave Laws. On the other hand, after about 1815, New England industrialists entered the market for cheap cotton, and defended slavery—at a distance.

Escapes before the Civil War (about 90,000 went North on the underground railroad) and movement North during and just after the Civil War added up to a sizable migration of blacks. Before 1850 most movement was to Baltimore, Philadelphia, Cincinnati, and other cities close to the South. After the Anti-Fugitive Slave Laws of 1850, migrants had to reach Canada to be safe.

Expansion of "Slave" and "Free" Territories. In 1787 the Northwest Ordinance forbade slavery in the territory that was to become Illinois, Indiana, Michigan, Ohio, and Wisconsin; but many of these areas restricted the entry of blacks. In 1820 the South, with its congressional majority, obtained the Missouri Compromise which would admit states to the West and South as slave states. Nevertheless, Oregon and California were admitted free, as were the territories of the Southwest, won from Mexico, which abolished slavery in 1829. The South won a temporary victory with the Kansas-Nebraska Act of 1854, but the feverish efforts of antislavery forces barely managed to keep Kansas free. By 1860, northern Republicans achieved a majority, Lincoln was elected, and Congress passed liberalized immigration, the Homestead Act, and protective tariffs for industry, all of which the South feared and opposed. In 1861 seven southern states seceded to form the Confederacy. The border slave states of Kentucky, Maryland, Delaware, and Missouri, with a low proportion of slaves, had prounion majorities and did not secede.

The Civil War. Sentiment in the North would not tolerate secession. For a time the war was between whites in the North and the South, and the issue was preservation of the Union, not abolition. As the war dragged on, attitudes hardened. Both North and South began to utilize blacks—some 300,000 in the North [18, p. 213]. The majority were limited to menial service activities, but some black combat forces were organized in liberated areas of the South and in New England. In 1863 Lincoln's Emancipation Proclamation freed the slaves in the occupied areas.

Immediately after the war, in spite of the Thirteenth Amendment abolishing slavery, the situation for blacks was little better, since southern governments enacted "Black Codes" which forced blacks into slavelike service for their former masters. However, northern "radical" Republicans soon had the power to force military government and Reconstruction regimes on the South. The Reconstruction governments quickly ratified the Fourteenth and Fifteenth Amendments, which restricted state powers and bestowed the right to vote on blacks [3, chap. 8]. Ironically, these amendments never could have been ratified if it had not been for the Reconstruction governments, since several northern states, particularly in the Midwest, did not ratify them.

BETRAYAL, LYNCHING, AND MIGRATION, 1865 TO 1940

The freeing of the slaves, the enfranchisement of the blacks, and in a few areas of more "radical" military administration, the allocation of some land to the former slaves, brought about a period of hope. For a few years after 1866, under military protection, many blacks were elected to Congress and to state legislatures and state offices in the South; they never in fact gained even temporary control of any state, but had enough influence at least to see a system of public education set up throughout most of the South. The blacks had little preparation for legal intrigue. As memories of the war receded, sentiment in the North ceased to support military intervention. Most people in the North, while opposed to slavery, also viewed blacks as inferiors, not to be given power. Thus, in the disputed election of 1876, Hayes became President on a promise to end Reconstruction and remove the northern "carpetbaggers." It took almost no time for southern whites to disenfranchise most blacks through the imposition of literacy tests and other devices, including sheer terror. In the early 1890s a hopeful alliance of poor whites and poor blacks under the banner of Populism emerged, but this alliance was short-lived.

Under slavery, social distance was automatic and institutionalized; spatial separation was needed less to maintain superiority of whites. After the Civil War, physical separation became legislated through a set of Jim Crow laws, forbidding miscegenation, providing for separate institutions and facilities, and depriving blacks of legal rights such as the right to be empaneled on a jury [3, chap. 9]. These laws became increasingly severe throughout the late nineteenth and early twentieth centuries.

Sharecropping Serfdom. Most former slaves remained on their former plantations. Even where they held title to the land, blacks depended on the plantation owners to market their cotton. In most cases, however, no ownership changed; black farmers were essentially landless peasants. A kind of serfdom emerged—the former slaves leased land, usually very little, from the plantation owner for a rent of from one-third to one-half of the crop. Very quickly, most sharecroppers became permanently indebted to the owner, and were then legally forbidden to move from the owner's holding. Not only was the sharecropper kept in abject poverty, but the system of agriculture was so inefficient (i.e., too many minute holdings, lack of uniform variety, inadequate care of land) that production fell, and landowners, too, were much worse off than before the war [23, p. 140].

The plantation was rearranged: the sharecroppers were now scattered about on small holdings throughout the former plantation. Gradually, too, many blacks drifted back into the direct employ of the plantation owner, a life materially not much better than slavery, but psychologically preferred, because the laborer was free to leave providing he was free of indebtedness.

Condition of Black People. Since the blacks were still overwhelmingly rural, perhaps even more scattered than before, scarcely educated or often illiterate, and extremely poor, organized resistance to the new forms of subjugation was difficult. The white community, both through grossly unfair local police power and through the terrifyingly effective tool of lynching, could keep the black man "in his place." Terrorist organizations like the Ku Klux Klan were effective in maintaining "correct" attitudes among whites as well as in terrorizing the black population. Lynchings, and other violent and arbitrary treatment of blacks, were most intense around 1905, especially in Mississippi and Georgia [12].

For evidence of the general condition of the black population in 1910, illiteracy statistics are useful. In the North and West, white illiteracy varied between 1 and 3 per cent, black illiteracy from 12 per cent (New England) to 25 per cent (West North Central, mainly Missouri). In the South, thirty-five years after the Civil War, white illiteracy was 12 per cent and black illiteracy was 48 per cent—casting doubt on the adequacy of the rigidly segregated school system operated for blacks, and reflecting the difficulty of regular or long attendance.

The situation had improved by 1930, but was still extremely discriminatory. In the South, white illiteracy varied from 1 to 6 per cent, and black from 11 to 27 per cent. The low level of educational achievement of blacks, while being used to support the white view of innate black inferiority, was mainly a function of discrimination in school expenditures per pupil. Despite the alleged "separate but equal" facilities accepted by the Supreme Court in Plessy vs. Ferguson in 1896, in the Deep South in 1931 expenditure for a black pupil was less than one third that for a white pupil. In Mississippi and South Carolina, it was only one sixth ($5 per pupil per year).

Naturally, the notion of leaving such a precarious life occurred to many. Proposals for a separate state were made, but to think that whites were going to make land available for such a venture was folly. Many blacks did attempt to establish colonies in the new territories of the West. In 1879, some 40,000 migrated to Kansas, in a partly successful venture [6, chap. 5]. In the South itself, some all-black communities were founded in isolated, marginal land not needed by whites. Other blacks revived the idea of migration to Africa, such as to the Liberian colony established originally in 1821. This proposal was encouraged by many whites, friendly and unfriendly; not many blacks, however, wanted to return to a continent whose culture they in fact no longer shared. Some blacks gradually drifted north, but they were unwelcome in the countryside, and were subjected to rough and discriminatory treatment by the city immigrants who feared the competition for jobs. Race riots were not uncommon.

More than 5,000 black cowboys went up the cow trails from Texas after the Civil War. Black men such as James Beckworth, Jacob Dodson, Saunders Jackson, "Pap" Singleton, and George W. Bush participated in the exploration and settlement of the West [11, 18]. Thousands of free blacks were among the "forty-niners" who flocked to the California gold fields. The western campaigns of the U.S. Army included four black units, the Ninth and Tenth Cavalries and the Twenty-fourth and Twenty-fifth Infantries. But whether as cowboys, cavalrymen, or settlers, blacks faced the same kind of discrimination and oppression in the West as they faced in the South and East. Black cowboys, for example, found race hatred stronger in Montana and Idaho than in other parts of the cattlemen's West [11, p. 140]. The black troops were discriminated against in terms of supplies, equipment, and assignments [37, p. 5]. Black settlers found discriminatory laws and restrictions in areas like Iowa, Illinois, and the Oregon Territory.

Population Redistribution (to 1910). During the period from 1850 to 1910, although the blacks remained almost totally rural and southern, there was a continuous shift of black farmers and farm laborers toward the Southwest. The number of blacks continued to grow moderately, especially in North Carolina and Georgia, but expanded rapidly in Mississippi, Texas, and Louisiana. In 1880 the black population reached its maximum proportion of about 45 per cent of the population of the South (but only 13 per cent of the nation, owing to massive European immigration into the North).

Blacks were a majority in Louisiana (51 per cent), Mississippi (57 per cent), and South Carolina (60 per cent) and closely approached half of the population in Alabama (47 per cent), Georgia (47 per cent), and Florida (47 per cent). By 1910, although the proportion of blacks had fallen slightly, the absolute size of the black population reached a maximum in Georgia, Kentucky, and South Carolina. In 1850 Virginia and South Carolina had the largest black populations; by 1880 Virginia had the third largest black population, below Georgia and Mississippi. By 1910 the dominance of the Deep South was clear: Georgia, Mississippi, Alabama, South Carolina, and Louisiana had the largest black populations, absolutely and relatively. The South still had 89 per cent of the black population, and 80 per cent of that was rural. In the North, where 11 per cent of the blacks lived, only 5 per cent of the population was black; these were already 80 per cent urban in 1910.

Migration (to 1910). Considering the large size of the black population in 1910 (10,000,000), the amount of lifetime migration does not show great mobility. Nevertheless, the out-migration from the South Atlantic states was large; the majority of people did not move too far to the northeast (especially to Baltimore, Philadelphia, and New York). There was a smaller net migration from the East South Central states, about half of whom went across the Mississippi to Texas and Louisiana and about half to the North and West, especially St. Louis, Chicago, Cincinnati, and Indianapolis.

A Slow Awakening, 1910 to 1950. The terrible conditions at the end of the century led on one hand to a prevailing black reaction of "accommodation," as enunciated by Booker T. Washington in 1895, and on the other to a strong current of bitterness and protest, led by W. E. B. Du Bois and others [3, 23]. Washington stressed gradual economic improvement through education and self-help; Du Bois stressed the denial of fundamental rights of blacks. After the NAACP was founded in 1910 and the Urban League in 1911, a more activist approach was accepted. The NAACP stressed legal challenges, and gains through the courts date from 1911. The Urban League worked to improve job opportunities and community relations—a difficult task.

As before, war led to an improvement in the position of the blacks [3, pp. 289–95]. The slowing of European immigration, particularly after 1914, and the increased demand for labor in shipyards and other war industries, for the first time opened up better industrial jobs to blacks. Many were actively recruited from the rural South, and went North, especially to Chicago, Detroit, Philadelphia, and to other industrial cities. Not surprisingly, when the war bubble burst, blacks were first to be fired. Unemployment increased and a period of severe race riots ensued, becoming worst in the Red Summer of 1919, when there were severe riots in Washington, Chicago, East St. Louis, Omaha, and Knoxville.

During the early 1920s, Garvey revived the idea of colonization, but few were interested [6, chap. 13]. Conditions for blacks in the cities slowly improved in the prosperous 1920s. Blacks, concentrated in large ghettos, such as New York and Chicago, had become so numerous that the idea of black separatism and black businesses became popular. Chicago elected the first black congressman in 1928.

The Great Depression destroyed the hopes of equality gained within "Black Metropolis." Again blacks were first to be fired, but since most blacks were desperately poor already, some side effects of the Depression eventually proved beneficial.

New Deal legislation, such as the minimum wage, social security, unemployment insurance, and the various work and training programs, while perhaps instituted for the benefit of white workers, greatly aided blacks as well [23, pp. 212–13]. Perhaps the agricultural programs were most significant. Designed to modernize and mechanize agriculture, especially in the South, the programs forced hundreds of thousands of black sharecroppers off the land. The tiny shareholdings were hopelessly inefficient, the sharecroppers unbelievably poor, terrorized by white vigilantes, and weakened by dispersal. Forced to migrate to the northern cities, they found adjustment hard, and life in the slum ghetto far from pleasant; but a move to a northern city was the only realistic means of improving income, obtaining an education, and gaining political power.

World War II, like World War I, greatly aided blacks by opening up far more industrial jobs than ever before, for example in the steel and automobile industries. And the military itself provided valuable education and training for many blacks, although in World War II segregated units were still required. Indeed, as of 1945, in the North as well as the South, most institutions and accommodations were still segregated.

MIGRATION AND URBAN GROWTH, 1910 TO 1970

Population Redistribution and Migration, 1910 to 1940. The "Great Migration" of 1915 marked the beginning of a significant shift in the distribution of black people from the rural South to the urban North [6, 16]. In the North, an increasing need for unskilled labor accompanied by a halt in European immigration opened the labor market. As a consequence, agents were sent South to recruit black labor for northern industry. In the South, the ravages of the boll weevil and floods reduced the income of the planters, thus cutting the income, supplies, and credit of the tenants. And many people wanted to escape the legal and educational systems and terrorism. From 1910 to 1940 the proportion of the black population in the South fell from 89 to 77 per cent and the black proportion of the South fell from 30 to 24 per cent, while it increased in the North from 2 to 4 per cent. The proportion of black people in cities rose from 27 to 48 per cent (35 per cent in the South, 88 per cent in the North). For the first time a northern state, New York, was a leader in total black population. After 1910, growth of the black population ceased in the East South Central states, and slowed markedly in the South Atlantic and West South Central, but increased greatly in the Northeast, exceeding 2 million by 1940. The rate and volume of black migration out of the South increased dramatically after 1910, so that by 1940 the Northeast had 1.3 million blacks (60 per cent of its total black population) who had been born in the South. The some 1.5 million blacks who left the South represented 10–15 per cent of its black population. States with largest in-migration were New York (308,000), Illinois (230,000), Pennsylvania (217,000), and Ohio (170,000); those with the largest net out-migration were Georgia (358,000), South Carolina (323,000), Mississippi (255,000), and Virginia (234,000). The pattern of migration followed the major rail corridors—up the Atlantic coast from the South Atlantic states, up the Mississippi and Ohio to the Great Lakes states, and from Arkansas, Louisiana, and Texas to the West Coast.

The Growth of Black Communities in Cities. By 1900 the black population in fourteen cities, ten of them in the South, had passed 25,000 (Table 2). The largest were those in or quite near the South: Washington (87,000), Baltimore (79,000), New Orleans (78,000), and Philadelphia (63,000). But in the next twenty years growth was rapid in the North and only moderate in the South; in 1920, of twenty-four cities having a black population over 25,000, ten were in the North, although the largest populations, except for New York (169,000), were still in or near the South—Philadelphia (134,000), Washington (110,000), New Orleans and Baltimore (101,000).

From 1920 to 1940, growth was marked in the South, but more so in the North and especially rapid in Chicago, New York, Detroit, and Cleveland, indicating a shift of emphasis to longer moves, and in the direction of the Great Lakes. New York's black communities comprised more than half a million, and those of Chicago and Philadelphia 250,000; there were more than 100,000 in New Orleans, Memphis, Birmingham, Atlanta, and

TABLE 2
Development of Black Population in Cities, 1880 to 1970

(*1940 Rank Order*) (*Population in 000s*)

City	City 1880	City 1900	City 1920	City 1940	% Black 1940	SMSA 1960	% City Black	% SMSA Black	SMSA 1970	% City Black
New York	28	68	169	504	6	1557	14	11	2368	21
Chicago	6	30	109	278	8	977	23	15	1343	33
Philadelphia	32	63	134	251	13	671	26	15	844	34
Washington	52	87	110	187	28	487	54	24	704	74
Baltimore	54	79	108	166	19	375	35	22	490	46
St. Louis	22	36	70	166	13	295	29	14	379	41
New Orleans	58	78	101	149	30	267	37	31	324	45
Detroit	3	4	41	149	9	559	29	15	751	44
Memphis	15	50	61	121	42	224	37	36	265	39
Birmingham		17	70	109	41	219	40	35	218	42
Atlanta	16	36	63	105	35	231	38	23	311	51
Houston	6	5	34	86	22	250	23	20	384	26
Cleveland	2	6	35	85	10	258	29	14	333	39
Los Angeles		2	16	64	4	465	14	7	763	18
Jacksonville	4	16	42	62	36	105	41	23	118	22
Pittsburgh	4	20	38	62	9	161	16	7	170	20
Richmond	28	32		61	32	103	42	26	130	42
Cincinnati	8	15	30	56	12	127	21	12	155	28
Indianapolis	7	16	35	51	13	100	21	14	137	18
Dallas	2	9	24	50	17	159	19	15	241	25
Nashville	16	30	36	47	35	78	37	19	96	20
Norfolk	10	6	43	46	32	149	26	26	168	28
Louisville	21	39	41	47	15	83	18	12	101	24
Savannah	16	28	39	43	40	67	35	34	64	44
Kansas City	8	18	31	42	10	116	23	11	151	22
Miami			9	37	21	137	22	15	190	23
Columbus (Ohio)	3	8	22	36	12	89	16	12	106	19
Shreveport	5	9	17	36	35	96	34	34	97	34
Montgomery	10	17	20	35	40	64	35	38	70	14
Charleston	27	25	32	32	40	78	51	37	95	45
Boston	6	12	16	24	3	88	9	3	127	16
Charlotte	3	7	15	31	28	61	28	35	95	30
Mobile	12	17	24	29	35	101	32	32	113	35
Fort Worth	1	4	16	25	14	61	16	11	83	20
Augusta	10	18	23	27	40	66	45	30	70	50
San Francisco	2	2	2	5	1	239	10	9	330	35
Tampa, St. P.		4	12	23	22	89	16	11	109	18
Columbus, Ga.	5	7	9	17	32	63	27	29	68	26
Baton Rouge	4	7	9	12	34	72	29	32	81	28
Jackson	3	4	10	24	39	75	35	40	96	40
Buffalo	1	2	5	18	23	83	13	7	109	20
Dayton	1	3	9	20	10	70	21	10	94	30
Columbus, S.C.	6	10	15	22	35	75	30	29	85	30
Beaumont		3	13	19	32	62	29	21	68	31
Milwaukee		1	2	9	1	63	9	6	107	15
Chattanooga	5	13	19	36	28	49	33	18	50	36
Macon	7	12	23	26	45	56	44	31	60	37
Winston Salem		5	21	36	45	45	37	24	118	34

Washington. In the cities of the South, the proportion of blacks was often
about 25 per cent; in the North, it was more than 10 per cent only in St.
Louis, Philadelphia, and Detroit.

Development of the Ghetto. Up to 1900, part of the black population
of cities was scattered, housed in the servants' quarters of the wealthy.
From colonial times on, however, there have also been areas of towns and
cities, both North and South, that have been designated by whites as
black parts of town [8, 31]. In the South, poor blacks often were found in
semirural slums on the outskirts of town, and in large cities in shacktowns
along the railroad. In the North around 1900, linear black communities
began to develop in old run-down houses, or shacktowns, mainly along
the industrial railways near the center of the city where no one else
wanted to live. With growth and after 1910, conflicts between poor
whites and poor blacks for poor living space were inevitable. Resistance
to expansion of the ghetto forced greater and greater overcrowding and
deterioration of existing housing; the black community had to grow,
block by block, into the neighboring white areas.

Ghetto expansion was made possible as overseas immigration slowed
after 1920 and as a portion of the white population escaped the inner-city
slums into newer, lower middle-class housing a little farther out. Jewish
communities were easier to move into than eastern and southern European Catholic communities. Moves were sometimes "concentric," that is,
into areas of similarly old and poor housing. Often the concentric move involved a jump over intervening more resistant groups or richer areas.
More commonly, growth was outward within the sector, along and between the railroads, and adjacent to less desirable industrial areas [10,
31]. Thus, the first to move were often middle-class blacks who could more
easily afford to penetrate the somewhat better and newer housing, whose
former residents again had the means to flee to the suburbs. In turn, the
poorest and most recent black migrants from the South moved into the
worst and oldest slums, which were to be found in the core areas of
the black community.

The term ghetto is appropriate to describe black residential space, a
segregated territory with boundaries enforced by both external and internal pressures. Interestingly, the black ghetto has been more rigidly
defined in the North where blacks have been feared as the unknown, than
in the South, where several smaller black sections were easier to control
than a single large section. There were numerous external pressures
against the dispersal of blacks: these included legal restrictions against
housing integration, enforced by the FHA itself until 1949; refusal by the
real estate industry to show or sell housing to blacks in white areas, and by
banks and insurance companies to finance such sales; white and black mu-

tual fear of being alone within the others' territory; lack of information about opportunities; building freeways and renewal projects, which serve as barriers to expansion; white protective organizations and violence perpetrated against blacks who attempt to enter white areas; and, the sheer poverty and political and legal weakness of blacks [27].

Internal pressures included, as they still do, the advantages of mutual protection within the ghetto, the convenience and preference for black churches, clubs, businesses, and especially friends and relatives, and the possibility of political power through spatial concentration. By 1928, the black ghetto in Chicago was large enough to elect the first black congressman since Reconstruction. In the larger New York ghettos, geographic separation and gerrymandering prevented black representation until 1940. Still, the solidarity of the ghetto has proved to be an important basis for growth of political power and activism in the more recent past.

The ghetto is mainly the product of social forces. It is true that the majority of the ghetto residents may be poor, but by no means all are. The ghetto contains all classes of blacks from the poorest slum dweller to the upper class professional. Social distinction by color is stronger than the usual economic determination of residential location. But the black ghetto is also an economic colony: the majority of residents rent from absentee landlords, and the majority of jobs and businesses are white-controlled. Understandably, the pattern provides the continuing potential for violent reaction.

Population Redistribution and Migration, 1940 to 1970. After 1940, the growth of the black population of the Northeast continued to accelerate, slowing only slightly in the Middle Atlantic states after 1960, and in the East North Central states after 1965. By 1960, the latter, with somewhat better job opportunities, had a larger black population than the Middle Atlantic states. By 1960 both regions passed the East South Central region, whose black population had been declining absolutely, and the West South Central, whose black population was growing only moderately. The black population of the Northeast passed 6 million by 1963, its proportion of the total black population rising from 22 per cent in 1940 to 40 per cent by 1968. After 1940 the black population of California grew rapidly, reaching one million by 1960. The West's proportion rose from 1 per cent to 8 per cent while that in the South fell from 77 to 53 per cent. The South will probably be the residence of less than half of the black population by 1972. At the same time, the black proportion of the total southern population fell from 24 to 19 per cent, while it increased in the Northeast from 4 to 8.5 per cent and in the West from 1 to 5 per cent. The proportion of the black population living in urban areas reached 95 per cent outside of the South and even 60 per cent in the South by 1968 (up from 35 per cent in 1940).

In 1940, only one of the eleven states with high black populations was to be found outside of the South and that was ninth-ranked New York. By 1960, New York had become the leading state. Illinois now ranked sixth, California ninth, and Pennsylvania eleventh. Within the South, a relative shift out of the Deep South (Mississippi, Alabama, Georgia, South Carolina) to Florida, Louisiana, and especially Texas occurred. By 1970, the three highest states were all located outside of the South: New York, California, and Illinois.

CIVIL RIGHTS AND BLACK POWER, 1950 TO 1970

The Civil Rights Movement. The twenty years from 1950 to 1970 might be described as a period of social revolution. A symbolic beginning was Truman's integration of the Armed Forces in 1949, his reversal of FHA housing segregation policy, and his demand for Civil Rights legislation. The latter was not acted upon until the period from 1964 to 1969, when persistent and increasingly strong black anger and protest made such action necessary. Many of the veterans returning from World War II and Korea were no longer easily intimidated. A number of more radical black groups and leaders emerged in the early 1950s. The crucial school desegregation of the Supreme Court in 1954, outlawing the "Separate but Equal" doctrine, and especially the Montgomery bus boycott in 1955–56 unleashed a flood of demonstrations, protests, and conflicts, without which no change would have been possible.

The dual system of public accommodations has been substantially eliminated, and that of schools partially broken. Blacks have become far more mobile. Since 1965, after some years of improving education and after the catalyst of severe riots, job opportunities in better industrial and white-collar occupations have finally begun to open. Blacks have been able to participate in the growth of industry in the South only since 1966. This, in turn, has led to a slowdown of the migration of blacks to the North, since many prefer to remain in their home region. The occupational shift has also led to the first real improvement in the income of blacks in relation to whites. The median income of blacks, which had hovered around one half that of whites from 1940 to 1964, increased to 63 per cent by 1969 (about 75 per cent in the North, 50 per cent in the South). The continuing reduction in employment in the lowest paying farm labor and domestic service categories is being offset by movement into other services and the hitherto almost closed clerical and professional categories.

But resistance by unions and small businesses to integration is great, and the battle for equality is far from over. Open housing bills and equal-opportunity employment laws have been passed, but often are unenforced or unenforceable. Anyone using the conditions of slavery as his base line might say that progress has been made; but to do so would be inadequate. The basic issue is not the progress of the black measured in terms of his conditions one hundred, or ten, or two years ago. Ours is a multiracial society. The basic issue is, as it has always been when the black man is compared to the white, whether the changes have been of such a magnitude as to alter the socioeconomic relationship between blacks as a group and whites as a group? In recent years, the rate of growth of income for blacks was rapid; however, the actual dollar increase of the white income was greater. Contrasted to the level of prosperity reached by much of the white population, the progress of the black seems less impressive [14, 26, 32].

Discrimination, Housing, and the Ghetto. The symbolic, legal, and rhetorical evidence of progress convince many that black progress is effectual. But there remains discrimination against blacks in virtually all American communities. Voting districts are gerrymandered to decrease the power of the black voter. School districts are so organized as to produce "white" and "black" schools. Health and welfare policies are used against the black family. And in many cities, services and facilities are not located where they would be readily available to the black population. Most hospitals, clinics, and physicians in Detroit [24], Chicago [9], and Los Angeles [17], for example, are located in or restricted to middle and upper class areas. This provides the poor, especially blacks, with inferior and infrequent care, with longer trips and longer waits, and consequently aggravates an already high incidence of disease and mortality.

Land use zoning has been used against blacks in Miami, Atlanta, and Philadelphia [38, 5, 4]. Physical barriers, whether natural or socially contrived, are also used to maintain the racial and spatial status quo. The Harlem, Cuyahoga, and Anacostia rivers, for example, have separated black and white residential areas in New York City, Cleveland, and Washington, respectively. Streets and railroads have been used to define and confine black areas in Durham, Detroit, Chicago, New Haven, Atlanta, and San Francisco.

Urban renewal and public housing have consistently fostered segregation, with the sanction or insistence of local governmental bodies. Research findings indicate, for example, that there have been political and social pressures to contain public housing within existing racial and poverty concentrations in Chicago, Cleveland, Detroit, Atlanta, New Orleans, Dade County (Florida), and Montgomery [22, 13, 21]. The

National Commission on Urban Problems [29] found that in six of the twelve case histories it studied, the policy was to locate public housing projects in such a manner as to identify with the existing racial pattern of the cities.

Besides government policy there are a variety of apparently "neutral" activities to maintain strictly white residential areas. These include building code decisions and inspection standards, location standards, location of water and sewer facilities, and zoning policies. Glendale, California, and Deerfield, Illinois, are examples of places in which building permits and inspections have been used to keep the community white. Dearborn, Michigan, on the other hand, tried to evict black families by terminating such public facilities as gas and garbage collection. Oklahoma City unsuccessfully attempted to exclude blacks from the city by redrawing the city boundaries [25].

Not only have federal and local governments sanctioned or forced the segregation of public housing, they have condoned the inferior quality of that housing. Wright Patman of the House Banking Committee has charged that the FHA has approved substandard housing as eligible for federal programs. Under these programs the government subsidizes interest payments on "safe, sanitary and decent" housing. The Southern Regional Council found that the welfare departments of the states of Virginia, Florida, North Carolina, and South Carolina are collectively the largest slum lords in the South.

Even the elimination of many legal and financial barriers to residential integration has not resulted in any diminution in the solidity of the ghetto. Some interracial housing developments have been built; integrated housing does exist in many cities and in certain professional, upper middle class areas. But white resistance and fear remain strong, so that when an area becomes partially black, the remaining white residents find reasons to move to the suburbs for newer housing.

An indirect benefit of the white flight to the suburbs and increased general affluence has been the dramatic extension of the ghetto into areas of better quality middle-class housing. Another benefit is that many central cities are heading toward a black voting majority—Gary by 1970, Detroit, Philadelphia, Cleveland, St. Louis, Baltimore, Atlanta, and New Orleans by 1980. This is a fascinating geographic result of minority concentration: from a pattern of dispersed sharecroppers, without political strength in 1900, to one possessing the political balance of power in major cities by 1980. Cities have tried to bring middle-class whites back into the city through urban renewal, but this has so far failed to stem the tide of white outflow.

At the same time, the emergence of a strong sense of black community and culture since 1964, and the development of the black power movement have increased the internal pressures for remaining spatially separate. This has paid off in the form of increased political power, even in the South, since 1965. For example, there are now twelve black members of Congress (New York City two; Chicago two; Detroit two; and Cleveland, Los Angeles, St. Louis, Oakland, Baltimore, and Philadelphia one each), more and more representatives in legislatures, in the South as well as the North, and even a few county sheriffs—holders of real power in the South.

Blacks recognize advantages in integration—particularly access to better schools, housing, and jobs; but they fear the dilution of power, the very real possibility of permanent subjugation as a dispersed minority. Logically, the white national majority of 89 per cent should avidly seek full integration, since they could successfully prevent the emergence of black separatism and black power; but irrationally and emotionally, the majority of whites still fear blacks socially and psychologically more than they do the prospect of a yet more racially divided and violent society.

CONCLUSION

In the century since Reconstruction, the majority of black Americans have abandoned a life confined to share-crop farming in the South, where they were numerically in the majority in many areas, but totally subjugated economically, socially, and politically. For many of those blacks who have remained in the South, the total subjugation remains. Out-migration has reduced the black population of the South, but black people are again becoming a majority, this time by concentrating in the ghettos of major cities, North and South. The long-term trend is toward an equalization of the black proportion of the population in the highly urban parts of the country, but in nonsouthern rural, small-town, and small-city areas the black population probably will remain small. The geographic concentration in urban ghettos has undesirable aspects both for blacks and whites. In the foreseeable future, this does not seem reversible, both because of the possible political advantages it offers blacks in terms of solidarity, and because of the abiding inability of whites and blacks to overcome deep-seated fears and prejudices. Evidently not until political, economic, and social equality are achieved, and perhaps not even then, will black and white no longer be the basis for this dominant geographic separation of peoples in America.

LITERATURE CITED

1. Aptheker, H. "Maroons Within the Present Limits of the United States," *Journal of Negro History*, 24 (April 1939), pp. 167–84.

2. Aptheker, H. *American Negro Slave Revolts*. New York: International Publishers, 1963.

3. Bennett, L., Jr. *Before the Mayflower*. Rev. ed. Baltimore: Penguin, 1964.

4. Blumberg, L. and M. Lalli. "Little Ghettos: A Study of Negroes in the Suburbs," *Phylon*, 27 (Summer 1966), pp. 117–31.

5. Blumberg, L. "Segregated Housing, Marginal Location, and the Crisis of Confidence," *Phylon*, 25 (Winter 1964), pp. 321–30.

6. Bontemps, A. and J. Conroy. *Anyplace But Here*. New York: Hill and Wang, 1966.

7. Brandt, L. "Negroes of St. Louis," *Journal of the American Statistical Association*, 8 (March 1903), pp. 203–68.

8. Clark, K. *Dark Ghetto*. New York: Harper and Row, 1965.

9. De Vise, P. et al. *Slum Medicine: Chicago's Apartheid Health System*. Chicago: University of Chicago Community and Family Study, 1969.

10. Drake, St. Clair and H. R. Cayton. *Black Metropolis*. New York: Harper and Row, 1962.

11. Durham, P. and E. L. Jones. *The Negro Cowboys*. New York: Dodd, Mead and Co., 1965.

12. Ginzburg, R. *100 Years of Lynchings*. New York: Lancer Books, 1969.

13. Glazer, N. and D. McEntire, eds. *Studies in Housing and Minority Groups*. Berkeley: University of California Press, 1960.

14. Good, P. *The American Serfs*. New York: Ballantine Books, 1968.

15. Green, C. M. *The Secret City*. Princeton: Princeton University Press, 1967.

16. Hart, J. F. "The Changing Distribution of the American Negro," *Annals of the Association of American Geographers*, 50 (September 1960), pp. 242–66.

17. Jacobs, P. *Prelude to Riot*. New York: Random House, 1966.

18. Katz, W. L. *Eyewitness: The Negro in American History*. New York: Pitman, 1967.

19. Kemble, F. A. *Journal of a Residence on a Georgia Plantation in 1838–1839*. Edited by J. A. Scott. New York: Alfred A. Knopf, 1961.

20. Kilson, D. "Towards Freedom: An Analysis of Slave Revolts in the United States," *Phylon*, 25 (Summer 1964), pp. 175–87.

21. Lowi, T. J. "Apartheid U.S.A.," *Transaction*, 7 (February 1970), pp. 32–39.

22. McEntire, D. *Residence and Race*. Berkeley: University of California Press, 1960.

23. Meier, A. and E. M. Radwick. *From Plantation to Ghetto*. New York: Hill and Wang, 1966.

24. Milio, N. *9226 Kercheval*. Ann Arbor: University of Michigan Press, 1970.

25. Million, E. M. "Racial Restrictive Covenants Revisited," *Open Occupancy vs. Forced Housing Under the Fourteenth Amendment: Symposium.* Edited by A. Avins. New York: Bookmailer, 1963.

26. Moore, W., Jr. *The Vertical Ghetto.* New York: Random House, 1969.

27. Morrill, R. L. "The Negro Ghetto: Problems and Alternatives," *The Geographical Review,* 55 (July 1965), pp. 339–61.

28. Myrdal, G. *An American Dilemma.* New York: McGraw-Hill, 1964.

29. The National Commission on Urban Problems. *More Than Shelter: Social Needs in Low and Moderate-Income Housing.* Research Report No. 8, Washington, D.C.: Government Printing Office, 1968.

30. Peskin, A., ed. *North Into Freedom: The Autobiography of John Malvin, Free Negro, 1795–1880.* Cleveland: Western Reserve University Press, 1966.

31. Rose, H. M. "Social Processes in the City: Race and Urban Residential Choice." Commission on College Geography Resource Paper No. 6. Washington, D.C.: Association of American Geographers, 1969.

32. Sloane, M. E. "The Housing Act of 1968: Best Yet But Is It Enough?" *Civil Rights Digest,* 1 (Fall 1968), pp. 1–9.

33. Stampp, K. M. *The Peculiar Institution.* New York: Vintage Books, 1956.

34. Still, W. *The Underground Railroad.* Philadelphia: People's Publishing Co., 1871.

35. Sydnor, C. S. "Life Span of Mississippi Slaves," *American Historical Review,* 35 (April 1930), pp. 566–74.

36. Taylor, O. W. *Negro Slavery in Arkansas.* Durham: Duke University Press, 1958.

37. Utley, R. W. "Pecos Bill on the Texas Frontier," *The American West,* 6 (January 1969), pp. 4–13, 61–62.

38. Virrick, E. L. "New Housing for Negroes in Dade County, Florida," *Studies in Housing and Minority Groups.* Edited by N. Glazer and D. McEntire. Berkeley: University of California Press, 1960.

39. Wade, R. C. *Slavery in the Cities; The South 1820–1860.* New York: Oxford University Press, 1964.

THE ORIGIN AND PATTERN OF DEVELOPMENT OF URBAN BLACK SOCIAL AREAS

Harold M. Rose

The urban geography of the city has historically focused on the city as a physical entity. But, as the city has evolved into an arena of complex social interaction and has increasingly become the locus of a host of ill-defined social and economic problems, geographers are beginning to view it from a different perspective. The title of Churchill's book, *The City Is The People,* is a good description of that new perspective. While many characteristics of the residents of the American city help to mold its character and affect its image, none are currently so important as race. Most major American cities are rapidly becoming the place of residence of the black population, as the white population continues to abandon the city for the open space of the suburbs. Thus, within one generation, the racial spatial patterns prevailing in large American cities have undergone very profound changes. In order to better understand the nature of the most recent social conflict that has evolved within the metropolitan complex, some understanding of the nature of existing racial spatial patterns will be helpful.

The evolution of social groups in urban space with an attachment to a territorial base has been a common phenomenon in American society. The classic example is associated with the rise of territorially based ethnic communities in eastern and midwestern cities during the late nineteenth century. Ethnic enclaves often occupied the least desirable parts of the city, but performed the function of providing a sense of community at a crucial stage in the life of its residents. Most of the old ethnic enclaves have disappeared or now occupy only remnants of their previous domain.

The previous territorially based social groups have been succeeded by the recent rise in the magnitude of urban black populations. At the present, these new territorially based social communities are rapidly growing entities which show no sign of diminishing. Communities of this type are often described as black ghettos. Thus, the geography of black urban populations most frequently coincides with the geography of the ghetto.

THE EVOLUTION OF THE GHETTO

The black ghetto, as an urban spatial form, is not new to major American cities, as there is historical evidence which attests to its presence as long ago as the early nineteenth century.[1] What has changed is the areal magnitude of the ghetto community and the social philosophy bearing upon its existence. The term "ghetto" has grown in popularity during the past two decades to describe those parts of large urban centers which are predominantly occupied by the black population. The appropriateness of the term has, on occasion, been challenged by those from both without and within who are offended by its implications.[2] Since the term tends to imply spatial restriction only indirectly related to housing costs and more directly related to race, one might logically expect this kind of reaction.

The black ghetto represents a social area or community occupied chiefly by persons of a single race and somewhat similar subcultural characteristics. The presence of the ghetto has led to social isolation and a strengthening of subcultural characteristics. A new generation of blacks is today attempting to capitalize on what was previously considered an undesirable situation by emphasizing the positive aspects of the subcultural differences which have evolved and spread within these social areas.

For the geographer, who is accustomed to delimiting areas on maps, the above definition does not ease his task. First, because of its failure to specify the intensity of black occupance necessary to qualify an area for membership in this social area, and second, because of rapid scale changes occurring within the ghetto community. Furthermore, there are regional differences which impinge upon a complex set of forces which ultimately lead to ghetto formation. To be more specific, it is generally agreed that the forces at work in the South are somewhat different from those which operate outside this region. Ultimately though, even though the ghetto forming process is variable, the same type of conceptual spatial form has evolved throughout the nation.

Black social areas which have come into existence in major northern urban communities might be described as type A, while those developing in the South might be thought of as type B ghetto areas. In the latter region land was initially set aside to be employed as housing sites for the black population. The type A ghetto is the result of one population replacing another in a common housing market, principally along racial lines. More recently the expansion of type B ghettos has followed a pattern similar to that which is characteristic of the North and West. The forces, which once permitted regional differences in the pattern of ghetto formation, appear to be weakening, as the ghetto formation process in the South more and more is beginning to resemble that prevailing outside the region.

In order for the geographer to translate a social concept into a valid spatial configuration, a decision has to be made regarding the minimal level of black occupance necessary for an area to become identified as a segment of the black ghetto. Not only is the intensity of occupance a prerequisite for establishing the areal extent of the ghetto, one must also agree on a suitable unit of occupance on which these measurements will be based. The most suitable unit for mapping purposes is the block concept employed by the Bureau of the Census, which is a cellular rather than linear block. This enables one to point out differences in intensity of occupance within short distances and is, therefore, a more sensitive measure of the spatial form of the ghetto at any given time. The question of the more appropriate minimum level of occupance for establishing the spatial limits of the ghetto is a difficult one and should be given careful consideration.

A more rational approach to the solution of this problem can be specified for type A ghettos than for type B. In the case of the former, there seems to be more evidence available which describes the expected behavior in a common housing market. Whites frequently refuse to compete with blacks in racial housing markets where blacks are in the majority. Since one's perception of what constitutes the majority is often impaired, it appears that some smaller value, that is, less than 50 per cent, would represent a more appropriate minimum. With this in mind, blocks containing a minimum of 40 per cent black household heads were designated for ghetto inclusion. Thus, the spatial form of type A ghettos might be described by including all contiguous blocks possessing a minimum of 40 per cent black occupance. The problem of establishing limits for B type ghettos is even more problematic.

The employment of the above specified level of black occupance as the outer limit of the ghetto, as a spatial configuration, implies much about the evolution of a territory as a social area. Black institutions will be principally confined to the core of the ghetto where the level of intensity of black occupance is higher and a threshold population has been present for a much longer period of time. Along the margin of the ghetto edge, white social and selective economic institutions will be beginning to disappear. Frequently, in type A ghettos, the black population inherits a set of institutional structures which were developed by and for the previous residential population.

The boundary separating the black community from its neighbor is in a

constant state of flux. A zone of transition of varying width tends to separate these social communities. In type A ghetto areas the zone of transition
will include blocks with a level of black occupance ranging from 20 per
cent to less than 40 per cent. Within this zone, many residents exhibit a
feeling of not holding membership in the zone of occupance. The boundaries in type B ghettos are generally more abrupt than those characterizing
the type A communities and in some there is almost a complete absence of
the zone of transition.

THE PERSISTENCE OF THE GHETTO

The ghetto or black social areas in urban space are not threatened by
the imminent possibility of disappearance. The areal magnitude of the
ghetto is one of continuous expansion.[3] One might point out that two most
rapidly expanding spatial configurations in the metropolitan complex are
the ghetto and the suburbs. While there are shifts in ghetto land use as an
outgrowth of competition with other urban land users, this simply results
in the more rapid inclusion of contiguous space as a part of the ghetto
configuration. The contiguous black occupance of vast areas of urban
space within our major metropolitan complexes works against any meaningful change in the pattern of development of social areas based on race.
While social areas evolve that are racially based, these areas are not
homogeneous. There exists within the ghetto community a spatial
stratification based on income differences.[4] Black social areas possess a
kind of internal structure which is a replica of that which prevails in the
larger urban community. The strength of stratification, though, is weaker
than that which exists outside, and thereby leads to a great degree of
social and economic heterogeneity.[5]

When one considers the persistence of this urban form, one wonders why
geographers have given it so little attention. This, no doubt, is a reflection
of the recency of recognition granted to the subfield of social geography,
an area which is not yet highly developed in the United States. The continued existence of black social areas largely rests on the future of race
relations. A combination of white backlash attitudes and the rise of the
concept of black awareness prolongs still further the continued existence
of social areas that are racially based. These social areas tend to evolve
into cultural areas and thereby reflect the areal consequences of cultural
pluralism.

The nondiminishing character of black social areas could play a major
role in the alteration of the structure of urban governments. As more and
more major urban centers become the place of residence of black populations spatially dispersed in the previously described manner, the possi-

bility of black political controls appears ever more likely. If traditional white behavior can be anticipated, there could be a widespread opting for a metropolitan form of government. If this does happen, one can attribute to the black ghetto the power to promote the development of a governmental form that has previously engendered only minor support.

THE GHETTO PATTERN

The pattern of ghetto development might be viewed in terms of its historical pattern of evolution and thereby emphasize the growth of black communities as a response to changes in the social and economic conditions in the larger community. The ghetto pattern viewed from this perspective would focus on the distribution of urban areas containing black communities having reached some predefined order of magnitude. Thus, if one was concerned with identifying the location of black communities in the United States on the basis of population size, then a map of such localities could easily be constructed.

In 1960, one third of the nation's black population resided in eighteen cities.[6] Each of these cities contained more than 100,000 Negroes in their populations. (Figure 1) At the same time, approximately two thirds of the nation's black population were residents of metropolitan areas. The size of the black community is highly correlated with the size of the total population among the ten ranking black communities. There are some slight differences in rank among the ten largest communities and the ten largest black communities.

Regional differences in the distribution of the nation's major black communities are also apparent. As is true of the nation's population as a whole, the Middle Atlantic and North Central cities are the locations of most of the large black communities. The South includes four of the eight second-order ghettos, but only two among the ten ranking black communities. The West, the most recently developed urban region in the nation, contains only one of the major black communities, and it is to be found in Los Angeles. The prevailing regional pattern reflects accessibility between the original source region, and that of the chosen destination. The pattern of black migration developing after the turn of the century has largely influenced the magnitude of the population prevailing within these communities.

An alternative way of viewing the external pattern of black communities might be to develop a map showing the racial imbalance in cities of more than 100,000. In this case one might employ as an index of imbalance a ratio that is, minimally, twice the national percentage of blacks in the total population. Such a distribution would include those

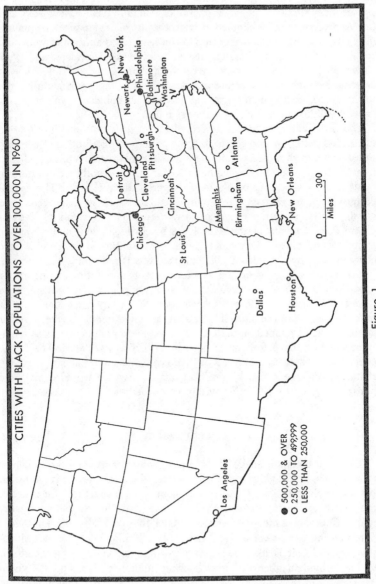

CITIES WITH BLACK POPULATIONS OVER 100,000 IN 1960

● 500,000 & OVER
◐ 250,000 TO 499,999
○ LESS THAN 250,000

Figure 1

places in which the Negro percentage is 22 per cent and above. Employing an index of this type, such enormous communities as New York and Los Angeles would be eliminated from the list of major black communities. The greatest imbalance occurs in southern cities and major industrial centers in the Middle West. The newer cities of the Southwest and West almost all contain a ratio of a lower order of magnitude. While such an index is instructive, it does not appear to be a suitable surrogate for the former, and, furthermore, regional indexes of imbalance might be of greater validity than a single national index.

The kind of point pattern described above does not actually describe the spatial pattern of the ghetto, but the pattern of distribution of communities which have nested within them ranking ghetto communities. The internal pattern of ghetto development is highly varied and tends to run the range from a single major cluster to several minor clusters. The spatial pattern of ghetto clusters is related to such factors as: 1) heterogeneity of housing costs in contiguous space; 2) pattern of employment; 3) stage of ghetto development; 4) the size of the black population; and 5) public policy. Many of the embryonic ghetto communities in major cities are characterized by a single cluster, but even this is not a universal pattern. Minneapolis, with one of the smaller black communities among major urban centers, has at least two distinctive black population clusters, while Denver and Seattle, whose black communities in 1960 contained fewer than 50,000, were the sites of essentially a single ghetto cluster. Smaller ghettos have developed on the fringes of the metropolitan area in some instances. These have sometimes been described as *ghettolets*. The fringe enclaves run the gamut in terms of their economic and social structure. No single generalization can be made at this time which would explain the pattern of ghetto distribution within central cities.

THE GHETTO CONDITION

The most common image of the ghetto, which is held by the public, is that of a slum or blighted zone. All too often the public image is not far off the mark. Nevertheless, the ghetto concept is not a substitute for zones of crumbling residential structures. It is true that the residential quality within those areas identified as elements of the black ghetto is constantly deteriorating because of age and the limited development of new residential structures. It is likewise true that within segments of the ghetto or within individual ghetto clusters housing quality is high, and the visual appearance of these areas does not differ perceptibly from that of adjacent areas. Unfortunately, the latter condition seldom constitutes the model condition of housing located within the ghetto context. A point to be made here is that the physical condition of the ghetto is in no way involved in establishing its territorial limits.

If quality of the ghetto environment is measured in terms of some index of residential quality, then one would have to accept as a truism that environmental quality is low. The low quality of the residential environment is generally associated with the fact that the ghetto, in its incipient state, is confined to zones of the oldest housing in the city. In type A ghettos, this housing is most often found nearest the city center, yet, in some of the B type ghetto clusters, alternative patterns sometimes emerge. In the latter situation, where basic shelter was often provided for segments of the black labor force, vacant land and accessibility to the job were major considerations; a situation which could easily lead to a pattern of ghetto development unlike the modal type evolving within type A ghetto areas.

As the ghetto expands from its interior location outward, it frequently will include the range of housing quality that is to be found within a single sector of the city. This range is clearly typified in the southern sector of black occupance in Chicago. The physical enormity of the area makes possible a wide range of housing quality. A second alternative is represented by the Boston ghetto. In this case, the age of the central city and the nature of the housing developed within the central city during the most recent building cycle, coupled with the size of Boston's black population, relegates it to a zone of little differentiation. The impact of age of the city and the size of the black population can also be seen in some of the newer western cities. The black ghetto in Denver, as a case in point, hardly resembles that of Boston in terms of residential quality. This younger city, with its prevalence of relatively new single family structures located in the path of ghetto expansion, is sometimes held up as a model black community, in terms of its physical quality.

Poverty in the black ghetto is all too commonplace and does much to help reinforce the existence of the ghetto, but is not the basic factor explaining its existence. The National Commission on Urban Problems recently revealed their findings on the areal extent of poverty, occurring within the nation's principal urban agglomerations. While the percentage of the total land area occupied by persons in poverty is highly variable, the percentage of black occupants situated within poverty areas is consistently high.[7] Blight is likewise an ever-present condition within poverty areas. An extreme example is represented by Birmingham, Alabama, wherein 45 per cent of the total land area of that city can be described as representing a landscape of poverty. More than 90 per cent of the occupants of the poverty area in Birmingham are black. McHarg's modification of a once proud national proclamation seems to be an altogether fitting description of today's urban condition: "Give us your poor and oppressed, and we will give them Harlem and the Lower East Side,

Bedford-Stuyvesant, the South Side of Chicago, and the North of Philadelphia—or if they are very lucky, Levittown."[8]

The physical quality of life in social areas described as black ghettos is far from heartening in most instances. Yet there are examples of segments of urban space that have had attached to them the ghetto label that are on par with many nonghetto areas. Needless to say, the former type of ghetto condition is that whose image is most widespread and to which more effective attention must be focused as a means of altering the quality of the environment.

CONCLUSIONS

The long-range future of urban black social areas is highly speculative. Although there is little evidence which would lead one to believe that they are anything less than semipermanent features in the urban landscape. The momentum associated with ghetto development in the nation's principal metropolitan complexes works against any short run reversal of the process. Thus, black social areas are likely to become increasingly territorially based at a time when territorially based social communities are diminishing in importance. One noted urbanist recently remarked that "Here in the slum blocks of the central cities may be the only pure place-based social neighborhoods we have left."[9] If this is the case, one can only expect a widening of the rift that has led to the social ferment in the cities.

Moves currently afoot could lead to the eventual invalidation of the employment of terms such as ghetto to describe black social areas. But until these areas are perceived differently both by their residents and outsiders, the ghetto designation tends not to be inappropriate. At the present there is some evidence that internal perceptions are being altered more rapidly than the external ones. To the contrary, there has been a sharp upsurge in the usage of the ghetto designation by the popular media in referring to spatially based black social areas.

While black social areas are not threatened by the immediate prospect of disappearance, there exists the possibility of an alteration in the pattern of social area development. In the future it is conjectured that a larger number of small black clusters dispersed throughout the metropolitan complex could represent the modal pattern. Such a pattern could lead to improvements in the quality of the environment in black social areas. Needless to say, because of the diminution of the perceived power base associated with expansive territorial control, the latter pattern might be rejected by blacks.

LITERATURE CITED

1. Gilbert Osofsky, "The Enduring Ghetto," *The Journal of American History*, September 1968, p. 244.
2. Karl R. Rasmussen, "The Multi-Ordered Urban Area: A Ghetto," *Phylon*, Fall 1968, pp. 283–90.
3. Theodore G. Clemence, "Residential Segregation in the Mid-Sixties," *Demography*, IV, 2 (1967), 562–68.
4. Karl E. Taeuber, "The Problem of Residential Segregation," *Proceedings, The Academy of Political Science*, XXIX (1968), 108–9.
5. James Q. Wilson, "The Urban Unease: Community vs. City," *The Public Interest*, No. 12, Summer 1968, pp. 33–34.
6. *The Negroes in the United States, Their Economic and Social Situation*, United States Department of Labor, Bulletin No. 1511, June 1966, p. 19.
7. Allen D. Manvel, *Housing Conditions in Urban Poverty Areas*, The National Commission on Urban Problems, Research Report No. 9, 1968, pp. 14–19.
8. Ian L. McHarg, "Values, Process and Form," *The Fitness of Man's Environment*, Washington, D.C., 1968, p. 211.
9. Melvin M. Webber, "The Post-City Age," *Daedalus*, Fall 1968, p. 1102.

CHAPTER II

Locational Aspects of Black Population

INTRODUCTORY NOTE

Population geography is a comparatively recent addition to the many subfields of geography. Since Trewartha's enunciation of population geography as a distinct specialization in 1953, much research on locational aspects of population has been accomplished. However, only in the last decade have population geographers turned their attention to studying characteristics of racial and ethnic populations.

Racial composition is a variable that population geographers have tended to neglect in their work. Contemporary demographers and other social scientists have found that population characteristics vary racially. Sex ratios, age structures, birth rates, mortality rates, and other demographic variables are not constant when racial groups are studied comparatively.

In the pluralistic society of the United States, blacks and whites often do not share common population characteristics, and it is only by analyzing pertinent socioeconomic data can geographers delimit accurately areal organization of America's black population. This task is imperative if geographers wish to understand all sectors of United States society.

Insights into locational aspects of black population are relatively few in number; however these contributions are increasing rapidly in the literature as is evidenced by the four works in this chapter. Although the chapter in general concerns racial population, each article treats a different facet of the subject. The changing national distribution of blacks is the topic of John Fraser Hart's research. Mark Lowry II deals with population and race in the state of Mississippi. Rose and Sanders and Adams focus their attention respectively on black populations of Miami and Cleveland. Thus, the chapter's structure proceeds from nation to state to city in an ascending scale of areal order.

In the "The Changing Distribution of the American Negro," John

Fraser Hart has written a lengthy and perceptive examination of one of the most dramatic aspects of population geography in twentieth-century America: migration of blacks from the rural South to the urban North and West. Hart examines in fine detail major migration trends by the nine census regions from 1860 to 1950, emphasizing massive northward migration after 1910. To provide a better understanding of relative locational importance of blacks, Hart combines density and intensity criteria into a single index that delimits the black core area in the United States through time.

Hart, prior to discussion of black interstate migration, presents a detailed account of the major techniques used to measure migration: mobility, census survival ratio, state of birth, and natural increase. The author then applies these techniques to develop a clear picture of nonwhite patterns of interstate movements in 1940–50.

In conclusion, Hart states that black Americans are becoming increasingly urbanized, and that three principal streams of migration from rural South to urban North and West can be defined. First, the Piedmont and Inner Coastal Plain of Georgia, the Carolinas, and Virginia are the sources of migrants to Middle Atlantic states. The second stream consists of migrants from the Delta and Black Belt of Mississippi who are moving to urban centers of the Midwest. The third flows from the Southwest westward to the Pacific states.

Hart's article is a classic in the geography of black Americans and one of the first major geographical works written concerning black America. However, several criticisms of this article must be made. First, for an article of this length, Hart's conclusions are disappointingly brief and cursory. Second, documentation of facts and figures contained in this extensive work is somewhat lacking. Lastly, Hart gives the subtle impression of viewing black Americans almost as objects, not human beings, and his population geography of race is not concerned with social variables as the bigotry and racial discrimination suffered so long by black Americans. Nonetheless, these are minor flaws in an otherwise well-written and significant work.

Mark Lowry II discusses the importance of race in southern society in "Population and Race in Mississippi, 1940–1960." Using the state of Mississippi as a case study, Lowry illustrates the manner in which a segregated plural society affects the state's population geography. Lowry discusses four specific topics: black and white regional population distributions, local residential segregation, areal arrangement of the two races at intermediate scales, and contemporary population trends.

Lowry's discussion of the distinct racial population geography of Mississippi as produced by a discriminatory society is both a timely and significant contribution to the literature of race. The purpose of the article is to assess significance of race in Mississippi's population by: placing the state in perspective with the surrounding area and nation, emphasizing population trends and racial percentages, and comparing patterns of total population and black and white races for 1940 and 1960 using minor civil divisions and urban places as units of areal observation.

Mississippi was selected as the study area for several reasons. The study period was a time of vast changes contrasting with prior decades. The area experienced rapid rural to urban immigration that caused faster rates of urban growth and rural decline than in the rest of the nation. And, finally, the state has a larger percentage of blacks than either region or nation.

The technique that Lowry utilizes in the article to analyze racial changes in population trends from 1940 to 1960 is multiple correlation. However, data from 1950 are not presented in the research and one wonders why they were excluded.

Lowry states in conclusion that causes for the pattern of race in Mississippi must be found in the social-economic milieu. Particularly important economically are the rapidly changing agricultural sector and growing secondary and tertiary sectors. Unfortunately, the author does not specify changes in the social sphere which have led to racial redistribution, perhaps because of the great difficulty in obtaining and measuring such data.

Harold M. Rose examines several factors responsible for atypical patterns in spatial distribution of black population of the Miami SMSA (Standard Metropolitan Statistical Area). A regional framework is used to view the population geography of a minority group in the urban environment. The factors which Rose utilizes to analyze the black population of Miami are age structure, sex composition, and educational levels.

The Miami SMSA has been divided somewhat subjectively into three areal units which designate major black settlements based upon the operation of socioeconomic conditions: Core, Inner Ring, and Outer Ring. For these subregions, Rose describes the situation and nature of each settlement area and character of the population contained therein. The Core area contains most of Miami's black population and is the most densely settled area in the region. The Inner Ring area constitutes a group of small black communities that can be thought of as black suburban ghettos. The Outer Ring is situated in a semirural setting and only a small number of impoverished blacks inhabit this area.

Using three population characteristics, Rose examines the black pattern of settlement, future growth, and economic considerations of labor force participation by blacks. Rose concludes that rapid growth of Miami's black population is due partially to great economic and social attractions found in Miami. Specific patterns of black settlement are affected by a number of social and economic forces, chief of which is proximity to place of employment. Lastly, Rose characterizes the emerging service-orientated metropolitan area as physically fragmented—at least as far as the black community is concerned.

Ralph A. Sanders and John S. Adams introduce their work on the age structure of Cleveland's black population by criticizing geographers as being traditionally disinterested in social attributes of population, over-concerned with forcing regional approaches onto their subject matter, and suffering from a landscape bias with a heavy rural orientation. Such criticism, although sharp, is justified and the authors perform a legitimate service in raising it. They are not content, however, with criticism alone, and offer a well-structured analysis of internal stresses operating within ghettos through time, thus avoiding the fallacies mentioned above. Sanders and Adams maintain that it is possible to outline systematic areal and temporal variations within the ghetto, and that basic age-selective residential moves originate from the ghetto core to the periphery.

Methodologically, the authors utilize characteristic age structures for local populations by imposing a best-fitting least squares line upon a population-age histogram. As a result, a generalized age structure is reflected in the slope parameter of that line. Completing the method, signs and decimal points are dropped giving the Age Structure Index Value (ASIV), which indicates ratios of youth to aged in a given population. The authors found that median ages of black residents vary systematically throughout the ghetto. As expected, the oldest age structures are found in the central ghetto area. Additionally, age structure increases with length of time that an area is part of the ghetto.

The authors conclude that in Cleveland pattern of age structure variation parallels ghetto territorial expansion. Or more simply, the ghetto core is inhabited by aging populations and the periphery or ghetto outliers are populated by young blacks who have migrated selectively from ghetto centers. According to Sanders and Adams, ghetto expansion is not so much a block by block transition but a pattern of "leapfrogging" and interstitial growth.

THE CHANGING DISTRIBUTION OF
THE AMERICAN NEGRO

John Fraser Hart

The changing distribution of its Negro population has been one of the most dramatic aspects of the population geography of the United States over the last half century. In 1910 the Negroes of the United States were concentrated mainly in rural areas on the plains of the southeastern part of the nation, but by 1950 most of the nation's Negroes had left the rural areas, and many of them had left the South as well. In 1910 only one Negro in four lived in an urban place, and Negroes comprised only 6.3 per cent of the urban population; by 1950 two thirds of the nation's Negroes lived in urban areas, and 9.7 per cent of the urban population was Negro.

It is the purpose of this paper to examine and describe the changing patterns of Negro distribution in the United States. Insofar as possible these patterns are analyzed and interpreted, but they are so complex, both temporally and areally, that no one person could be fully competent to analyze them adequately, and in some instances the paper has had to be limited to descriptions of patterns rather than attempt interpretation.

In describing the redistribution of Negroes, this paper treats three separate but closely interrelated aspects of this redistribution: (1) changes in the distribution of Negroes between 1910 and 1950, with a delimitation of the Negro area of the United States; (2) areal variations in the date of maximum Negro population; and (3) patterns of Negro migration in the decade 1940–50, with a discussion of techniques for measuring migration.

DISTRIBUTION OF NEGROES IN 1910 AND 1950

The distribution of the Negro population in 1910 is of considerable importance. On the regional level it was essentially where it had been for some fifty years, albeit thicker on the ground. The massive northward migration was about to start, but had not yet gotten under way. In short, the census of 1910 records the high tide of the rural Negro in the South, and any comprehension of the subsequent redistribution must be based on an understanding of the situation in 1910.[1]

The distribution of Negroes in 1950 provides a useful basis for comparison with the 1910 distribution, and also, despite the more recent data of the 1960 census of population, it merits consideration in its own right. The turbulent decade of 1940–50 witnessed the greatest Negro redistribution, both relatively and absolutely, that has ever been recorded in the United States. Existing trends were intensified by wartime mobilization and industrialization, and by 1950 every major metropolitan area had a sizable Negro population.

When considering the distribution of Negroes—or any other minority group—in the United States, neither density per square mile nor percentage of Negroes in the total population is a completely satisfactory index, if used alone.[2] Some urban areas, for example, have almost astronomical Negro densities; yet the percentage of Negroes in the total population is quite low. Conversely, Negroes comprise an extremely high percentage of the total population in some sparsely settled areas; yet there may be less than one Negro person per square mile. It is necessary, therefore, to consider both indices in order fully to comprehend the distribution of Negroes.

The major area of Negro population in the United States in 1910 was a belt some two hundred miles wide which spanned the plainsland South[3] from the Black Prairies of Texas to Virginia, and then tapered to a narrow tip in Megalopolis. This belt widened perceptibly where it crossed the Mississippi River bottomlands, sent a finger curling into northern Florida, and had outliers in the middle Tennessee River Valley–Nashville Basin–Pennyroyal Plain area and in the Kentucky Bluegrass. The greatest rural densities within the belt were in the Mississippi Delta country, in the Black Belt, on the Piedmont of Georgia and South Carolina, and on the Inner Coastal Plain of South Carolina. Relatively few counties had urban densities of more than seventy Negroes per square mile, and urban Negro communities in the Middle West were still relatively small.

Southern Florida and the Appalachian uplands had few Negroes in 1910, but there was more than one Negro per square mile in western Tennessee, western Kentucky, and the part of southwestern Ohio which centers on the old Virginia Military District. There were two or three Negro families per square mile along the lower Missouri River, in the eastern part of the new state of Oklahoma, and along the Gulf Coast. Farther afield only Chicago and Pittsburgh had more than thirty-three Negroes per square mile, but there was a hint of things to come in the increasing

Negro population of many northern cities, especially those in the Pittsburgh-Cleveland area.

Two major changes are apparent in 1950: the shrinkage of the major belt and the increased number of counties with urban densities. The number of urban Negroes increased notably in the Middle West and the trans-Mississippi South, and the Negro population also increased in parts of the High Plains of Texas, western Oklahoma, peninsular Florida, and the Inner Coastal Plain of the Carolinas. But there were fewer Negroes in much of eastern Texas, in the southern Appalachians, and in three areas which had a dense rural Negro population in 1910: The Mississippi Delta, the Black Belt, and the Piedmont of Georgia and South Carolina.

The same broad patterns are revealed by maps of Negro intensity. In 1950 the counties which were more than half Negro were concentrated in the Mississippi Delta, in the Black Belt, on the Piedmont of Georgia and South Carolina, on the South Carolina Coastal Plain, and in areas centering on the peanut country of Virginia–Carolina and Georgia–Florida. The large number of counties which dropped out of this category between 1910 and 1950 are scattered throughout the South, but the greatest losses were in areas isolated from the main belt, or along its fringes.

The counties in which at least one third of the population was Negro tend to fill the interstitial areas of the preceding pattern. The largest additional areas are in eastern North Carolina, northern Florida, southern Arkansas, Louisiana, and eastern Texas. The counties which dropped below this percentage between 1910 and 1950 are almost entirely peripheral, with the largest number in the Piedmont, northern Florida, Louisiana, and Texas.

Virtually the entire plainsland South, from Texas to southern Maryland, had at least one Negro for every five persons in 1910. The small outlying areas in which Negroes comprised at least 20 per cent of the total population included the Kentucky Bluegrass, the Middle Tennessee River Valley–Nashville Basin–Pennyroyal Plain area, and east central Oklahoma, but these areas had shriveled considerably or even completely disappeared from the map by 1950. Otherwise, as in the two higher percentage categories, the counties whose Negro intensity dropped below the 20 per cent mark between 1910 and 1950 were strung along the margins of the main area. This is the highest percentage category, however, to which counties were added between 1910 and 1950, with the major area of accretion in southern Florida. It is also noteworthy that, with the exception of Lake County, Michigan, and Howard County, Missouri, there has been no county outside the traditional South in which more than 20 per cent of the population is Negro.[4]

Apart from the upland areas, in virtually every county in the South in 1910 at least one person in ten was a Negro. There was little change on the plains between 1910 and 1950, but along the margins of the uplands the Negro intensity dropped below 10 per cent in many counties. It is much more significant, however, that in the same period, between 1910 and 1950, the number of Negroes exceeded 10 per cent of the population in many northern cities, including Chicago, Detroit, Indianapolis, Cincinnati, Columbus, Cleveland, Philadelphia, and Newark. Parenthetically it might be noted that in 1950 Negroes comprised exactly 10 per cent of the population of the United States.

Approximately half the counties of the United States had two or more Negroes per hundred persons in 1910 or in 1950, if not in both years. The South is so solid that the main interest lies in those counties whose Negro numbers have climbed above or dropped below the 2 per cent level. Most of the losses are in the border area, and they call attention to the early role of the Missouri and Ohio rivers in the distribution of American Negroes. Although the Negro population has declined along the Ohio, at one time that river was lined, as the lower Missouri still is, by counties in which at least one person in fifty was a Negro.

The great majority of counties whose Negro population surpassed the 2

TABLE 1
Negro Population in Selected States, 1950

State[1]	Negro population	
	In selected urbanized areas	Elsewhere in state
California (7)	402,281	59,891
Washington (2)	19,870	10,821
Arizona (1)	13,406	12,568
Colorado (1)	15,611	4,566
Nebraska (1)	17,011	2,223
Oregon (1)	10,664	865
Minnesota (1)	12,561	1,461
New Mexico		8,408
Nevada		4,302
Utah		2,729
Wyoming		2,557
Montana		1,232
Idaho		1,050
South Dakota		727
North Dakota		257
Total	491,404	113,657

[1]Numbers in parentheses indicate the number of urbanized areas included in the calculation.

per cent level between 1910 and 1950 are in the North and in the southern part of the West. North of the Ohio River and the Mason-Dixon line all but a few of these counties contain a major urban center. In the West, however, the pattern is complicated by the large size and sparse population of many counties. In western Texas, for instance, many counties have fewer than 10,000 people, and 2 per cent of the population is only 200 persons.

Despite the appearance of the map, to the north and west of a line from San Antonio through Kansas City to Milwaukee the Negro population actually is highly localized (Table 1). Fifteen states in this area had a total Negro population of more than 600,000 persons in 1950, but over four fifths of the total number lived in only thirteen urbanized areas, and well over half lived in the Los Angeles and San Francisco urbanized areas. Outside the thirteen urbanized areas the total Negro population of these fifteen states is far less than half the Negro population of the eleven counties between the Mississippi and Yazoo rivers in the Mississippi Delta country.

But whereas the percentage of Negroes has been increasing in other parts of the nation, the Negro population intensity has been decreasing in the South. Fewer counties had extremely high percentages of Negroes in 1950 than in 1910, but at the lower percentage levels there were about the same number. For example, the number of counties in which more than half the population was Negro dropped from 285 to 163, but the number of counties with more than three Negroes per hundred persons rose from 1,211 to 1,244.

THE NEGRO AREA IN 1950

Combining density and intensity criteria into a single index provides a better understanding of the relative importance of the Negro population of the United States than can be gained by the use of either criterion alone. From the previous discussion one may conclude that the Negro area of the United States includes those counties which meet two criteria: (1) a density of at least one Negro per square mile, and (2) an intensity of at least 2 per cent. Negroes patently are of minimal importance in counties which fail to meet both these criteria.

Within the Negro area one must recognize a core of counties in which the density is at least nine Negroes per square mile, and in which at least 20 per cent of the people are Negroes. Furthermore, there are two types of counties intermediate between the core of the Negro area and those outlying areas which barely meet the criteria for inclusion. Many highly urbanized counties have a density of more than nine Negroes per square mile, but an intensity of less than 20 per cent; conversely, numerous sparsely settled counties have an intensity greater than 20 per cent but fewer than nine Negroes per square mile.

The core of the Negro area in 1950 swings in a great arc across the plainsland South from eastern Maryland to eastern Texas. There are scattered outliers in Texas, Florida, and the area extending north and south through Nashville, but the core consists of a group of impressively contiguous counties. The sparsely settled counties of the Negro area—those with low densities and high intensities—are largely in eastern Texas, Florida, and along the Gulf Coast near Mobile Bay. Conversely, the counties with high densities and low intensities, which are the highly urbanized portions of the Negro area, lie north of the core area. The largest concentration is in Megalopolis, but there are smaller clusters in the Pittsburgh–Cleveland area, in the Detroit–Chicago area, in southwestern Ohio, and on the Piedmont of Georgia and North Carolina.

Some counties of the lowest category are scattered through the core of the Negro area, but for the most part the counties of this category lie around the margins of the area or are completely separated from it. They are strung along the Great Valley, from Hagerstown to Birmingham, and festoon the eastern front of the Blue Ridge from Virginia to Georgia. They cover much of northern Alabama, middle Tennessee, and western Kentucky, and extend northward into the old Virginia Military District of Ohio. Farther west they are found along the lower course of the Missouri River, in central Oklahoma, in eastern Texas, and scattered over the High Plains. And there are a number of counties in this lowest category on the West Coast.

For the most part, those counties which were in a lower category in 1950 than in 1910 are those which were in the lowest category in 1950, or had dropped completely out of the Negro area. There was a decline throughout the uplands; the Blue Ridge Mountains, the Appalachian Hills, the Highland Rim–Pennyroyal Hills, and the Ozark–Ouachita borders are all areas in which the Negro population was of less importance in 1950 than in 1910. Interestingly enough, however, the Great Valley held its own, as did several other more favorable areas in the hill country. There was also a decline in many counties of the western South, and along the Gulf Coast, with concentrations in south central Texas, the marshlands of southern Louisiana, and the flatwoods country east of Mobile Bay and in southeastern Georgia and northern Florida.

The Negro area of 1910 lay almost entirely to the south and east of a line from New York City to Kansas City, and thence to San Antonio, and the Negro redistribution after 1910 might almost be described as an eruption across this line. The analogy is strengthened by the way in which counties of a higher category in 1950 than in 1910 are splattered across the map; they are on the West Coast, in the western part of the South, in the North, and in Florida. There is a cluster in southern Missouri, several in coal-mining areas of Kentucky and West Virginia, and one on the industrial Piedmont of North Carolina.

But most impressive of all, perhaps, is the fact that such a large proportion of the counties of the Negro area were in the same categories in 1950 as they had been in 1910. Although there was some attrition of counties along its northern fringes, the core area in particular remained remarkably stable, and so did the sparsely settled areas of eastern Texas and northern Florida. This is not to say, quite obviously, that there were no changes, because there were many and they were far-reaching, but it does indicate that the Negro area as here defined, and its core in particular, had a considerable degree of stability between 1910 and 1950.

Censal Year of Maximum Negro Population

Although 1910 is a critical year for any general consideration of Negro redistribution in the United States, it would be foolhardy not to assume that other years might be equally critical in various parts of the nation. It seems logical, therefore, to discover whether there actually is any great variation in the censal year in which various counties attained their maximum Negro population, and if so, to determine whether these variations have any areal significance.

Deciding the areal extent of the area to be investigated poses an immediate problem. Although the Negro area has shown a surprising degree of areal stability between 1910 and 1950, there still have been enough changes to warrant extension of the investigation beyond its outer limits. On the other hand, there seems little point in extending the investigation to the entire nation, as the Negro population of a large number of counties has always been small and subject to fairly great fluctuations; the censal year of maximum Negro population for these counties would be almost meaningless.[5] After some experimentation, it became evident that the requirements of this study would be satisfied if the investigation included all counties which at some time have had a Negro population density of at least one person per square mile.

The question of the censal year in which to begin the investigation was easily answered by the notorious differential under-enumeration of Negroes in the South in the ninth census in 1870. Some years afterward Francis A. Walker, who had been superintendent of the ninth census, told a legislative committee:

> When the appointments of enumerators were made in 1870 the entire lot was taken from the Republican Party, and most of those in the

South were Negroes. Some of the Negroes could not read or write, and the enumeration of the Southern population was done very badly. My judgment was that the Census of 1870 erred as to the colored population between 350,000 and 400,000.[6]

The first step in investigating the censal year of maximum Negro population, therefore, was the preparation of a map of the maximum Negro population density attained by each county in any census between 1880 and 1950. This map holds relatively few surprises. A few counties are added in New England, and there are minor accretions all along the upland margins. There are also a number of marginal counties with higher densities than they had in 1910 or in 1950, but no large blocks of counties are added to the areas already considered previously. Furthermore, the counties west of the 100th meridian were so uniform in attaining their peak Negro population in 1950 that they were omitted from further consideration, and the investigation was restricted to the eastern portion of the country.

It soon became apparent that the maximum Negro population was attained almost simultaneously in large contiguous groups of counties with an impressive degree of regional concentration. The peak was reached at a surprisingly early date in the four border states of Missouri, Kentucky, Tennessee, and Virginia, where large numbers of counties had their maximum Negro population in 1880 or in 1890. These counties are concentrated in the lower Missouri Valley, in middle Tennessee and middle and western Kentucky—including most of the Bluegrass and Nashville basins—in southwestern Ohio, in the Great Valley, and on the Virginia Piedmont. This period was the Negro high tide in the central hilly belt of the eastern United States, and by 1950 Negroes had almost disappeared in many of these counties.

In 1900 many additional counties around the margins of the hills attained their maximum Negro population, but this year is more notable because a few plainsland counties also reached their peaks. They are strung along the Fall Line in Georgia, a dozen are in the Alabama Black Belt, a few are along the lower Mississippi River, and some sixteen are in southern East Texas. But in 1900 the Negro population of most of the Cotton South was still growing.

The tide turned in 1910 and in 1920. Perhaps the boll weevil was pushing Negroes off the farms; perhaps wartime labor shortages in northern cities were pulling them off; in any event, three fifths of the counties of South Carolina and Georgia, half in Arkansas and northern Florida, a third in Alabama, and a quarter in East Texas had more Negroes in 1910 or in 1920 than they have ever had before or since. North Carolina counties held their own, but throughout the rest of the Cotton South, from South Carolina to Oklahoma and Texas, the Negro population of many counties reached its peak at this period.

The years 1930 and 1940 were the heyday of the Negro population in the western parts of the South, with heavy concentrations in central Oklahoma, on the sandy lands of Texas–Arkansas–Louisiana and of southern Mississippi, and on the alluvial lands along the Mississippi River. In this same period the Negro population curve reached its apex in coal-mining areas of Pennsylvania and West Virginia, in Piedmont and mountain areas of western North Carolina, and in parts of the Georgia–Florida flatwoods.

At this point attention needs to be called to the relationship between peak Negro population and the regional trends which have already been discussed. The sharp drop in the percentage of the Negro population in the South Atlantic states after 1920 corresponds with the fact that so many South Carolina and Georgia counties had their peak Negro population in 1910 or in 1920. The steady decline in the East South Central region's share between 1920 and 1950 is mirrored in the counties of Alabama, which had their peak years in 1920 or 1930, and in the counties of Mississippi, which had theirs in 1930 or 1940. The sharp decline in the West South Central region's share after 1940 is closely related to the fact that so many counties in Texas, Louisiana, and Arkansas had their peak Negro population in 1930 or 1940.

The counties whose Negro population was at its zenith in 1950 are rather less concentrated than those counties whose Negro population crested earlier. True enough, there are some quite obvious concentrations of counties with a 1950 peak—in the tier of states from Illinois to the Atlantic Seaboard, in eastern North Carolina, and in peninsular Florida—but a large number of such counties are scattered through the South.

Outside of North Carolina and Florida the counties which had their maximum Negro population in 1950 are urban, for the most part, and their distribution is closely related to the distribution of major urban centers. Some city counties—especially north and west of Chicago—lacked the one Negro per square mile necessary for inclusion in this investigation, and some city counties in the South had fewer Negroes in 1950 than in some previous census year. By and large, however, one may conclude that those counties which contain a major city also attained their major Negro population in 1950.

This conclusion, of course, led to the refined grouping of areas used above in discussing regional trends in the Negro population, because in the South the trends of the metropolitan and nonmetropolitan Negro populations quite obviously are diverging. Furthermore, the trend of the

Negro population in Florida and in North Carolina differs from other parts of the South.

A number of factors presumably contribute to the fact that such a large part of peninsular Florida recorded its maximum Negro population in 1950. The absolute increase in the Negro population between 1940 and 1950 was not large, and the Negro density in Florida is still sparse. Counties are comparatively large, and many have urban centers which have retained the natural increase of their Negro population and even attracted immigrants. These urban centers have rather large numbers of retired persons, representing an unusually good opportunity for Negro employment in personal services, and presumably the influx of people from the North has created a social climate rather more acceptable to Negroes than in other parts of the South.

The concentration of counties with a 1950 peak Negro population in eastern North Carolina is more puzzling, and thus far no completely satisfactory explanation for it has been discovered. It has been suggested that a more enlightened political climate might have played a role in providing more acceptable conditions for Negro life, but this concentration is in the politically more conservative part of the state; furthermore, it includes eight counties in South Carolina, a state not especially renowned for the excellence of its race relations. Later in this paper it will be suggested that the agricultural system and demographic history of the area might provide some explanation, but the unique character of the rural Negro population trend in eastern North Carolina unquestionably warrants further investigation.

To what extent has the Negro population declined since its peak year in those five of every six southern counties which had fewer Negroes in 1950 than in some previous year? Although the relationship is not as close as might have been suspected, there is general correspondence between the length of time since the peak was reached and the amount of subsequent decline. The simplest rule of thumb, which has almost as many exceptions as instances, is that the decline has been approximately 10 per cent per decade in those counties whose Negro population was at its maximum before 1950.

One is immediately tempted to wonder about the extent to which Negro depopulation has continued, and about where Negroes go when they leave. Our attention thus far has been focused on changes in the numbers of Negroes living in specific areas, with little mention of migration. Before we can discuss Negro migration in the United States, however, we need to consider the various techniques by which it can be measured, the types of data which are available, and the pitfalls to heed.

TECHNIQUES OF MEASURING MIGRATION

Four more or less standard techniques might be used for measuring migration in the United States during the decade 1940–50. Each of these techniques makes use of a different set of data, and each has its own strong points and weaknesses. These techniques consist in an analysis of four criteria:

(1) *Mobility:* A representative 20 per cent sample of persons one year old and over at the time of the 1950 census were asked their place of residence one year previously. On the basis of their responses, data have been published on the numbers and some selected characteristics of nonwhite migrants for State Economic Areas.[7] It can be argued, however, that the State Economic Area is not an especially satisfactory unit of area for geographic purposes. Furthermore, these data pertain only to a single year, and unfortunately it was a year in which mobility appears to have been relatively low for the postwar years because of the mild economic recession of 1949 and 1950. A final minor objection is the difficulty of distinguishing the specialized migration of college students. For these reasons it was concluded that this measure of migration would contribute little or nothing to the present study, and consequently it has not been used.

(2) *Census Survival Ratio:* The prime exemplar of the census survival ratio as a measure of migration is the monumental work of Everett S. Lee in estimating migration data for each state for each decade since 1870.[8] A survival ratio for each age-sex group is calculated by dividing the number of persons in the age-sex group by the number of persons in the age-sex group ten years younger at the previous decennial census. This ratio is calculated for the entire population of the nation; if it is assumed that age-specific mortality rates are uniform throughout the nation, then this ratio represents the intercensal change which would occur in the age-sex group within each unit of area if there were no migration. The actual population of the younger age-sex group at the earlier census is multiplied by the survival ratio to provide an estimate of the number of persons in the group who would have lived to be enumerated in the older age-sex group at the succeeding census. The difference between this estimate and the population actually enumerated in the age-sex group is attributed to migration.

For instance, the number of nonwhite males aged twenty to twenty-four in the United States in 1950 (603,511) is divided by the number of

nonwhite males aged ten to fourteen in the United States in 1940 (693,-
322) to give a survival ratio of 0.8703. When the number of nonwhite
males aged ten to fourteen in Sunflower County, Mississippi, in 1940
(2,302) is multiplied by the survival ratio of 0.8703, one obtains an estimate that 2,003 nonwhite males in this group should have lived to be enumerated in the age-sex group aged twenty to twenty-four in 1950. In
1950, 1,539 nonwhite males aged twenty to twenty-four were actually
enumerated in Sunflower County, and it is assumed that the difference
represents a loss of 464 persons from this group by migration. The process
is repeated for each age-sex group to determine the total gain or loss by
migration.

Although they are obligatory under this method, any geographer would
wince at the assumptions (1) that there are no areal variations in the age-
sex pyramids of states and counties in the United States, and (2) that
there are no areal variations in age-specific mortality rates of states and
counties in this country. Lee himself points out that "there are considerable differences in relative survival ratios among the states,"[9] and it is
only logical to assume that there are even greater differences between
counties. There is the further objection that this technique yields estimates only for persons ten years old or older, and further complicated
calculations are necessary to estimate the migration of persons born during the intercensal period.

For these reasons the census survival ratio technique of measuring
migration has not been used in the present study, despite its very great
value for certain types of investigation.[10] If adequate age data are available the survival ratios are easily computed and applied to provide a
wealth of information on the age-sex composition of migrants. It should
also be noted that estimates obtained by the survival-ratio technique are
not affected by the migration of previous decades, as are those obtained
by the state-of-birth technique. Lee concludes, however, that correspondence between data obtained by these two methods is remarkably
good for major migrations, although there may be discrepancies on small
movements.[11]

(3) *State of birth:* In the census of 1950 a representative 20 per
cent sample of the population were asked their state of birth, and the
resulting data have been published with a complete cross-tabulation of
state of birth by state of residence.[12] For any state, therefore, it is possible
to determine the states of which all of its residents are natives, and the
states in which all of its natives are resident.

Unfortunately, albeit for understandable reasons of economy, data on
state of birth—and also on vital statistics, which are discussed below—are
published only for nonwhite population, without separate tabulation for

Negroes, Indians, Japanese, Chinese, and others. The Taeubers suggest, however, that "since the Negroes are such a large portion (95.5 per cent) of all nonwhites, the trends in numbers, structure, and distribution in the nonwhite population are essentially those of the Negro,"[13] and demographers generally appear to find no fault with this assumption. It is not precisely correct, however, to equate the nonwhite and Negro populations, especially at the county level,[14] and in this paper the terms "Negro" and "nonwhite" are specifically differentiated. Data for the Negro population are used whenever possible, but when data for Negroes alone are not available in published form, data for the nonwhite population are used, and the population is referred to as "nonwhite" rather than as "Negro."

Data on state of birth must be used with a certain degree of caution, because they indicate only the net resultant of migration during the widely variant lifetimes of the persons enumerated, and give no information in intermediate or intra-state moves. They also tend to be heavily weighted toward adjacent states because of the ease with which persons move their residences across state lines, especially when the state line transects a metropolitan area.

State of birth data have been published for every census from 1850, however, and it is possible to circumvent some of the difficulties described above by computing intercensal change. For instance, if the 34,653 nonwhite natives of Georgia residing in New York in 1940 are subtracted from the corresponding 62,605 in 1950, it would appear that 27,952 nonwhite natives of Georgia had moved to New York in the decade of 1940–50. A problem of indeterminate proportions is created, however, by the intercensal deaths of migrants from previous decades. In 1940, for example, Arkansas residents included 2,166 nonwhite natives of South Carolina, whereas the number had declined to 1,315 in 1950. The loss of 851 persons may be attributable either to back-migration or to deaths of earlier migrants.

Nevertheless, despite the defects which require that they be used and interpreted with the greatest caution, state of birth data are indispensable to any study of migration, for they are the only available source of information on the direction of movement, and even of the very existence of migration streams. Furthermore, the user can take considerable comfort in Lee's conclusion, cited above, that data obtained by the census survival ratio and the state of birth computations are reasonably comparable insofar as major movements are concerned.

(4) *Natural increase:* The number of people in any given area can be changed only by births, deaths, and migration. The technique of using natural increase to measure migration assumes that any intercensal population increase greater than the natural increase—the surplus of births over

deaths—must result from in-migration, and that a population increase less than the natural increase must result from out-migration.

The amount of natural increase is determined easily enough from data contained in the annual volumes of *Vital Statistics of the United States,* which give the number of births and deaths each year, by place of residence, for every county in the United States and for every city with a population of at least 10,000 persons at the preceding census. In the years 1940–49, for example, Marshall County, Mississippi, had 6,413 nonwhite births and 1,655 nonwhite deaths for a natural increase of 4,758 nonwhite persons; Peach County, Georgia, had 1,799 nonwhite births and 796 nonwhite deaths for a natural increase of 1,003 nonwhite persons (Table 2). Unhappily, the vital statistics data, like the state of birth data, make no distinction between Negroes and other nonwhite persons, and even separate nonwhite data are published only for those counties and places in which the nonwhite population formed at least 10 per cent of the total population or numbered 10,000 or more persons at the last census. Where published, however, they are the best available source for measuring migration at the county level.

The number of migrants from any given county is determined by subtracting the natural increase from the population increase; it is necessary to perform this operation algebraically, because either quantity may actu-

TABLE 2

Nonwhite Natural Increase in Two Selected Counties, 1940-49[1]

Year	Marshall County, Miss.		Peach County, Ga.	
	Deaths	Births	Deaths	Births
1940	201	605	85	165
1941	165	572	83	166
1942	193	654	89	187
1943	158	626	83	172
1944	155	594	88	180
1945	167	588	81	174
1946	160	616	86	154
1947	165	710	59	171
1948	146	714	67	219
1949	145	734	75	211
Total	1,655	6,413	796	1,799
Natural increase		4,758		1,003

[1] Source of data: Vital Statistics of the United States, Births and Deaths by Place of Residence, for appropriate years.

ally represent a decrease rather than an increase, and hence must be treated as a negative quantity. The result indicates in-migration if positive, out-migration if negative. The population increase must be corrected, where appropriate, for the change in place of enumeration of college students, who in 1950 were enumerated in the college community rather than in the community of parental home, as in 1940. As there is no possibility of "restoring" college students to the home community in 1950, this correction is best made by adding the resident college enrollment during the regular session, 1939–40, to the 1940 population of the college community.

In 1940, for instance, Marshall County, Mississippi, had a nonwhite population of 17,966 persons, plus 118 students in Rust College at Holly Springs, for a total population of 18,084 (Table 3). The nonwhite population in 1950 was only 17,730 persons, a loss of 354 persons, whereas the natural increase, as we have seen in Table 3, was 4,758 persons. Algebraic subtraction of the natural increase shows that there were 5,112 nonwhite migrants from Marshall County in the decade 1940–50. Peach County, Georgia, illustrates the calculation of migration when the population has increased. The migration rate is calculated by dividing the number of migrants by the 1940 population, and is given the same sign as the number of migrants; in-migration is indicated by a plus sign, out-migration by a minus.

TABLE 3

*Nonwhite Migration From Two
Selected Counties, 1940-50*

	Marshall Co., Miss.	Peach Co., Ga.
1940 population	17,966	6,366
Number of students in 1940[1]	118	225
Total in 1940	18,084	6,591
1950 population	17,730	7,173
Population increase	−354	582
Less natural increase	−4,758	−1,003
Number of migrants	−5,112	−421
Migration rate	−28.5%	−6.6%

[1] Data on resident college enrollment during the regular session, 1939-40 in Rust College (Holly Springs, Miss.) and Fort Valley State College (Fort Valley, Ga.) from Table 18, "Faculty, Students, and Graduates, 1939-40," in U.S. Office of Education, Biennial Surveys of Education in the United States, 1938-40 and 1940-42, Vol. II, Chap. IV, "Statistics of Higher Education, 1939-40 and 1941-42."

NONWHITE INTERSTATE MIGRATION, 1940–50

Both state of birth and natural-increase measurements must be used to develop a clear picture of nonwhite migration patterns in the decade 1940–50. State of birth data reveal the dominant patterns of interstate movement, but give no indication of source or magnet areas within states. The magnitude of migration in each county can be computed from the natural increase, but this gives no indication of the origin or destination of migrants. Comparison of the patterns revealed by the two sets of data, however, appear to justify conclusions which are not warranted on the basis of either set of data alone.

As measured by the state of birth data, Mississippi was the leading producer of nonwhite migrants in the decade 1940–50 but was not far ahead of the other seven states from North Carolina to Florida. Smaller numbers were produced by Oklahoma, Tennessee, and Florida, and even fewer by the four border states from Virginia to Missouri. Pennsylvania was the lone state outside the South to produce more than 10,000 out-migrants.

Interstate nonwhite migration is highly selective regionally; that is, a large percentage of the migrants from each region select the same region of destination. In each of the South Atlantic states except Georgia, for instance, more than three quarters of the nonwhite migrants went to the Northeast, which also attracted just over half of the nonwhite migrants from Georgia. The Northeast attracted less than a quarter of the nonwhite migrants from Alabama, however, and had virtually no attraction for migrants from other states.[15]

In similar fashion, the largest proportion of nonwhite migrants from the East South Central states went due northward. The majority of nonwhite migrants from Mississippi, Alabama, Tennessee, and Kentucky, as well as almost half of those from Arkansas, were attracted into the East North Central states. The pull of the Pacific states was felt slightly in Mississippi, somewhat more strongly in Arkansas and Oklahoma, and most strongly of all in Louisiana and Texas; to a lesser degree the westward surge from the West South Central states is indicated by the extent of intra-regional migration, which is directed almost entirely into Texas.

The other side of the coin reveals the same high degree of regional selectivity in nonwhite migration; just as each source region has a dominating region of destination, so each migration magnet region pulls primarily from a single region of origin. Three fourths of the nonwhite migrants to the Pacific states hailed from the four West South Central states. Illinois and Indiana received almost three fourths, and Wisconsin, Michigan, Ohio, and Missouri rather more than half their nonwhite migrants from the four

East South Central states. And three of every four migrants to Megalopolis had come up the Atlantic Seaboard from the South Atlantic states.

These data indicate that there were three great streams of nonwhite migration in the United States in the decade 1940–50. One moved westward from the trans-Mississippi South toward the Pacific Coast. A second flowed northward from the middle South into the Middle West. The third moved up the Atlantic Seaboard from the South Atlantic states into the Northeast. The existence of these three streams reinforces our earlier conclusion about reciprocal trends in the Negro population of pairs of regions, one in and one outside the South. This reciprocal relationship quite obviously is based on the flow of migrants, and the length of time over which these trends have existed gives some indication also that the streams of migration follow relatively old routes; it has even been pointed out that the streams fairly closely follow the old route of the Underground Railway!

If we wish to trace the origin and destination of nonwhite migration streams with greater geographic precision, on a county rather than a state basis, we must turn from state of birth data to natural increase data. In varying degree, nonwhite out-migration characterized the large majority of counties for which data could be computed in the decade 1940–50. The largest number of migrants came from the counties with the densest rural Negro population. The leading migrant producing area was the Delta country of Mississippi, with the Black Belt fairly close behind. Large numbers of migrants also came from the sandy lands of Louisiana and Texas, and the Inner Coastal Plain and Piedmont of Georgia and South Carolina.

At least three areas of apparently heavy out-migration—Iredell County, North Carolina, Jefferson County, Alabama, and East Baton Rouge Parish, Louisiana—seem to be simply a product of changes in city boundaries.[16] On the other hand, nonwhite overspill from cities or migration into cities of less than 10,000 persons—for which data are not available—appears to account for some counties of anomalously light out-migration, such as Macon County in Alabama or Dougherty, Bibb, Baldwin, and Richmond counties in Georgia.

There is relatively close areal relationship between those areas with large numbers of out-migrants and those areas with the heaviest rates of out-migration, although the rates in sparsely settled eastern Texas are higher than might have been suspected from the total number of migrants. A large number of counties lost more than one third of their nonwhite population by migration between 1940 and 1950, and the majority of counties from South Carolina to eastern Texas lost more than a quarter of their nonwhite population. The impressive implications of this figure, when it is remembered that the majority of migrants are in the younger age groups, are best realized by consideration of counties farther north which had much lower rates of out-migration in the decade 1940–50.

In the rural areas of ten Kentucky Bluegrass counties, for instance, there were 24,490 Negroes in 1940 and only 20,736 in 1950, a loss of 3,724 persons. More than a fifth of the loss, however, can be attributed to the fact that these counties had 796 *more nonwhite deaths than births.* The explanation lies in the age structure which has been produced in these counties by long-continued out-migration. The migrants are most commonly young people, in the reproductive ages, and their departure by removing part of the reproductive potential of the county reduces the number of births. The number of births is reduced still farther as the remaining population ages and passes the reproductive years. In 1950, for example, 34 per cent of the Negroes of the rural Bluegrass were aged forty-five or older, as compared with 22 per cent of the total Negro population of the nation. The migration rate from the aging and dying Negro population of the rural Bluegrass was low because, quite literally, there was no one left to migrate! The same is true for other counties along the northern fringes of the South, especially in Virginia. And if the 1940–50 migration rates are maintained, it is reasonable to expect that similar demographic conditions will characterize much of the rural South within a generation or so.

Paradoxically, the low migration rates of the eastern Carolinas appear to be attributable to a youthful population which has not been artificially aged by migration. For some reason (perhaps related to the difficulties involved in mechanizing various cultivational and harvesting operations required by such labor-hungry crops as peanuts, cotton, and flue-cured tobacco) the counties of this area appear not to have experienced heavy out-migration in the past, and the population is still young. In twenty counties selected at random from this area, only 16 per cent of the Negro population was aged forty-five or older, as compared with 22 per cent in the nation, and 34 per cent in the Bluegrass. It would appear that a youthful Negro population with a high rate of reproduction accounts for the low migration rate, despite the fact that relatively large numbers of migrants have left the area. It is further suggested that the age structure of the population might be a clue to the problem of why this area should have attained its maximum population in 1950.

On the urban side, many southern cities had negative or only very low positive migration rates for the decade 1940–50. Nonwhite migration from urban areas was especially pronounced in the Border states and on the Piedmont, but every southern state had at least one city whose nonwhite population declined as a result of migration. Furthermore, relatively few southern cities had high rates of in-migration, although there were exceptions in the Norfolk area, along the Gulf Coast, and in the western South. As a general rule, it appears safe to conclude that cities in the South had surprisingly little attraction for Negro migrants, whereas cities outside the South typically had high rates of in-migration.

Unfortunately, these data give only the net resultant of migration, and it is therefore impossible to tell whether cities in the South act as "staging points" for Negro migrants. It would be interesting to know, for instance, whether the Negro migrant from the rural South goes straight from the cotton fields to the asphalt jungle of the metropolis, or whether he first spends an acclimatization period in a smaller city. It is possible that a southern city could experience considerable in-migration which would not appear here if it had been balanced by migration "up the ladder" to a larger town on the part of natives or in-migrants of an earlier decade.

There is no question that the major metropolitan areas were the major magnets for Negro migrants in the decade 1940–50. The Houston area, greatest magnet in the South, attracted less than fifty thousand nonwhite persons during the entire decade, greater Norfolk attracted only thirty-seven thousand, Memphis, Atlanta, and New Orleans only twelve thousand each, and Birmingham only eight thousand. These six metropolitan areas, combined, attracted fewer nonwhite persons than did metropolitan Detroit alone, and only half as many as metropolitan New York. Metropolitan Los Angeles attracted almost as many nonwhite persons during the decade as the three most attractive metropolitan areas in the South.

The vast bulk of Negro migrants, in short, are moving to cities outside the South. South of a line from Norfolk through Cincinnati and St. Louis to Los Angeles only a very few cities attracted as many as a thousand nonwhite migrants a year over the decade. But Baltimore and St. Louis averaged four thousand a year, Washington six thousand, San Francisco eight thousand, Los Angeles nine thousand, Philadelphia ten thousand, Detroit thirteen thousand, and Chicago twenty thousand a year. And metropolitan New York attracted an average of two thousand nonwhite migrants each *month* for the entire decade.

Within the South only the towns and cities are attracting Negro migrants, and the Negro population increase of the South is concentrated almost entirely in the cities. Virtually all nonmetropolitan counties in the South had a smaller Negro population than at some previous census, whereas the majority of the metropolitan counties had more Negroes than they ever had before. As noted earlier, these divergent trends within the South suggested the desirability of refining the areas originally used in discussing regional trends in the Negro population.

Conclusion

The American Negro is becoming increasingly urbanized, and largely as a result of migration from the rural South to metropolitan areas outside the South. In light of the information here presented, the three major streams of Negro migration in the United States can be defined more precisely. Natural increase data indicate that the great majority of Negro migrants from the South Atlantic states come from the Inner Coastal Plain and the Piedmont of Georgia, the Carolinas, and Virginia; state of birth data show that the vast majority of migrants from these states move to the Northeast; and natural increase data indicate that migrants to the Northeast settle almost entirely in the metropolitan areas of Megalopolis.

In the same fashion, we may conclude that the second major stream consists of migrants from the Delta, the Black Belt, and virtually the entire state of Mississippi who are moving toward Chicago, Detroit, and the other urban centers from Cleveland to St. Louis. This stream, like the first, is fed partially from the Georgia-Alabama Coastal Plain, which also appears to send migrants to peninsular Florida. The third stream of Negro migration originates in the sandy lands of southern Arkansas, northern Louisiana, and eastern Texas, and flows westward toward Los Angeles, San Francisco, and Seattle; some migrants from the Delta also appear to join this stream.

Examination of Negro population trends by regions shows a reciprocity between regions which would seem to indicate that these streams of migration have existed for at least half a century, although their volume was not so great in the earlier years. Migration has nonetheless decimated the Negro population of many areas as is revealed by the study of peak years. First, Negroes left the hills, which had reached their peak by 1900; then they left the South Atlantic states, where 1910–20 peaks are most common; next came heavy migration from the central South, where most counties have peaks between 1910 and 1940; more recently heavy migration from the trans-Mississippi South has been associated with peaks in 1930 and in 1940. But the cities—the major magnets for Negro migrants—had more Negroes in 1950 than they had ever had before, and are increasing their share of the nation's increasing Negro population.

Urbanization for the American Negro has come more belatedly than it came for his white neighbor, but now that it has started it is proceeding with a rush. Negroes have almost disappeared in some rural areas where once they were numerous. Virtually every nonmetropolitan county in the South had fewer Negroes in 1950 than in some previous year, whereas metropolitan areas throughout the nation had their maximum Negro population in 1950. But Negro migrants are attracted mainly to cities outside the South. In short, the American Negro, who was a rural Southerner two generations ago, is rapidly becoming an urban Northerner or Westerner.

LITERATURE CITED

1. With almost uncanny prescience, after completion of the census of 1910, the Bureau of the Census sponsored a monumental study of the Negro: John Cummings, *Negro Population, 1790–1915* (Washington: Government Printing Office, 1918).

2. Although the term "density" is universally accepted for describing the concept of number of units per unit of area, there appears to be no equally suitable and generally accepted term for the concept of proportionality, such as the percentage of Negroes or of older persons. It is suggested, therefore, that the term "intensity" might be used in describing the concept of the percentage of components of a population. Hereafter in this paper the term "Negro intensity" will be considered synonymous with "percentage of Negroes in the total population."

3. "Plainsland South" appears preferable to the more common "deep South" or "lower South," and is rather less cumbersome than "Piedmont and Atlantic and Gulf Coastal Plain Physiographic Provinces" as a name for that part of the South in which level to rolling topography, a sizable rural Negro population, and an agricultural economy dominated by production of cotton or tobacco are more or less coextensive. The plainsland South is quite different from the "hill-land South" of the Blue Ridge, Ridge and Valley, Appalachian Plateau, Interior Low Plateau, Ozark, and Ouachita Physiographic Provinces, in which a predominantly native white population practices "general farming" in areas of hilly topography.

4. For a discussion of the Negro population of Lake County, Michigan, see John Fraser Hart, "A Rural Retreat for Northern Negroes," *Geographical Review*, Vol. 50 (April 1960), pp. 147–68.

5. An excellent illustration is provided by Chittenden County, Vermont, whose Negro population soared from 153 in 1900 to 1,114 in 1910, then dropped abruptly to 175 in 1920, and has never exceeded 208 persons at any other time. The explanation apparently has to do with the stationing of Negro troops at Fort Ethan Allen.

6. As quoted in James P. Munroe, *A Life of Francis Amasa Walker* (New York: Henry Holt, 1923), p. 113. Although great improvements have been made since 1870, partisan considerations still play too large a role in the appointment of enumerators.

7. *U. S. Census of Population: 1950.* Vol. IV, *Special Reports,* Part 4, Chapter B, "Population Mobility—States and State Economic Areas" (Washington: Government Printing Office, 1956).

8. Everett S. Lee, "Migration Estimates," pp. 7–361 of Everett S. Lee, Ann Ratner Miller, Carol P. Brainerd, and Richard A. Easterlin, *Population Redistribution and Economic Growth: United States, 1870–1950.* Vol. I, *Methodological Considerations and Reference Tables* (Philadelphia: American Philosophical Society, 1957).

9. Ibid., p. 34.

10. For instance, see Gladys K. Bowles, *Farm Population: Net Migration from the Rural-Farm Population, 1940–50,* U. S. Department of Agriculture Statistical Bulletin No. 176 (Washington: Government Printing Office, 1956).

11. Lee, op. cit., p. 95.

12. *U. S. Census of Population: 1950.* Vol. IV, *Special Reports,* Part 4, Chapter A, "State of Birth" (Washington: Government Printing Office, 1953).

13. Conrad Taeuber and Irene B. Taeuber, *The Changing Population of the United States* (New York: John Wiley & Sons, 1958), p. 71.

14. Wesley C. Calef and Howard J. Nelson, "Distribution of Negro Population in the United States," *Geographical Review,* Vol. 46 (January 1956), pp. 82–97.

15. West Virginia has highly complicated patterns of nonwhite inter-regional migration primarily because the state is contiguous with four geographic divisions, and a considerable part of the nonwhite migration from the state may well consist merely of short shifts of residence across nearby state lines. To some extent this is also true of Arkansas.

16. It is impossible to estimate compensating corrections for changes in city boundaries because population and vital statistics data are not available for the annexed area *alone.* Thus one cannot compute the decennial population change or the amount of natural increase within either the old or the new boundaries. The simple and admittedly unsatisfactory technique used here is utilization of data actually reported for both population and vital statistics. This has the effect of treating the entire 1940 population of the annexed area as migrants from the county to the city (which, in a sense, perhaps they were), thus producing high out-migration rates in the county and high in-migration rates in the city.

POPULATION AND RACE IN MISSISSIPPI, 1940–1960[1]

Mark Lowry II

The population geography of the southeastern United States has been affected significantly by the discriminatory plural society of that area.[2] That influence is manifest in white and Negro regional distributions, in local residential segregation, in spatial arrangements of the races at intermediate scales, and in contemporary population trends.

The purpose of this study is to assess, in more detail than previous geographical works provide, the significance of race in Mississippi's population geography.[3] First, the state is set in perspective with the surrounding area and the nation, emphasizing population trends and racial percentages, and the period 1940 to 1960 is identified as one of great change. Second, comparisons are made among patterns of the total population and the Negro and white races for 1940 and 1960 and the patterns of their rates of change, using minor civil divisions (beats) and urban places as units of areal observation.[4] Third, some findings are amplified, and directions for further research are suggested.

Several works treating the population of the conterminous United States, or large parts of it, have included Mississippi.[5] Two papers have concentrated exclusively on the state's population and socioeconomic characteristics.[6] All these works used the county or larger divisions as units of areal observation, and where urban places have been studied the emphasis has been on the relatively large places. The present study reveals important contrasts among urban, suburban, and more distant rural areas, and points to significant racial differences which are not readily apparent when only one race or the total population is considered.[7]

MISSISSIPPI AND THE NATION

Mississippi is an excellent study area for several reasons. The study period witnessed vast changes contrasting with prior decades. Rapid rural to urban migration caused faster rates of urban growth and rural decline than the nation experienced (Table 1); it was the fastest rate of rural to urban migration in the state's history. From 1880 to 1940 the percentage crept steadily upward from 3.1 to 19.8. About 1940 the trend changed sharply, and the percentage soared to 37.7 in 1960. Whereas between 1930 and 1940 seventy-one of the eighty-two counties gained population, the next decade saw fifty-eight, mostly rural, counties lose, and the trend continued through the 1950s.

Lying at the core of the Negro area in the United States, Mississippi has a larger percentage of Negroes than the region or nation (Table 1).[8] In 1940 the state had 49.2 per cent, whereas the region and nation had 39 and 9.8 per cent, respectively. By 1960 the percentages had changed to 42.3, 33, and 10.6. The change in Mississippi was greater than the change in the entire century prior to 1940 (in 1850 the state was 51.2 per cent Negro).[9] This same period "witnessed the greatest Negro redistribution, both relatively and absolutely, that has ever been recorded in the United States."[10] The proportion of Negroes in Mississippi's population is trending toward that of the region and nation.

After a century and a half of uninterrupted growth (except during World War I when the state experienced a slight decline), Mississippi's population declined by 0.2 per cent between 1940 and 1960, whereas the Southeast and the United States grew by 21 and 35.5 per cent. The state has been losing population to the rest of the nation through a net outmigration of both races. In 1960 the cumulative net loss was 960,496, over two thirds of whom were Negroes (this includes all migrants still living in 1960). For every white migrant to Mississippi, there were 2.5 white outmigrants; about a third of all living whites born in the state resided elsewhere. By contrast, for every Negro inmigrant there were sixteen Negro outmigrants; about four of every nine living Negroes born in Mississippi lived outside the state in 1960.[11] During the decade following 1940 Mississippi produced more Negro outmigrants than any other state.[12]

Outmigrants have been selective in choosing their destinations. Whereas most whites have gone to other southern states, a great majority of Negroes have gone to the North. Sixty per cent of the Negroes and only 10 per cent of the whites have gone to the North Central area, and of the western states California has gained most Negroes and whites.

TABLE 1

Population Comparisons: Mississippi, the Southeast,[a] and the United States

	Mississippi	Southeast	United States
Total population, 1940	2,183,796	12,405,000	131,669,275
Total population, 1960	2,178,141	15,028,000	178,464,236
Percentage change total population 1940-1960	−.2	21.0	35.5
Percentage urban[b] 1940	19.8	31.0	56.5
Percentage urban 1960	37.7	52.0	69.9
Percentage change urban population 1940-1960	90.0	106.0	67.6
Percentage change rural population 1940-1960	−22.5	−21.8	−6.1
Percentage Negro 1940	49.2	39.0	9.8
Percentage Negro 1960	42.3	33.0	10.6
Percentage change Negro population 1940-1960	−14.8	2.5	46.9
Percentage change white population 1940-1960	13.7	33.5	34.1

[a] Arbitrarily defined as Louisiana, Mississippi, Alabama, Georgia, and South Carolina.

[b] The change in urban definition between 1950 and 1960 altered Mississippi's urban population by only 0.3 percent; therefore the current definition is used.

Source: United States Census Bureau publications.

TOTAL POPULATION

Mississippi's total population (Negro and white) has patterns and trends which differ significantly from those of each individual race. Worthwhile perspective can be gained from an initial view of the two races in the aggregate.

Today's population distribution evolved over many decades. At the beginning of settlement the hinterland around Natchez was marked off and tilled; then followed the Pearl and Tombigbee river (Black Belt) valleys.[13] After the boom of the 1830s and the coming of the railroad, cotton farmers settled the hill country of north and central Mississippi. The last large unsettled part of the state was the flat, fertile Yazoo Basin, popularly called the Delta. As late as 1860 less than one tenth of this area was cleared for cultivation, and even up to 1900 fully two thirds remained in virgin wilderness.[14] Therefore most of the Yazoo Basin was never worked by slaves, but Negroes poured in after the Civil War, and the trend continued into the late 1930s.[15]

In 1880 only three urban places had more than 5,000 people, and several of today's largest cities had not yet come into being. At about the same time counties with larger urban centers began to stand out as high population density counties, but it was not until 1910 or 1920 that the pattern of urban counties came to real prominence.[16] Few urban places in 1960 were large enough to be of national significance; Jackson, the state capital, was the only metropolitan place. Lying near the center, and with its governmental function, it had become to a very considerable degree the crossroads of the state its founders envisioned.[17] In the next category (40,001–50,000) there were three cities, Biloxi, Greenville, and Meridian, and four cities were in the third category (25,001–40,000), Gulfport, Hattiesburg, Laurel, and Vicksburg. Thus only eight cities had more than 25,000 people. There were, however, 138 urban places, incorporated and unincorporated, with more than 1,000 people. Since the smallest category (1,000–2,500) includes so many places, and since the Census Bureau definitions of urban and rural are arbitrary, hereafter all places which were as large as 1,000 in 1960 will be considered urban, and all people living outside those places will be termed rural.[18] By this definition the state was still only 42.6 per cent urban in 1960 (Table 2).

Population changes from 1940 to 1960 were characterized by urban growth, rural decline, and a shifting of heaviest concentrations of both urban and rural population. The most obvious change was a general thinning of rural population resulting from a net loss of 399,863 rural people (Tables 2 and 3). The state's total population declined by 5,456. The

TABLE 2

Characteristics of White, Negro, and Total Population in 1940 and 1960[a]

	White		Negro		Total	
	1940	1960	1940	1960	1940	1960
Total number	1,108,839	1,262,397	1,074,757	915,743	2,183,596	2,178,140
Percentage urban[b]	29	46	20	36	24.4	42.6
Urban number	317,397	589,846	216,020	337,979	533,417	927,824
Average urban number	2,299	4,273	1,566	2,449	3,865	6,722
Rural number	791,442	672,551	858,737	577,764	1,650,179	1,250,316
Average rural population density	18.1	15.9	18.5	12.4	36.6	28.3
people per square mile (square kilometer)	(6.98)	(6.14)	(7.15)	(4.78)	(14.12)	(10.92)

[a] Minor differences between these and Census Bureau figures are the result of data gathered in the field.

[b] Urban people are those who live in places which were as large as 1,000 in 1960.

Source: United States Census Bureau publications supplemented by field survey.

remaining people leaving rural areas moved into cities, towns, and villages, contributing to a 74 per cent increase in urban areas.[19]

The great rural decline notwithstanding, some rural areas grew. Increases, for the most part, were associated with suburban growth which resulted from two kinds of migration. Some people, mostly those leaving farms, vacated the countryside and gathered around the city, whereas others moved from inside the city to the suburbs. The only large area of rural growth is along and back from the coastal urban strip. Other notable areas are around Jackson, Natchez, Hattiesburg, Laurel, Columbus, and Starkville. Of the losing areas, the lowest loss rates were experienced around urban places.

Urban trends were quite different, with all but four of the 138 urban places growing considerably.[20] However, ninety-two places with fewer

TABLE 3

Characteristics of White, Negro, and Total Population Changes, 1940 to 1960[a]

	White	Negro	Total
Net change total number	153,558	−159,014	−5456
Net change urban[b] number	272,448	121,959	394,407
Net change rural number	−118,890	−280,973	−399,863
Percentage change total number	13.7	−14.8	−.2
Percentage change urban number	86	56	74
Average percentage change urban number	76	64	68
Percentage change rural number	−15	−32	−24
Average percentage change rural number	−10	−28.6	−20.6
Change in average urban number	1974	883	2857

[a]Minor differences between these and Census Bureau figures are the result of data gathered in the field.

[b]Urban people are those who live in places which were as large as 1,000 in 1960.

Source: United States Census Bureau publications supplemented by field survey.

than 1,000 people in 1960 lost population.[21] Since most places larger than 1,000 grew, and most smaller places declined, it seems logical to include the former in urban population and the latter in rural population.

RACIAL COMPARISONS

Insights into the impact of a plural society may be gained from comparisons of the maps of the proportion of Negroes in the total population, of white and Negro rural densities for 1940 and 1960, and of their rates of change.

Percentage Negro

In 1960 there were considerable differences between urban and rural racial percentages for the state (the urban population was 36.4 per cent Negro and the rural population was 46.2 per cent Negro), but the two varied similarly from area to area (Table 4).[22] Nevertheless, there were local contrasts between urban places and rural areas. Where rural areas had highest percentages of Negroes, urban places had slightly lower percentages; where rural percentages were lowest, urban percentages were slightly higher. Thus urban places moderated the broader patterns, but their effect was not strong enough to obscure them.

Each race clearly preponderated in different areas. High percentages of Negroes were in the best agricultural areas, including the Yazoo Basin, the Black Belt, the interfluve between the Pearl and Big Black rivers, the loess hills south of Vicksburg and Natchez, the Bluff Hills, and the Jackson Prairie. Whites predominated in the Fall Line Hills, the Red Hills, the Pine Hills, and along and back from the coast. The north-south zone between the two broad racial areas corresponded closely with the eastern limit of the thin loess belt. This regional orientation was established during early settlement.[23] Several areas, some as large as counties, were more than 80 per cent Negro, and there were comparable white enclaves. These areas illustrate an important advantage of the minor civil division in mapping population.

Even though there was a sharp reduction in the state's percentage Negro from 1940 to 1960, the general spatial orientation of racial percentage did not change significantly (Tables 1 and 4). However, there were considerable changes at a more local level. Some highly Negro areas receded, some expanded, and some shifted; the same is true of predominantly white areas. The local areas of most pronounced drop in percentage Negro are around large urban places such as Greenville, Vicksburg, Natchez, Jackson, Starkville, Columbus, and McComb.

One might expect some relationship between size of urban places and the proportion of Negroes in the population, but places of all sizes had high and low percentages of Negroes (Table 5). The determinants of

TABLE 4
Correlation of Population Variables by Beat

	Percentage Negro 1960	Density rural white 1960	Density rural Negro 1960	Density total rural 1940	Density total rural 1960	Percentage change rural Negro	Percentage change rural white	Urban[a] percentage Negro 1960
Percentage Negro 1940	.96							
Density rural Negro 1940			.88	.82		−.15	.05	
Density rural Negro 1960					.50	.07	.08	
Density rural white 1940		.65		.57		−.03	−.04	
Density rural white 1960					.85	.02	.59	
Rural percentage Negro 1940						−.15	.04	
Rural percentage Negro 1960						−.02	−.14	
Percentage change total rural						.29	.82	.83

[a] Urban people are those who live in places which were as large as 1,000 in 1960.

Source: Calculated by author.

Negro percentages in urban places seem to be regional in nature, and they probably are linked closely with historical causes. Extreme cases of racial separation are all-white and all-Negro towns.[24] The seven all-white towns, Waveland (95 per cent), Longbeach (95 per cent), D'Iberville (100 per cent), Petal (98 per cent), Pearl (98 per cent), Wesson (95 per cent), and University (98 per cent) are adjacent to larger, more racially mixed cities. Wesson, one of the original mill towns inhabited almost entirely by whites, is a very small place with an all-white junior college.[25] At University is the University of Mississippi, until recently completely white.

The four all-Negro towns, Tunica North (92 per cent), Mound Bayou (99 per cent), West Gulfport (90 per cent), and McComb South (83 per cent) are separated from larger cities by physical barriers such as commercial areas, roads, or open spaces. The one exception is Mound Bayou, an independent all-Negro town originally established as such.[26] Tunica North illustrates the spatial separation.[27] In October 1968 it was separated from the white community of Tunica by an open field of soybeans. The houses were unpainted, weathered, dilapidated, and largely set in weeds and unkept, junk-littered yards. It was crowded by Delta standards, and was bordered on all sides by roads. In contrast, white Tunica had large, modern houses set back in spacious, well-kept yards shaded by gigantic oak and pecan trees. The observable gap in living conditions between the races seems even wider than the spatial gap between their living areas—the most symbolic example I have found.[28] Whereas predominantly white places usually have comparatively high living standards, predominantly Negro places are often pockets of poverty.

Rural Densities

This analysis considers white and Negro rural population only, a majority of both races (Table 2). Urban places are included on the maps to emphasize the relationship of rural concentrations to urban places. Negro rural population has been concentrated for decades in the Yazoo Basin and the Black Belt, with smaller concentrations in the Southwest. The dense Negro area in the Yazoo Basin, with more than forty-eight Negroes per square mile (1940), and less than 20 per cent white, has the "highest density and largest number of rural Negroes in the United States."[29] This can be considered the eye of the Negro core area, a clear reflection of Negro labor intensity in plantation type agriculture. Notable smaller areas are around Memphis (Tennessee), north and west of Jackson, north of Natchez along the Mississippi River, and around McComb. Between 1940 and 1960 the average Negro density dropped sharply, but the broader orientation of rural Negroes did not change significantly (Tables 2 and 4).

TABLE 5

Correlation of Population Variables by Urban Place[a]

	Total population 1940	Total population 1960	Percentage Negro 1940	Percentage Negro 1960	Negro absolute change	Percentage change white
Total population 1940						
Total population 1960			.04	−.03		
Percentage change white	.02	.10	−.005	−.09		
Percentage change Negro	−.03	.05	−.16	−.04		
White absolute change					.92	.74

[a] Urban people are those who live in places as large as 1,000 in 1960.

Source: Calculated by author.

By contrast, rural whites have been heavily concentrated in the relatively poor Fall Line Hills, Red Hills, and Pine Hills, characterized by yeoman farmers. Between 1940 and 1960 average white rural density declined less sharply than Negro, and suburban areas grew around Jackson, Columbus, Greenville, Natchez, Hattiesburg, and the coastal urban strip (Table 2). Suburban growth partially offset the rural loss and moderated the average white density decline. There was a shifting of rural whites, rather than a mere thinning, such as rural Negroes experienced. The orientation of rural whites in 1960 was considerably different from 1940 (Table 4).

The racial disparities are reflected in the changing pattern of total rural population. In 1940 the total rural pattern resembled the Negro pattern more than the white, but by 1960 the relationship had reversed (Table 4). In 1940 Negroes were a majority of the rural population, but by 1960 whites were a majority (Table 2).

Percentage Change

During the study period Mississippi lost 14.8 per cent of its Negroes while experiencing a 13.7 per cent gain of whites (Table 1). Whites had urban growth of 272,448 and rural loss of 118,890 for a net gain of 153,558; Negroes logged a 121,959 urban gain and a 280,973 rural decline for a net loss of 159,014. Between 1950 and 1960 white people constituted 95 per cent of net migration into urban places, but that is misleading if taken as representative of urban growth.[30] In fact, 30.9 per cent of urban growth between 1940 and 1960 was due to Negro increases. Although the white rate was higher than the Negro rate, there was not as much difference between them as one might expect (Table 3). Even so, the proportion of Negroes in the total urban growth was smaller than the proportion in the total population (Table 1).

Whereas racial discrepancy is clearly evident in the aggregate, Negro and white changes varied similarly from urban place to urban place with a very high correlation, even though there were some anomalies (Table 5). Furthermore, there was no significant relationship between size of urban places and rates of change of either race. The racial percentage in urban places had no relationship with the rate of change of either race; neither predominantly Negro places nor predominantly white places showed a tendency to have growth rates of one race greater than the other (Table 5). Neither race of rural-to-urban migrants, as a rule, chose its cities of destination on the basis of the racial percentages in those cities.

Rural percentage change was considerably different for the races. Both races generally experienced high rates of rural decline across the state, but suburban areas around Natchez, Vicksburg, Greenville, Memphis

(Tennessee), Jackson, Starkville, West Point, Columbus, and back from the coastal urban strip had astounding white growth rates and equally drastic Negro loss rates. Whereas one might assume that these discrepancies reflect an effort to further segregation in the suburbs, the causes lie elsewhere (Table 4). Apparent exceptions can be seen around Columbia and Columbus.

Negroes and whites unquestionably did not enjoy equally the benefits of economic advances in and around urban places. White people generally had growing employment opportunities, but those opportunities were in practice relatively closed to Negroes, because of discrimination as well as the Negroes' lack of preparation for more skilled employment, one of the tragic consequences of the plural society.[31] Without opportunities or means of taking advantage of them, Negroes had less reason to gather around urban places. Furthermore, in general they did not have means to live in most growing suburban areas, or access to housing there if they did have the means. Most Negro growth inside urban places contributed to ghetto expansion characterized by very low socioeconomic standards.

It is not surprising that relative spatial variations in rate of total rural change correlate much closer with white rates than with Negro rates (Table 4). Once again the aggregate glosses over some most significant racial differences.

PERSPECTIVE

The idea that population distributions and changes mirror certain aspects of society has been expressed by some scholars, and mounting awareness of it is manifest in a continuing flow of geographical literature.[32] Analysis of momentary distributions can yield useful results, but only through the historical or dynamic approach can cause be found, for, as Zelinsky has said, "that any explanation, with the rarest exception, will be historical in nature is probably the most basic of all . . . assumptions," and he has stanch allies on this point.[33]

In seeking causes for population trends, those trends must be related to changes in other phenomena, or to push and pull forces in the social-economic milieu.[34] During the period of this study the primary economic push forces within Mississippi were associated with the changing agricultural sector, and the primary pull forces were associated with the changing secondary and tertiary sectors. In the social sphere the forces are expected to be reflected in spatial patterns of living conditions, socioeconomic status, and other social phenomena.[35]

Since the push-pull concept applies to the total population, it can be logically assumed that it applies to each race. But trends of change are quite different for the races. Whereas both races are being redistributed, the influencing conditions are not affecting them equally inside the state or on the interstate level. Attractive conditions in and around urban places favor whites much more than Negroes, and the predominantly Negro long-range migration is evidence of the same kind of situation nationally. Through comprehensive analysis of social and economic forces as they relate differently to Negro and white population changes, we can learn more about the discriminatory nature of society.

The impact of race probably could be important in other matters, such as central place theory and the development of formulae which attempt to account for population distribution by reference to other variables.[36] If two areas have significantly different racial percentages and/or types of race relations, it is likely that such formulae would apply differently to those areas, and they might apply differently to two races in the same area.

This study provides a datum plane reflecting the effect of the plural society on the population geography of Mississippi up to 1960. This datum plane could be used in the future as a base from which to assess the impact of social legislation and implementation of subsequent decades as that impact is manifested in the changing geography of the races.

LITERATURE CITED

1. Appreciation is extended to my friends in Mississippi who assisted during field research, and to the staff and graduate students of the Department of Geography, Syracuse University, for useful ideas.

2. Social pluralism, as considered here, is distinct from cultural pluralism, which "results from the presence within a society of several ethnic groups, or, at least in the minimum case, of several distinguishable varieties of the same cultural tradition (such as class-based subcultures). Social pluralism, however, is present in pure form to the extent that a society is structurally compartmentalized into analogous and duplicatory but culturally alike sets of institutions, and into corporate groups which are differentiated on a basis other than culture. In practice, social and cultural pluralism often go together and can thus be regarded as two facets of the same phenomenon. The analytical distinction, however, remains useful, for although cultural pluralism is almost invariably accompanied by social pluralism the latter can be found in the nearly total absence of cultural pluralism. Such is the case in the United States where rigid and persistent racial cleavages (an important instance of social pluralism) have persisted in spite of relatively great cultural homogeneity," Pierre Louis Van den Berghe, *Race and Racism* (New York: John Wiley and Sons,

1967), pp. 35–36. For a discussion of the spatial ramifications of pluralism in South Africa, see M. Ernest Sabbagh, "Some Geographical Characteristics of a Plural Society: Apartheid in South Africa," *Geographical Review*, Vol. 58 (1968), pp. 1–28.

3. For background on the social significance of race in the South, see Gunnar Myrdal, *An American Dilemma: The Negro Problem and American Democracy* (New York: Harper and Brothers, 1944).

4. The minor civil division as a spatial unit in mapping population is discussed in Robert E. Nunley, "Population Geography and Problems of Areal Units: Some Results From a Study of Central America," *Annals*, Association of American Geographers, Vol. 59 (1969), p. 197.

5. For example, see T. J. Woofter, "Migration in the Southeast," *Demography* (1967), pp. 532–52; C. Warren Thornthwaite, *Internal Migration in the United States* (Philadelphia: University of Pennsylvania Press, 1934); Wesley C. Calef and Howard J. Nelson, "Distribution of Negro Population in the United States," *Geographical Review*, Vol. 46 (1956), pp. 82–97; and John Fraser Hart, "The Changing Distribution of the American Negro," *Annals*, Association of American Geographers, Vol. 50 (1960), pp. 242–66.

6. Herbert Vent, "Some Population Trends in Mississippi," *The Journal of Geography*, Vol. 53 (1954), pp. 141–43; and Mark Lowry II, "Race and Socioeconomic Well-being: A Geographical Analysis of the Mississippi Case," *Geographical Review*, Vol. 60 (1970), pp. 511–28.

7. To generalize about a total population from data on a segment, or about a segment from data on the total, is to risk significant fallacies. The danger of committing the group fallacy is "present when the unit to which the inference refers is smaller than the unit of observation or of counting. . . . The danger of the individualistic fallacy is then present when the units of observation or counting are smaller than the units to which inferences are made," Richard L. Merritt and Stein Rokkan, *Comparing Nations: The Use of Quantitative Data in Cross-National Research* (New Haven: Yale University Press, 1966), p. 164.

8. Hart, op. cit., footnote 5.

9. Charles S. Sydnor, *Slavery in Mississippi* (Baton Rouge: Louisiana State University Press, 1966).

10. Hart, op. cit., footnote 5, p. 244.

11. G. L. Wilber and T. W. Rogers, "Interstate Migration of Mississippi Population 1960," *Bulletin 717* (Mississippi State University: Agricultural Experiment Station, 1965), p. 7; and Ronald Freedman, *Population: The Vital Revolution* (New York: Doubleday and Company, 1964), p. 133.

12. Hart, op. cit., footnote 5, p. 260.

13. "The term Black Belt bears a definite association with the dark prairie

soil." The regional identification is not based on human factors, racial or cultural, J. Sullivan Gibson, "The Alabama Black Belt: Its Geographic Status," *Economic Geography*, Vol. 17 (1941), p. 1.

14. Robert L. Brandfon, *Cotton Kingdom of the New South* (Cambridge: Harvard University Press, 1967), pp. 40 and 142. For a discussion of the ravaging floods which constantly threatened the Yazoo Basin up to the late 1920s, see William A. Percy, *Lanterns on the Levee* (New York: Alfred A. Knopf, 1966).

15. The population maps were constructed using the 410 minor civil divisions (beats) and 138 urban places. Where two or more contiguous beats fell in the same category they were grouped together. The lines between categories were smoothed slightly to improve the appearance of the maps. If a map of civil boundaries were overlaid on any of the population maps, the category of each beat would be clear. Data for the maps were calculated from United States Census Bureau publications supplemented by my field survey for 1940 total population in thirteen small urban places and Negro population in thirty-five small urban places.

16. For example, see Charles O. Paullin, *Atlas of the Historical Geography of the United States*, John K. Wright, ed., Publication No. 401 (Washington: Carnegie Institution, 1932).

17. For historical background on many urban places, see *Mississippi: A Guide to the Magnolia State* (New York: Federal Writers' Project of the Works Progress Administration, 1938).

18. Hereafter when the Census Bureau definitions of the terms urban and rural are used, it is so noted. For discussion of problems in population classification, see Leon E. Truesdell, "Problems Involved in the Classification of Population as Farm and Nonfarm," *Rural Sociology*, Vol. 12 (1947), pp. 419–23; and Wilbur Zelinsky, "Changes in the Geographic Patterns of Rural Population in the United States, 1790–1960," *Geographical Review*, Vol. 52 (1962), pp. 492–524.

19. Nearly all rural decline was due to migration, and urban increases were due to migration, natural increase, and expanding city limits. If natural increase had not been a factor, rural decline would have been greater, and urban growth would have been less. No distinction is made in this study in mapping population changes. On the basis of migration and natural increase figures, it is assumed that all areas of percentage loss experienced that loss because of outmigration, and that areas of gain, with few exceptions, experienced a majority of that gain because of inmigration. E. S. Bryant and G. L. Wilber, "Net Migration in Mississippi 1950–1960," Bulletin 632 (Mississippi State University: Agricultural Experiment Station, 1961).

20. This seems to concur with findings that, contrary to expectations, many small places in the Middle West are growing rather than declining. For example, see John Fraser Hart, Neil E. Salisbury, and E. G.

Smith, Jr., "The Dying Village and Some Notions About Urban Growth," *Economic Geography*, Vol. 44 (1968), pp. 343–49.

21. Ray M. Northam, "Declining Urban Centers in the United States: 1940–1960," *Annals*, Association of American Geographers, Vol. 53 (1963), p. 53.

22. When the Census Bureau definitions of urban and rural are applied, the percentages are 36.1 and 46.0, respectively.

23. For example, see Paullin, op. cit., footnote 16; Federal Writers' Project, op. cit., footnote 17; Sydnor, op. cit., footnote 9; James F. Woodruff, "Some Characteristics of the Alabama Slave Population in 1850," *Geographical Review*, Vol. 52 (1962), pp. 379–88.

24. All-white and all-Negro towns are arbitrarily defined as those more than 90 per cent white or 90 per cent Negro, with the one exception listed. Rose defined all-Negro towns as with more than 1,000 population and 95 per cent nonwhite, Harold M. Rose, "The All-Negro Town: Its Evolution and Function," *Geographical Review*, Vol. 55 (1965), pp. 362–81. For other studies on all-Negro towns, see John Fraser Hart, "A Rural Retreat For Northern Negroes," *Geographical Review*, Vol. 50 (1960), pp. 147–68; and William H. Pease and Jane H. Pease, "Organized Negro Communities: A North American Experiment," *Journal of Negro History*, Vol. 47 (1962), pp. 19–34.

25. For a discussion of race relations in mill towns, see W. J. Cash, *The Mind of the South* (New York: Alfred A. Knopf, 1941).

26. Rose, op. cit., footnote 24.

27. This is an agricultural ghetto somewhat different from those studied previously by geographers. For example, see James O. Wheeler and Stanley D. Brunn, "Negro Migration into Rural Southwestern Michigan," *Geographical Review*, Vol. 58 (1968), pp. 214–30; idem, "An Agricultural Ghetto: Negroes in Case County, Michigan, 1845–1968," *Geographical Review*, Vol. 59 (1969), pp. 317–29; Richard L. Morrill, "The Negro Ghetto: Problems and Alternatives," *Geographical Review*, Vol. 55 (1965), pp. 339–61; and Harold M. Rose, "Metropolitan Miami's Changing Negro Population, 1950–1960," *Economic Geography*, Vol. 40 (1964), pp. 221–38.

28. For an analysis of racial disparities in socioeconomic conditions, see Lowry, op. cit., footnote 6.

29. Calef and Nelson, op. cit., footnote 5.

30. By Census Bureau definition of urban. See Bryant and Wilber, op. cit., footnote 19, p. 9.

31. Numerous interviews with government officials, educators, and others in Mississippi reveal that the shortage of adequate labor is a significant hindrance to industry, even though there are more than enough people.

32. "Population is the point of reference from which all other elements

are observed and from which they all, singly and collectively, derive significance and meaning. It is population which furnishes the focus," Glenn T. Trewartha, "The Case For Population Geography," *Annals,* Association of American Geographers, Vol. 43 (1953), p. 83. "The superficially simple yet profoundly complicated question—'Why are people where they are?'"—is the most crucial one in geography today. "By focusing on the central problem of distribution of population, one can also avoid the necessity for using and defining much of what might be called geographical jargon. For instance, abstract or general terms like 'areal differentiation' or 'space relations' . . . become redundant," D. J. M. Hooson, "The Distribution of Population as the Essential Geographical Expression," *Canadian Geographer,* Vol. 17 (1960), pp. 10–20. In the study of population, "with few exceptions . . . the question is the interpretation of the distribution map —the classic geographical problem," H. C. Brookfield, "Questions on the Human Frontiers of Geography," *Economic Geography,* Vol. 40 (1964), p. 292.

33. Wilbur Zelinsky, *A Prologue to Population Geography* (New Jersey: Prentice-Hall, 1966), p. 27. "The study of historical background becomes an essential feature of any functional appraisal of population distribution," H. H. McCarty, "A Functional Analysis of Population Distribution," *Geographical Review,* Vol. 32 (1942), p. 293. "Momentary numbers and densities, while important, are not sufficient; population must be treated dynamically," Trewartha, op. cit., footnote 32, p. 75. Most lasting and valid interpretation will be based on relations of population changes to other changes, Donald J. Bogue, "The Geography of Recent Population Trends in the United States," *Annals,* Association of American Geographers, Vol. 44 (1954), p. 134; and Emrys Jones, "Cause and Effect in Human Geography," *Annals,* Association of American Geographers, Vol. 46 (1956), pp. 369–77.

34. For discussions of the push-pull concept, see Dennis H. Wrong, *Population and Society* (New York: Random House, 1967), pp. 88–89; J. Beaujeu-Garnier, *Geography of Population* (New York, 1966), pp. 216–17; Carter Goodrich, *Migration and Economic Opportunity* (Philadelphia: University of Pennsylvania Press, 1936); Everett S. Lee, "Internal Migration and Population Redistribution in the United States," in Ronald Freedman, ed., *Population: The Vital Revolution* (New York: Doubleday and Company, 1964), pp. 123–36.

35. F. T. Bachmura, "Migration and Factor Adjustment in Lower Mississippi Valley Agriculture, 1940–1950," *Journal of Farm Economics,* Vol. 38 (1956), pp. 1024–42; Allen D. Grimshaw, "Relationships Between Agricultural and Economic Indices and Rural Migration," *Rural Sociology,* Vol. 23 (1958), pp. 397–400; Herbert G. Kariel, "Selected Factors Areally Associated with Population Growth Due to Net Migration," *Annals,* Association of American Geographers, Vol.

53 (1963), pp. 210–23; Woofter, op. cit., footnote 5; O. E. Baker, "Rural-Urban Migration and the National Welfare," *Annals*, Association of American Geographers, Vol. 23 (1933), pp. 59–126; Richard Hartshorne, "Agricultural Land in Proportion to Agricultural Population in the United States," *Geographical Review*, Vol. 29 (1939), pp. 488–92; Edward L. Ullman, "Amenities as a Factor in Regional Growth," *Geographical Review*, Vol. 44 (1954), pp. 119–32; Lowry, op. cit., footnote 6; and Joseph J. Persky and John F. Kain, "Migration, Employment, and Race in the Deep South," *The Southern Economic Journal*, Vol. 36 (1969–1970), pp. 268–76. Social and cultural factors may be more important than economic ones. It is not easy to measure them because they cannot be evaluated in pecuniary terms, McCarty, op. cit., footnote 33, p. 292.

36. Edward Ackerman, "Population and Natural Resources," in Philip M. Hauser and Otis Dudley Duncan, eds., *The Study of Population: An Inventory and Appraisal* (Chicago: University of Chicago Press, 1959), pp. 621–48.

METROPOLITAN MIAMI'S CHANGING
NEGRO POPULATION, 1950-1960

Harold M. Rose

The population geography of the American Negro at the local level is a frequently neglected aspect of the field, and to date only one study of note has focused attention upon this subject,[1] although within the last decade other studies have been concerned with the population geography of the Negro at the national level.[2] The present study will examine the factors responsible for population change within a large southern metropolitan area. The factor of Negro out-migration from the South during the previous decade has been cited frequently, and numerous consequences of this phenomenon have been predicted. Less attention has been accorded to Negro population growth in southern metropolitan areas, as the growth rates there were generally slow at a time when growth rates characterizing northern metropolitan areas were unusually high.

Selected for analysis was the Miami Standard Metropolitan Statistical Area,[3] which is coincident with Dade County, Florida. Miami was the twenty-fifth largest SMSA in the nation in 1960, with slightly fewer than one million residents; at the same time, it embraced the twentieth largest Negro aggregate, numbering slightly fewer than 140,000. Miami, the nation's largest tropical metropolis, is essentially a product of the twentieth century and Negroes have constituted a significant element in the population since its inception. The primary purpose of this paper is to examine the factors responsible for the spatial distribution of the population in Miami and the factors responsible for its abnormal growth.

REGIONAL FRAMEWORK

The Miami SMSA consists of twenty-seven independent municipalities and numerous unincorporated places which are in some way directly involved in the economic development of the central city. The rise of these municipalities on the fringe of the central city has virtually halted the possibility of any significant areal expansion, other than in those areas where unincorporated areas serve as a buffer between central city and suburb. Negro settlements within the SMSA are similarly dispersed and twenty-six individual clusters can be identified. Since almost 95 per cent of the population is concentrated in ten settlements, attention will be focused on these.

In view of the fact that we are dealing with a metropolitan region, rather than a single city, it appears desirable to develop some regional frames of reference based on variations in the character of the settlements. This approach to the study of urban phenomenon would not have been necessary fifty years ago, as the city itself was an adequate unit of analysis.[4] Employment of the SMSA concept allows us to view the operation of the process of urbanization in its entirety. The major Negro settlements within the SMSA have been placed in three spatial units. Their designations imply the operation of special social and economic conditions that characterize the communities therein. The unit designations are the Core, the Inner Ring, and the Outer Ring.

THE CORE

The Core areas of the nation's larger urban centers are traditionally the places of residence of the lower income groups. More recently, Core areas have become the place of residence of Negroes and members of other minority groups. This situation has created a number of social, economic, and political problems that are likely to remain with us for some time. In this regard, Miami's situation is not unlike that of any of the nation's other large metropolitan centers.

Situation and Nature of Settlements

The Urban Core of the Miami SMSA includes the political city of Miami and a segment of unincorporated area found along the city's northwestern margin. Within the Urban Core, the Negro population numbers 84,000, or 61.3 per cent of the population of the SMSA. Two separate Negro communities, locally referred to as the "Central Negro District" and the "Liberty City–Brownsville area," house 39,000 and 45,000 respectively. These two settlements constitute the nucleus of the SMSA's Negro population.

The Central Negro District, which is located in downtown Miami in close proximity to the central business district, was until the 1950s the largest single Negro cluster in the metropolitan region. By 1960, it had lost this position to the rapidly growing community in the northwestern sector of the Core. In both 1940 and 1950, this original node contained more than half of the SMSA's Negro population,[5] but in 1960 fewer than 30 per cent resided here. Although its rate of growth was slow, it still managed a net increase of 10,000 residents.

The Central Negro District is the most densely settled area in the region, with more than 30,000 persons per square mile in an area of slightly greater than one-half square mile. The district is presently the site of a maze of apartment buildings which replaced most of the area's former "shotgun" houses. Fewer than 5 per cent of the area's residents were home owners in 1960. The area is yet referred to as a permanent slum even though most of the original housing has been cleared. Virrick, an authority on local housing conditions, has indicated that while these developments are not classified as substandard by the Census Bureau they are in fact substandard when one considers the intensity of their use.[6] A recently proposed urban renewal project, if initiated, would result in the elimination of this historic center of Negro settlement, which has been blamed for stifling the economic growth of the central business district.

The second Negro settlement within the Core is northwest of the Central Negro District and extends beyond the margin of the political city of Miami into an unincorporated area. This settlement, the Liberty City–Brownsville area, is currently the single largest community in the SMSA, having experienced a 318 per cent increase during the fifties. In 1950, Liberty City and Brownsville were separate communities, with populations of 12,000 and 5,000 respectively. By 1960, these two communities had become one continuous settlement. The stage was set for the fusion of these two communities in the winter of 1957, with the invasion of a Negro resident into a previously all-white neighborhood, a phenomenon more common in northern cities than in the South. By 1960, the zone previously separating these two communities had been eliminated. As a result of this initial success, Negroes are continuing to expand the margin of the community. The transfer of dwellings from white to Negro ownership is a phenomenon previously rare in Miami,[7] as most of the housing occupied by Negroes was developed specifically for their use. Continued areal expansion of this community might be hampered by the presence of physical obstacles to the north and west which might serve as effective racial boundaries. The northern boundary is a major highway artery, while to the west the presence of the Seaboard Air Line Railroad might serve as an effective barrier, as railroads often serve to separate the races in southern communities.[8]

Liberty City–Brownsville, like the previous Core settlement, is characterized by a low index of home ownership and a high incidence of multiple dwellings. Slightly fewer than three fourths of the residents are renters, but rents here average slightly higher than in the Central Negro District. The higher percentage of single family dwellings and the greater areal extent of this community has resulted in a density of only 12,000 per square mile, which is significantly lower than that prevailing in the Central Negro District, but higher than that for the SMSA as a whole. The southward expansion of the community into an area of single-family dwellings could result in lowering its density. However, if urban renewal results in the elimination of the original Negro Core, the Liberty City–Brownsville area is considered the logical relocation area because of its proximity to the residents' place of employment. This would necessitate the development of numerous additional multiple dwellings and thereby increase density conditions, as well as create a demand for additional space.

Character of the Population

The character or quality of the population is frequently as important as numbers in attempting to determine the contribution that a group will make to society. The factors which will be treated here are age structure, sex composition, and educational levels. These are the factors which often determine the level of efficiency at which a group will operate.

The age structure of the group reflects the level of dependency, as well as the labor force potential. Franklin recently reported that geographers are beginning to lend implicit recognition to age structure as an important index to the social and economic life of a community.[9] The Negro population of the Urban Core is characterized by a median age of 23.6 years, which is slightly higher than that of either the Inner Ring or the Outer Ring. The low median age of the population is associated with a high level of fertility. In 1960, more than 47 per cent of the residents of the Core represented a dependent population. In other words, approximately 53 per cent represented what is generally considered the labor productive period, twenty to sixty-four. At the national level, 48 per cent of our population was dependent in 1960.

There are some significant variations in the age structure of the Core's two principal settlements. The Central Negro District is characterized by a smaller proportion of its population under five and a larger proportion over sixty-five than is the case with the Liberty City–Brownsville area. The former likewise has a population pyramid characterized by a narrow waist, which represents the fifteen to nineteen age group. This probably reflects shifts in residential occupancy by parents of children in this age bracket, as well as the fact that this area is the principal place of residence of the newcomer, a factor that would cause a depression in the proportion in this age category. The larger percentage of older people here can be partially attributed to the availability of lower cost housing. The higher percentage of persons over sixty-five and the lower fertility index of the Central Negro District has resulted in a median age that is more than three years higher than that of the Liberty City–Brownsville area.

The Liberty City–Brownsville area shows a greater variation in its sex composition than does the rival Core settlement. In the age category twenty to forty-four, females exceed males by almost 3.5 per cent in the northwest Core community, while variation in the sex ratio in the Central Negro District appears to be insignificant. The larger concentration of women in the twenty to forty-four age group in Liberty City–Brownsville probably indicates a more favorable situation with respect to place of employment. In no other age category is there a significant difference in the sex ratio.

The Core is characterized by a higher level of educational attainment than the SMSA's two other major regions. The median number of years of education completed by the Core's residents is 8.2. This is likewise the median level of education attained by nonwhites at the national level. Almost 14 per cent of the area's residents are high school graduates, but less than 3 per cent are college graduates. The Central Negro District produces its proportionate share of the Core's high school graduates; but it is the place of residence of less than one quarter of the Core's college graduates.

More than 20 per cent of the Core's population is "functionally" illiterate, a situation which severely restricts the nature of available job opportunities.[10]

INNER RING

The presence of Negro communities beyond the margin of the Central City is partially indicative of the desire of the group to participate in the process of suburbanization; although it must be kept in mind that some of these communities have developed primarily in response to proximity to place of employment. The prevailing pattern of Negro settlement is typical of that which characterizes most of the nation's urban areas.

Situation and Nature of Settlements

The Inner Ring constitutes a group of smaller communities located on the margin of the Central City which range in size from 2,700 to almost 12,000. Within the Inner Ring, there are five distinct Negro communities which have more than a thousand residents. These communities are the

Bunche Park community of Opa Locka; Coconut Grove, a community that straddles the Miami–Coral Gables boundary; the Negro community in South Miami; Richmond Heights; and Perrine. The latter two communities are located in an unincorporated area.

The Inner Ring communities are less dependent upon the Central City as a source of employment than was the case with the Core communities. The degree of dependence appears to be a function of distance. Coconut Grove, which is partially situated within the Central City, sends more than 61 per cent of its workers to Miami for employment, while Richmond Heights–Perrine, which is located more than fifteen miles south of the Central City, sends only 21 per cent of its workers there.

The communities within the Inner Ring show much variation in housing quality, but the extent of home ownership is higher than in the Core. Only South Miami shows an unusually low proportion of home owners, 20 per cent, while Richmond Heights and Opa Locka, both middle-class, suburban developments, show home ownership ratios of 87.5 and 78.2 per cent, respectively. There is a positive correlation between the extent of home ownership and the existence of sound housing. More than one third of the housing in South Miami is considered substandard, while less than 1 per cent falls in this category in the community of Richmond Heights. The prevalance of single family dwellings in this region has resulted in lower densities than those prevailing in the Core. Only Coconut Grove, among the Inner Ring communities, is characterized by an unusually high density.

Character of the Population

The age structure of the Inner Ring population reveals the extreme youth of the group. The median here is only 21.8 years; it is associated with high fertility and with the recency of development of some of these communities. Only Coconut Grove and South Miami, among the Inner Ring communities, show a significant number of older people in the population. Both Richmond Heights and Bunche Park are recent developments and show concentrations in the lower age groups (zero to fourteen) and the middle age groups (thirty to forty-four). Only 47.5 per cent of the group is considered dependent, on the basis of age. Coconut Grove, one of the older Negro communities in the SMSA, is characterized by a relatively low proportion of dependents, whereas Perrine shows the highest percentage of dependence among the group.

The older Inner Ring communities appear to be more attractive to women in the twenty to forty-four age category than to men. The availability of jobs in close proximity to these communities is probably responsible for this phenomenon. In the older age categories, there does not appear to be any significant differences in sex ratios.

The level of educational attainment in the Inner Ring is slightly less than that of the Core. Almost 13 per cent of the group represent high school graduates, but more than one quarter of the population over twenty-five is functionally illiterate. While the median level of education is only 7.8 years, the Inner Ring has more college graduates than does the Core. This reflects the greater degree of heterogeneity among Inner Ring communities.

THE OUTER RING

Outer Ring communities frequently represent zones situated within a semirural setting and occupied by a less affluent group than that inhabitating the Inner Ring. For this reason, Negroes are infrequently residents of this zone since employment in the service trades will be at a minimum.

Situation and Nature of Settlements

The Outer Ring communities are located more than twenty miles south of the Central City and demonstrate little direct dependence upon the Central City as a source of income. The Outer Ring contains fewer than 10,000 Negroes or less than 8 per cent of the SMSA's Negro total. The major communities in this sector are Goulds, Homestead, and Florida City, with Negro populations of 4,189, 3,152, and 2,328, respectively. Both Homestead and Florida City are independent municipalities in which Negroes constitute more than one half and one third of the respective totals. Goulds, an unincorporated place, is more than 80 per cent Negro.

The physical appearance of the Outer Ring communities reveals a high degree of substandardness. This can be attributed to an unusually low rate of home ownership and to the nature and age of the structures. To some extent, physical blight has been reduced by the recent development of the ubiquitous stucco apartment buildings which are common to all of the major Negro communities, with the exception of Richmond Heights. So, even in the smaller communities in which we normally expect to find single family dwellings, multiples tend to provide the principal accommodations. It is in these smaller communities that the "imageability" of the urban form tends to reflect what might best be considered the "vernacular image."

Character of the Population

The age structure of this group, like that of the previous groups, reflects a pattern of high fertility which results in a median age of only 20.5 years.

Because in-migration has not been a principal source of growth, there is here a fairly uniform decline in the proportion of the population in the age bracket twenty to forty-four. The limited opportunities for women in these smaller communities is reflected in a slight surplus of males in the productive years.

The level of development of the Outer Ring communities will probably remain low as a result of the low level of educational attainment of its residents. The median level of educational attainment of the group is only 6.1 years and almost 40 per cent of the adult population is illiterate. Fewer than 5 per cent of the population is represented by high school graduates, while college graduates comprise approximately 0.2 per cent. High fertility and limited formal education should mark this as a persistent problem area.

LABOR FORCE PARTICIPATION

The present pattern of Negro distribution within the SMSA can probably be best explained by carefully observing changes in labor force participation, for most often the initial establishment of a Negro community is directly related to the proximity of major sources of employment. Only within the last decade, with the creation of new communities, has the source of employment lost ground as one of the determinants dictating the spatial distribution of Negroes within the metropolitan area.

In 1960, Negroes represented 16.9 per cent (62,000) of Dade County's labor force. More than 80 per cent of all eligible Negro males were in the labor force, while 59 per cent of the Negro women were active participants in the employment market. The proportion of Negro males in the labor force is only 5 per cent higher than that of white males, whereas the proportion of Negro females is more than 22 per cent higher than that of their white counterparts. However, the Negro female is also a more frequent participant in the national employment market. The age structure of the white population probably accounts, at least in part, for its lower index of labor force participation.

The effects of the national economic recession were felt in the Miami SMSA during much of 1960, when almost 6 per cent of the labor force was unemployed; this was cause for much alarm, especially in the building-construction industry. The level of Negro unemployment, which is traditionally higher than that of whites, reached 7.4 per cent, but was lower than the high rates of Negro unemployment reported by Hill[11] for such large urban centers as Chicago, Pittsburgh, St. Louis, and Philadelphia. This might be partially attributed to the fact that service industries are characterized by greater employment stability,[12] although domestic-service workers have a higher unemployment ratio than do other service workers. The labor market in the SMSA has become saturated, primarily as a result of the massive influx of more than 100,000 Cuban refugees. This has led the Negro laborer to raise claims that the Cuban newcomer is undercutting him in the traditional jobs and thereby creating problems of economic dislocation.

The occupational structure of the Negro population of the SMSA reflects the city-serving functions of Miami and associated municipalities. Nelson, in his "Service Classification of American Cities," based on major economic activities, placed Miami in the personal services, retail trade, financial category.[13] In a more recent study which included only 50 major United States cities, classified on the basis of metropolitan function and regional relationships, Miami was one of nine cities cited as representing a special case,[14] although it was emphasized that Miami's industrial profile reflected its function as a major resort.[15] Nelson has likewise implied that cities throughout the South in the personal services category have a strong attraction for Negroes, and that only cities in the public administration category have a higher mean ratio.[16]

In 1960, personal services remained the most important occupation in which Negroes were employed, but some minor variations in the traditional Negro occupational profile could be observed. Increasing employment in retail trade and manufacturing occur probably as a result of changes in the population structure and in the economic structure. In these two categories, Negro males were represented most strongly in eating and drinking establishments and food services, but had failed to gain employment on a significant scale in Dade's major manufacturing activity, aluminum fabrication. In 1960, this industry employed 10,000 workers,[17] but it has recently encountered production problems. Negro women have done only slightly better in the rapidly growing garment industry that employs more than 5,800 people.[18] There was also a sharp increase in the number and proportion of Negro professionals during the decade, principally teachers. The growth of Negro professionals can be attributed to the rapid rise of the Negro population, which constitutes their primary market.

If the labor force is broken down on the basis of sex, we find that Negro males have made the greatest strides in the category of operatives as this category now includes slightly more males than did the previous leader among employment categories, viz., laborers. More than 52 per cent of the employed Negro males are now in these two categories, with another 17 per cent classed as service workers. In both 1950 and 1960, approximately one half of the Negro women in the labor force were classed as private household workers. The relative importance of this job category declined during the decade, but there was an absolute increase of more than 4,300 such jobs. Negro women monopolize the domestic situation as more than three fourths of all of the jobs in this category are held by them. The domestic jobs appear to hold greater attraction for women in the thirty-five to fifty-four age group. The relatively high increase in the number of in-migrant women in this age group might possibly be associated with the increase in the number of jobs in this category. Private household employment in the Miami SMSA is more remunerative than in other selected southern SMSA's.[19]

In 1960, 5,300 Negro females were classified as service workers. This includes quasi-domestic employees. Among this group there was a sharp increase in hospital personnel, which probably reflects the high incidence of illness among the SMSA's high proportion of older people. The clerical category, which accounts for almost 30 per cent of all employed females in the SMSA, gives employment to only 1.7 per cent of the SMSA's Negro women. The increase in the total population of the SMSA during the decade has made available an increasing number of opportunities for Negro females in the traditional categories, but the more desirable and remunerative jobs were not open to Negro women because of a lack of necessary skills, imperfect knowledge, or social restraints.

Because of the nature of the occupational structure, the Negro could hardly be expected to attain a high level of living; consequently, the median family income for the SMSA is only $3,367. While this exceeds the median family income of Negroes in the South by more than a thousand dollars, it is far below the $5,350 median family income for the total SMSA. Among the several Negro subcommunities within the SMSA, the median varies from a low of $2,262 in the Outer Ring community of Goulds, to a high of $4,670 in the Inner Ring community of Richmond Heights. The two Core communities possessed a median only slightly lower than that for the total Negro population.

Variations in median family incomes reflect variations in the occupational structure within these subcommunities. If it is agreed that the primary function of each of these subcommunities is consumption rather than production, then we might classify them on the basis of the dominant occupation of their residents. The mean and standard deviation for the major employing occupational groups were determined. These were represented by the following categories: (1) private household workers, (2) operatives, and (3) laborers. When the percentage of workers in any community was more than one standard deviation above the mean percentage for all workers in one of the above-specified occupational categories, the subcommunity was designated by its dominant occupation.

Of the ten major Negro subcommunities in the SMSA, two were classified as residences of operatives, three as residences of laborers, two as residences of private household workers, and three as units of diversified employment. The communities of diversified employment showed little dispersion around the mean in any of the above categories. This is a reflection of their more heterogeneous population composition. The two private household-workers' communities are located on the margins of the high-income, residential community of Coral Gables; the dominance of laborers in the Outer Ring seems to imply a lack of economic opportunity. The future of the Outer Ring communities appears to be more uncertain than that of the others.

The jobs represented by the large increase in the number of operatives and of other personal-service workers were largely filled by newcomers who settled in the Core, which is in close proximity to the employing centers. Many second generation Miamians shifted their place of residence from the original Core community to the new Core community or out of the Core completely, as a result of occupational mobility and the establishment of employment tenure.

The small relative increase in the number of persons in the labor productive ages in the older and smaller communities in the Inner Ring reflect a fairly stable situation in the adjacent employing centers. At this time, the remote communities of the Outer Ring appear to be in a tenuous position as a result of the slow development of employment opportunities within this sector of the metropolitan area. The southward push of new middle-class suburban developments onto lands formerly given over to crop production can hardly be expected to provide the kind of opportunities associated with the older and affluent communities on the periphery of the Central City.

The development of new industries within the SMSA has occurred principally on the western fringe of the urbanized area. This has been one of the fastest growing areas within the metropolitan region, yet the Negro community in Hialeah has not attained the minimum size to be included in this study. If, in the future, Negroes are able to secure employment within this changing employment market, the pattern of distribution of the Negro population will be slightly altered.

METROPOLITAN GROWTH

The rate of growth of metropolitan Negro populations in the South during the previous decade lagged far behind the growth of this component of the population in the metropolitan areas of the North. Of the larger southern SMSA's, only Miami and Atlanta were characterized by Negro growth rates which resembled those of the larger northern SMSA's. The nonwhite population of the Miami SMSA increased from 65,000 in 1950 to almost 140,000 in 1960, an increase of 114.5 per cent. The rate of growth of the Negro population in metropolitan Miami exceeded that of any of the other clusters that comprise the twenty largest Negro aggregates in the nation. The factors responsible for this growth will be viewed in some detail in order to attempt to predict Miami's future color composition.

The high birth rate of the Negro population of Dade County coupled with rapid in-migration played prominent roles in producing a local population explosion. In 1955, the crude birth rate of Dade's nonwhite population was 37.7 per 1,000, while the death rate was only 8.8 per 1,000. It appears unlikely that the death rate can be lowered significantly, but changes in economic and social status will likely result in altering the fertility differentials which exist between whites and Negroes, as has occurred on a national scale during the last several decades.[20] A projection of the present rate of annual increase would result in an additional 40,000 individuals in 1970, owing to an excess of births over deaths.

Some variations in the pattern of fertility can be observed within our regional framework. Employing the index of fertility known as the child-woman ratio[21] or replacement ratio, we find that the Outer Ring communities are characterized by the highest fertility levels, while the Core is characterized by lower levels of fertility. The lowest fertility level among the several communities prevails in the Central Negro District, which registered a ratio of 618 (Table 1). The lowest Negro fertility ratios are more nearly similar to those of the white communities of Carol City (694) and Cutler Ridge (652), which possess the highest indexes of fertility among

TABLE I

Variations in Negro Fertility Patterns in the Miami SMSA

Areas	Fertility ratios
Core:	
The Central Negro District	618
Liberty City-Brownsville	756
Inner Ring:	
Opa Locka	639
Coconut Grove	689
Richmond Heights	766
Perrine	768
South Miami	800
Outer Ring:	
Goulds	789
Homestead-Florida City	800

Source: compiled from U.S. Census Bureau reports.

the SMSA's white population. Westoff reported the average fertility ratio of urban whites at the national level was 540 in 1950, while the urban nonwhite ratio was 584.[22] Thus the high fertility ratios which prevail in the SMSA's Negro communities are not typically urban, but resemble more closely the fertility ratios of white rural farm residents.

The second, growth-producing factor, in-migration, has been only slightly less important than the first. The attraction of Negroes to Miami is difficult to explain in an era when paths of migration extend predominantly North and West. Miami's situation along Florida's lower east coast is a minimum distance of four hundred miles from its nearest major reservoir of in-migrants. More than 76 per cent of its in-migrants during the decade were southern Negroes from states outside of Florida, and approximately 4 per cent were from areas outside of the South. Opportunity for economic betterment is generally the principal force motivating individuals to break with previous ties and to select a new place of residence. But when we consider the nature of the job market and the Negro occupational structure in Dade, it seems strange that this factor would serve as a strong magnet, but this does not seem to be the case. Hart is of the opinion that the creation of a favorable social climate, as a result of the influx of people from the North, might be a significant factor.[23] It is generally agreed that Miami's pattern of race relations is an improvement over that of other southern cities, but for the person who is only able to acquire a menial, low-paying job this may be of little psychic value. One might also wonder how important climate is as a drawing force; Ullman considers it the most important single amenity factor contributing to regional growth.[24]

In-migration varies in its importance as a growth-producing factor within the established regional framework. Only in the Core has migration been more important than natural increase in promoting growth; here, in-migration accounted for almost 60 per cent of the increase during the decade. In both the Inner Rings and the Outer Rings, in-migration was responsible for only about one third of the total growth. Thus, the traditional pattern, in which the newcomer is found primarily in the Urban Core, prevails here. The pattern of distribution of the newcomer in the Miami SMSA reflects the economic status of the migrant, as well as his desire to locate as near to the employment market as possible.

SUMMARY AND CONCLUSIONS

If the factors responsible for growth continue to operate at the 1950 to 1960 level, the SMSA will record a Negro population in excess of 200,000 by 1970. But birth rates should decrease during the decade, without a significant change in the death rate, thereby reducing the rate of natural increase; continued high birth rates would likely depress incomes. The more rapid growth of the Negro population in the Miami SMSA, in comparison to that of other southern metropolitan areas, is a function of Miami's greater economic and social attractions. If the social factor is an overriding element in attracting Negroes to Miami, the improvement of the social climate in other southern centers may do much to divert migrants who in the past might have selected Miami as a place of residence. But it appears that the extent and nature of the employment market will be the principal factors affecting future in-migration. Competition with Cuban refugees for many of the traditional jobs has allegedly hurt the Negro population economically and may do much to hamper in-migration. The fastest rate of growth is likely to continue to prevail in the Core, but with the expansion of suburban communities in the Inner Ring this area should also experience more rapid growth. The Outer Ring communities will continue to be the slowest growing in the area.

The pattern of settlement within the SMSA will be determined by the operation of a number of social and economic forces, the chief of which will continue to be proximity to place of employment. The status of the agricultural industry in South Dade and alternative employment opportunities in the Central City will affect the vitality of the Outer Ring communities. The old Core area will likely give way to the new Core in the northwest as urban renewal becomes a reality. This move will result in uprooting many established Negro commercial enterprises with the disappearance of the "Negro Main Street." Continued improvements in the area's transportation network will enable the Negro to settle at greater distances from his primary source of employment in the Central City and will likely contribute to the further expansion of the Inner Ring's suburban communities.

In characterizing the settlement pattern of the Negro population in the Miami SMSA, one factor stands out, *viz.*, its physical fragmentation. Thus, in the Miami metropolitan area we do not find a single Negro community, but a number of Negro communities of which ten include more than one thousand residents. This physical fragmentation is essentially a function of proximity to places of employment in a service-oriented metropolitan area, but could hardly have occurred in anything other than a newly emerging metropolitan community.

LITERATURE CITED

1. John F. Hart, "A Rural Retreat for Northern Negroes," *Geogr. Rev.*, Vol. 50, 1960, pp. 147–68.

2. Wesley C. Calef and Howard J. Nelson, "Distribution of the Negro Population in the United States," *Geogr. Rev.*, Vol. 46, 1956, pp. 82–97; and John F. Hart, "The Changing Distribution of the American Negro," *Annals Assn. Amer. Geogrs.*, Vol. 50, 1960, pp. 242–66.

3. Prior to 1960 the Census Bureau employed the term Standard Metropolitan Area to represent this concept. Hereafter, in this paper the terms Standard Metropolitan Statistical Area and SMSA will be used interchangeably.

4. Edgar M. Hoover and Raymond Vernon, *Anatomy of a Metropolis*, New York, 1962, p. 1.

5. Reinhold P. Wolff and David Gillogly, *Negro Housing in the Miami Area*, Coral Gables, Fla., 1951, p. 4.

6. *The Miami Herald*, Feb. 26, 1961.

7. Elizabeth Virrick, "New Housing for Negroes in Dade County, Florida," *Studies in Housing and Minority Groups*, Berkeley, Calif., 1960, p. 136.

8. Nicholas J. Demerath and Harlan Gilmore, "The Ecology of Southern Cities," *The Urban South*, Chapel Hill, North Carolina, 1954, p. 157.

9. S. H. Franklin, "The Age Structure of New Zealand's North Island Communities," *Econ. Geog.*, Vol. 34, 1958, p. 77.

10. The term functional illiterate refers to persons with less than 5 years of formal education.

11. Herbert Hill, "Racial Discrimination in the Nation's Apprenticeship Training Programs," *Phylon*, Vol. 23, 1962, p. 216.

12. D. E. Diamond, "The Service Worker in United States' Manufacturing and Employment Stability," *Oxford Econ. Papers*, Vol. 14, 1962, p. 81.

13. Howard J. Nelson, "A Service Classification of American Cities," *Econ. Geog.*, Vol. 31, 1955, pp. 189–209.

14. Otis Dudley Duncan and Others, *Metropolis and Region*, Baltimore, 1960, p. 270.

15. Ibid., p. 258.

16. Howard J. Nelson, "Some Characteristics of the Population of Cities in Similar Service Classifications," *Econ. Geog.*, Vol. 33, 1957, p. 177.

17. *Metropolitan Miami*, South Miami, Florida, 1962, p. 44.

18. Ibid.

19. Only Miami, of a group of selected southern SMSA's, might be equally as attractive in terms of real income to Negro women seeking private household employment as such centers as Chicago, Detroit, Philadelphia, Los Angeles, or Cleveland.

20. For an extensive treatment of differential fertility in the United States, see Charles F. Westoff, "Differential Fertility in the United States: 1900 to 1952," *Amer. Soc. Rev.*, Vol. 19, 1954, pp. 549–61;

and Everett S. and Anne S. Lee, "The Differential Fertility of the American Negro," *Amer. Soc. Rev.*, Vol. 17, 1952, pp. 437–52.

21. The child-woman ratio is computed by calculating the number of children in the population under 5 years of age born per 1,000 women between the ages of 15 to 44 or 15 to 49, during one census period.

22. Westoff, op. cit., p. 551.

23. Hart, op. cit., p. 256.

24. Edward L. Ullman, "Amenities as a Factor in Regional Growth," *Geogr. Rev.*, Vol. 44, 1954, p. 123.

AGE STRUCTURE IN EXPANDING GHETTO SPACE:
CLEVELAND, OHIO, 1940–1965

Ralph A. Sanders and John S. Adams

INTRODUCTION

In recent years, Negro ghettos have become increasingly conspicuous in American cities. Geographic insights into patterns of urban "ghettoization," however, are few. In part, this geographic ignorance derives from a traditional disinterest in the social attributes of population, from constricting regional approaches to the subject matter, and from a landscape bias with heavy rural orientation.[1]

Geographical studies have emphasized two well-defined directions: (i) the location of ghettos within large white-dominated cities,[2] and (ii) patterns of ghetto expansion into hostile white residential areas, with heavy attention on the role of housing in the process.[3] While further study is needed along these lines, other focuses must be sought to direct geographical attention toward unresolved social issues. To date, geographic research into other aspects of Negro ghettos in the United States is highly fragmentary.[4]

For the most part, scholarly research implicitly assumes a general uniformity of demographic and social characteristics for ghetto residents and pays little attention to internal differentiation. Yet it is reasonable to think that many of the forces which sort and stratify the urban population as a whole are operative within the ghetto as well. The ghetto population is subject to two broad sets of ordering forces: those *external* to the ghetto which impose spatial confinement upon the population, and those *internal* forces which act to differentiate the population within the ghetto, some of which of course, provide the motive power for ghetto expansion. It is these internal forces, operating within ghetto space and through time, which occupy our attention here.

A top geographical priority for studying ghetto populations is to establish characteristic age structures for local populations. Only Rose[5] has looked at age structure differentials for a ghetto, and yet the importance of age in understanding behavior is well established for other kinds of work.[6] By finding regularities in age structure variations, significant behavioral questions in the ghetto context can be asked.[7]

Limited attention has been paid to age structure in geographical research partly for methodological reasons. Wilson[8] thoroughly reviews methods for measuring age structure in geography, but these techniques, deriving indices of age structure from population pyramids, fail either to reflect the pyramid faithfully or to generalize it adequately. Coulson[9] offers an alternative solution to these longstanding difficulties. A best-fit, least squares line is imposed upon a population-age histogram, and a generalized age structure is reflected in the slope parameter of that line. Signs and decimal points are dropped, and the Age Structure Index Value (ASIV) is found.[10] Low values for the ASIVs reflect a low ratio of young to old in a population (old population), and high values indicate a high ratio (young population).[11]

STUDY AREA

The black ghetto of Cleveland, Ohio, is well suited to substantive investigations of this kind. First, in addition to data from the regular dicennial censuses, detailed information about the central city is also available for 1965.[12] Second, the growth of Cleveland's Negro population in the past three decades has been spectacular. This growth can be seen in Cleveland having been one of the first large cities in the United States to elect (and re-elect) a black mayor. And third, the black/white dichotomy in Cleveland is not clouded by the presence of other racial groups.[13]

Definitions of ghetto space are based generally upon the degree of racial

TABLE 1
Percent of the Total Nonwhite Population Represented in the Study

Year	Total Nonwhite Population	Total Population in Census Tracts Containing at Least 500 Nonwhites	Percent Represented in the Study
1940	84,919	77,751	91.55
1950	149,544	141,848	94.85
1960	250,818	245,630	97.93
1965	279,222	272,222	97.44

domination in residential areas. Here, where census tracts of approximately 4,000 population are used, 500 blacks is considered the minimum for that tract's inclusion in "ghetto space." Measurements of population attributes on smaller figures generally are unreliable and, in any case, this figure usually indicated racially homogeneous census tracts, since "tipping points" are surpassed below this level (Table 1).[14]

PATTERN OF AGE STRUCTURE

For the Cleveland ghetto, ASIVs are found for each census tract in the four study years. Least squares fits, significant at the .05 level, occur for all but eight of the 214 tracts, and these eight cases were discarded with little loss of information (Table 2).

Accompanying the increase in the number of census tracts contained within the ghetto is a tendency for populations to become more youthful.

TABLE 2
Aggregate Age Structure Index Values for
206 Cleveland Census Tracts by Year

| | Old Population | | | | | | | Young Population | | | |
	000-024	025-049	050-074	075-099	100-124	125-149	150-174	175-199	200-224	Total Tracts	Median ASIV
1940	0	1	2	7	13	3	3	0	0	29	111
1950	0	0	5	9	14	9	4	2	2	45	115
1960	0	1	5	4	13	14	9	17	2	65	140
1965	1	3	4	7	9	11	12	15	5	67	145

Median age structure values increase irregularly throughout the study period, and the skewness of the distribution of ASIVs shifts from left to right. The greatest change in median age structure values occurs in the period 1950–60 and appears to be associated with the pronounced bimodal tendency in the ASIVs for 1960.

Using this information, maps were constructed for each of the census years using an isopleth convention. A strong spatial differentiation of age structures can be seen.

Age structure varies systematically through ghetto-space. The oldest age structures are found in central ghetto locations, either within the main body of the ghetto, or at the center of small areas some distance from this main body. During later years, black settlement between these outlying areas and the core tracts is associated with youthful population. Within the confines of the ghetto at any time period, the greater the distance from areas of old population age structure, the younger the age structure of the population.[15] One exception to this rule is found in the western portion of the ghetto near the Central Business District of Cleveland. A concentration of youthful population is found in close proximity to the portion of the ghetto where the oldest age structures are found. This is an area of public housing development, and as such represents a spatial incursion of public policy into the ghetto, and is seen, therefore, as an anomaly.

Through time, the differentiation of age structures within the ghetto intensifies. There is a direct relation between low ASIVs and the length of time a census tract has been occupied by Negroes. The "depression" of old age structures at the center of the ghetto is deepening. Mean ASIVs for the ten lowest values recorded in each year, in chronological order, are 081, 075, 074, and 058. This increasing differentiation extends, in fact, throughout the ghetto. By standardizing ASIVs to a common scale and comparing the range of age structure values of each year, a surprisingly constant trend is pinpointed.

The degree of ASIV differentiation increases at a more or less regular rate through time; age structure contrasts within the ghetto are strengthening. But because the ghetto has territorially expanded during this period, the age structure *gradient* from core to periphery probably has not altered appreciably. No measurement of this gradient is attempted because of the indeterminacy of ghetto boundaries. Net population changes, expressed as a percentage of the population in the tract at the beginning of a time period and mapped in isopleth fashion, provide some insight into the process of age structure differentiation through time and ghetto space.[16]

A clear correspondence between population losses and old age structures is established. For the most part, tracts which have suffered the most severe depletion of population numbers have experienced the greatest drops in ASIVs and generally are found in positions central to the ghetto as a whole. Additional population declines are found in the central portions of outlying ghetto areas which invariably have experienced drops in ASIVs as well. Places where in-migration is recent (tracts newly added to the ghetto in any time period) have the youngest population. These are the places at the periphery of the main body of the ghetto, at newly established areas of black population, and, in the later periods, at the fringes of these outlying areas.

An important element of these structural relationships is the apparent stratification of population on the basis of age-selective migration. Census tracts with depleted population appear to be source areas for migrants whose destinations are the ghetto fringe and the ghetto "outlier." Associated changes in age structure, furthermore, taken in conjunction with the spatial pattern on net population changes, imply that selective migration of the young is taking place. Where outmigration of the young occurs, the aging process for the remaining population will be accelerated, due not only to the loss of the young but also to lowered rates of reproduction and survival.

On these grounds it is reasonable to argue that systematic spatial and temporal variations in migration behavior within the ghetto have been outlined. Basic age-selective residential moves occur from the ghetto core to its periphery, or from the core to ghetto "outliers." After these outlying areas have been established as areas of black residence, they may also become significant source areas for intraghetto migrants. But because information regarding the origins and destinations of black intracity migrants is lacking, and especially because the destinations of large numbers of incoming Negro migrants from outside the system are not known, a great deal of caution is in order for postulating mechanisms of this kind.

Summary and Comment

A high degree of regularity in the distribution of age structures is found within the Cleveland ghetto, reflecting credit upon the sensitivity of Coulson's method of measuring age structure and, more importantly, indicating a fundamental regularity in spatial processes at work in the black ghetto of Cleveland. There exists a pattern of age structure variation which parallels ghetto territorial expansion. Rough inferences made about the patterns of intraghetto migration, seen as streams of residential movers flowing from the core to the fringes of the ghetto, reflect the causal link between migration and age structure composition.

Population age structure variations within ghetto space reveal that substantial structural changes take place not only at the edges of the ghetto, where territorial expansion is apparent, but also at the core of the long established ghetto. Occasional leaps into noncontiguous areas of the inner city characterize ghetto territorial expansion, with simultaneous if less spectacular accretions at the edge of the ghetto. This basic growth process forms cores of old age structure surrounded by "rims" of young population both within the main body of the ghetto and in the outlying areas of black residence.

Although it is beyond present objectives to explore the issue systematically, the pattern of expansion of the Cleveland ghetto appears to possess substantial regularity of a kind not described in geographic literature. Ghetto expansion has been viewed as a "block by block total transition"[17] where contiguity is preserved in territorial growth. While there is nothing in this discussion which tends to refute that assertion, *at a different scale* the primary pattern appears to be one of "leap-frogging."[18] The pattern can be illustrated in a sequence of repetitious growth stages (Fig. 1):

1. The ghetto begins to expand in contiguous fashion (Fig. 1A).

2. Noncontiguous ghetto "outliers" are established, and population numbers at the center of the ghetto fall (Fig. 1B).

3. Coalescence between the outlying areas and the main body of the ghetto follows. Further population depletions occur at the core of the ghetto and at the center of the "outliers" established in Stage 2. Ghetto contiguity is re-established (Fig. 1C).

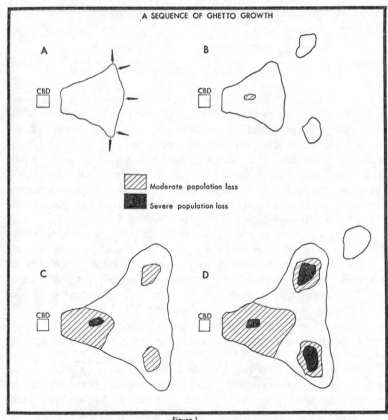

A SEQUENCE OF GHETTO GROWTH

Moderate population loss

Severe population loss

Figure 1

4. Either during Stage 3 or after it has been completed, new "outliers" are formed and the process begins again (Fig. 1D).

The extent to which black ghettos in American cities follow this description is, of course, unknown, but new hypotheses concerning determinants of expansion patterns are needed. A large number of behavioral variations for small populations (e.g., in commuting patterns for work and school, and in shopping and recreation activities) are implied by an underlying ghetto space differentiated on the basis of population patterns. The study of many of these variations, however, may well have to be postponed until further structural relations within the "typical black ghetto" of American cities are found. In this sense, work in geography on ghettos is long overdue, and it is vital that we should continue the task of updating our knowledge on the little understood spatial framework for black population patterns and activities within the metropolitan area.

LITERATURE CITED

1. Rose, Harold M., "Social Processes in the City: Race and Urban Residential Choice," Commission on College Geography, Resource Paper No. 6, Association of American Geographers, Washington, D.C., 1969, p. 1.

2. Rose, Ibid., pp. 7–10.

3. See, for example, Richard L. Morrill, "The Negro Ghetto: Problems and Alternatives," *The Geographical Review*, Vol. 55, 1965, pp. 339–61, and Harold M. Rose, "The Development of an Urban Subsystem: The Case of the Negro Ghetto," *Annals*, Association of American Geographers, Vol. 60, 1970, pp. 1–17.

4. See, for example, A. Pred, "Business Thoroughfares as Expressions of Urban Negro Culture," *Economic Geography*, Vol. 39, 1963, pp. 217–33; B. J. L. Berry, "Commercial Structure and Commercial Blight," Department of Geography, Research Paper 85, University of Chicago, 1963; P. F. Lewis, "Impact of Negro Migration on the Electoral Geography of Flint, Michigan, 1932–1962: A Cartographic Analysis," *Annals*, Association of American Geographers, Vol. 55, 1965, pp. 1–25; W. Bunge, "Field Notes," Detroit Geographical Expedition, Detroit, 1968 (mimeographed); and Stanley D. Brunn and Wayne L. Hoffman, "The Spatial Response of Negroes and Whites Toward Open Housing: The Flint Referendum," *Annals*, Association of American Geographers, Vol. 60, 1970, pp. 18–36.

5. Rose, op. cit., 1969.

6. Huff, David, "A Topographical Model of Consumer Space Prefer-

ences," Papers and Proceedings, Regional Science Association, Vol. 6, 1960, pp. 159–74.

7. See, for example, "Profile of a Rioter," *Report of the National Advisory Commission on Civil Disorders* (Kerner Report), 1968, Government Printing Office, Washington, D.C., p. 129. In this key statement, place of residence and relevant spatial behavior, among other things, are not mentioned. The Kerner Report draws little upon scholarly research and not at all from geography. The Commission's failure to include any maps within its 400 page report reflects badly upon that investigation, and equally poorly upon the efforts of geographers to deal with these questions, from whose work the Commission otherwise might have drawn.

8. Wilson, M. G. A., *Population Geography*, Thomas Nelson, Melbourne, 1968.

9. Coulson, M. R. C., "The Distribution of Population Age Structures in Kansas City," *Annals*, Association of American Geographers, Vol. 58, 1968, pp. 155–76.

10. Where no positive values are found, it is unnecessary to add 100 points to the ASIVs. See Coulson, Ibid., p. 168. Because in this study no positive slope values occur, the ASIVs are 100 points lower than those values for identical populations in Coulson's study of Kansas City.

11. Sensitivity tests indicate that the technique faithfully reflects most important features of the population pyramid. See R. A. Sanders, "Spatial Trends in Age Structure Changes within the Cleveland Ghetto: 1940–1965," unpublished M.S. thesis, Pennsylvania State University, 1968, pp. 10–23.

12. U. S. Bureau of the Census, "Special Census of Cleveland, Ohio," *Current Population Reports*, Series P-28, No. 1390, Nov. 5, 1965, Government Printing Office, Washington, D.C.

13. Because the U. S. Census makes no distinction between nonwhites after 1940, except at aggregate levels, it is necessary to employ figures which are not specific to the Negro population itself. However, since non-Negro nonwhites comprise approximately 1.0 per cent of the total nonwhite population in Cleveland, we can disregard this inconsistency.

14. Wolf, Eleanor P., "The Tipping Point in Racially Changing Neighborhoods," *Journal,* American Institute of Planners, Vol. 29, 1963, pp. 217–22.

15. Some important implications of this statement should not be overlooked. Stress levels within the ghetto may be partly a function of age structure, an argument only minimally appreciated in the Kerner Report, op. cit., p. 130. On this point see John S. Adams and Ralph A. Sanders, "Urban Residential Structure and the Location of Stress in

Ghettos," *Earth and Mineral Sciences,* Pennsylvania State University, Vol. 38 (4) 1968, pp. 29–32.

16. The maps of population changes are comparable to those of age structure (Fig. 1). By adding 100 points to all percentage figures, a range of values closely corresponding to Age Structure Index Values is obtained, and the same contour interval is used.

17. Morrill, op. cit., p. 348; see also Rose, op. cit., 1970, footnote 24.

18. The term is derived from a description of a similar observation noted much earlier: "This main Negro district expanded somewhat during and after the war, but current invasions do not seem to be following the traditional pattern. Rather . . . they seem to be rather saltatory, leap-frogging over white areas to establish minor Negro districts in deteriorating outlying areas." Brussat, W. K., "Incidental Findings on Urban Invasion," *American Sociological Review,* Vol. 16, 1951, p. 96. Brussat offers an explanation: "In many cities today, blight has reached the periphery while interior sections have been redeveloped. If Negro migration followed blight (and white bias notwithstanding, it is more liable to follow than to precede), the saltatory invasion pattern might be so explained." p. 96.

CHAPTER III

Black Ghetto Space

INTRODUCTORY NOTE

The ghetto as locational focus of urban black experience in the United States is examined in this chapter. As Morrill and Donaldson, and Hart revealed in preceding articles, migration of blacks from the rural South most frequently resulted in accumulation of blacks in the nation's northern and western cities.

Today, the American black population, as a result and continuation of this migration, is urbanizing at a rapid rate. Much of this population lives within specialized urban areas known as ghettos. The ghetto generally is a territorially unified area of the urban community, often located near the Central Business District. It is an area in which inhabitants have similar racial, social, economic, and cultural attributes distinguishing them from the majority of the city's population. The ghetto as a social location is characterized by discrimination and inferior status and is maintained by suppressive forces of white majority over black minority.

The word "ghetto" usually is accompanied by the connotation of a slum; however, this is not always the case. A slum is caused and controlled by economic factors, a ghetto adds cultural and social restrictions to those already present in the slum. A slum can be a ghetto, but a ghetto need not be a slum.

Historically, in the United States, cities have always contained slums. The newest immigrants to cities have had the misfortune to habitate the most dilapidated, lowest cost housing stock. In many instances, they were able to improve the condition of their lives and leave the slum, and consequently were assimilated into mainstream American culture.

The black population of the United States has been one of the last minority groups to locate in these slums. But for black Americans, unlike their ethnic predecessors, the combination of racial prejudice and discrimination in employment opportunities, housing, and education has literally imprisoned them in the slum, transforming it into a ghetto. Geographers have been slow recognizing their responsibility to analyze this situation and contribute solutions to modern social problems, especially those of a racial nature. However, a certain few geographers have concentrated their efforts in racial and ethnic research and the list of social geographic works is growing in number and relevance.

The first article, by Louis Seig, defines and delimits the term "ghetto" and presents the historical derivation of the word. The problem of operationally defining concepts of ghetto is elucidated by Seig, who introduces his work by excoriating geographers for ignoring the spatial significance of minority groups in the United States. Further, Seig suggests strongly that geographers should recognize their responsibilities and become involved in crucial social issues and problems of the day.

The approach that Seig advocates is study of racial and ethnic urban population successions and residential segregation as they affect intra-urban mobility and interaction. One key concept which must be understood in the geography of such minority groups is ghetto. For Seig, definition of ghetto revolves around intimately related locational concepts of interaction and mobility. These concepts are expressed as social action—group awareness of consciousness in kind—and physical isolation either externally or internally imposed. Seig, for the purpose of his paper, uses these ideas to define ghetto in terms of external sanctions and pressures enforced through legal or extralegal means.

In the second part of the article, Seig examines the derivation of the word ghetto and compares medieval Jewish ghettos with modern black ghettos. This comparison is made using the above-mentioned concepts of mobility, interaction, isolation, and enforcement. Both types of ghettos have their similarities, and residents entrapped within have suffered from the effects of segregation and also found strength and unity in their community.

In the conclusion, Seig maintains with Oscar Lewis that it is the culture of poverty which identifies and unifies blacks within a larger urban context, allowing them to develop a community based upon their own subculture.

In "The Development of an Urban Subsystem: The Case of the Negro Ghetto," Harold M. Rose proposes a model which attempts to describe and predict changing scale and future state of the black ghetto in Milwaukee, Wisconsin. The problem dealt with by Rose is that internal development of individual urban places has not been a central focus in geography. Rose's paper provides insights on the spatial dynamics of one single internal subsystem within a metropolitan system: the black ghetto. The basic concern of the study is areal expression of processes responsible for ghetto changes in scale in northern urban centers.

Rose stresses two themes in this work. First, he analyzes intra- and inter-urban population mobility, using the somewhat discredited physical analogue of centrifugal and centripetal forces, the network of urban transport links, and the nature of population movements which have molded the social ecology of the urban system. Second, Rose posits the existence and persistence of the black ghetto as an areally based social community that can be explained best within the framework of social assignment of territory.

To simulate ghetto development, Rose uses a behavioral model based on three components: demographic, producer, and consumer. The demographic component provides a reasonable estimate of housing demand by applying age-specific birth and death rates, by color, to the population at one-year intervals for ten years. The producer component, based on white residential leaving rates, is employed to simulate housing vacancies which might allow black households to establish residences in given blocks somewhat remote from the main body of the ghetto. The consumer component is derived from the potential number of household formations deduced by applying an appropriate set of age-specific marriage rates to that portion of the population classified as single.

The model, although an oversimplification of residential household allocation, generally appears to provide a closer approximation of racial residential patterns than an open system operating without social constraints. Principal benefits of models of this type are not in their sophisticated predictive power, but in understanding gained of complex realities of processes involved in ghetto expansion.

Sources of variation in housing values in Washington, D.C., are the subject of the article by J. Tait Davis. Examined cartographically, the District of Columbia shows a random pattern with reference to urban land use values in the CBD; however, housing values tend to follow the sector model developed by Homer Hoyt. Davis attempts to relate patterns of housing value in Washington to social and economic factors which have affected the city, especially the factor of race. In the article, Davis considers three hypotheses: variations in value of residential units will be related to variations in: proportion of high income families; relative age of houses; and proportion of nonwhites.

In analyzing sources of variation of housing values, Davis first uses a multiple correlation technique to examine interrelationships among variables, then a factor analysis is made using the more significant variables as determined by correlation. Generally, all variables tested were confirmed as significant. However, the pattern of association of housing values with proportions of high income families is not consistent throughout the range of the percentage of high income families. A significant variation in housing values does not appear with variations in the proportion of high income families between 5 per cent and 10 per cent of the total families in the tract.

In classifying census as young, middle-aged, or old, Davis found that increments in the proportion of older housing units up to 40 per cent appear to be associated with rising housing value, and increments between 40 per cent and 80 per cent are clearly associated with moderate declines in housing values. Also, variation in white-nonwhite ratio in relatively young neighborhoods was not statistically significant; however, the proportion was significant in middle-aged and old neighborhoods.

Davis concludes that patterns in housing value in Washington, D.C., in 1960, represent more than a decade of accommodation to a locationally confined population; a feature which appears to have distorted normal thresholds of value relationships.

William H. Brown, Jr., examines one aspect of racial discrimination in "Access to Housing: The Role of the Real Estate Industry." He maintains that racial discrimination in housing is a serious and fundamental aspect of white racism in contemporary American society. Brown proposes to examine racial practices of real estate brokers to determine the profession's political, economic, social, and fundamental moral responsibility and the extent to which the profession is implicated in creation and development of the problem in its present dimensions.

The background of racially separate housing patterns in the United States is presented to provide historical perspective to the problem. White perception of blacks in a caste structure rather than a class system is shown to be one of the early determinants in the refusal of whites to live with blacks.

Historically, Brown maintains the real estate industry, firmly led and organized by the National Association of Real Estate Boards, has long been one of the major institutions in the country whose policies and practices have been particularly racist in attitude. The National Association of Real Estate Boards' employment of race restrictive covenants and their eventual adoption by the Federal Housing Administration mark a singular low point in legalized and institutionalized racism in the United States. However, with the Supreme Court's disallowal of race covenants, new and more insidious techniques of racial restrictions on the housing market have appeared. Real estate boards have financed opposition to fair housing ordinances, firms have refused to hire black agents or to license black brokers, and individual agents alert other realtors as to a buyer's race before showing black clients a multiple listing of available housing.

Brown is concerned with the real estate industry's constant maintenance of racist attitudes in their brokerage activities. First, salesmen and brokers, many who are middle-aged and have attained only a minimal educational experience, possess an "exclusion ideology" concerning conducting business with black Americans. Second, and more important, there is a considerable profit to be made in maintaining a segregated housing market. With this system, blacks are forced to pay dearly for available housing and whites can be manipulated through racial fear in selling their homes for a low price. Brown realistically concludes that neither legislation nor good will is sufficient to compel the real estate industry to abandon its long-established practices of racial discrimination in housing.

CONCEPTS OF "GHETTO":
A GEOGRAPHY OF MINORITY GROUPS

Louis Seig

Geographers are at last becoming cognizant of spatial variations in urban residential patterns based on racial, ethnic, or social factors. The discipline has generally ignored the introduction of minority groups into America with their subsequent assimilation and acculturation, however, Morrill[1] and Rose[2] have already begun work in one aspect of what might be called the geography of minority groups. Clearly, geography should become involved in the great social issues and problems of the day. One approach would be through the study of urban population successions and residential segregation which has to do with intraurban mobility and interactions. To insure mutual understanding, standardized terminology must be established.

One key term to an understanding of the geography of minority groups is "ghetto." In recent years, the idea of ghetto as a Negro slum area in American cities has been brought sharply into focus, yet no clear-cut definition exists which expresses the ideas of the many people who use the term. In other words, we are lacking a meaningful generalization to give us a useful picture of what ghetto really means.

There are different kinds of definitions which can be used for the term ghetto—social, including racial, ethnic, and religious; economic; and institutional. According to the *American Heritage Dictionary*, a ghetto is a section or quarter in a European city to which Jews are or were restricted, or a slum section of an American city occupied predominantly by members of a minority group who live there because of social or economic pressure.

Some would argue that the definition has to be social based on residential segregation due to some quality such as race, religion, or ethnic background. If true, this would mean that 50 per cent of Washington, D.C., would have to be called ghetto. It seems that one would also have to consider the perception of the residents. Upper- and middle-class black residents of Washington clearly see the boundary of what they consider to be a black ghetto; it is an inner core of urban blight containing economically disadvantaged people who have neither the income nor the education to break out.

A question which must be raised in this context is whether people really do want to leave the ghetto or whether they only want economic betterment within their area of residence. Does the idea of integration into American society necessarily carry with it the prerequisite to destroy cultural characteristics or racial solidarity which some groups may wish to maintain?[3]

Obviously, with blacks there is a definite visual identification, one which does not occur with Poles, Jews, Italians, or Czechs. No outsider has attempted to break up the ethnic enclaves of these European groups in order to fully integrate them into American society. Granted, it is much easier for individuals within these groups to assimilate if they so desire, yet nonblack ethnic colonies still exist within many of the larger American cities. Spear points out that as late as 1910, Italian immigrants in Chicago were more highly segregated from native whites than were blacks.[4]

It would seem that the real problem revolves around mobility and interaction—the ability of the individual to move about freely anywhere within the urban milieu and to interact on a person-to-person basis if he so desires. In addition, there are other ideas which may apply: (1) Social action—the idea of the group working together to obtain rights, to achieve common goals, or to protect its interests. (2) Physical isolation—either imposed from the outside or maintained from the inside. There is an internal perception of the boundaries of the area, almost an idea of territoriality, perhaps a kind of sanctuary where the group can maintain its integrity. In this paper, ghetto is defined in terms of external enforcement through legal or extralegal means.

For a long time, the use of "ghetto" as descriptive of the Negro situation was questioned because of the derivation of the term. But study seems to indicate a strong similarity between the medieval Jewish and present-day black situation both morphologically and institutionally. Perhaps it would be useful to look at the medieval Jewish ghetto as described by Sachar.[5]

MEDIEVAL JEWISH GHETTOS

Ghettos were formed during the Middle Ages to isolate the Jews in a restricted area of the city. This is not meant to imply that there was no prior residential segregation. Indeed, Jews tended to cluster together because they felt more at ease with each other and could more readily perform religious and social functions. In addition, they felt more secure in numbers rather than being scattered throughout a hostile community. The main difference between this type of clustering and ghetto is the difference between free choice and enforced segregation.

Compulsory segregation was established in the Middle Ages. The Salerno ghetto was formed in the eleventh century and in 1480, the Spanish *Cortes* ordered Jews and Moors segregated from Christians. The true ghetto age, however, was the sixteenth century when the institution diffused at a very rapid rate. Ghettos were generally relegated to the most undesirable portion of town. Areas were not enlarged as population grew, creating tremendous overcrowding as well as hotbeds of disease.

The medieval ghetto molded Jewish life. It created physical degeneration due to lack of recreational facilities. The people had no touch with nature; they could hardly see the sun from the narrow, dingy streets. The enforced segregation of the ghetto deepened the prejudice against Jews. Lack of social interaction gave each group a profound ignorance of the other. The ordinary Christian had little knowledge of the mysterious life behind the walls and, therefore, he gave credence to the ignorant and malicious stories told about Jews.

The isolation of ghetto life, with its attendant hardships, weakened Jewish loyalty to the rulers. As Sachar writes, "It would have been unnatural for the Jews to give their love to the monsters who bled them with every opportunity."[6] Thus personal and group loyalty became the rule of the day. In addition, isolation provided a natural medium for the creation of separate languages. By the fifteenth century, Yiddish, a mixture of German and Hebrew along with other languages, was in use in eastern Europe. Many Yiddish speakers could not speak the language of the country in which they lived. In southern Europe the new language was Ladino, a corruption of Spanish and Hebrew. The introduction of these new languages reinforced the solidarity of the group and increased their isolation from the rest of the community.

Isolation, on the other hand, did have some positive effects. Because the Jews were thrown closely together with a strong unifying religious faith, an *esprit de corps* developed. There was a strong Jewish consciousness, a new folk life with folkways, which was remarkably virile for a people with no land of their own and little opportunity in the land where they lived.

Walls were built to enclose the ghettos for two reasons—first, to keep Jews in and, second, to keep Christians out. There was complete interaction and mobility within the walls; interaction with the outside was minimal. Ghetto properties were owned by Christian landlords. Due to overcrowding and lack of interest in maintenance, ghetto housing deteriorated at a very rapid rate. Because Jews could not be readily recognized visually, they were required to wear badges or armbands as identification.

By the time European Jewish ghettos had reached their peak, the structure was institutionalized to an extremely high degree. Isolation was the primary factor in development of a specialized subculture. The inability of the Jews to interact socially with the dominant cultural group did not cause them to stagnate; rather they sought their own cultural goals. The experience of black Americans has been much the same in northern urban centers, although their isolation has been produced through discriminatory practices and *de facto* segregation rather than legal promulgation. Many of the manifestations of black ghettos correlate with those of Jewish ghettos.

BLACK GHETTOS

There is no evidence to indicate that blacks clustered together early as a protective measure in northern cities. As their numbers grew, however, white pressure forced them into a ghetto situation. According to Spear:

> The development of a physical ghetto in Chicago . . . was not the result chiefly of poverty; nor did Negroes cluster out of choice. The ghetto was primarily the product of white hostility. Attempts on the part of Negroes to seek housing in predominantly white sections of the city met with resistance from the residents and from real estate dealers.[7]

It must be argued that such discriminatory practices are based purely on racial grounds since there are no common cultural attributes which can be assigned to the American Negro. In the past, blacks had not joined together because of common linguistic, cultural, or religious traditions; the systematic pattern of discrimination left them no other option.

All of the physical and social ills of the medieval Jewish ghetto are extant. Black ghettos are found in the most undesirable sections of American cities. They are overcrowded, tend to be filthy, and are disease-ridden to some extent. There is a lack of recreational facilities and the people have no touch with nature. There is minimal social interaction between the ghetto dwellers and the outside community. Prejudice against the black deepens because the ordinary white has little knowledge of the people in the ghetto. People tend to be afraid of the unknown.

Because black loyalty to the establishment has been weakened, it is now focused on the ghetto group and, therefore, new organizations have been formed to take up independent leadership. The isolation which created a separatist movement also provided a medium for linguistic change. Although not yet speaking a separate language, there is a tendency to use mutually understood terms and signs which are alien to the formal language of the majority group. As pointed out previously, this device helps to reinforce the solidarity of the group.

There are, however, some positive effects of isolation. A strong black consciousness has developed. The idea of introducing folkways is enhanced, even though a common cultural heritage does not exist. Thus there is a desire for learning Swahili and for wearing Afro-dress and Afro-hairstyles. A type of soul music has been introduced—in fact, the very concept of "soul" itself. There is a need and desire for developing and maintaining an internal black culture rather than integrating into the surrounding white culture. As Spear says, "Racial solidarity is a response rather than a positive force. It is an attempt to preserve self-respect and foster self-reliance in the face of continual humiliations and rebuffs from white society."[8]

It would seem that blacks are considered to be a distinct class within American society. As such they have no status in the dominant social order. In many instances they have created their own institutions. According to Spear:

. . . despite their emphasis on the positive aspects of separate development, Negro leaders did not make a free choice when they opted for separatism. Their action was necessitated by white hostility and oppression. They built the institutional ghetto only after whites had created a physical ghetto, after Negroes had been barred from white neighborhoods and from the facilities of white Chicago.[9]

One of the stronger institutions has been religious; blacks have developed their own branches of Christianity, e.g., the African Methodist Episcopal Church, and have created the black Muslim movement as an expression of African culture.

White society has built walls around black ghettos—walls of prejudice, economic walls, and, in some instances, physical barriers. In many cases, the boundaries of ghettos are reinforced by construction of freeways. This type of physical barrier restricts interaction. As in the case of the Jewish ghetto, most properties are owned by people who live outside of the area.

It would seem that the term ghetto has to be defined in terms of *enforced* residential segregation whether it be *de facto* or *de jure*. In this context, then, there are certain ethnic and racial areas which must be called colonies or enclaves because the groups live in them by choice. If one considers the perceptual view of the residents, both inside and outside the ghetto, there are modifications to the definition. To the resident of a predominantly black middle-class neighborhood, ghetto would be a black area overlaid with the culture of poverty. Enforcement of segregation in this sense consists of those economic and social factors which force the disadvantaged to remain inside. The culture of poverty in this circumstance provides a unifying force which ties the group together in a sense of community, leading to the development of a strong subculture. The group in the middle-class area may not be unified by anything but race and social status in the black community. Considering the way most black areas expand, the middle-class area has become segregated by default; therefore, it is not actually ghetto.

The black people in the circum-ghetto area are in a better position to interact with the community at large. They may have the option to move outside the area based on the local enforcement of open housing laws. An important measure in determining whether or not an area is ghetto is the freedom of choice available to the residents.

The institution of the ghetto provided a strong cultural base for the Jews of Europe. The same process is now occurring among black Americans. Geographers are uniquely qualified to study spatial variations of cultural groups in both urban and rural contexts. The development of a geography of minority groups would help to explain how the various groups played roles in the American experience. Such study might also help to provide answers to the problems of ghettos, cultures of poverty, Indian reservations, and the like.

LITERATURE CITED

1. Morrill, R. L., "The Negro Ghetto: Alternatives and Consequences," *Geographical Review*, Vol. 55, 1965, pp. 221–38.
2. Rose, H. M., *Social Processes in the City: Race and Urban Residential Choice*, Commission on College Geography, Resource Paper No. 6. Association of American Geographers, Washington, 1969 and "The Development of an Urban Subsystem: The Case of the Negro Ghetto," *Annals*, Association of American Geographers, Vol. 60, 1970, pp. 1–17.
3. See Anthony Downs, "Alternative Futures for the American Ghetto," *Daedalus*, Vol. 97, Fall 1968, pp. 1331–78.
4. Spear, A. H., *Black Chicago; The Making of a Negro Ghetto: 1890–1920*. University of Chicago Press, Chicago, 1967, p. 26.
5. Sachar, A. L., *A History of the Jews*. Alfred A. Knopf, New York, 1966, 5th ed., pp. 251–55.
6. Ibid., p. 253.
7. Spear, op. cit., p. 26.
8. Ibid.
9. Ibid.

THE DEVELOPMENT OF AN URBAN SUBSYSTEM:
THE CASE OF THE NEGRO GHETTO

Harold M. Rose

The internal development of individual urban places has not traditionally been one of central focus in geography. This probably stems in part from the overriding emphasis on regions in general and the urban geographer's concern with the interrelationships among individual urban nodes. American geographers have only recently turned their attention to the internal structure of urban areas, no doubt an outgrowth of general interest in central place theory. Increasing interest in urban subsystems has resulted in a concomitant interest in the spatial structure of these systems. This paper attempts to provide insights on the spatial dynamics of a single subsystem within the metropolitan system, the Negro ghetto.

The Negro ghetto, as a universal and viable urban subsystem within the American urban system, has evolved with the rise of the Negro population in northern urban centers beginning with the decade prior to World War I.[1] The almost continuous flow of Negroes from both the rural and urban South to the North and West has permitted and promoted the development of Negro ghettos in all of the nation's major population centers. By 1960 more than 30 per cent of the nation's Negro population resided in twenty metropolitan areas. Whereas the Negro ghetto is found in nearly all two hundred metropolitan areas in the United States, the basic concern of this study is with the processes responsible for its change in scale in northern urban centers. The previous legality of a system of racial separation in the American South served as an exogenous factor, overriding all others, in the promotion and maintenance of residential clusters based on race. For a brief period there existed laws which were specifically designed to maintain residential segregation based on race. The Supreme Court outlawed attempts to maintain a legal system of residential separation in 1917, in the case of Buchanan *versus* Warley.[2] Such a legalized role-prescription tends to reduce the fruitfulness of a behaviorally oriented study, and thereby accounts for the limiting of this investigation to northern cities.

To date, only Morrill's pioneer work might be described as a spatial behavioral approach to the study of the changing state of the ghetto.[3] The model he assembled was employed to replicate the process of ghetto development in Seattle. Other researchers are beginning to show increasing concern for the general problem, with emphasis on the spatial dimension. Beauchamp recently suggested the use of Markov Chain Analysis as a means of specifying or identifying territorial units as ghetto or nonghetto by investigating the dynamic changes taking place in the racial composition of areas.[4]

The process of the changing ghetto state has been described elsewhere as a diffusion process.[5] Diffusion models have attracted the interest of a small number of geographers who have employed them as a means of describing the spatial spread of an innovation. The more notable of these are associated with the work of Hägerstrand. The suitability of diffusion models as a means of describing the spread of the ghetto, however, is questionable. It appears that the spread of the ghetto is a phenomenon of a different type. More specifically, it appears that the spread of the Negro ghetto is a function of white adjustment to a perceived threat. The distinction between adjustment and diffusion was recently reviewed by Carlsson.[6] He averred that motivation and values transcend knowledge, in importance, in explaining certain types of behavioral change.[7] If the diffusion thesis is accepted as a means of explaining rather than describing the expansion of the Negro ghetto, then it must be assumed that each metropolitan system operates as a closed system. Since this is not the case, the adjustment hypothesis which Carlsson supports is undeniably more appealing than the diffusion hypothesis as a means of explaining the spread of the ghetto. Admittedly, whites must first be aware of the presence of Negroes if a change in their normative mobility pattern is to occur, but awareness here promotes the kind of behavior which has also become accepted as normative. Thus, the necessary adjustment is made as a means of maintaining the steady state condition. The kind of behavior inferred here was described by Zelinsky as social avoidance.[8] Morrill, who previously described the ghetto development process in terms of diffusion, now describes processes of this general type, which are interactional in nature, as quasi-diffusionary.[9]

INTRAURBAN POPULATION MOBILITY

The spatial mobility of the American population, both in terms of long-distance moves and intraurban shifts, was intensified during the decade of the 1950s. As major metropolitan systems were the target of most long-distance moves, these moves resulted in the rapid dispersion of population into what was previously part of the rural countryside. The latter phenomenon has attracted the attention of researchers from a vast array of disciplines, geographers included. Geographers have also focused particular interest on the centrifugal flow of population, as this flow has had the most obvious impact on the form and areal magnitude of urban systems. But to consider the latter and ignore the role of the centripetal movement weakens the analysis of population shifts within the system and of the ensuing patterns which evolve.

Movements toward the periphery of the urban system, both from within the system and from without, have been principally responsible for the increase in the size of individual metropolitan aggregates. At the same time many central cities within metropolitan systems have suffered absolute losses in their populations. Thus, the centripetal flow into the central cities of metropolitan systems has seldom been sufficiently large to offset the counter flow. The most rapid and easily observed flow into the nation's larger central cities is that of Negro in-migration, a phenomenon which has had far-reaching effects on the color composition of metropolitan areas.[10] By the mid-sixties there was official evidence that this process was continuing. The city of Cleveland, Ohio, undertook a special census on April 1, 1965. The results showed that the city had lost 91,436 white residents during the five years that had elapsed since the last census, while gaining an additional 26,244 Negro residents.[11] The Negro proportion of Cleveland's population rose by five percentage points during that period, from 29 to 34 per cent. Since the census was confined to the political city of Cleveland, it is impossible to determine the extent to which Negroes entered the stream of movers destined for suburbia.

In response to the changing magnitude and composition of metropolitan populations, a network of transport links has evolved to facilitate the spatial redistribution of the population. Where an individual chooses to locate himself within the urban system is a function of occupational status, income, place of employment, and social taste. The operation or interaction of these factors has produced a strongly segmented pattern of urban occupance. A change in an individual's socioeconomic status frequently results in relocation within the metropolitan system. As the nation's occupational structure is being rapidly altered in the direction of a larger proportion of white collar workers, especially technical and professional workers, with a concomitant alteration in the income structure, spatial mobility is further accelerated. Changes of this nature tend to produce shifts in territorial status assignment in urban space. Davis, in a recent study, described the magnitude of territorial shifts in the location of middle-class housing areas in a selected group of American cities.[12] With the redistribution of the population toward the periphery, there has subsequently been an outward shift of the inner boundary of the zone of middle-class housing. As a consequence, these shifts frequently create gray areas which act as zones of transition or buffers between middle and lower class occupance. It is within these gray areas, with their high vacancy rates, that most of the centrifugal Negro flow is destined. The growing intensity of mobility within the metropolitan system has affected all segments of the population, although somewhat differentially. The pattern of movement of whites and nonwhites in urban space is akin to the pattern of interregional movement within the nation as a whole. In both instances nonwhite moves are characterized by short distance, whereas whites are more frequently engaged in long-distance moves.

The nature of population movement within the urban system is highly related to the magnitude and form of the set of urban subsystems which evolve. The Negro ghetto which comprises one such subsystem or social area is directly related to this process. Since spatial mobility is related both to age and income, one would expect to observe the evolution of a series of patterns which reflect the economic health of a specific metropolitan system, the nature of its economic base, and its subsequent ability to attract population through the process of internal migration; the latter phenomenon has the effect of altering the age distribution of the population. If ability to purchase was the single most significant variable influencing the distribution of population in metropolitan space, it should be easy to predict the kind of sorting-out which eventually occurs. Although this can be done in a rather general manner, purchasing ability alone is far from adequate in explaining the development of the ghetto.[13] The relative stability of the Negro's economic position vis-à-vis the white's during the last several years may have reduced or severely limited the ability of individual Negroes to cross critical rent isolines. On the other hand, the brisk hiring of Negroes to salaried positions by an increasing number of firms, pledged to the goal of equality of opportunity, could have the effect of increasing the length of the individual move. It is impossible at this time to specify with any degree of precision the effect of either factor upon the pattern of Negro movement, even though they both may be significant.

Territoriality

The existence and persistence of the Negro ghetto as a spatially based social community may best be explained within the framework of the social assignment of territory. Once a slice of physical space is identified as the territorial realm of a specific social group, any attempt to alter this assignment results in group conflict, both overt and covert. Stea recently described this behavior in the following way: "We have reason to believe that 'territorial behavior,' the desire both to possess and occupy positions of space, is as pervasive among men as among their animal forbears."[14] Weber attributed this kind of behavior simply to working class groups for whom physical space is an extension of one's ego.[15]

Human ecologists have employed terms such as invasion and succession to describe the process of residential change in which members of competing groups struggle for territory. Henderson recently questioned the employment of the term invasion to describe the process of Negro entry into areas bordering on the ghetto.[16] Admittedly the term invasion appears to be appropriate only within the context of territorial conflict. Viewed outside this context, the term does not appear to be meaningful. A further point, no doubt the one which concerned Henderson, is that the term invasion not only reflects the white resident's perception of events, but the perception of the researcher as well. It has been said, "When our own tribe engages in this behavior we call it nationalism or aggression."[17] From another vantage point, it would appear that the term retreat describes the process more accurately. Since both terms, invasion and retreat, refer to territorial conflict, no major point is settled by substituting one for the other. Nevertheless, it should be kept in mind that the nature of the behavior which occurs within this context does so within the context of a fear-safety syndrome.

The territorial acquisition by advancing Negro populations cannot always be viewed as a gain in this game of psychological warfare, for once the territory is transferred from one group to the other, it is perceived by the white population as having been contaminated and, therefore, undesirable. The formalization or codification of this attitude is associated with the Federal Housing Administration's policy of promoting racial homogeneity in neighborhoods during the period 1935–50.[18] Hoyt's classic study on the growth of residential neighborhoods strongly supported this position, and possibly served to support and justify the government's position.[19] Thus, the whole notion of stable property values revolves around the transfer of the status designation from a group to the territory occupied by the group. More recently Bailey observed in one case that unstable property values were associated with those zones located in the shadow of the ghetto rather than in the ghetto itself.[20] However, it is the slack demand for housing in a racially changing neighborhood that is likely to drive down housing values. The unwillingness of whites to compete with nonwhites for housing in a common housing market, coupled with vacancy rates which frequently exceed Negro demand, could eventually lead to a lessening of values. Thus, land abandoned by whites on the margins of the Negro ghetto at some single point in time is almost never known to be retrieved by such residents.

The behavior described above is rapidly leading to the development in the United States of central cities within which territorial dominance is being relinquished to the Negro population. This fact has undoubtedly had much to do with the increasing demand by Negroes for black power, and logically so. If one inherits a piece of turf it is only natural for him to seek control of the area of occupance. Thus, both the critics and supporters of black power have traditional white behavior and the public decisions stemming therefrom for its overt crystallization. Grier recently noted that it was not until President Kennedy signed his executive order of 1962, which treated the problem of discrimination in housing, had the federal government ever gone on record as opposing discrimination in housing.[21] Yet even today, as the nation's ghettos continue to expand, public policy abets their existence and expansion.

The Model

The previous description of a set of general processes goes far in explaining the continuous expansion of the Negro ghetto. The processes described reflect the values of society and, as Pahl recently pointed out, residential patterns are a reflection of the functioning of a social system.[22] It is possible within the framework of systems analysis to devise a model which replicates the total process of metropolitan systems development, but such an understanding exceeds the skills of a single researcher or the knowledge and focus of a single academic discipline. However, a single researcher might attempt to develop a simple model which replicates some aspect of the development of the metropolitan system. A model of this nature, although promoting keener insights into an understanding of processes operative at the microlevel, is characterized by serious shortcomings as it basically reflects the operation of endogenous processes. Nevertheless, the advantages emanating from the development of such models outweigh the previously specified shortcomings.

Components of the Model

A model of ghetto development is of the type described by Chorley and Haggett as normative.[23] An effective model describing ghetto development should include at least three basic components: 1) a demographic component, 2) a producer component, and 3) a consumer component. The data employed to describe these components serve as input for the model. The demographic component is employed to determine housing demand, the producer component to determine availability, and the consumer component to determine allocation. The operation of and subsequent interaction associated with these components permits the model to be placed in the category of behavioral models. The demographic and producer components are generated deterministically, whereas the consumer component is generated probabilistically. Thus, the spread of the ghetto is described in an indeterminate manner. The weakness of the simulation lies primarily in the gross assumption employed in the producer component and secondarily in the projections derived from the operation of the demographic components, both of which acutely affect the emerging pattern of ghetto development.

THE DEMOGRAPHIC COMPONENT

Gross changes in the magnitude of the ghetto are associated basically with the changing demographic character of the Negro population. The demographic characteristics of the white population residing in ghetto space will likewise influence the pattern or form of the ghetto at any point in time. The competition for housing and its subsequent allocation is largely influenced by the demographic characteristics of both the white and Negro populations. In order to better understand the role of population dynamics on ghetto development, interest is focused on the population occupying what is here identified as "ghetto space."[24] Ghetto space in the city selected for testing the model, Milwaukee, Wisconsin, spreads out over a twelve square mile area extending north and west from the central business district. The area in 1960 contained approximately 217,000 persons of which only 20 per cent was nonwhite. Nested within ghetto space was a much smaller area, approximately four square miles in extent, which had already become identified as the ghetto. This smaller area included 92,000 persons of whom approximately 68 per cent were nonwhite. Thus, the area identified as the Negro ghetto was slightly more than two thirds Negro and included many blocks which did not contain a single Negro household. In identifying the twelve square mile area as ghetto space, an assumption is posited that the spread of the Negro population will be largely confined to this area in the city of Milwaukee during the current decade and no doubt the decade which follows. By adopting this assumption it is clear that the model being developed here is a strict segregation model.

The principal reason for incorporating a demographic component in the model is to arrive at a reasonable estimate of housing demand. Demand is generated through the employment of an appropriate set of age-specific rates. Age-specific birth and death rates, by color, were applied to the population at one year intervals for a ten-year period. This procedure permitted the recording of year by year changes in the population resulting from an excess of births over deaths. Since in-migration is also an important aspect of population change in the Negro population, a migration factor was included. Migration was not thought to contribute significantly to net changes within the white population residing in ghetto space and was omitted as a growth producing factor.

A major weakness of the above described procedure is that it allows a piling up of population in census tracts. This condition is an outgrowth of the absence of a mechanism which would generate data on white out-movement at the tract level. The application of age-specific intracounty mobility rates could be applied to the white population as a means of generating a more accurate measure of the population actually in residence in a census tract at any given point in time. The employment of a correction factor of this type possesses the added advantage of enabling one to compare the actual rate of white movement from tracts with the expected rate; the expected rate would represent the number of movers generated through the use of intracounty mobility rates.

THE PRODUCER COMPONENT

The producer component is employed to create housing vacancies which might allow a Negro household to establish residence in a given block located in ghetto space. As few new housing units are constructed in older neighborhoods, residential space is essentially made available by white abandonment. It is generally agreed that there exists some level of tolerance beyond which whites will no longer continue to share a common residential space with Negroes. On the other hand, there is no general agreement on what whites perceive to be an acceptable residential mix. Nevertheless, a curve in which the leaving rate of whites is a function of the increase in the proportion of Negro households in a block may be described intuitively. Although it would be more logical to describe the leaving process as indeterminate rather than determinate, there is an absence of sufficient data upon which a stochastic process might be based. As the general leaving process becomes better understood, it may be described stochastically.

A shortcoming of the producer component based on assumed white leaving rates is that it produces an excessive number of vacancies in those parts of the ghetto space which are somewhat remote from the main body of the ghetto. The social distance effect is not as pervasive over space as the vacancy-creating mechanism suggests. Some constraints should be placed upon the territorial limits of ghetto space that would be open to Negro occupancy during any given time interval, under conditions of strict segregation (in order to effect a more realistic description of the actual process). The problem by nature suggests that ghetto space should be made available incrementally. These increments, which are unlikely to fall within the sphere of Negro residential search behavior during the initial time period, should not be influenced by the vacancy creating mechanism. The creation of vacancies on the periphery of ghetto space results in a series of random residential assignments which leads to a more dispersed settlement pattern than that which actually occurs. This suggests that interaction along what is perceived as the ghetto edge during any single time period is far more pervasive in its impact upon the actual ghetto form than interaction about individual clusters, which might evolve under conditions of random residential assignment if the total ghetto is available for entry throughout a ten-year time interval.

CONSUMER COMPONENT

The consumer component of the model is a residential assignment mechanism. The housing demand of the Negro population during any one-year period is derived by means of determining the number of households formed during the interval. Household formation is deduced by applying an appropriate set of age-specific marriage rates to that segment of the population classified as single. In a situation where in-migration is responsible for a significant proportion of the increase in the local population, it is difficult to choose the most appropriate marriage rates to be employed. In this case the rates characterizing the North Central region were employed. It is suspected that the employment of such rates under conditions of heavy in-migration is likely to produce a larger than actual number of marriages. The existence of a sizable number of single persons in a new environment is thought to have a depressing effect on the formation of new households.

Negro household assignments were made annually on the basis of the group's known propensity to purchase (or rent) housing in specific price categories. In order to generate household assignments, every block in ghetto space was assigned a probability of receiving a Negro home seeker. The highest probabilities were assigned to those blocks in which the median rent was in the $60–69 range, as blocks characterized by such rents housed the largest percentage of the Negro population in 1960. An assignment could not be made in a block wherein an appropriate number of vacancies did not exist.

The model oversimplifies the process of housing competition in ghetto space in not permitting whites and Negroes to compete for housing in a common market. Obviously, whites continue to seek housing in ghetto space until some critical threshold level is attained. Data on white entry into census tracts in ghetto space which had a minimum of 40 per cent Negro occupancy by 1960, confirms that whites continue to seek housing in close physical proximity to Negroes until Negro occupancy attains a level of approximately 30 per cent. And even then about one fifth of the housing seekers continue to be white, but falling off sharply thereafter. In the one census tract in ghetto space which exceeded 70 per cent Negro occupance in 1958, there was only a negligible number of white entrants; less than 2 per cent. Thus, the exodus of whites at the tract level takes place within a very short period of time, seemingly as a function of the Negro buildup in contiguous space. This fact implies an initial saturation at the block level, proceeding outward from blocks with an already heavy Negro concentration (Fig. 1). Changes in Negro-white relations during the past few years may have altered the expected behavior in contiguous physical space.

The continual expansion of the ghetto is essentially dependent upon the collective behavior of individual residents of ghetto space, white and black. A strict segregation model, such as that developed here, is an attempt to add to an understanding of the operation of the residential market existing within ghetto space. Although knowledge of the behavior of individuals based on race aids in this understanding, it is by no means the only force operating to promote the expected pattern of residential behavior. The operation of exogenous forces are more unpredictable, but

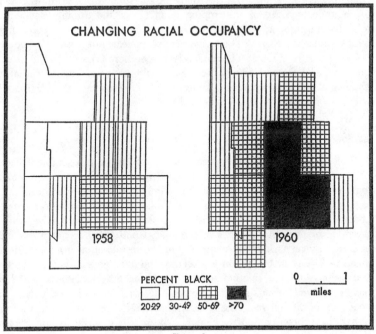

Figure 1

critically affect the ensuing pattern of racial residential development. In order to better understand the operation of the internal variables it is necessary to gain insights into the residential search behavior of prospective Negro home seekers as well as white propensity for residential desegregation. Morrill's ghetto residential assignment model was basically governed by the former consideration, whereas the model developed here emphasizes the latter as a means of shedding light on the dual problem.

Whereas Negroes move more often than whites, the lengths of the moves are usually shorter. A sample of Negro movers occupying units on the edge of the ghetto in 1950 exemplifies the pattern of intraurban movement attributed to Negro home seekers. Only 4 per cent of the Negro movers selected housing located more than ten blocks beyond the original ghetto neighborhood, 39 per cent selected housing within five blocks of the ghetto, while 41 per cent acquired housing within the same neighborhood. A similar pattern apparently continued to persist as is evidenced by the number of Negro households occupying units located on the fringe of the ghetto in 1960. It seems safe to say that whites and Negroes seldom compete for housing in a common market over an extended period of time. Wolf, in analyzing the concept of the tipping point in neighborhood change, was concerned with the following question as one of those critical to an understanding of the tipping point: Does the tipping mechanism refer to the point at which whites begin to leave, or the point at which whites refuse to enter?[25] The answer is yet unclear, but it is apparent that both factors are at work. The model developed here is based on the former question, and some of its weaknesses undoubtedly stem from an initial ignorance of the latter question. An examination of the success of the model will demonstrate this more effectively.

Evaluation of the Model

Once a model of the type described above has been assembled, it can be treated in one of two ways. It may simply be judged on the basis of the logic employed in its construction or it might be made operational as a means of actually testing its validity. The latter course of action has been chosen in this instance. The construct described here is recursive, and is designed to generate changes in the spatial pattern of Negro occupance over a ten-year period. An evaluation of the results of such a model is no mean task. The first problem is selecting the most appropriate method of evaluation. Opinion relative to this matter is mixed. Some researchers have employed various statistical techniques as a means of evaluating the goodness of fit between the simulated pattern and the actual pattern. Others have been content to evaluate the results empirically. Because of the nature of the data and the lack of precise information which can be employed to describe the actual pattern, an empirical analysis will be conducted. The lack of precise information in this case stems from the fact that the model which utilizes census data as input has been calibrated by employing the results of the 1960 census. The yearly changes in the spatial pattern of residential occupance occurring after the base year can only be crudely evaluated at this time. Only after the results of the 1970 census are available can the modal output be subjected to a more rigorous analysis.

A second question concerns the appropriate spatial unit to be employed in the evaluation. Data have been assembled at the block level, for it is generally assumed that race as a factor in the promotion of residential mobility has its most pervasive impact at this level. Yet the prevalance of other forces located within what Wolpert identified as the action space of the individual must not be overlooked.[26] Any meaningful analysis on a block-by-block basis would strongly suggest the use of statistical rather than empirical treatment. Even then, the results of statistical tests applied to the aggregation of blocks constituting ghetto space could prove misleading. In order to eliminate a modicum of the chaos which might arise in this type of analysis, a subaggregation of blocks has been chosen for investigation. These subaggregations may be considered housing market areas.

Only two of the housing market areas in ghetto space have been chosen for intensive observation. One of these is situated on the western edge of the ghetto, and the other is situated several blocks to the north of the original Negro core. Considering the characteristics of these areas at the beginning of the period, they may be described as a declining blue collar housing area and a stable housing area of skilled and semiskilled workers, respectively. These two prospective appendages of the ghetto are identified, respectively, as the West-Central housing market area and the Keefe-Capitol-Congress housing market area.

These two housing market areas contained approximately 7,500 housing units in 1960, a number sufficient to satisfy approximately one half of the anticipated Negro housing demand during the following ten years. The quality of housing in the two market areas differs significantly, with the quality in the West-Central market being generally lower than that which Negroes had previously inherited on the northern margins of the ghetto. Thus, given a choice of housing available in close proximity to the existing ghetto boundaries, the Keefe-Capitol-Congress market area, with its more attractive housing, should prove to be the major target area for Negro occupance during the ensuing ten-year period.

The Keefe-Capitol-Congress area is in many ways similar in housing quality and population characteristics to the Baxter area of Detroit, an area whose pattern of racial change was recently described by Wolf.[27]

The Keefe-Capitol-Congress area includes the only sizable volume of single family detached structures in close proximity to the ghetto.

In 1960 the total number of Negro households situated in these two housing market areas numbered less than 150, with the great majority of these located in blocks contiguous to the ghetto. The northern and western margins of the market areas were beyond the distance which most Negro movers travel to seek housing accommodations. This being the case, one would normally expect a block by block filling in, proceeding from areas heavily built up with Negro households to those without Negro households in the initial time period. As a means of comparing the actual process of racial change with the results generated by the simulation model, it was necessary to devise a sampling frame. The question of the type of sample to be employed had to be confronted. Because of the nature of the question to which answers are being sought, it was finally decided that two different sampling techniques would be employed. As a means of gaining insights into the general pattern of household mobility in the two market areas, a stratified random sample stratified by block was employed. In order to reveal more clearly the changes in the pattern of racial occupance, a quadrat or cluster sample was also introduced. The latter technique allowed observation of all changes taking place within a micro-housing environment through time.

The results of the stratified random sample demonstrate that the West-Central housing market area is far less stable than its northern counterpart. Samples drawn from the two census tracts which largely comprise the West-Central market showed that 60 per cent of the 1960 residents in the tract nearest the ghetto, and 52 per cent of the residents of the tract more distant from the ghetto, were no longer residents of this housing market area by 1965. Likewise, Negro householders served as the basic replacement population in the eastern half of the housing market area, which in 1965 possessed a vacancy rate of 20 per cent. The western segment of this market, although exhibiting signs of instability, was not yet receiving large numbers of Negro householders. Negroes at this date constituted fewer than 10 per cent of the housing market entrants. The fact that five years had elapsed and Negro entrance into the western segment of the market was minimal, strongly supports the contention that Negroes do not search for housing far beyond the margins of already heavily built-up Negro areas. The vacancy rate in the western segment of this housing market area was considerably less than that which characterized the east.

In the Keefe-Capitol-Congress housing market, residential mobility was less than half that which characterized the West-Central market. In the northern segment of this market only 20 per cent of the original residents had abandoned the area by 1965. The higher level of stability in this housing market was no doubt influenced by its greater physical attractiveness, its higher incidence of owner occupancy and the prevalence of older families. The latter factor is only a temporary contributing factor which will have the opposite impact on stability at a later time. As was true in the eastern half of the West-Central housing area, Negro families represented the chief replacement households in the southern half of the Keefe-Capitol-Congress area. Only about one third of the replacement households in the northern segment of the market were Negro. The peripheral segment of each of these housing market areas received a smaller number of Negro households during the five-year interval than did those segments of the market contiguous to the ghetto.

A number of blocks were selected at random within the two housing areas in which to observe the pattern of residential mobility of the universe of occupants located within those blocks. The city directory was employed as the basic source of information on the moves of individual occupants of the sample blocks on a year by year basis. It is often possible to determine the race of entering households on the basis of name, place of previous residence, and occupation data, all of which can be derived from the city directory. Although this technique is not without its shortcomings, it does enable one to arrive at crude index of racial change within a local housing environment.

Twenty-one sample blocks, or in this case quadrats, as the block configuration employed here is the census block rather than the linear block, were selected for intensive investigation. Eleven of these quadrats are located in the Keefe-Capitol-Congress housing market area, and the remaining ten are in the West-Central housing market area. The sample blocks in the West-Central area are characterized by rental levels which were prevalent in areas already heavily Negro in 1960. The median rental levels of the sample blocks in the northern market were generally higher than those occupied by the Negro population in the initial year. Thus, the probability of a Negro household receiving an assignment in the latter market area is less than that of receiving such an assignment in the former area.

A sequential running of the model over a five-year period allowed comparison of the simulated pattern of Negro entry in the sample blocks with the observed actual pattern. In all but one of the sample blocks in the Keefe-Capitol-Congress area, the model underpredicted the number of entrants. The basic flaw leading to underprediction in these blocks is the lack of an owner-occupancy mechanism in the model. These are blocks in which most homes are owner occupied structures. This results in high median rental values being assigned them, thereby reducing the probability of a Negro occupant receiving an assignment. In actuality, this area is one in which Negro home purchases have been rather substantial, as Negroes constituted the principal entrants by 1965. A combination of distance and high rents led to a nearly congruent relationship between the actual and simulated pattern in the northernmost blocks in the housing market area.

In the West-Central housing market area the model tended to underpredict in those blocks nearest the ghetto edge and to overpredict in those blocks farther removed. In only three of the sample blocks was there any real similarity between the actual and simulated pattern of Negro entries. Overprediction near the margins of the ghetto suggests that the vacancy-creating mechanism in the model requires modification as a means of improving its sensitivity to the presence of small numbers of Negro households within blocks. This lack of sensitivity results in too little concentration along the ghetto edge and too much dispersion in the outer areas of ghetto space, especially when blocks in the outer areas possess similar rental characteristics to those in the ghetto. This weakness was apparent in the overall simulation pattern characterizing ghetto space, as well as in individual housing market areas.

In evaluating the model it is apparent that the model's performance in the Keefe-Capitol-Congress housing market surpassed its performance in the West-Central market. This fact partially reflects the lack of constraints other than housing costs, to access to all housing in ghetto space. The sequential opening of segments of ghetto space within a time frame should result in a general improvement in the level of model performance. This further indicates that the ghetto resident is engaged in a series of short-distance moves, seldom exceeding a ten-block distance and most frequently confined to distances of less than six blocks. This practice permits whites to continue to compete for housing only a short distance from the margin of the ghetto, as the slow process of filling-in occurs along the ghetto edge.

The Validity of the Conceptual Model

The previous discussion which dealt with the behavior of whites and nonwhites in a common housing market was an attempt to demonstrate the soundness of the use of the previously specified components as input in a ghetto developer model. As the behavior of the individual decision maker operating within a common market is based on a host of factors, it is an inconceivable task to disaggregate all factors impinging on one's decision to move. Nevertheless, the role of the racial composition of the population in housing submarkets has been employed as the principal factor generating a reduction of white demand and a corresponding intensification of Negro demand in such areas. The question which arises here concerns the validity of the assumptions employed as the basis for model calibration. Since the model described here is a strict segregation model, employing the terminology of Thompson, it may be considered by many to be a distortion of the real-world process of residential household allocation.[28] Admittedly, it is an oversimplification of the process, but it generally appears to provide a closer approximation of racial residential patterns than an open system operating without social constraints.

Unless there is a radical departure in the behavior of individual householders, both white and black, as well as the innumerable exogenous forces whose impact is heavily felt in influencing the racial makeup of residential space, the strict segregation model will be effective in simulating the pattern of ghetto development for some time to come. Ghetto maintenance is strongly rooted in the nation's institutional mores. Whereas some question the wisdom of maintaining the ghetto intact, especially after a series of very hot summers, it appears that many professionals and a much larger segment of the lay population feel either that the task of breaking it up is an impossible one or that its maintenance is desirable. The recent flurry of open occupancy laws, at both the state and national level, do not alter this fact.

It appears that many social scientists, regardless of their basic motivations, currently support what Downs describes as a ghetto enrichment strategy.[29] Piven and Cloward, writing recently, strongly suggest that efforts at integration have worked against the Negro's acquisition of adequate housing.[30] This same type of reasoning was recently but somewhat more subtly stated by Spengler, who tends to emphasize the role of a satisfactory social environment.[31] Keller, a planner and strong advocate of the promotion of homogeneous communities, denied that one must favor complete segregation, but admitted that one should use caution in mixing neighborhoods in light of the evidence assembled.[32]

Thus, those in the ghetto who strongly advocate the development of black power and likewise opt for an enrichment strategy, and who consequently tend to be generally opposed to dispersion, seem to have strong professional backing. Downs, unlike Piven and Cloward, in evaluating the enrichment strategy, expressed uncertainty about its potential for success. Yet Grier has openly stated that public policy in the United States should be aimed at allowing the Negro to enter the mainstream of American life and not to solidify the structure of the ghetto.[33] After reviewing the evidence there appears to be strong support for the conceptual validity of something approaching a strict segregation model.

Depending upon the direction and impact of public policy on individual residential location choices, an alternative model might be developed. Such a model might generate specific levels of ghetto escapement on the basis of changing patterns of behavior, growing out of modified economic policies and social relations. But even if all future housing demands on the part of a rapidly growing urban black population are satisfied outside of the ghetto, the ghetto configuration will continue to generate conditions which may be thought to be inimical to the best interests of the nation. There is little question that the phenomenon treated here is complex and transcends the more simplistic problem of understanding housing markets. The ghetto is not simply a spatial configuration, but a social and ideological configuration that has spatial expression.

Models of the type described here might be employed with some modifications to aid in the planning process, if the ghetto enrichment strategy is chosen. Similarly, with additional modifications, such models might be employed as an aid in predicting the location and intensity of certain types of economic and social problems. If one opts for a strategy of dispersal, the strict segregation model will no longer represent a conceptually valid construct. An open system model might be developed which could generally be described as a "ghetto destroyer" model. At the moment there exists no body of information which might serve as a foundation for the development of a model of this type. Furthermore, such a model could only be employed to generate residential spatial patterns which do not currently exist on any meaningful scale. Yet, these currently nonexistent patterns could become a reality by altering human behavior as a result of major decisions emanating from both the public and private sectors of the economy.

SUMMARY AND CONCLUSIONS

An attempt has been made here to describe the basic behavior of individuals which gives rise to residential ghettos in northern metropolitan systems. After gaining limited insights into the behavioral dimension, a model was developed using these basic insights as input. The model, described as a ghetto-developer model, was employed to predict the future state of the ghetto. The state of the ghetto reflects the intensity of the spatial concentration of the Negro population within a contiguous area. Although models of this type can never be expected to duplicate the existing pattern, they can replicate in a general way the real-world process, which leads to the development of spatial patterns that bear varying degrees of similarity to the actual pattern. Whereas models of this type have some predictive value, the real merit derived from them is the gaining of additional understanding of the processes one is attempting to simulate.

The ghetto-developer model was run using data from Milwaukee, Wisconsin. The results provided evidence of deficiency in some of the basic assumptions incorporated in the model, both in terms of the aggregate simulated ghetto spatial pattern, as well as the resulting pattern occurring within individual housing market areas. The employment of the model to generate ghetto expansion in a series of urban systems should permit one to ascertain if a general set of assumptions might be employed to describe fairly accurately the process of ghetto formation.

Models of the type described above are attempts to replicate an actual ongoing process. The initiation of strategies designed to alter the existing process would tend to invalidate the model. At the same time, models may be developed based on the behavior necessary to modify the existing residential spatial pattern. Models of this type could very well serve as planning models, providing that in this case there is a national opting for an alternative strategy. The strict segregation model currently generates a spatial pattern that approaches the actual pattern, even though, in reality, ghetto escapements occur. But the extent of such occurrences are not sufficiently significant to alter the spatial configuration of the ghetto.

LITERATURE CITED

1. A. Meier and E. M. Rudwick, *From Plantation to Ghetto* (New York: Hill and Wang, 1966), pp. 191–92.
2. R. L. Rice, "Residential Segregation by Law," *The Journal of Southern History*, Vol. 34 (1968), pp. 194–99.
3. R. L. Morrill, "The Negro Ghetto: Problems and Alternatives," *The Geographical Review*, Vol. 55 (1965), pp. 339–61.
4. A. Beauchamp, "Processual Indices of Segregation: Some Preliminary Comments," *Behavioral Science*, Vol. 11 (1966), pp. 190–92.
5. Morrill, op. cit., footnote 3, p. 348; R. L. Morrill, *Migration and the Spread and Growth of Urban Settlement* (Lund, Sweden: C. W. K. Gleerup, 1965), p. 186.
6. G. Carlsson, "Decline of Fertility: Innovation or Adjustment Process," *Population Studies*, Vol. 20 (November 1966), pp. 149–50.
7. Carlsson, op. cit., footnote 6, p. 150.
8. W. Zelinsky, *A Prologue to Population Geography* (New York: Prentice-Hall, 1965), pp. 45–46.
9. R. L. Morrill, "Waves of Spatial Diffusion," *Journal of Regional Science*, Vol. 8 (Summer 1968), p. 2.
10. See H. Sharp and L. F. Schnore, "The Changing Color Composition of Metropolitan Areas," *Land Economics*, Vol. 38 (1962), pp. 169–85.
11. Special Census of Cleveland, Ohio, April 1965, *Current Population Reports*, Series p-28, No. 1390 (1965).

12. J. T. Davis, "Middle Class Housing in the Central City," *Economic Geography*, Vol. 41 (1965), pp. 238–51.

13. For a methodological discussion of this point see K. E. Taeuber and A. F. Taeuber, *Negroes in Cities* (Chicago: Aldine Publishing Co., 1965), pp. 78–95.

14. D. Stea, "Space, Territory and Human Movements," *Landscape*, Vol. 15 (1965), p. 13.

15. M. M. Weber, "Culture, Territoriality and the Elastic Mile," *The Regional Science Association Papers*, Vol. 13 (1964), pp. 61–63.

16. G. C. Henderson, "Negroes Into Americans: A Dialectical Development," *Journal of Human Relations*, Vol. 14 (1966), p. 537.

17. Stea, op. cit., footnote 14, p. 13.

18. E. Grier and G. C. Grier, "Equality and Beyond: Housing Segregation in the Great Society," *Daedalus*, Vol. 95 (1966), p. 82.

19. H. Hoyt, *The Structure and Growth of Residential Neighborhoods in American Cities* (Washington, D.C.: Government Printing Office, 1939), pp. 62 and 71.

20. M. J. Bailey, "Effects of Race and Other Demographic Factors on the Values of Single-Family Homes," *Land Economics*, Vol. 42 (1966), pp. 214–18.

21. G. C. Grier, "The Negro Ghettos and Federal Housing Policy," *Law and Contemporary Problems* (Summer 1967), p. 555.

22. R. E. Pahl, "Sociological Models in Geography," in R. J. Chorley and P. Haggett (Eds.), *Models in Geography* (London: Methuen and Co., Ltd., 1967), p. 239.

23. Chorley and Haggett, op. cit., footnote 22, p. 25.

24. Ghetto space represents the area presently identified as the ghetto as well as that expanse of contiguous territory thought to be sufficiently adequate to house the net increase of Negro households over a ten-year period.

25. E. P. Wolf, "The Tipping Point in Racially Changing Neighborhoods," *Journal of American Institute of Planners*, Vol. 29 (1963), p. 219.

26. J. Wolpert, "Behavioral Aspects of the Decision to Migrate," *The Regional Science Association Papers*, Vol. 15 (1965), p. 163.

27. E. P. Wolf, "The Baxter Area: A New Trend in Neighborhood Changes?" *Phylon*, Vol. 26 (1965), pp. 347–48.

28. W. R. Thompson, *A Preface to Urban Economics* (Baltimore: The Johns Hopkins Press, 1965), pp. 309–13.

29. A. Downs, "The Future of American Ghettos," *Daedalus*, Vol. 97 (1968), pp. 1346–47.

30. F. F. Piven and R. Cloward, "The Case Against Urban Desegregation," *Social Work*, Vol. 12 (1967), p. 12.

31. J. J. Spengler, "Population Pressure, Housing Habitat," *Law and Contemporary Problems*, Vol. 32 (1967), p. 172.

32. S. Keller, "Social Class in Physical Planning," *International Social Science Journal*, Vol. 18 (1966), pp. 506–7.

33. Grier, op. cit., footnote 21, p. 560.

SOURCES OF VARIATION IN HOUSING VALUES
IN WASHINGTON, D.C.

J. Tait Davis

The distribution of housing values in Washington, D.C., displays an apparently random pattern with reference to the traditional basing point for describing urban land use structures in the central business district.[1] In broad terms there is evidence of the patterning of housing values after the sector model developed by Homer Hoyt,[2] who described the pattern in 1955 in these terms:

> The Map of Home Values of the Washington Metropolitan Area in 1953 does not show a rigid geometric pattern in which every high priced home is in one sector and the slums are all in another sector. It does reveal, however, the great concentration of higher valued homes in the Northwest sector of Washington, which extends into the fashionable home areas in Chevy Chase and Bethesda in Montgomery County and faces a high income area in Arlington and Fairfax Counties across the Potomac River. . . .
> In all American cities, the high value homes are found in one sector of the city, and the expansion of the higher income families tends to move outward in this one sector. In Washington, D.C., the highest income families tended to locate in the Northwest sector; west of 16th Street and Rock Creek Park. This trend became established by 1904 when there was a movement away from an early fashionable area east of the Capitol to a new center of social prestige beginning at the White House and extending down Sixteenth Street and westward to Connecticut and Massachusetts Avenues to Florida Avenue. By 1938 the sector of high grade residences had extended to the District of Columbia line at Chevy Chase and into Montgomery County.

The map to which this description refers is representative of conditions at the midpoint of a decade of deep social and economic change for the

District of Columbia. In 1950 the population of the District totaled 802,178 persons of whom 35 per cent were nonwhite, 65 per cent, white. By 1960 the total population had declined 4.8 per cent to 763,956 persons. But of this population 55 per cent were nonwhite. Given the substantial changes in the social composition, and, by inference, the economic composition of the District population it seemed reasonable to attempt to relate housing value patterns to social and economic conditions.

In turning attention to the pattern of housing values in 1960 and recollecting that the previous decade was one of profound social change in the District of Columbia, a change perhaps reflected in the different pattern of housing value in the latter year, it seems reasonable to postulate that the 1960 pattern of housing values might be explained in terms of some of those social features.

SELECTION OF HYPOTHESES

We can be reasonably certain that a large part of the variation from neighborhood to neighborhood in housing values might be explained in terms of variations in income.

There is no particular point in arguing here which of income or housing value is the independent variable, although given the relative age of housing units throughout most of the District of Columbia it is probably housing value which is the independent variable with the population sorting itself out in terms of the housing that it can afford. What might be more profitably explored here is the proposition, originating with Hoyt, that "leaders of the community" might have something to do with the patterning of housing values. Unfortunately, there is no consensus satisfactory to all interested parties as to who comprise the "leaders of the community" in Washington, D.C.[3] One thing common to all definitions of this group, however, is their relative affluence. Generally, the leaders of the community are in the higher-income brackets, and thus, the proportion of relatively affluent in a neighborhood has been selected as a proxy for the "leaders of the community."

In many residential subdivisions average housing values show a pattern of change over time. Basic to this pattern is a rise in value over the first few years of life followed by a prolonged and gradual decline in value. Unlike most other durable goods a house does not depreciate regularly in value over time. The explanation for this phenomenon might lie in the importance of numerous other factors in explaining housing value. Such considerations as location with respect to employment and shopping centers, whether or not the streets are lined with shade trees are examples of these other factors. Also of significance in determining housing value is the neighborhood in which the unit is located. In Washington, D.C., partly because of the diversity of such considerations it is not expected that there would be a high correlation between the relative age of a residential neighborhood and the values of housing units. Nevertheless, a second hypothesis to be explored is that variations in housing values might be associated with the relative age of residential neighborhoods. As explained above a high correlation between the two is not expected. But, in the Washington situation it seems likely that there might be a combination effect of age of neighborhood and relative affluence. If, for example, it can be demonstrated that housing values in older neighborhoods are little affected by variations in the proportion of high-income families within a certain range one might generate some insights into the selective effect of neighborhood age on housing values. A third relationship, possibly important in Washington and other cities having significantly large Negro populations, is that between the changing proportions of this group and variations in a neighborhood's residential values. As with the variables, age of neighborhood and high-income families, some combination effect of Negro and age of neighborhood is to be expected. It might be postulated, for example, that the effect of changing proportions of Negroes in a neighborhood upon housing values would be different in older neighborhoods that are predominantly white than in other neighborhoods.

In summary, the hypotheses to be explored here are as follows:

1. Variations in housing values from census tract to census tract may be attributed to variations in:
   a. proportion of high-income families in census tract population,
   b. relative age of housing units in the census tract,
   c. proportion of nonwhites in census tract population.

2. The effect of these suggested sources of variation in housing values will vary for different ranges of each of the three variables. For example, the effect of the proportion of nonwhites in the population on housing values will be different in old neighborhoods than in relatively new ones. The interactions of the selected variables will themselves be significant sources of variation in housing values.

The data unit used for this analysis is the census tract and the measure of housing value used throughout is median housing value by census tract.

As a preliminary step in analyzing these relationships an examination was made of the intercorrelations among the variables. These are suggestive of the validity of some of the reasoning outlined in the development of the working hypotheses (Tables 1 and 2).

INTERCORRELATIONS OF SELECTED VARIABLES

Although the hypotheses outlined above are examined here only in reference to 1960 it is interesting to note differences in the correlations between 1950 and 1960. In 1950, for example, the correlation between the proportion of housing units more than twenty years old and median family income was reasonably high, $-.60$; in 1960 it was $-.09$. Also significant is

TABLE 1
Inter-Correlations of Selected Social and Economic Measures, District of Columbia, 1950

	1	2	3	4	5	6	7
1. Median value of owner-occupied housing unit	—	.70	.20	.62	.75	.05	−.27
2. Median monthly rent		—	.18	.57	.79	.13	−.32
3. White-nonwhite ratio			—	.35	.29	.10	−.27
4. Median family income				—	.81	.32	−.60
5. % of families with incomes above $7,000					—	.16	−.47
6. % housing units < 10 years old						—	−.83
7. % housing units > 20 years old							—

TABLE 2
Inter-Correlations of Selected Social and Economic Measures, District of Columbia, 1960

	1	2	3	4	5	6	7
1. Median value of owner-occupied housing unit	—	.81	.51	.85	.80	.19	.01
2. Median monthly rent		—	.40	.81	.79	.35	−.07
3. White-nonwhite ratio			—	.52	.59	.09	−.24
4. Median family income				—	.92	.20	−.09
5. % of families with incomes > $8,000					—	.25	−.18
6. % housing units < 10 years old						—	−.74
7. % housing units > 20 years old							—

the higher correlation between the white-nonwhite ratio and median housing value and median monthly rent, in 1960 than in 1950, suggesting that
this element might be relatively important as a predictor of housing value
in the latter year where it was not in the earlier.

A factor analysis which was performed on larger correlation matrices
incorporating the elements listed in Tables 1 and 2 suggested that the pattern of intercorrelations in 1960 and 1950 was explicable in terms of similar factors although the relative importance of the different factors
changed. Measures of income, housing value and rents, and of educational
achievement were heavily weighted in the first factor extracted in both
years; the age of neighborhood residential units was heavily weighted in
the second factor extracted for both years.

Of the variables tested for their relationship to variations in housing
values only the white-nonwhite ratio changed in its relative importance
from 1950 to 1960, being heavily weighted in the fourth factor of the
1950 matrix and in the fifth factor of 1960. What the factor analysis demonstrated was the likelihood that each of the variables examined here is
distinguishable from the others in the sense of reproducing the patterns of
intercorrelation in Tables 1 and 2.

Design for a Factorial Experiment

The relationships between housing values from tract to tract and the
proportion of higher-income families, age of residential units and the ratio
of whites to nonwhites in the tract population has been examined in a factorial experiment. The model used is an adaptation of a similar model
used to test the effect of location with respect to a roadway on land values.[4]

The results of this experiment are presented in Table 3. Generally all the
variables tested are confirmed as significant sources of variation in housing
values. The only exception is the white-nonwhite ratio in relatively new
residential areas (W_k in A_1). To a limited extent the pattern of inter-
correlations presented earlier suggests these conclusions. What the correlations do not show, however, is the nature of the association, which for
several elements is not adequately described by the correlation
coefficients. Nor do they suggest a classification of the housing value pattern in terms of the three variables examined. It is these last two aspects
which are discussed below.

VARIATIONS OF HOUSING VALUES WITH PROPORTIONS OF
HIGH-INCOME FAMILIES

Generally, housing values are higher where the proportion of high-income families is higher. But, the pattern of association is not consistent throughout the whole range in the proportions of high-income families.

TABLE 3

*Significance of Selected Measures on Variations in Housing Values,
District of Columbia, 1960*

Source due to	d.f.	Sum of Squares	Mean Sum of Squares	Significant at .05 level
I_j	3	33,577.2	11,192.4	Yes
A_j	2	3,096.6	1,548.3	Yes
$(IA)_{ij}$	6	912.5	152.1	Yes
W_k in A_1	2	8.2	4.1	No
W_k in A_2	2	1,738.8	869.4	Yes
W_k in A_3	2	1,593.5	796.8	Yes
$(IW)_{ijk}$	4	51,059.6	10,132.8	Yes
error	79	11,652.0	31.9	—

Where I_j = Income classes
A_j = Age of Housing classes
$(IA)_{ij}$ = Interaction of Income with Age
W_k in A_1 = White/Nonwhite ratio in Age Class 1
W_k in A_2 = White/Nonwhite ratio in Age Class 2
W_k in A_3 = White/Nonwhite ratio in Age Class 3
$(IW)_{ijk}$ = Interaction of income with White/Nonwhite ratios

There does not appear to be a significant variation in housing values with variations in the proportion of high-income families between approximately 5 per cent and 10 per cent of the total families in the tract. Below and above this range there is a clear tendency for variations in the proportion of high-income families to be reflected in variations in housing values.

The general trend in the relationship between high-income families and median housing values is not surprising. It is to be expected when we consider that income levels and housing values are highly correlated and that the number of high-income families is highly correlated with average income for census tracts. An interesting question which might be inferred from this particular pattern is the following: Are housing values more sensitive to variations in the proportion of high-income families when these proportions are relatively low or relatively high than when the proportion is in between?

VARIATIONS OF HOUSING VALUES WITH AGE OF NEIGHBORHOOD

In examining the relationship between housing values and age of neighborhood a simple notion was initially adopted, namely, that census tracts could be characterized as young, middle-aged or old in terms of the proportion of housing units in the census tract that were more than twenty years old. The determination of the actual proportions which would constitute the dividing points between these classes proceeded by trial and error toward a set of three classes which were as different from each other, in terms of median housing values, as seemed possible.

VARIATIONS IN HOUSING VALUES WITH WHITE-NONWHITE RATIOS

In establishing the class limits of the white-nonwhite ratios to be tested the objective was, as in the case of the age of housing, to maximize class to class variations in housing values. Conceptually, absolute nonwhite areas are at one end of the scale and absolute white areas at the other. The effect of the white-nonwhite ratio has been examined here in terms of the young, middle-aged and old neighborhoods of the preceding section. The results of the factorial experiment suggested that variation in the white-nonwhite ratio in relatively young neighborhoods (those with less than 40 per cent of housing units more than twenty years old) was not statistically significant (Table 3).

In both middle-aged and old neighborhoods there is a tendency for housing values to be higher when the nonwhite population is proportionately smaller. There is a tendency for housing values in middle-aged neighborhoods to be more sensitive to variations in the ratio so long as nonwhites constitute a majority, than when they are not. Conversely, older neighborhoods tend to be more sensitive to variations in the ratio when whites constitute a majority of the populations.

Overall, however, variations in housing values associated with variations in the white-nonwhite ratio operate within a much smaller range than do variations attributable to the proportions of high-income families or age of neighborhood. And, as noted above, there is no evidence of a significant variation in housing values with variations in the white-nonwhite ratio in relatively young neighborhoods, as these have been defined here.

VARIATIONS IN HOUSING VALUES SEGREGATED BY AGE AND INCOME

The factorial experiment suggested a combination effect on housing values attributable to the interaction of age of neighborhood and proportion of high-income families. Generally the pattern is replicated here, but there are some interesting additional relationships illustrated. For example, housing values in relatively young neighborhoods are consistently lower than those in other age classes. For lower proportions of high-income families the newer areas are most sensitive, while the older neighborhoods appear relatively insensitive. When the proportions of high-income families vary above approximately 10 per cent the implication of these data is that housing values in neighborhoods behave in similar fashions.

VARIATIONS IN HOUSING VALUES SEGREGATED BY INCOME AND WHITE-NONWHITE RATIO

Also identified as a significant source of variation in housing values was the combination effect of the proportion of high-income families and the white-nonwhite ratio. Considering the nature of this association in terms of neighborhoods which are predominantly nonwhite, predominantly white, or in approximate racial balance some interesting relationships reveal themselves.

The general tendency for housing values to increase with increases in the proportion of high-income families is most evident in the case of census tracts which have a nonwhite majority. The lowest housing values in Washington are associated with racially balanced areas which have low proportions of high-income families. Curiously, the highest values of housing are associated with predominantly white areas, but these values are not greatly different from the highest values associated with racially balanced census tracts. Certainly the greatest range in housing values is associated with racially balanced neighborhoods.

There is a curious tendency for housing values to be lower in all white tracts as the proportion of high-income families ranges from approximately 5 to 10 per cent. The result is that housing values in all white tracts with 8, 9, or 10 per cent of their families in higher-income classes are not much different from housing values in all white neighborhoods with less than 3 per cent of their families in this category. It seems possible that this pattern might be explained in terms of the inertia of a resident population which stays in a house purchased some years ago although individual income levels have risen in the meantime. Also worth noting here is the observation that housing values in predominantly nonwhite, high-income areas are substantially below those of other categories of high-income areas.

SUMMARY

The analysis of housing values in the District of Columbia for 1960 largely confirms the initial working hypotheses. Variations in housing value are associated with variations in the proportion of high-income families, with the relative age of housing in a census tract, and with variations in the white-nonwhite ratio. More significant would seem to be the differences in the nature of the associations which require that the original hypotheses be qualified. For example, housing values in predominantly nonwhite areas do tend to be lower than those in either racially mixed or predominantly white census tracts, but there is no significant variation in housing values with changing proportions of nonwhites in census tracts with relatively young housing stocks. Again, housing values do tend to be higher in tracts having relatively higher proportions of high-income families. But, there are significant exceptions to this generalization, particularly among predominantly white areas where the proportion of high-income families ranges between approximately 5 and 10 per cent of the total. The class limits used in this analysis are of interest in interpreting the results reported here and may be useful in the exploration of similar problems elsewhere.

Class Limits for the Proportion of High-Income Families

Low: fewer than 3.5 per cent of families above $8,000 in 1959

Medium: between 3.5 per cent and 7.5 per cent of families above $8,000 in 1959

High: between 7.5 per cent and 11.5 per cent of families above $8,000 in 1959

Very High: more than 11.5 per cent of families above $8,000 in 1959

Class Limits for Age of Housing Stock

Young: less than 40 per cent of housing units over twenty years old

Middle-aged: between 40 per cent and 80 per cent of housing units over twenty years old

Old: more than 80 per cent of housing units over twenty years old

Class Limits for White-Nonwhite Ratio

Nonwhite: white-nonwhite ratio less than .75

Racial balance: white-nonwhite ratio between .75 and 1.50

White: white-nonwhite ratio greater than 1.50

It would be desirable from several points of view to develop a finer classification than the crude one employed here. The main limitation in studying a single city is the factorial design itself which requires a minimum number of observations in each cell. While the design can be accomodated to a few missing observations it cannot cope with a great many. Such findings as those presented here are subject to some reservation. It is conceivable that Washington, D.C., is an atypical city in respect to housing as it is atypical in other respects. Postwar residential developments have largely accrued to a suburban periphery. In the case of Washington the suburban periphery is in two different states, Maryland and Virginia. Until recently, and in some cases not even yet, suburban housing areas have not been available to nonwhites. This has meant that a rapidly expanding Negro population has had to be accommodated within the confines of the central city. But this expansion had not proceeded so far in 1960 that several areas of predominantly white population were not available for comparative purposes. Obviously, in those cities where there are no predominantly white areas available for testing in the several income and age categories this variable cannot be tested in the manner described here.

The housing value patterns of Washington in 1960 represent the results of a decade of accommodation to an increasingly pent-up population. This feature might be expected to have distorted some of the value relationships from some threshold of normality. With this reservation, and the qualifications of the various relationships described briefly above, the results of this analysis appear consistent with findings of other studies of variations in housing values.

LITERATURE CITED

1. Davis, J. Tait, "Middle Class Housing in the Central City," *Economic Geography*, 41 (1965), 238–51.

2. Homer Hoyt Associates, "The Pattern of Home Values in Washington, D.C. Standard Metropolitan Area," in *Economic Survey of Montgomery and Prince Georges Counties, Maryland.* 1955, pp. 92–93.

3. Smith, A. Robert and Eric Sevareid, *Washington: Magnificent Capital.* Garden City, N.Y.: Doubleday and Company, 1965. Ch. 6, 8, 10, and 12.

4. Davis, J. Tait, "Parkways, Values and Development in the Washington Metropolitan Region," *Research Record No. 16,* National Academy of Sciences/Highway Research Board (1963), 32–43.

ACCESS TO HOUSING:
THE ROLE OF THE REAL ESTATE INDUSTRY

William H. Brown, Jr.

Racial discrimination in housing is perhaps the most serious and basic aspect of white racism manifest in American society today. It provides not only the basic structure for most other forms of institutional segregation, but also the resulting pattern of racially separate residential areas fosters the persistence of private prejudices and mythologies by which the entire structure is undergirded. The result is a seemingly impenetrable, "vast, silent, and automatic system directed against men and women of color" [9, p. 80]. One need not feel intimidated by this conceptualization of the problem if attention is focused on the word "automatic." In the complex chain of events which perpetuates racial discrimination there are many connections which are far from automatic, but persist primarily because of the conscious acts and decisions of individuals and organizations. By attempting to determine the basis for this behavior we should be able to make some progress in deciding how to intervene most effectively. The racial practices of real estate brokers offer one such point of intervention.

HISTORICAL BACKGROUND

The real estate industry has long been recognized as one of the major institutions in American society whose policies and practices have consistently and forcefully worked to perpetuate racial discrimination in housing. So consistent and tenacious have the industry's activities been in this respect that it has been interpreted as being either conspiratorial or ideological [4, 10]. The nationwide uniformity of the industry's position in opposition to racially integrated housing and fair housing legislation, as represented by the National Association of Real Estate Boards (NAREB), has given abundant evidence to support both interpretations. The two are obviously interrelated—and are derived from basic forces within the nation's social and economic system. To be sure, there have been minor modifications of the industry's position on the matter of race and housing over the past half century, but by and large, since World War II, these have been attempts to adapt an ongoing policy of racial separation to evolving civil rights legislation as applied to housing. Also, distinctions are to be made between the industry as a whole and individual real estate dealers.

In this period of the twentieth century it hardly seems necessary to present yet another recitation of the obviously destructive effects on our society of enduring racial prejudice and segregation, particularly against black Americans. Yet many, perhaps most, Americans, schooled as they have been in the melting-pot theory of ethnic assimilation, are as yet only dimly aware of the depth and pervasiveness of this prejudice.

Central to the racial crisis in all of its manifestations is the pattern of racially segregated housing. And here history has cast the real estate dealer as the leading actor: not simply as a broker in real estate, but as the chief broker between the races in what has become one of the most acute political, social, economic, and fundamentally moral issues in twentieth-century America. Just how he has measured up to this responsibility, and the extent to which he is implicated in the creation of the problem in its present dimensions are two of the basic questions with which this paper is concerned. But we should first of all briefly consider the background of racially separate housing patterns in America.

Among the prescient and incisive observations of mid-nineteenth-century America by Alexis de Tocqueville was the following:

> If I were called upon to predict the future, I should say that the abolition of slavery in the South will, in the common course of things, increase the repugnance of the white population for the blacks. I base this opinion upon the analogous observation I have already made in the North. I have remarked that the white inhabitants of the North avoid the Negroes with increasing care in proportion as the legal barriers of separation are removed by the legislature [20, p. 390].

It is of course a mistake to interpret as simplistic Tocqueville's prediction of the white southerners' increasing "repugnance" for blacks in the post-Civil War period. There was no instinctive repulsion between the races. "Churches and schools had become racially separate during Reconstruction, but afterward, for a decade or two, Negroes and whites generally continued to use the same facilities for eating and drinking, transportation, and recreation" [14, p. 257]. With the failure of Reconstruction, however, all of this was to change drastically, except the pattern of scattered black residences and settlements which tended to persist in most southern cities until well after World War II in spite of relentless constraint.

Until 1900, less than 10 per cent of the country's black population lived in the North. Yet a pattern of racial segregation in housing had long been in the process of development. Many factors, particularly economic ones, were responsible. But in Philadelphia, whose nearly 63,000 blacks then represented the largest black community in the North, Du Bois [7] observed the racial residential pattern and attributed it to "a curious effect of color prejudice." More specifically he blamed real estate agents for an increase in this prejudice "by refusing to discriminate between different classes of Negroes."

Du Bois assumed that the racial prejudices of whites would be softened if real estate agents selected for occupancy only those black families whose class status was compatible with the given residential area. The apparent inability or reluctance of whites to make distinctions between different classes of blacks proved, however, to be a most formidable obstacle. To little avail, middle and upper class blacks attempted to persuade whites to understand that social and economic class differences existed within the black community as well as within the white community, and that class alone should be the criterion of social position.

The idea of *caste* rather than *class* as more relevant in analyzing the problem of race relations in America developed somewhat slowly, and did not gain widespread acceptance until about the time of World War II [5, 6, 15]. As early as 1932 Frazier [8] showed that upper class blacks were actively putting as much distance as possible between their residences and those of the black lower classes, yet they have generally remained within the boundaries of a predominantly or totally black residential area. The poverty which has characterized the black community as a whole has been most often cited as the explanation for this segregation. But in fact, class heterogeneity has always characterized black residential areas [43].

Between 1900 and the Great Migration of 1915–18, when tens of thousands of southern blacks were recruited to work in the wartime industries, black urban populations were too small to arouse much concern or activity aimed at limiting or restricting settlement. In Chicago, for example, the black population in 1910 was only 44,000, just 2 per cent of the total, consisting of widely scattered settlements located for the most part on the city's south and west sides. New York City, however, proved a dramatic exception—and a symbolic one—in the rapid growth and consolidation of black Harlem. Here were all of the elements of today's pattern of ghetto development: black population pressure generated by migration and relocation (for subway construction), panic sales, white flight and black invasion, "blockbusting," real estate speculation, and profiteering [17].

Meanwhile, the South was devising legal weapons with which to control black residential patterns. The first attempt took the form of segregation ordinances which would precisely define urban residential areas in which blacks would be permitted to live. Efforts along this line were ultimately blocked in 1917 when the Supreme Court decided that such statutes were in violation of the Fourteenth Amendment [13, p. 176]. In the same year, however, in the face of an expanding black population, Chicago's Real Estate Board threw its weight on the side of segregation by declaring:

> It is desired, in the interest of all, that each block shall be filled solidly [with Negroes] and that further expansion shall be confined to contiguous blocks, and that the present method of obtaining a single building in scattered blocks be discontinued. Promiscuous sales and leases here and there mean an unwarranted and unjustifiable destruction of values [11, 14, p. 244].

As if to underscore the Real Estate Board's position, black buyers, real estate agents, or anyone selling a home to blacks in areas where they were not wanted were subject to having their homes and offices bombed. The Chicago Race Relations Commission reported a pattern of "systematic" bombing which lasted from July 1, 1917, to March 1, 1921, averaging one every twenty days [3]. Shortly thereafter there appeared, for the first time in Chicago, the most effective device ever to be employed in the control of black residential areas—the race restrictive covenant.

NAREB AND THE RACE RESTRICTIVE COVENANT

The race restrictive covenant was a deed restriction which stated that the subject property could not in any manner be conveyed to certain racial group members for their use or occupancy. This most effective of all residential restrictive devices had a variety of shaky legal precedents going back as far as 1890 [12, p. 173; 22, pp. 1–29; 14, pp. 253–90]. But not until 1926, in *Corrigan v. Buckley*, did the United States Supreme Court render a decision which permitted the covenant's implementation to continue unchallenged. Its employment was assiduously promoted not only by the real estate industry but eventually even by the Federal Housing Administration which, as Weaver pointed out, was an inevitable consequence of its being staffed by "the very financial and real estate interests and institutions which led the campaign to spread racial covenants and residential segregation" [24, p. 70]. Spearheading this movement was the NAREB of Chicago and its affiliated boards across the nation. As Weaver [24, p. 217] further showed, their position was clearly and unequivocally stated in the board's own code of ethics: "A Realtor should never be instrumental in introducing into a neighborhood a character of property or occupancy, members of any race or nationality, or any individuals whose presence will clearly be detrimental to property values in that neighborhood."

The spirit of this article was echoed fourteen years later in the FHA Underwriters Manual of 1938 which, in specifying valuation criteria, stated that "a high rating should be given only where adequate and enforced zoning regulations exist or where effective restrictive covenants are recorded against the entire tract, since these are the surest protection against undesirable encroachment and inharmonious use" [21].

So effective had the race restrictive covenant become in limiting the housing opportunities available to blacks that Weaver [24] was led to condemn them as "the villain" in the creation of black ghettos. Even Myrdal [15, p. 624] was led to believe that should the Supreme Court declare illegal "the private restrictive covenants, segregation in the North would be nearly doomed, and segregation in the South set back slightly."

Two basic patterns emerged in the development of covenanted areas: the neighborhood scheme and the community scheme [13]. In the former plan, one easily adapted to new subdivisions, a single covenant was sufficient to cover certain compact neighborhoods thus delineated. The community scheme, devised to cover larger and less compact areas, depended upon enough property owners signing the agreement to bring a certain percentage of the community's land area under the restriction. At this point the agreement became binding upon the entire community.

More important than the actual number or percentage of residences covered by covenants was their strategic location. Since areas of black urban settlement were most frequently bounded in part by other barriers such as industrial areas, natural boundaries, or even worse housing, it was usually necessary only to provide covenant protection to those areas in the paths of black expansion. In Chicago, for example, it was found that just over half the residential area not occupied by blacks was covenanted against them. But it was an area which effectively (at least for a time) sealed off natural avenues of expansion [13].

In 1948, the Supreme Court held the race restrictive covenant to be judicially unenforceable. Yet today, as has been made manifest by the tempo of urban racial violence, well documented by U.S. census data, a steady and often steepening increase in residential segregation has characterized American cities in the North and South.

INTRODUCTION OF NEW RESTRICTIVE TACTICS

In 1950 the first concession made by the National Association of Real Estate Boards to the changed legal situation was to alter the offending Article 34 of its 1924 Code of Ethics. As Article 5, Part I, it now reads: "A Realtor should not be instrumental in introducing into a neighborhood a character of property or use which will clearly be detrimental to property values in that neighborhood" [16]. Although deletion of the phrase referring to race was hailed as a "milestone" by the national board, it was privately conceded that a character of property or use covered the introduction of Negroes [10, p. 201]. Not until 1959 did a realtor bring the issue to a head by going to court over a charge of unethical conduct concerning his introduction of a nonwhite buyer into a white neighborhood. When the court ruled in the realtor's favor, and against the local board, "it caused inquiry from some boards surprised to learn that Realtors no longer could be subjected to disciplinary action if they assisted minority families in finding homes in all-white neighborhoods" [37, p. 2]. As McEntire [14, p. 239] said: "Racial discrimination in real estate is much more than a practice of individual brokers and salesmen. It is one of the standards of the real estate business to which individual businessmen are expected to conform and are liable to sanctions if they do not."

A question that naturally arises at this point concerns the kind of sanctions that could possibly be imposed on black real estate agents who, one assumes, would be very unlikely to abide by any such race restrictive policies. The answer is simply that black agents, until fairly recently, have generally been excluded from membership on real estate boards. Black realtors responded to this exclusion by establishing in 1948 their own boards and a National Association of Real Estate Brokers. But even this did not make available, at least at the beginning, the Multiple Listing Services (MLS), by which lists of properties within local boards' areas were distributed to member brokers. Although an increasing number of blacks were being admitted to local boards, they were generally excluded from the policy-making committees of these boards. In Oakland, California, after trying for eight or ten years, blacks were first admitted to membership in the white-controlled Oakland Real Estate Board in 1962. Yet black members are expected to abide by the parent organization, NAREB, that is, to refrain from selling blacks property in white neighborhoods. Shortly after becoming a member of the Oakland Real Estate Board, one well-known broker in the city made the following statement in testimony before the U.S. Commission on Civil Rights [42, pp. 2–3]:

> One and a half years ago we became members of the Oakland Real Estate Board and thus had access to MLS. I was amazed to discover that the OREB (Oakland Real Estate Board) used "Caucasians Only" on their multiple listings. Not only was this used on listings that supposedly did not fall under the Rumford and Unruh laws but also from time to time on listings that did fall in this category. . . . I related to the OREB my concern about this situation. I have never had a response

to this letter from MLS. The only response I had was a phone call from the executive secretary during which conversation he disagreed with my interpretation of the laws and furthermore informed me that it was incumbent on an office such as ours that is well known for its integrationist philosophy to check with brokers prior to showing a property in an area which might be all-white in character. He stated that *it was our ethical duty to our fellow Realtors to inform them of the color of the buyer before showing a multiple listing.* (Emphasis supplied.)

The witness testified further that in order to avoid exposing listings to black brokers, separate listing services were developed privately among white realtors, particularly among those who operated in the white suburban neighborhoods.

In line with this development has been the exclusion of black brokers from membership in suburban boards. The methods employed to accomplish this in the San Francisco Bay Area are described in a recent joint study carried out by the National Committee Against Discrimination in Housing and the Department of Housing and Urban Development. That part of the study dealing with the listing practices of real estate agents [28] finds that high board fees appear to be widely employed, as a means of discouraging black membership. Fees range from $50 to $1,000. As expected, the highest fees are found in suburban areas. But even for the city of Oakland with a 30 per cent black population, the fee is $600. Of the 376 brokers in the city, less than 50 are black. In southern Alameda County, which, as we shall see, has been extremely successful in limiting black settlement, the broker's fee is $1,000.

As a rule, however, control of black entry into the profession has been effected by racial discrimination in the hiring of salesmen. In California,

most candidates for the broker license base their claims for qualification upon two years of experience as a real estate salesman. However, the commissioner does not allow any person who has been a licensed salesman for two years to qualify unless the applicant can submit proof that he was actively employed full time as a salesman. A form is provided the applicant so that he may obtain the signature of his employing broker, who must certify that the applicant has been employed for the required time on a full time basis [1, p. 5].

Since white brokers have rarely employed black salespeople, the effect is apparent.

REALTORS AND OPEN HOUSING

The commitment of the real estate industry to the usual discriminatory practices in spite of changes in the law was nowhere more clearly demonstrated than in its opposition to the various city and state fair housing law campaigns which took place across the nation during the 1960s. The threat to subject any such legislative proposals to popular referendum and to actually carry out the threat should any such law be passed was the basic tactic. A particularly acrimonious and free-swinging campaign, for example, was waged against California's 1963 fair housing law, the Rumford Act. In an editorial [25, p. 1] entitled "The Forced Housing Issue," the California Real Estate Association announced:

> Representatives of the CREA, the California Apartment House Owners Association and the Home Builders Association have filed an initiative (Proposition 14 on the statewide ballot) for an amendment to the State Constitution. . . . If voted in at the next general election, the amendment will restore the right of choice to the property owner in the state.

This right, as conceived by the CREA's "Americans to Outlaw Forced Housing Committee," was described, in part, as follows:

> Neither the State nor any subdivision or agency thereof shall deny, limit or abridge, directly or indirectly, the right of any person, who is willing or desires to sell, lease, or rent any part or all of his real property, to decline to sell, lease, or rent such property to such person or persons as he, in his absolute discretion, chooses [25, p. 1].

The thrust of the realtor's campaign was to question the patriotism of those who would deny this right. Indeed the "idea and phrase 'fair housing' . . . was born in the communist press" according to the executive vice president of NAREB [27].

While it would be somewhat unfair to take too seriously things that were said in the emotional heat of a campaign, it is difficult to dismiss this kind of destructive politicking as simply a "gimmick" as did one prominent realtor with whom this matter was discussed. More important, however, was the opportunity the campaign gave for observing inconsistencies in the stated position of realtors with respect to race and housing. Admitting that realtors "have not been in the forefront of changes which have followed step-by-step as government accorded and supported recognition of civil rights," the responsibility for the industry's position at various times was blamed on the "prevailing sentiment." Article 34 of its 1924 Code of Ethics only "mirrored the 'separate but equal' doctrine of the time," and its stated alterations of that policy were not adhered to by realtors because "the resistance of homeowners (was) at that time almost universally adamant" [27]. Yet, according to its own survey, "77 of the 80 multiple listing systems in California showed during a 90-day period that less than one percent were restricted by the owner as to the race of the buyer" [40, p. 7]. Although this survey was revealed in 1966, after the victory of Proposition 14 at the polls, the fight was not yet over. The constitutionality of the law was subsequently challenged and the California Real Estate Association had allocated $110,000 for its defense. The amendment was nevertheless struck down by the California High Court the same year. An analysis of variations within the State of California in support of, or opposition to, Proposition 14 revealed a complex pattern of responses intimately related not only to race, but to region, education, and income levels, as well as to political ideology [45]. In the last instance, the role of the realtor was taken specifically into account when the California Democratic Council passed a resolution in 1964 urging that only those realtors who supported the Rumford Act be patronized. While this resolution found strong support among Democrats generally, leading Republican groups were active in endorsing repeal of the act. But here again regional differences came into play. It was determined that in the San Francisco Bay Area 33 per cent of Republicans actually planned to vote "no" on Proposition 14, as opposed to only 14 per cent of Republicans in southern California. As might be expected, *the clearest line of opposition to Proposition 14 was drawn with respect to race.* It was found that "by October [1964] Negroes were uniformly opposed to Proposition 14, a vote intention consistent with their equally unanimous support of the Rumford Act" [45, p. 757]. In statewide balloting, the San Francisco Bay Area voted 42 per cent against the proposition, compared with a 32 per cent "no" vote in the Los Angeles area.

The divisive, highly emotional campaign in California did little to enhance the realtor's image in California, or the rest of the nation for that matter. Indeed, it was a source of genuine concern to the industry. As anyone who is familiar with its literature is aware, realtors see themselves as salesmen first and foremost; and great stress is constantly placed on creating a positive public image. However this may be gilded, there is an approximate profile of reality which can be gained from a look at those who are recruited for the profession.

The Making of a Realtor

Those who have been concerned with professionalization of the real estate industry are faced at the outset with a basic problem, according to Fred Case [26], namely that the profession does not enjoy a particularly high status among college students. Assuming that there is a body of specialized real estate knowledge which can be acquired through institutions of higher learning, it was found that real estate is almost never considered as a career by the great majority of students now attending California state colleges. Only one half of 1 per cent, in fact, was prepared to choose real estate for a career; upper division students ranked it eleventh out of fifteen selected professions. It was concluded, in part, that "unless a quite significant proportion of the students majoring in business administration plan to enter real estate, it is quite improbable that the needs for new salesmen in the real estate industry can be met from the ranks of college students in the foreseeable future" [26, pp. 9–10].

Case further indicated that "a major reason for entering the field is based on economic values as opposed to values concerned with service to others, interest in the work itself, and so on. Economic values are usually more often held by older and perhaps more mature individuals" [26, p. 10].

This observation coincided with a study by Wilson and Cleveland on real estate turnover which stated as its first major conclusion: "Individuals in the age brackets between 30 and 55 whose motivations are economic and materialistic as opposed to being social or selfish [sic], for example, 'liking to work with people,' or 'regulating own hours,' appear to have a good chance of success" [44, p. 22]. With respect to professionalization and the question of realtor education, the findings indicated that "formal education was not an important factor in determining whether an individual would remain in real estate sales or leave the field once he had decided to change his employing broker" [44, p. 20]. Allowing that these findings would be "difficult" to accept, the authors "welcomed" them, saying: "It substantiates our opinion that real estate sales is one of the few remaining opportunities for intelligent, ambitious men and women who have not had the opportunity for a college education" [44, p. 20]. If, in addition to the educational picture, we add the fact that of the 234 individuals sampled in the Wilson-Cleveland study the average age was forty-five, the profile of a middle-aged individual with a minimal formal educational background begins to emerge as a typical real estate agent.

With particular respect to race, Rose Helper's [10] study on the racial policies and practices of the real estate industry helps to complete the picture. Using what she terms an "ideological" approach in a study of racial attitudes of brokers as well as the real estate board itself, she concluded that the majority of brokers share an "exclusion ideology" expressed as follows:

> White people do not want Negroes as neighbors, property values decline when Negroes enter an area, residential integration is not likely for a long time to come if at all, there are harmful consequences for the people of a white community when Negroes enter, and it is morally wrong or violates some principle or value of the real estate business or of the country to sell or rent to Negroes in a white area [10, p. 144].

Although descriptive of a majority of brokers, it does not apply to all of them. The exclusionist grades into the "integrationist" which at the extreme end is the "deviant," or, as one black appraiser in Oakland described him, "the renegade broker. They're the ones that open things up."

Yet many people today number among their acquaintances someone who "practices a little real estate." He, or she, may be a full-time professional, or may practice only on occasion. Educational levels range from those with less than a high school diploma to those with university graduate degrees [18].

Typically, the broker's office is a small one, managed by the broker himself with perhaps the assistance of one or two salesmen. In Oakland, for example, there are 376 brokers listed and 548 salesmen, which averages roughly one and a half salesmen per broker. One of the largest firms employs 83 brokers and salesmen operating from three branch offices, and grossed $125 million in 1969. Its interests are of course diversified into commercial and industrial real estate as well as residential. The small broker's practice, on the other hand, is confined primarily to residential property. He usually "works" an area or neighborhood of limited extent. Since he gets to be well known, and his income is usually modest, he is rather well attuned to the private wishes and prejudices of his area. And should he violate any of the "ethics" of his profession, especially that one regarding the showing of property to black buyers in white neighborhoods, any pressures brought to bear or sanctions imposed upon him could be financially disastrous. Not so with the larger firms whose larger diversified resources enable them to resist such pressures more successfully, and who, at the same time, do not relish the adverse publicity that might attend a lawsuit which more and more frequently is being resorted to by blacks in order to overcome racial prejudice in obtaining housing. On the other hand, the larger firms have not used their greater leverage to bring about fair housing practices among realtors. The National Association of Real Estate Boards still sets policy, and this policy is not much more forward looking than it was a quarter of a century ago.

CURRENT ATTITUDES OF THE INDUSTRY

The total outlawing of racial discrimination in housing was achieved through the Supreme Court's decision of June 17, 1968 (*Jones v. Mayer*, 1968), which established, under the Civil Rights Act of 1968, the fact that *all* racial discrimination in housing is illegal. In response to this decision, the executive secretary of NAREB called upon all realtors to comply with the decision saying: "The Negro in America is henceforth a free man, or, if there be any further impediment to that freedom in the future, the court noted the means by which it would be struck down" [38]. Pointing out that the position of those who opposed open housing laws had been "forever negated," he called upon the nation's realtors to consider the means by which the new mandate would be implemented. In practice, however, the industry's social concern assumed a somewhat different focus. In his 1969 acceptance speech, the new president of NAREB stated, "The first civil right for all Americans is to be safe from personal assault" [39]. He urged further that a more energetic prosecution of "Light the Night" and other "anti-crime" programs be undertaken.

But let us return to the San Francisco Bay Area for an example of current industry practices.

In the thirty years since the start of World War II, the black population of Oakland, California, has increased enormously, both absolutely and proportionately. Less than 9,000 black residents made up 2.8 per cent of the city's population in 1940. By 1966 these figures were 110,850 and 29.7 per cent, respectively. In 1950, 70 per cent of Oakland's black population, approximately 33,000, were crowded into the "traditional" West side ghetto. With the postwar resumption of housing construction, new opportunities for blacks to acquire housing developed in the city, particularly in East Oakland, as the white population began moving into new tract developments appearing in southern Alameda County: San Leandro, Castro Valley, and Hayward. In spite of some leapfrogging southward, particularly into Castro Valley and Hayward, initially by middle-class professionals, black settlement was effectively stopped at the San Leandro boundary.

In 1968, a study was made of integration in southern Alameda County concentrating on Hayward, which had a somewhat larger black population than either San Leandro or Castro Valley. A total of fifty-five families were interviewed. "Many clients mentioned 'getting the runaround from realtors,'" the report said in part, citing reasons given by realtors as the clients were "too young" or "too old," that they had nothing for the clients and weren't likely to, or that the realty company was afraid to take a Negro client [33, p. 6]. In its conclusions the report made the following important observation:

> Once moved in, only five clients had a hostile or distinctly cold reception, and in each case the acceptance improved to normal within a matter of months. Children found a normal acceptance level fairly quickly (with few exceptions) and generally encountered only normal school problems. The black family moving into an all-white neighborhood got a cooler reception than in an "integrated" neighborhood, but as time passed there became no appreciable difference in attitudes [33, pp. 12–13].

This conclusion is in accord with findings that the basic racial attitudes of white Americans have indeed been changing [31, 32, 43], yet they remain markedly ambivalent. According to one survey [31], only 23 per cent of southerners indicated that they would actually move, sell, or get out. Even in Chicago, the nation's "most segregated city," one study has shown that there are thousands of homes that are available on a non-discriminating basis in that city's suburbs [29, p. 259].

Why, then, does the real estate industry remain apparently so intransigent and so hostile to the idea of racially integrated housing?

In seeking an answer—or answers—to this question, it should be kept in mind that individually the "typical" realtor as he has been described is probably not a great deal less vulnerable to changing racial attitudes than anyone else. If he assumes the mantle of protector of white neighborhoods, it would seem that the motives lie deeper than simply a wish to maintain racially pure neighborhoods. With the perpetual and heavy emphasis placed on the profits to be gained in the business, and considering the motives for entering the profession that we have examined earlier, something more than simple racism seems to suggest itself as the essential reason for the desire to maintain racial separation in housing. What, in fact, is the realtor selling above and beyond the physical structure of the residence we may ask. The answer is: private knowledge as to the location of available desirable residences. And within this body of private knowledge is a premium item to many prospective buyers: the all-white neighborhood.

> What they [realtors] fear is that any reduction in their power to keep minority families out of all white neighborhoods will increase the volume of direct dealing between buyers and sellers. In home sales, constituting the entire business of 90 percent of the agents, direct deals are usually assumed to be about 30–40 percent of all transactions, and when they can be brought to a frank discussion of the issues, many realtors said . . . that they believed this figure would be much higher if there were any way in which all brokers could be forced to make their services available on a nondiscriminatory basis [28, p. Ja 10].

Even as the Taeubers and others have pointed out, there is still a considerable profit to be made in maintaining a dual housing market.

> It can be assumed that the supply of housing for nonwhites is restricted in terms of both numbers of units and quality of units. For nonwhites, then, demand is high relative to supply, and this situation is aggravated by the rapidly increasing urban Negro population. Housing within Negro areas can command higher prices than comparable housing in white residential areas. Furthermore, there has been a continual need for Negro housing which has been met by transferring property at the periphery of Negro areas from the white housing market to the Negro housing market. The high demand among Negroes for housing,

combined with the relatively low demand among whites for housing in many of these peripheral areas, makes the transfer of housing from whites to Negroes profitable [19, p. 25].

The successful prosecution of such a policy necessarily entails the exploitation of white fears of blacks as neighbors. This lends an important element of certainty and control—the flight response—in a unique type of sales market where uncertainty is the rule. A house is the major purchase of a lifetime for most families, and the closing of a sale can be forestalled by countless developments—illness or death, a "cloud" on the title, financing problems, or simply a change of mind. Bringing a sale to a successful close is not a simple matter, and the broker managing the transaction has few controls over the numerous variables that affect the ultimate decision of the potential buyer or seller. The ambivalent racial attitude of most Americans is a powerful weapon upon which he can count with certainty. There is no doubt but that the caste mentality is very much alive in spite of evident moderation over the years in overtly expressed forms of racial prejudice. Yet there are some signs of change even here.

In 1969, five years after a black realtor testified before a Civil Rights Commission concerning the discriminatory practices of Oakland's Real Estate Board [42], a new executive officer was hired. Under his leadership the board has been moving in a different direction. An Equal Rights Committee has been formed headed by that same realtor, and through it black members have been particularly active in "pressuring and educating" white members as to the present laws concerning civil rights in the sale and rental of housing. It was found that a great many of the white brokers were almost totally ignorant of the new laws. Their efforts have received substantial support in the expanding number of young white brokers. Private listing services, which have been used to avoid giving black brokers access to housing information in certain suburban areas, have come under heavy pressure from the board. Further, it is expected that in 1972 the board will, at its annual election, elect a black president for the first time in its history.

SUMMARY AND CONCLUSIONS

The firm control that NAREB has historically exerted over racial policies and practices of the real estate industry could never have remained so effective had these policies not found a sympathetic response in the racial attitudes of the vast majority of workaday white real estate agents. But there are also numerous other individual practitioners who have exerted wholehearted efforts and made great personal sacrifices in order to see racial equality in housing put into practice. These "friendly brokers," as they are referred to by the fair housing groups, have been instrumental in helping to break down entrenched residential segregation in many urban areas. But it is questionable it seems, to depend upon these people of good will as being the solution to the problem.

In 1966, the Department of Justice did in fact begin an investigation of the racial policies and practices of real estate boards [30, p. 1]. These began as investigations of anti-trust violations. Now, with the additional machinery of the 1968 Civil Rights Act, abolishing all forms of racial discrimination in housing, legal attacks upon housing discrimination can be more widely based. The real estate industry indicated that it was alert to the dangers of these developments, preferring to settle matters when they arose, and out of court, to avoid setting yet more restrictive legal precedents.

What then can be done?

Obviously a continuing effort must be made to provide immediate and effective legal redress in all cases of racial discrimination in housing. But the fundamentally economic motives underlying the behavior of the real estate industry and the great majority of its brokers and salespeople should not be overlooked. In eliciting support from this vast industry some indication as to what is possible stems from its about-face with respect to low income housing. Having formerly opposed "Turnkey" developments, NAREB realizes the advantages of a guaranteed income from the leasing of existing privately owned housing and thus now supports such programs. It still believes, however, that "public housing should be terminated and existing projects liquidated by sale to private taxpaying ownership" [36, pp. 8–9].

When the choice has to be made between racial discrimination and profits, discrimination is very likely to suffer. An example of the economic muscle that can be exerted in this direction is afforded in the case of IBM, which located a large new typewriter plant in Lexington, Kentucky [34]. When, in the late sixties, it was pointed out that IBM was not using its influence to stop local discrimination in housing, not even in assisting its own black employees, the firm's local vice-president sent a letter to Lexington's First Security National Bank concerning IBM's policy of nondiscrimination. The president of the bank sent a letter to the Lexington Real Estate Board which, in turn, contacted its Multiple Listing Service participants (the local real estate brokers).

> Within two days after the IBM letter went out, one black IBM employee who had made no progress in finding housing after two weeks of effort received nine phone calls from real estate dealers. A local realtor stated that IBM's stand would carry more weight than either Kentucky's open-housing law or the recent decision banning all discrimination in housing.

Experience has clearly demonstrated that neither legislation nor good will is enough to compel the real estate industry to abandon its long established practice of racial discrimination in housing, particularly in view of the general reluctance or inability of officials to adequately enforce such legislation. The industry has shown itself to be clearly responsive to economic pressures. But perhaps the most substantial and lasting support must come from within the industry itself and from the internal pressures generated by black members themselves, supported by a more progressive membership of young white brokers and salesmen.

LITERATURE CITED

1. Berston, H. M. *California Real Estate Practice*. Homewood, Ill.: Richard D. Irwin, 1968.

2. Case, F. E. *Real Estate Brokerage*. Englewood Cliffs: Prentice-Hall, 1965.

3. Chicago Commission on Race Relations. *The Negro in Chicago*. Chicago: University of Chicago Press, 1922.

4. Denton, J. H. *Apartheid American Style*. Berkeley: Diable Press, 1967.

5. Dollard, J. *Caste and Class in a Southern Town*. New Haven: Yale University Press, 1937.

6. Drake, St. Clair and H. Cayton. *Black Metropolis*. New York: Harper and Row, 1962.

7. Du Bois, W. E. B. *The Philadelphia Negro*. New York: Schocken Books, 1967.

8. Frazier, E. F. *The Negro Family in Chicago*. Chicago: University of Chicago Press, 1932.

9. Harrington, M. *The Other America*. Baltimore: Penguin Books, 1964.

10. Helper, R. *Racial Policies and Practices of Real Estate Brokers*. Minneapolis: University of Minnesota Press, 1969.

11. Hughes, E. *A Study of a Secular Institution: The Chicago Real Estate Board*. Unpublished Ph.D. dissertation, University of Chicago, 1928.

12. Johnson, C. S. *Patterns of Negro Segregation*. New York: Harper and Brothers, 1943.

13. Long, H. H. and C. S. Johnson. *People vs. Property; Race Restrictive Covenants in Housing*. Nashville: Fisk University Press, 1947.

14. McEntire, D. *Residence and Race; Final and Comprehensive Report to the Commission on Race and Housing*. Berkeley: University of California Press, 1960.

15. Myrdal, G. *An American Dilemma*. New York: Harper and Row, 1944.

16. National Institute of Real Estate Brokers. *Real Estate Salesman's Handbook*. Fifth rev. ed. Chicago: National Institute of Real Estate Brokers of the National Association of Real Estate Boards, 1969.

17. Osofsky, G. *Harlem: The Making of a Ghetto*. New York: Harper and Row, 1963.

18. Pierovich, A. and H. O. Bain. *A Survey of California's Real Estate Industry: Its Characteristics and Information Sources*. Berkeley: University of California, Institute of Urban and Regional Development, Center for Real Estate and Urban Economics, 1963.

19. Taeuber, E. E. and A. F. Taeuber. *Negroes in Cities*. Chicago: Aldine, 1965.

20. Tocqueville, A. *Democracy in America*. 2 vols. New York: Vintage Books, 1965.

21. U. S. Federal Housing Administration. *Underwriting Manual; Underwriting and Valuation Procedure under Title II of the National Housing Act*. Washington, G.P.O., 1938.

22. Vose, C. E. *Caucasians Only; The Supreme Court, the NAACP, and the Restrictive Covenant Cases*. Berkeley: University of California Press, 1959.

23. Wade, R. C. *Slavery in the Cities*. New York: Oxford University Press, 1964.

24. Weaver, R. C. *The Negro Ghetto*. New York: Russell and Russell, 1948.

25. *California Real Estate Magazine*, 44 (December 1963).

26. Case, F. E. "Is Professionalization Necessary for Real Estate Success," *California Real Estate Magazine*, 50 (June 1970), pp. 6–8.

27. Conser, E. P. *Historical Background of the Realtor's Position in Race Relations*. National Association of Real Estate Boards, n.d. Reprint of a series of editorials published in *Realtor's Headlines* (January–March 1965).

28. Denton, J. H. "Study and Report on the Listing Practices of Real Estate Agents." Appendix J of National Committee Against Discrimination in Housing and U. S. Department of Housing and Urban Development, *Urban Renewal Demonstration Project, 1970* (No. Calif., D-8), Phase I Report. n.d., pp. Ja–1–Ja–36. (Mimeographed.)

29. Freeman, H. M. "Desegregation of Chicago Suburbs," *Journal of Intergroup Relations*, 4 (Autumn 1965), pp. 259–68.

30. Gall, P. "Government Plans Fight Against Bias in Housing Using Monopoly Laws," *Wall Street Journal*, February 4, 1968, p. 1.

31. Gallup, G. "Shift of Views on Interracial Marriage?" *San Francisco Chronicle*, September 10, 1970, p. 55.

32. Gross, L. "America's Mood Today," *Look*, 29 (June 29, 1965), pp. 15–21.

33. Lewis, A. "Integration in Southern Alameda County." San Francisco, Council for Civic Unity of the S.F. Bay Area, 1968. (Typescript.)

34. Lowe, J. R. "Race, Jobs, and Cities; What Business Can Do," *Saturday Review*, 52 (January 11, 1969), pp. 27–30; 91–92.

35. Morrill, R. L. "The Negro Ghetto: Problems and Alternatives," *Geographical Review*, 55 (July, 1965), pp. 337–61.

36. National Association of Real Estate Boards, "Statement of Policy," *California Real Estate Magazine*, 50 (January 1970), pp. 8–9.

37. *Realtor's Headlines* (National Association of Real Estate Boards), 32 (March 15, 1965).

38. *Realtor's Headlines* (National Association of Real Estate Boards), 35 (July 1, 1968).

39. *Realtor's Headlines* (National Association of Real Estate Boards), 36 (February 3, 1969).

40. "Realtors' Image Wilts Under Magnifying Glass," *Trends in Housing* (National Committee Against Discrimination in Housing), 10 (March–April 1966), p. 7.

41. Sheatsley, P. B. and H. H. Hyman. "Attitudes on Desegregation," *Scientific American*, 211 (July 1964), pp. 16–23.

42. Slaughter, A. M. "Testimony before the U. S. Commission on Civil Rights, Oakland, California, May 12, 1964." (Typescript.)

43. Taeuber, K. "Residential Segregation," *Scientific American*, 213 (August 1965), pp. 12–19.

44. Wilson, J. E. and T. Cleveland. "A Case Study of the Causes of Real Estate Turnover," *California Real Estate Magazine*, 50 (July 1970), pp. 20–22.

45. Wolfinger, R. E. and F. I. Greenstein. "The Repeal of Fair Housing in California: An Analysis of Referendum Voting," *American Political Science Review*, 42 (September 1968), pp. 753–69.

CHAPTER IV

Race, Economics, and the City

INTRODUCTORY NOTE

Although geographers have long examined locational aspects and areal patterns of economic activities, they have not exhausted all possibilities for worthwhile study. It is well known and documented that economic phenomena vary from country to country and regionally within a single nation. However, economic variations resulting from cultural and racial differences are not so well recognized or understood.

The economic situation of blacks in the United States is regarded by several social scientists as pathological in nature. Many blacks are members of lower economic classes. Living in dilapidated housing and owning little personal property, blacks are heavily unemployed, underemployed, and large numbers are on the verge of starvation.

One important factor in continuance of a plural society in the United States is economic discrimination, relegating to ethnic and racial minorities lower wages, entry level jobs, token employment, and high rates of unemployment and underemployment. Widespread practices of economic discrimination (coupled with discrimination in education, housing, etc.) are all the less tenable in a country that steadfastly maintains it is the land of equality, where everyone ostensibly is accorded the same treatment under law. However, social scientists have demonstrated repeatedly the absurdity of such idealistic claims of freedom and equality, especially for members of minority groups.

White economic exploitation forcing blacks into vicious circles of poverty is one aspect of economic geography that must be examined fully. However, until recently, this has not been the case. The following articles are among the few to explore this new research frontier on social geographic aspects of economics. Allan Pred's research illustrates that commercial land use patterns provide microcosms of material features of culture that are ideal bases for cross-cultural comparison. Harold Rose investigates effects of race on retail structure in racially changing neighborhood trade areas. James Wheeler is concerned with different locational aspects of journey-to-work in black areas.

Business thoroughfares and commercial centers often reflect the culture of an area's inhabitants. Inherent attributes of an ethnic community are easily visible in its business district. "Chinatown," "Little Italy," "Latin Quarter," and the "Black Belt" are all examples of cultural uniqueness in locational expression of ethnicity.

To corroborate this notion, Allan Pred investigates, compares, and contrasts three culturally distinct business thoroughfare land use patterns in Chicago, Illinois. His specific purpose is to identify phenomena which distinguish commercial land use patterns of the black community from two white areas, one low income and one middle income, and to determine which factors underlie these differences.

In classifying commercial land use data, Pred utilizes four subjective categories: land uses which appear to be characteristic of black areas; uses which appear to be characteristic of white areas; uses which appear to be characteristic of low-income business areas; and those which are common to all three areas. This methodology has several procedural difficulties. It is difficult to identify features typical of a certain area and even more difficult to avoid falling into the trap of using stereotypical images instead of factual characterizations based on empirical evidence.

Pred concludes that the atmosphere of low-income black business thoroughfares is more than a result of externally imposed economic conditions. The author maintains these commercial establishments are expressions of aggregate behavior and needs of an individual subculture. Thus, examination of land use patterns constitutes a valid cross-cultural technique in social and geographic ethnic-racial research.

Harold Rose analyzes locational significance of commercial trade in a racially changing neighborhood, with the social characteristic, race, an important factor affecting retail trade structure from both consumer and retailer viewpoints. Specifically, Rose examines changes in retail structure of a given trade area in relation to entry of black economic participants. The study area consists of three contiguous black neighborhoods in Milwaukee, Wisconsin, containing several unplanned shopping centers. Rose maintains analysis of racial factors in structure of retail trade is complicated because areas of black economic expansion are also areas of decline and decay, factors basically unrelated to racial situation.

Rose uses a Markov Chain model to analyze effects of areal development of a black ghetto on retail structure of trade. The model assumes dependency between predicted occurrence and immediately preceding events. A matrix of transitional probabilities is constructed for retail trade areas for 1955, 1960, and 1965. Analysis shows shifts in retail trade over the five-year periods and reflects changing racial composition of the area's population. Markov's analysis proves successful in predicting changes in retail character of the study areas and also predicting black entry into commercial areas.

Because of competition decline for business space in older areas of the city, small low-order businesses are entering at a rapid pace, hastening evolution of the area to commercial blight. Rose views race as a catalytic in this commercial transition. He concludes continuous expansion of ghettos also indicates continuous spread of commercial blight.

Inadequate transportation facilities and opportunities limit blacks in many everyday activities and perpetuate black isolation in ghettos. Poor transportation minimizes black social interaction with whites and restricts economic opportunities open to blacks. James O. Wheeler focuses on journey-to-work trips in Tulsa, Oklahoma, to illustrate differences in black and white travel behavior. In addition he outlines some major barriers to locational mobility among urban blacks. His major hypothesis is travel differences between blacks and whites may be explained by the fact that blacks are forced to travel considerable distances to find employment because they are limited in choice of residential location. Initial transportation and occupation advantages of living near the central business district are sharply curtailed by suburbanization of work places.

Wheeler uses a travel time index to compute black work trips in Tulsa. He establishes the average black work trip is approximately one-half mile longer than the white work trip. Factors aggravating this problem are that blacks live in areas serviced by inadequate transportation and congested with considerable vehicular traffic. Because of low per capita ownership of automobiles, they must rely upon poor public transportation facilities or are forced to walk to work.

Wheeler concludes that black employment patterns are spread more widely over the metropolitan area than their residential patterns. Blacks living near the CBD move counter to major commuter streams, both morning and night, depending in large part for their transit needs on buses, whose travel patterns are highly circuitous and correspondingly slow.

The principal hypothesis of forced mobility is upheld only for black women, as black and white men show no significant differences in travel to work. According to Wheeler, resolution of racial inequities in journey-to-work patterns involves the larger problem of urban transportation and upward social mobility of blacks. Thus, solutions to these complex problems are not limited to the ghetto alone but are enigmas which face the total urban community.

BUSINESS THOROUGHFARES AS EXPRESSIONS OF
URBAN NEGRO CULTURE

Allan Pred

An engulfing wave of cacophonous sound: from jazz and swinging syncopations blaring-pulsating over loudspeakers recessed in the interiors of bars, liquor stores and record shops; from a shabbily dressed pseudoblind mendicant, rhythmically shaking his collection box, repeatedly droning out his life song in rasping tones—"I beat the devil runnin' and I'm so glad"; from sidewalk chatterers, the hat-crowned idle and unemployed in front of billiard parlors and barbershops; the shoppers and merchants going about their business; from the agonizing roar of the rapid transit overhead; from the honking, crowded traffic.

A dazzling montage of contrasting colors: melanous folk, ebony, bronze and tan; golden toreador slacks clinging closely to an undulating frame; sport shirts ablaze with fiery versions of every spectral hue; automobiles reflecting their turquoise-crimson-fuchsia tones on sunlit shop windows; garish signs and window paintings fronting loan banks, fundamentalist churches and unctuous eateries.

A melange of confusing odors emanating from open-doored markets and establishments; smoky-stuffiness from pool rooms and "recreation parlors"; the penetrating fumes of frying oil and "mumbo" sauce from makeshift dining places; alcoholic aromas expiring from beneath bloodshot, hungry-looking eyes.

Thus, one may impressionistically describe the commercial complex in Chicago's "Black Belt" on 47th Street, between Cottage Grove Avenue on the east and State Street on the west. Yet to think of this business street, or similar streets in other urban Negro communities, solely in such terms is to fall victim to stereotypes and to ignore features which are common to all commercial areas.

The Nature of the Study

As the "principal business thoroughfare" or "neighborhood business street"[1] is the center of human activity in any residential area its land use patterns of store types provide a telescoped expression of the material features of culture[2] and an ideal basis for comparing such features from community to community.

Contrasts between the commercial land uses of a city's residential areas are likely to be most striking when they are between those of the slum areas and other areas. Whether dealing with the "Black Belt" of Chicago, the Arab quarter of Marseilles, the rocky ridges overlooking Rio de Janeiro's business district, the maze of makeshift structures lying at the periphery of Calcutta, or the slum area of any contemporary metropolis, one is usually speaking of an area whose population is not completely acculturated, not totally assimilated into the prevailing urban way of life.

Even in those instances where a great proportion of the slum population has been in residence for a considerable period of time, rather than being of recent in-migrant status, the daily pattern of existence in the slum is one which, in varying degrees, normally manifests some vestiges of a subculture or way of life which is foreign to the particular city—whether the subculture in question be that of a nearby rural area, of another section of the country, or of another land. This being the case, it is to be expected that these subcultural differences will find some expression in patterns of consumer behavior and thereby be reflected in the land use structure of the slum's principal business thoroughfare or market.

The main body of this paper is devoted to investigating, comparing, and contrasting the business thoroughfare land use patterns—as external expressions of culture—of a Chicago Negro area and two nearby white areas. The primary objective is to establish those phenomena which distinguish the commercial land uses of the urban Negro subculture, and to determine what factors underlie their differences. In a broader sense, the paper may be viewed as a case study of the slum as a mirror of other subcultures. Its approach is perhaps also of some importance to the even more general problem of categorizing subjective field observations.

Numerous drawbacks and problems are inherent in the approach and objectives of this study. Previous works on the American Negro written by geographers are strikingly small in number and provide no methodological assistance. Four articles have considered different spatial and temporal variations in the distribution of Negro population in the United States.[3] Hart's note on a Negro resort area in Michigan makes passing references to commercial establishments.[4] An article by Nelson contains a short note on the distribution of Negroes in cities of different service classifications.[5]

The type of data being dealt with, namely store-front characteristics, and the necessity of compartmentalizing this data into a few categories, presents a considerable problem. In striving to capture outward expressions of culture in the urban landscape, one must group and classify data which are essentially subjective, impressionistic, raw, and unrefined. Consequently, in the initial stages of investigation it is difficult to avoid making some highly arbitrary decisions which, in the end, may or may not prove to be inconsistent. Only after considerable field work does it become even remotely possible to establish more precisely defined categories which, though still subjective to some degree, are yet capable of lending themselves to statistical analysis.

An additional obstacle is that of avoiding stereotypes in attempting to explain the presence or absence of given phenomena in Negro areas. Of particular complexity is the problem of distinguishing between phenomena which are "typical" of Negro areas in general, those which are "typical" of low-income Negro areas, and those which are "typical" of all areas that are inhabited by a population of low socioeconomic status. However, the desire to avoid stereotypes should not be overdone since, through the research of competent sociologists, many widely held preconceptions have been proven to be reasonably accurate for certain Negro economic classes and personality types.[6]

AREAS OF STUDY AND LAND USE CATEGORIES

At one time it could be said that "The present shopping center of the [Chicago] Negro community is 47th Street, having moved south through the years from 35th Street until it is now at the center of density of the 'Black Belt.' On this street is the largest retail business owned and operated by Negroes."[7] A portion of this street, between Cottage Grove on the east and State on the west, serves as the focal point of this study. Forty-seventh Street is the most important commercial ribbon development in Chicago Community Area 38.[8] That 47th Street still maintains its position of primacy within the "Black Belt" is highly dubious. In 1954, the retail sales volume of the commercial complex on 63rd Street, between Stony Island and Cottage Grove, was at least eight times that of the 47th Street strip.[9] However, the 47th Street ribbon actually extends considerably east of Cottage Grove, meaning that its total retail sales volume is actually larger than that indicated in available sources, and the clientele on 63rd Street is not as overwhelmingly composed of Negroes as that of the 47th Street complex. While 47th Street may not be the most important ribbon development in the entire "Black Belt," there is no disputing that it

TABLE I

Population and Income Characteristics of Selected Areas in 1950[a]

	Community area 38 (47th Street)		Community area 61 (Ashland)		Census tracts 636–638 (71st Street)	
	Number	Per cent	Number	Per cent	Number	Per cent
Total population	114,557	100.0	75,917	100.0	18,056	100.0
Native white	892	0.8	62,947	83.0	b	—
Foreign born white	183	0.2	12,829[c]	16.9	b	—
Negro	113,374	98.9	112	0.1	0	0.0
Median family income (dollars)	2,527		3,727		6,000	
Land area (sq. miles)	1.76		5.0		0.5	
Length of business thoroughfare (miles)	1.0		0.9		0.5	

[a]Sources: Local Community Fact Book for Chicago, op. cit., pp. 158-161, 178-181, and 250-253; and Chicagoland's Retail Market, op. cit., pp. 55, 81 and 125.

[b]Not available.

[c]Of which 5416 were Poles, and nearly 3000 of other Slavic nationalities.

is the principal business thoroughfare of a community inhabited by well over 100,000 Negroes (Table I).

Two relatively nearby business thoroughfares in white communities were selected for examination and comparison. One of these comprises a segment of Ashland, from 46th Street on the north to 51st Street on the south, as well as another portion of 47th Street which runs from Ashland on the east to Wood on the west. This is the largest commercial development in Chicago Community Area 61—an area which is dominated by Poles and other Slavic groups.[10] This business development serves as an almost ideal basis for comparison, since the income level of the community area which it dominates is extremely low for a white residential area.

The other white community business thoroughfare is located in a middle-class neighborhood on 71st Street, between Jeffrey on the west and South Shore Drive on the east. This is the most important business thoroughfare in census tracts 636–638, which are in Chicago Community Area 43. Because of the much higher income level in this Community Area, the contrasts between it and the Negro area are much more glaring than those between the low-income Ashland complex and the Negro area.

Preliminary mapping of land uses on each of the thoroughfares was carried out by using the personal service, business service, and retail categories set forth in the Census of Business. The result was a land use map showing no less than sixty-five commercial and professional uses; it is of little value because of its complexity and consequent inability adequately to show the areal differences which were so apparent in the field. After some hesitation and deliberation the diverse uses were subjectively classified into four major categories: (A) those uses which appeared to be more characteristic of, although not necessarily unique to, the Negro area; (B) those uses which appeared to be most characteristic of low-income area business thoroughfares; (C) those uses which were common to all three areas; and (D) those uses which appeared to be more characteristic of, although not necessarily unique to, white areas. A not inconsiderable number of uses were left uncategorized because of their rare occurrence or other complicating factors. In no case was there any possibility that the unclassified use was one unique to 47th Street.

The difficulties in distinguishing between the four major categories, and particularly between the first two, were often quite intricate and involved. It is no mean task to distinguish that which is "typical" of a Negro area and its culture from that which is "typical" of low socioeconomic areas; consequently the decisions made are to some degree at variance with one another. The following two examples may be given:—(1) Bars were found to be of approximately the same relative frequency on both 47th Street and in the Ashland complex, and were consequently classified in the second category, namely most characteristic of low-income area business thoroughfares. This was done despite the fact that the bars in the two neighborhoods present a totally different appearance to the observer in the field. Bars in the white area have, more often than not, a very unimposing exterior which tends to give an impression that very little is going on inside. In contrast, those in the Negro area tend to exude a character which is distinctly their own—music blasting from an open doorway, an off-beat name, and a window cluttered with colors and advertisements. (2) Dry-cleaning and other "valet" services are striking in their number and unimpressive appearance on 47th Street, and for this reason were classified as more "typical" of the Negro area. However, it is questionable whether this land use reflects an aspect of urban Negro culture (something inherent to the Negro's self-directed pattern of existence) or an aspect of the limited economic horizons of a large proportion of the urban Negro population (an externally imposed characteristic). On the one hand, there is some evidence that certain Negro personality types are quite concerned with personal appearance,[11] whereas, on the other hand, it has been shown that this business type attracts Negro investors because it does not require a large capital outlay.[12]

MORE CHARACTERISTICALLY NEGRO LAND USES

The land uses in this category, which is summarized in Table II, presumably distinguish the low-income Negro area business thoroughfare from all other residential area business thoroughfares in Chicago. In addition, it may be anticipated that these land uses occur frequently in low-income Negro communities in other American cities.

Beauty parlors and barbershops are the most frequently occurring store-front phenomena on 47th Street, between Cottage Grove and State. The beauty shops (which are twice as common as the barbershops) are generally drab in appearance though they are occasionally distinguished by their exotic names, such as "Tropical Beauty Nook," "The Treasure Chest," "Sarah's Beauty Box." The barbershops are typified by a somewhat neater appearance, by small groups of men idling outside, and by the presence of additional functions such as bail bonding and shoeshining. If undocumented sources are correct, these shops also serve as "fronts" for the negotiation of various illegal activities. The high rate of occurrence of beauty parlors and barbershops seems to be attributable to at least two factors. First, the stereotype of the Negro's concern about the woolly or "kinky" quality of his hair is apparently true for certain Negro economic groups and personality types.[13] This is substantiated by advertisements for "hair processing" which appear in the majority of establishments, and by the fact that expenditure for barbershop and beauty parlor services, at

TABLE II

Distribution of Land Uses in Category A: More Characteristic of 47th Street

	47th Street		Ashland		71st Street	
	Number	Per cent	Number	Per cent	Number	Per cent
Total store-fronts	343	100.0	250	100.0	165	100.0
Total in Category A	132	38.7	17	6.8	31	18.8
Beauty parlors and barbershops	37	10.8	4	1.6	14	8.5
Dry cleaners and other "valet" services	31	9.1	4	1.6	12	7.3
Tailor-made men's clothing	6	1.7	0	0.0	0	0.0
Disassociated uses	16	4.7	1	0.4	0	0.0
Independent groceries	17	5.0	5	2.0	4	2.4
Billiard parlors	9	2.7	0	0.0	0	0.0
Record stores	7	2.0	2	0.8	1	0.6
Store-front churches and spiritual consultants	9	2.7	1	0.4	0	0.0

given income levels, have been found to be "somewhat higher for Negro than white families in urban areas."[14] Second, these businesses fall into Frazier's category of "personal services" which attract Negro investors because of the absence of any need to make large capital outlays.[15] However, because of the first factor this commercial land-use type may be considered a reflection of a segment of urban Negro culture.

It is evident, from Table II, that beauty parlors and barbershops have a relatively high rate of incidence on the middle-class white business thoroughfare (71st Street). There is, however, such a distinct contrast in physical appearance between the shops on 47th Street and 71st Street that there is no need to question the misleading nature of the comparative percentages shown in the table for this phenomenon. Beauty parlors on both the white commercial streets present a very aseptic exterior, whereas those on 47th Street are usually located in obviously decrepit quarters.

The frequency of dry-cleaning and associated valet service establishments on 47th Street has already been mentioned. In addition to a more frequent occurrence, particularly in comparison with the low-income white Ashland complex, dry-cleaning establishments on 47th Street have an external aspect which clearly sets them apart from their counterparts on 71st Street and on Ashland. These establishments are generally unimposing, often to the point of being rundown, and perform additional valet functions, usually hat blocking. As previously indicated, the number of valet services on 47th Street may or may not be a reflection of the concern for personal appearance held by certain Negro personality types. To the extent that this concern for personal appearance may be held responsible, the frequent occurrence of valet services may be considered as a component of urban Negro culture.

Stores selling tailor-made men's clothing were found to be unique to 47th Street. An explanation for this stems partly from the fact that Negroes "may attach more importance than whites to clothing,"[16] and from the fact that some male Negroes, particularly those of darker skin in the lower income classes, are inclined to be "flashy" in dress.[17] Because of this factor, custom-made men's clothing stores may be considered along with beauty parlors, barbershops, and valet service establishments as a single subcategory—all three uses being, to some extent, a response to the needs of different Negro personality types who are in one way or another concerned with personal appearance.

The next two land uses which are more characteristic of 47th Street may also be grouped into a subcategory, insofar as they both mirror extremely low economic conditions. The first is the not uncommonly occurring group of disassociated uses within one store possessing a single entrance. The following are but a few examples of the combinations which are to be encountered on 47th Street: record shop and beauty parlor, radio-TV repairs and shoe repairs, barbershop and insurance agent, and barbershop and billiard hall. On the side streets off 47th Street, the juxtaposed uses are sometimes even more bizarre: a "restaurant" and coal-hauling service, a sandwich shop and extermination service, for example. These combinations are apparently related to the marginal character of some of the businesses and the inability of most of the businessmen involved to bring in enough revenue to pay rentals by themselves.

The second store type in this subcategory is that run by the independent grocer or food merchant. The profusion of these stores (which often stay open twenty-four hours per day) is presumably a reflection of the willingness of many Negroes to pay high prices on credit, rather than lower prices in cash at large chain stores. Independent groceries on 47th Street, and their less numerous Ashland counterparts, may be distinguished by certain items which they carry. Neck bones or chicken necks are the most conspicuously advertised items to be found in 47th Street groceries or butcher shops; they contrast starkly with the choice meats, poultry and sea food displayed in 71st Street butcher-shop windows. Other food consumption patterns of low-income urban Negroes also determine the merchandise carried by independent grocers (for example, turnip greens and other leafy, green, and yellow vegetables).[18] However, as such commodities are not prominently advertised or arranged in store windows, they do not make an impact upon the urban landscape and are not, therefore, of such interest as the more obviously displayed items. In speaking of such "interesting differences" in food consumption, Myrdal points out that: "One may call these . . . differences 'cultural,' but that does not mean that they have nothing to do with economics. In part they may depend on traditions from a time when the Negro's economic conditions were different. In part they may depend on circumstances inherent in the Negro's present economic status."[19]

The remaining land uses which are more characteristic of 47th Street all conform in some way to stereotypes commonly held by various segments of the American white population. Although Table II shows billiard parlors to be unique to 47th Street, such establishments are occasionally encountered in white communities. However, 47th Street's preponderance of these "recreation centers" (and the groups of milling men in their interiors) would, at first sight, seem to confirm the stereotype of the Negro as idle and "shiftless." Obviously, if the stereotype is accurate in any way it does not apply to Negroes as a group, but only to poolroom "hang-abouts" and other unemployed types. Once again we are confronted by the question of whether a particular land use reflects an aspect of urban Negro culture (something inherent in the Negro's self-directed pattern of existence) or an aspect of the limited economic horizons of the urban Negro population (an externally imposed characteristic). More specifically, the question to be answered in this instance is whether or not the relatively high frequency of billiard parlors is attributable to the inherent "shiftlessness" of the Negro or to the high rate of unemployment amongst Negro males, the latter being a condition often externally imposed directly via the color line in some firms and occupations, and indirectly by restricted educational opportunities.

The record shop is not an unusual sight on 47th Street, whereas its infrequent occurrence on Ashland or 71st Street is rarely if ever characterized by jazz music blaring from an open doorway. Because of their numbers, these shops could conceivably serve as a prop for the popular image of the Negro as a happy-go-lucky, carefree, music-loving individual. Yet the greater frequency of such stores on 47th Street would give little credence to this stereotype, even if it could be shown that the per capita dollar sales significantly exceed those of the smaller number of shops in the less densely populated white areas.[20] If any explanation is to be found for this phenomenon it probably lies within the subtle and complex intricacies of the Negro's cultural heritage,[21] and not within the stereotyped happy-go-lucky, carefree personality. Regardless of the underlying explanation, the noisy record shop is one of the most singular characteristics of the low-income urban Negro business thoroughfare.

The presence of store-front churches and spiritual consultants on 47th Street may be interpreted by some as an affirmation of the Negro's basically simple, if somewhat "primitive," spiritual needs. Again this is a generalization which lacks validity because it looks at Negroes as a single group rather than as a vast complex of personality types. As a rule, the store-front churches cater to first-generation migrants from the South. "The denominational churches do not always offer to the migrant the satisfaction which he found in the Church of the South. The store-front church comes into existence as a result of an effort to maintain the face-to-face relationships of the South."[22] The store-front church is not as common on 47th Street as it is on less intensely developed business thoroughfares, since the distribution of such churches is intimately related to the availability of cheap rentals.[23] In accordance with this fact, several of these fundamentalist churches were to be seen on the unmapped side streets, off 47th Street, where rents are naturally somewhat cheaper.

LAND USES MORE CHARACTERISTIC OF LOW-INCOME AREA BUSINESS THOROUGHFARES

In some respects, these uses are of greater interest than those in the previous category, in that their near-equal rate of occurrence on the low-income Negro and low-income white thoroughfares aids in dispelling certain widely held and preconceived notions of Negro behavior. On the other hand, similar frequencies of given land uses are sometimes misleading because their form and function are far from being coincident on the two thoroughfares. Therefore, it may be argued that some of these uses, once they had been more rigorously defined, could be placed in the previous category because they reflect certain aspects of urban Negro culture and because they create a singular sense of impression to the field observer.

The dingy-looking restaurant or eating place, often referred to in the vernacular as a "greasy spoon," is a commonplace on 47th Street and in the Ashland complex. Though establishments on both streets specialize in cheap foods, there are some important distinctions to be noted. Stores on Ashland have a pronounced tendency to deal in such items as hamburgers, fountain orders, and frankfurters. A few of the more decrepit-looking places on Ashland sell pizza. The menu listings on 47th Street are more often characterized by such items as fried or barbecued chicken (the acrid-odored barbecue sauce is often referred to as "mumbo" sauce in window advertisements), pigs' ears, and frog legs. It is to be recalled that Myrdal pointed out that such dietary discrepancies may be thought of as "cultural," although this does not mean that they are divorced from economic factors. In the light of these differences, as well as of the dismal aura of most of the Negro eating places, it should be recognized that a stricter definition of terms can permit the reclassification, into Category A, of most of the dining establishments on 47th Street.

The large number of bars and liquor stores on 47th Street might be offered as a substantiation of the argument that a high percentage of Negroes are large consumers of alcohol. However, Table III shows that there is approximately the same percentage of bars on the commercial streets of the low-income Slavic neighborhood. Of course, one bar on Ashland is not necessarily the equivalent of one bar on 47th Street, though in fact, the numbers in attendance at 47th Street drinking places might serve to reinforce arguments concerning Negro alcoholism. In any case, the obvious differences in external appearance between bars on 47th Street and those on Ashland have already been brought to light. The sedate appearance of the two 71st Street drinking places offers an even more striking contrast. These visual differences once again demonstrate that a more precise definition, which would distinguish between bar types, could allow for the reclassification of most of the drinking establishments on 47th Street into Category A.

Loan offices or loan "banks," and pawnshops are scattered along both low-income area business thoroughfares at about the same frequency. Loan establishments on Ashland are usually operated on a cash on interest basis, whereas stores on 47th Street are usually of the variety which

TABLE III

Distribution of Land Uses in Category B: More Characteristic of Low-Income Area Business Thoroughfares

	47th Street		Ashland		71st Street	
	Number	Per cent	Number	Per cent	Number	Per cent
Total store-fronts	343	100.0	250	100.0	165	100.0
Total in Category B	86	25.0	53	21.2	6	3.6
Cheap restaurants	20	5.8	13	5.2	2	1.2
Bars	19	5.5	14	5.6	2	1.2
Liquor stores	13	3.8	5	2.0	2	1.2
Loan and pawn establishments	8	2.3	7	2.8	0	0.0
Shops advertising credit	26	7.6	14	5.6	0	0.0

exchange cash for material articles. Here it might prove rather difficult to reclassify establishment types in order to identify those which are more typical of 47th Street, since both varieties (pawnshops and loan offices) are present on each of the low-income area streets. However, it is likely that a detailed inventory of the items pawned on 47th Street would differ significantly from one for those pawned on Ashland. Regardless of the outcome of such an inventory, the fact to be re-emphasized is that a profusion of loan and pawn establishments is not peculiar to Negro areas.

Likewise, the credit sign is by no means unique to Negro business thoroughfares. If establishments, regardless of type, offering credit do not form as high a proportion of the total number of store-fronts on Ashland as on 47th Street, they still make a very noticeable impression. On Ashland, credit signs most often appear in stores selling higher priced items, such as jewelry shops and appliance stores. On 47th Street, credit signs are apt to be in the windows of stores selling items in all price ranges, though they appear with the greatest consistency in shops which sell clothing. Without drawing any further conclusions concerning the relative occurrence of credit signs on the two business thoroughfares, it is to be observed that, in a business development which caters to neighborhood clientele, there is no reason to conclude that the absence of a credit sign in a given establishment means that there is no credit offered there. Similarly, the total absence of credit signs on 71st Street does not mean that none of the establishments there offers credit.

No attempt was made to quantify another characteristic which is common to both low-income area business thoroughfares, namely, shops which are in various states of dilapidation. The feeling here was that impulse rather than reason was likely to reign in making decisions with regard to such a highly subjective question.

LAND USES COMMON TO ALL THREE BUSINESS THOROUGHFARES

The land uses in this category, which is summarized in Table IV, were found to be ubiquitous in business thoroughfares located in all community areas, regardless of racial composition or socioeconomic level. They thereby presumably support the contention that there are features which are commonplace to all urban commercial areas. Yet, even in this category, there are establishment types for which there exists a distinct possibility that a redefinition of terms would result in their reclassification into one of the first two categories.

Some independent corner drugstores tend to differ in appearance from one business thoroughfare to the next, whereas the chain drugstores have a fairly uniform appearance regardless of location. Drugstores situated on

TABLE IV

Distribution of Land Uses in Category C: Common to All Three
Business Thoroughfares

	47th Street		Ashland		71st Street	
	Number	Per cent	Number	Per cent	Number	Per cent
Total store-fronts	343	100.0	250	100.0	165	100.0
Total in Category C	58	17.3	46	18.4	26	15.6
Miscellaneous business services[a]	12	3.5	11	4.4	8	4.8
Jewelers and optometrists[b]	15	4.4	15	6.0	5	3.0
Shoe stores	15	4.4	14	5.6	6	3.6
Corner drug stores	9	2.7	2	0.8	4	2.4
Automatic laundromats	4	1.2	3	1.2	2	1.2
Gas stations	3	0.9	1	0.4	1	0.6

[a]Currency exchanges, realtors, insurance agencies, etc.

[b]Often found in conjunction.

47th Street are sometimes in a more run-down state, and are often a little more blatant in conveying the fact that they carry alcoholic beverages. Therefore, if drugstores are differentiated into subtypes a few additions could be made to Category A. Whether these distinctive drugstores are a result of external economic forces, of traits inherent in urban Negro culture, or of some other factors is not easily established.

Shoe stores, on both 47th Street and Ashland, on occasion advertise extremely cheap merchandise with such signs as "2 Pair for $5." Clearly, such shops could have been reclassified into Category B. In addition, some of the styles displayed in 47th Street shoe store windows are quite distinctive. Once again they may be interpreted as being demonstrative of the inclination which some Negro personality types have to be "flashy" in dress.

At least two other major features were found to be common to all three commercial thoroughfares. One such feature was the second-story professional office of doctors, dentists, and lawyers. The second phenomenon was a decrease in the intensity of use of space toward the periphery of each business thoroughfare. General concepts of land economics would point to the expectation of this second feature; consequently there is no necessity for considering the deterioration of use on the margin of the 47th Street complex as a possible concomitant of urban Negro culture. The remaining land uses in Table IV appear to show no significant variations from one business street to the next and, therefore, require no interpretation.

LAND USES MORE CHARACTERISTIC OF BUSINESS THOROUGHFARES IN WHITE AREAS

The land uses in this category, which are summarized in Table V, are presumably more representative of Ashland and 71st Street, that is, of white areas regardless of socioeconomic composition.

A relatively low percentage, or total absence, of women's apparel shops, which are neither run-down nor display credit signs in their shop windows, could probably be pointed to as another singular characteristic of the low-income urban Negro business thoroughfare, but the origin of this phenomenon appears to be economic rather than cultural. The better women's shops on 47th Street are not unlike those on 71st Street and Ashland, save for the frequent occurrence of credit signs in their windows. Such signs are certainly not manifestations of subcultural traits; and, as already mentioned, the absence of a credit sign in a white neighborhood shop does not preclude the possibility that credit is given.

The small number of confectionaries, cigar stores, florists, gift shops, and miscellaneous specialized-retail establishments on 47th Street could also be interpreted as being peculiar to the low-income urban Negro shopping street. In this instance, the peculiarity may be, at least in part, attributable to subcultural differences, especially since there are some noticeable differences between the merchandise lines carried in the few shops on 47th Street and those on the two white thoroughfares. Differences in general appearance, however, would suggest that economic factors, including consumer buying power, are also at work. Clearly, if such establishments are to be used for describing differences in the urban landscape then there again arises the problem of reclassifying land uses on the basis of more precisely defined terms.

The total absence of stores selling fresh-baked goods on 47th Street is in accord with the observation that Negro homes in general have smaller expenditures for baked goods than "white homes of the corresponding income class."[24] Therefore, assuming that this dearth of bakeries on 47th Street is characteristic of other Negro low-income business thoroughfares, this dietary difference may be thought of as something "cultural."

Although, in all probability, there is some cultural factor underlying the rarity of "presentable" restaurants (or restaurants which have an attractive exterior and serve moderately to expensively priced dinners) on 47th Street, the number of such establishments on all three thoroughfares was so small that it would be foolhardy to draw any conclusions.

It is more than likely that the less intense development of Ashland and 71st Street, as indicated in Table V by the greater preponderance of store-fronts which are either vacant or for rent, is not due to any cultural factor, but is instead a result of the fact that these two thoroughfares serve communities which are less densely populated than 47th Street.

Although they do not belong to this category, unclassified land uses merit some discussion. Several of them were arbitrarily left uncategorized; others may well have been placed in Category C; whereas the remainder of omitted uses have little or no bearing on the over-all theme of this paper. Some of the unclassified uses include governmental functions (post offices, military recruiting stations, and police stations), hardware and building materials stores, and furniture and appliance stores which were neither run-down nor outwardly offered credit.

OBSERVATIONS ON A HARLEM STREET

The distinctive character of the low-income Negro business thoroughfare is apparently derived from both the economic and cultural attributes of its customers, that is, the over-all impression created by 47th Street is caused not only by the fact that it is used by Negroes, but also by the fact that it caters to a low-income population. In several instances, it

TABLE V

Distribution of Land Uses in Category D: More Characteristic of White Area Business Thoroughfares

	47th Street		Ashland		71st Street	
	Number	Per cent	Number	Per cent	Number	Per cent
Total store-fronts	343	100.0	250	100.0	165	100.0
Total in Category D	31	9.0	69	27.6	64	38.8
Women's clothing stores (neither run-down nor advertising credit)	14	4.1	22	8.8	31	18.8
Confectionaries, gift shops, florists, cigar stores and related misc. shops	8	2.3	19	7.6	15	9.1
"Presentable" restaurants	1	0.3	2	0.8	6	3.6
Bakeries	0	0.0	6	2.4	3	1.8
Vacant or for rent	8	2.3	20	8.0	9	5.5

TABLE VI

Comparison of Land Uses in Categories A and B on 47th Street (Chicago) and 8th Avenue (New York)

	47th Street		8th Avenue	
	Number	Per cent	Number	Per cent
Total of store-fronts	343	100.0	284	100.0
Total in Category A	132	38.7	102	35.9
Beauty parlors and barbershops	37	10.8	34	12.0
Dry cleaners and other "valet" services	31	9.1	18	6.3
Tailor-made men's clothing	6	1.7	0	0.0
Disassociated uses	16	4.7	12	4.2
Independent groceries	17	5.0	26	9.2
Billiard parlors	9	2.7	3	1.1
Record stores	7	2.0	2	0.7
Store-front churches and spiritual consultants	9	2.7	7	2.5
Total in Category B	86	25.0	51	18.3
Cheap restaurants	20	5.8	19	6.7
Bars	19	5.5	16	5.6
Liquor stores	13	3.8	6	2.1
Loan and pawn establishments	8	2.3	5	1.8
Shops advertising credit	26	7.6	5	1.8

has been rather difficult to choose between the economic and cultural bases of features singular to 47th Street. Therefore, in checking to see whether or not the atmosphere created by the land uses on 47th Street is similar to that of other low-income Negro business thoroughfares in northern cities it is necessary to compare the frequency of land uses in Category B, as well as in Category A.

Land uses on 8th Avenue (between 125th Street on the south and 135th Street on the north),[25] in the Harlem area of Manhattan were examined and found generally to conform with those on 47th Street (Table VI). Beauty parlors and barbershops, almost without exception, displayed "hair processing" advertisements, were in general somewhat more dilapidated than their "Black Belt" counterparts, and were sometimes found in almost staggering numbers on certain side streets off 8th Avenue (not included in Table VI). Cheap restaurants and bars also had a higher rate of occurrence; and again important distinctions (based on appearance and foods sold) could be made between these establishments and those with similar functions in low-income white neighborhoods. The highly peculiar incidence of store-front churches, as well as of disassociated uses within a single establishment, was nearly equal on the low-income Negro thoroughfares of both Chicago and New York. Tailor-made men's clothing stores did not occur on 8th Avenue, and record stores, liquor stores, and loan and pawn establishments occurred somewhat less frequently there than on 47th Street. As it might be expected that little difference in the frequency of these store types would occur from one low-income Negro business thoroughfare to another (particularly since the rate of occurrence of record shops and tailor-made men's clothing stores on 47th Street was considered to be in some way reflective of urban Negro culture), it should be mentioned that all four of these establishment types are clustered in numbers on 125th Street, and near that street's intersection with 8th Avenue. Billiard parlors and "valet" services also appear less often on 8th Avenue than on 47th Street. No adequate explanation for these differences appears available in either case, although it must be emphasized that a good number of the "valet" services on 8th Avenue had the same characteristics as those on 47th Street; that is, they were generally run-down and performing more than one "valet" function, such as shoe repairing and hat blocking. A noteworthy discrepancy exists between the occurrence of shops advertising credit on the two Negro business thoroughfares, and this may or may not be totally explained by the fact that on 47th Street such shops usually dealt in new (as opposed to secondhand) women's clothing. Stores selling previously unused women's clothing are again to be found in greater numbers on 125th Street rather than on 8th Avenue.

Conclusion

Many of the observations and interpretations in this study have been presented in a most tenuous terminology. To some degree this has been done intentionally. The singular atmosphere imparted to the low-income Negro business thoroughfare by its shopkeepers and clientele is more than a result of cultural characteristics and externally imposed economic conditions. It is also a consequence of the aggregate behavior and needs of a particular group of individuals. When interpreting a landscape whose impact is to some extent determined by the unique behavior of individuals one cannot employ ultimates, absolutes, or incontrovertible arguments.

Nevertheless, the distinctive (but *not* necessarily unique) land uses of the "Black Belt's" 47th Street, Harlem's 8th Avenue, and other low-income Negro business thoroughfares, may be grouped into four categories. First, there are those land uses which to some extent are a response to the needs of certain Negro personality types which are in one way or another concerned with personal appearance: beauty parlors and barbershops, dry cleaners and associated "valet" services, and stores specializing in tailor-made men's apparel may be included in this category. Second, there are those land-use types whose very preponderance mirrors extremely low standards of living; independent groceries and stores with disassociated uses are included in this category. Third, there are those uses whose rate of occurrence in some way tends to confirm stereotypes of the Negro held by various segments of the white population; this group comprises billiard parlors, record shops, and store-front churches, and, in each case, there is evidence to suggest that the explanation does not necessarily lie within the framework of stereotyped personality traits. Finally, there are those land uses which have the same relative frequency on business thoroughfares located in both low-income white and low-income Negro areas, but whose exterior appearance differs considerably between areas; bars, cheap restaurants, and possibly loan and pawn establishments fall into this classification.

Literature Cited

1. Proudfoot defined principal business thoroughfares and neighborhood business streets in terms of store types, vehicular traffic, and customer origins. See Malcolm J. Proudfoot, "City Retail Structure," *Econ. Geog.*, Vol. 13, 1937, p. 427.
   Urban commercial concentrations occurring in residential areas are

also referred to as "string-streets" or "business ribbons." See Brian J. L. Berry, "Ribbon Developments in the Urban Business Pattern," *Annals* Assn. Amer. Geogrs., Vol. 49, 1959, p. 149.

2. The relationship between the distribution of store types in a residential area and the "psychology" of its inhabitants has been considered by French sociologists, amongst others. For example, see P.-H. Chombart de Lauwe, et al., *Paris et L'Agglomération Parisienne*, Presses Universitaires de France, Paris, 1952, Vol. I, pp. 142-45, and Vol. II, pp. 66-73.

3. Wesley Calef and Howard Nelson, "Distribution of Negro Population in the United States," *Geogr. Rev.*, Vol. 46, 1955, pp. 147-68; J. Fraser Hart, "The Changing Distribution of the American Negro," *Annals* Assn. of Amer. Geogrs., Vol. 50, 1960, pp. 242-66; James F. Woodruff, "Some Characteristics of the Alabama Slave Population in 1850," *Geogr. Rev.*, Vol. 52, 1962, pp. 379-88; and Richard Hartshorne, "Racial Maps of the United States," *Geogr. Rev.*, Vol. 28, 1938, pp. 276-88.

4. J. Fraser Hart, "A Rural Retreat for Negroes," *Geogr. Rev.*, Vol. 50, 1960, pp. 147-68.

5. Howard Nelson, "Some Characteristics of the Population of Cities in Similar Service Classifications," *Econ. Geog.*, Vol. 33, 1957, pp. 95-108.

6. Perhaps the most significant of such works is the dated, but still relevant, investigation made by Warner and his associates: W. Lloyd Warner, Buford H. Junker, and Walter A. Adams, *Color and Human Nature*, Washington, D.C., 1941.

7. St. Clair Drake, *Churches and Voluntary Associations in the Chicago Negro Community*, Works Projects Administration No. 3, Chicago, 1940, p. 179. (Mimeographed.)

8. The selection of business thoroughfares was facilitated through the use of two sources: Paul M. Hauser and Evelyn Kitagawa, *Local Community Fact Book for Chicago*, Chicago Community Inventory, Chicago, 1957; and Evelyn Kitagawa and De Ver Sholes, *Chicagoland's Retail Market*, Chicago Association of Commerce and Industry, and Chicago Community Inventory, Chicago, 1957.

9. Kitagawa and Sholes, op. cit., pp. 11 and 81.

10. Hauser and Kitagawa, op. cit., p. 205.

11. Warner, et al., op. cit., pp. 65-66.

12. E. Franklin Frazier, "Negro Harlem: An Ecological Study," *Amer. Journ. Sociology*, Vol. 43, 1937, p. 87.

13. Warner, et al., op. cit., *passim;* and J. T. Johnson, *The Potential Negro Market*, New York, 1952, pp. 37 and 158.

14. Richard Steiner, *The Negro's Share*, New York, 1943, p. 142.

15. Ibid.

16. Sterner, op. cit., pp. 137–38.

17. Warner, et al., op. cit., pp. 65–66.

18. See the discussion of Negro food consumption patterns in Sterner, op. cit., pp. 102–27.

19. Gunnar Myrdal, *An American Dilemma,* New York, 1942, Vol. I, p. 372.

20. It has been established that certain racial differences in phonograph ownership exist, with a higher percentage of Negroes in comparable income groups owning such appliances. Sterner, op. cit., p. 159.

21. See Melville J. Hershkovits' discussion in *The Myth of the Negro Past,* New York, 1941, pp. 261–69.

22. E. Franklin Frazier, *The Negro Family in Chicago,* Chicago, 1932, p. 113.

23. Drake, op. cit., p. 300.

24. Sterner, op. cit., p. 105.

25. The ribbon development along 8th Avenue was selected in preference to that of 125th Street, which is clearly the busiest thoroughfare in Harlem, because the latter has so many uses which are characteristic of an entertainment center.

THE STRUCTURE OF RETAIL TRADE IN A
RACIALLY CHANGING TRADE AREA

Harold M. Rose

During the period following World War II a revolution occurred in the pattern of retail location in U.S. cities. The decline of the central business district and the subsequent rise of regional shopping centers have often been topics of in-depth research by retail location analysts. A lesser concern of researchers has been the future of unplanned shopping districts in the older neighborhoods of central cities. Of the limited attention devoted to these areas, one recent study described them this way: "Many are Sick, Many are Dying . . . What Can Be Done?" [10].

The most frequent death of unplanned centers is taking place within areas undergoing racial change. This has prompted a spate of statements which indicate major commercial institutions are not serving the needs of ghetto populations, and anger in the black community is frequently an outgrowth of dissatisfaction with ghetto merchants [17]. The complexity of these and other forces operating in metropolitan areas has dictated that a closer look be given at the role of race on retail structure in racially changing trade areas.

In this study race will be viewed as a social characteristic. That it is an important factor affecting retail structure was pointed out by Rolph [16] more than a generation ago. Further, Bucklin [7] has found that race, like distance, is a variable which affects one's choice of a place to shop. Yet, to date only Pred [15] among American geographers has sought to investigate this phenomenon.

The specific objective of this study is to attempt to relate changes in retail structure to the entry of Negroes into a given trade area during the period 1950–65. The problem of isolating changes emanating from a changing racial composition in a retail subsystem is difficult, since numerous other forces are at work which prompt change in the character and structure of a retail trade area. The problem is further compounded by the fact that retail trade areas of the type that are becoming predominantly Negro have been going through states of decline for some time, a trend which is only incidentally related to the racial character of the market. This factor was mentioned by writers assessing the possibility of commercial redevelopment along the riot ravaged commercial strips of Detroit [18].

THE STUDY AREA

The area selected for this investigation lies approximately two and one-half miles northwest of the central business district in the city of Milwaukee, Wisconsin. It is a rectangular area embracing less than two square miles, and in both 1950 and 1960 it contained approximately 42,000 persons. The study area does not represent a precisely delineated trade area, but a series of contiguous neighborhoods. One assumes that the residents of the area will seek to satisfy as many of their basic retail needs as is possible from the set of commercial outlets found in close proximity to their places of residence, although there is growing evidence [13] that residents of low-income areas possess a keen awareness of price differences in stores located beyond the margins of the local neighborhood, a factor which could have a demonstrated impact upon shopping patterns.

The vast majority of retail outlets in the area under investigation are situated along four major arterials which transect the district. Two of these, North Avenue and Center Street, run east-west, while the other two, Fond du Lac Avenue and Teutonia Avenue, run to the northwest. Since many of the retail outlets which have evolved along these roads cater to the local residential market, they are more than simple string streets or ribbon developments. The retail character of the area is best reflected in the small, unplanned shopping centers found nested along stretches of the arterials. In 1950, there were seven unplanned shopping centers located along various stretches of the transecting roads. The seven individual centers were spaced at approximately one-quarter mile intervals. The spaces separating these centers were also largely commercial, generally performing urban arterial functions, although along some stretches residential land uses tended to predominate. The unplanned centers included approximately one half of the retail establishments located along these radials. This ratio coincides with Boal and Johnson's [6] assessment of the higher importance of hierarchic functions along commercial ribbons situated in the older parts of the city. Among the seven centers or districts, there were present in the initial period a small shopping goods center, a community center, and five neighborhood centers.

Since the principal objective of this study is to consider the impact of the changing racial composition of the trade area on retail structure, it is useful to subdivide the trade area into smaller segments in line with the community area designations developed for Milwaukee by Tien [19]. The study area embraces two complete community areas and parts of a third.

The racial composition of the population within the trade area moved from a Negro share of approximately 7 per cent in 1950 to 49 per cent in 1960. If racial composition does in fact produce a significant impact on the number of operating establishments, then the racial threshold reflecting the decision of an existing operator to relocate or terminate his operation was not reached prior to 1955. This view is supported by the fact that there was only a 4 per cent decline in the number of establishments within the area during the initial five-year interval. Berry [5] recently demonstrated the catalytic effect of racial turnover on the retail structure in several community areas in Chicago, but like others, he has pointed out the difficulty of separating race from income.

MARKOV ANALYSIS AND RETAIL CHANGE

To answer the question "What effect does the spatial development of the Negro ghetto in major central cities have on the retail structure of business clusters situated within its area," it was necessary to search for a method or technique which is sensitive to processes having an impact on retail character. Berry and his colleagues have developed models to describe changes in a given aspect of retail character as a function of certain status variables measured at some specified point in time. But these models have been found to be inadequate for predicting retail change in small unit areas [4] and, also, they do not include social variables among the independent variables. In areas undergoing racial change the models were least able to predict satisfactory results [3].

Certain features of Markov Chain models appear to offer more satisfactory alternatives for predicting changes of the type with which this study is concerned. Markov Chain models have found only limited use among geographers, although their utility has been demonstrated by both Marble [14] and Clark [9]. These models are used here to describe the changes of commercial structures from one retail category to another over time.

A five-year interval was selected as an appropriate time period for describing shifts in retail character. Transition probability matrices were constructed which described shifts among some twelve retail categories for the set of commercial structures located along each ribbon.

These matrices demonstrate the stability or lack of stability of the various retail types. They likewise reflect the suitability, in terms of rents or character of physical facilities, which might readily allow shifts in retail types to occur. The existence of zeros in cells indicates that it is not possible for a unit in the ith state to transfer to the jth state; for example, a unit which housed an automotive service in the initial time period cannot house a clothing store at the next time period.

Depending upon one's objectives, Markov models can be employed in a number of ways. Both Marble and Clark focused their attentions solely on the transition matrix as a clue to expected behavior. Other researchers have utilized the matrix of transition probabilities to predict future outcomes. In this case, the matrix of transition probabilities is multiplied by a vector describing each category's share of the set of businesses in the present time period as a means of predicting future shares.

A matrix of transition probabilities was constructed for each of the commercial ribbons in the study area for the times 1955, 1960, and 1965. In each instance, the matrix reflects shifts in states over the preceding five years. The construction of a series of transition matrices (1950–55, 1955–60, 1960–65) reflects a desire to illustrate the impact of changes taking place during the immediate past period on retail stability. A conventional Markov Chain analysis which might use only the initial transition probability matrix (1950–55) to predict future changes would not get at this principal concern. Besides, in anticipating the impact of racial composition upon the structure of retail trade, it appears logical to expect that the dispersion of the Negro population within the trade area over subsequent five-year intervals, would distort the predicted results associated with a given transition matrix. This logic is based on recognized subcultural differences reflected in differential propensities to consume specific items [1, 2, 8] and the traditional behavior of white entrepreneurs engaged in the provision of social services. Eventually, the transition matrices should begin to reflect the changing racial composition of the population although the role of race cannot be precisely specified. Galloway [12], using a Markov model, encountered a similar problem in attempting to partition the role of specified variables in explaining differences in the propensity for poverty on the basis of race.

The retail structure along all commercial ribbons in the study area during the period 1950–55 can be described as stable. Some of the more important conditions leading to the retail stability were residential stability, limited change in the income characteristics of the local consumer population, and the absence of attractive alternative retail locations. These conditions are essentially related to the subsystem itself.

TABLE 1
Transition Probabilities For The North Avenue Businesses

Retail Category	1950	S_1	S_2	S_3	S_4	S_5	S_6	1955 S_7	S_8	S_9	S_{10}	S_{11}	S_{12}
Professional	S_1	1.00											
Personal	S_2		.80		.05							.15	
Financial	S_3			.57	.13						.13		.17
Eating & Drinking	S_4				.95								.05
Groc. & Rel. Goods	S_5		.08			.84			.04				.04
Clothing	S_6		.10				.60			.20			.10
Auto Sales & Serv.	S_7				.04			.78		.04			.04
Multifunctionals	S_8								1.00				
Specialty	S_9		.06							.75	.06	.06	.06
Household Furnish. & Related Goods	S_{10}					.07					1.00		
Miscellaneous	S_{11}		.07								.13	.60	.13
Vacancy	S_{12}												1.00

TABLE 2

Transition Probabilities For The Teutonia Avenue Businesses

Retail Category	1950	1955 S_1	S_2	S_3	S_4	S_5	S_6	S_7	S_8	S_9	S_10	S_11	S_12
Professional	S_1	1.00											
Personal	S_2		.75							.25			
Financial	S_3			1.00									
Eating & Drinking	S_4				.95							.05	
Groc. & Rel. Goods	S_5					.80				.10	.10		
Clothing	S_6						1.00						
Auto Sales & Serv.	S_7							.91			.09		
Multifunctionals	S_8								1.00				
Specialty	S_9				.07				.08	.50	.08	.17	.17
Household Furnish. & Related Goods	S_{10}										.85	.07	
Miscellaneous	S_{11}									.09	.18	.63	.09
Vacancy	S_{12}												1.00

Tables 1 and 2, examples of the matrices of transition probabilities, demonstrate the stability that characterized retail activity in the trade area during the initial interval. Although conditions along only two arteries are shown, there was little variability within the whole area during the interval. The rate and character of change along these two arteries in the following two five-year periods, however, is quite disparate. Teutonia Avenue (Table 2) lies along the main axis of ghetto development, whereas North Avenue (Table 1) is situated at a right angle to this major direction of ghetto spread. The physical orientation of these axes accounts for far-reaching changes in the later time periods.

The entries along the main diagonals of the matrices give the probabilities of remaining in the same state over the one time interval and are called the *retention probabilities*. It is clear from observing these matrices that the structures housing certain retail categories are often ill-suited to house other categories. The nature of the structures which house categories S_9–S_{11} seem to permit most readily changes of state among categories.

The development of a set of transition probability matrices for each ribbon permits one to begin to look for causal factors which would explain the differential shifts in the retail character along these ribbons. The transition matrix has been employed as a predictive device in order to test for the homogeneity of processes occurring through time (Table 3).

TABLE 3.

*Predicted Percentage Retail Mix 1960, as Function
of Processes Operating 1950-55*

Retail Category	North Avenue		Teutonia Avenue	
	Observed	Predicted*	Observed	Predicted*
S_1 Professional	0.6	0.0	2.1	0.0
S_2 Personal	10.4	10.9	5.3	4.5
S_3 Financial	1.2	4.7	3.2	2.0
S_4 Eating & Drinking	15.3	15.3	20.2	20.2
S_5 Groceries	9.2	9.9	6.6	9.9
S_6 Clothing	3.1	9.5	4.3	10.0
S_7 Auto Sales & Serv.	9.8	10.6	8.5	10.7
S_8 Multifunctionals	4.9	6.3	3.2	4.0
S_9 Specialty	7.9	9.0	5.3	8.6
S_{10} Household Furnish.	11.0	11.7	10.6	17.5
S_{11} Miscellaneous	14.1	12.3	8.5	10.7
S_{12} Vacancy	12.8	11.6	22.3	0.0

*Product of 1955 state vector and transition probability matrix for 1950-55.

Along both sample ribbons, the differences between the observed and predicted shares of S_4 (Eating and Drinking) and S_2 (Personal Services) are minor. Some other differences are, in part, a function of the original retail character of the ribbons themselves. The predictive ability of the model is less satisfactory for Teutonia than for North Avenue. While a general decline in retail functions can be detected along both ribbons, the more serious decline along Teutonia is probably related to the facts that it contained fewer establishments originally, had less retail diversity, and greater residential instability during this interval.

The matrices describing shifts in the retail mix during each successive five-year interval show a general decline in the retention probabilities among states. This condition, no doubt, is basically related to the economic decline of old neighborhoods. But variations in the sensitivity of some retail categories reflect changing social characteristics.

In the transition probability matrices for those ribbons which cut across the principal axis of ghetto development, such as North Avenue and Center Street, the impact of changing racial character is less evident. Changes taking place along one stretch of the axis are masked by entry decisions occurring elsewhere on the street, since the racial factor has a less pervasive impact along the total length of the ribbon in any given year.

NEIGHBORHOOD SHOPPING CENTERS

As a means of highlighting the role of the racial composition of the trade area on retail structure, a set of transition probability matrices has been developed for the two retail conformations situated along North Avenue. Both of the conformations represent neighborhood retail centers. Since the retail changes there were minor during 1950–55, attention is focused on structural changes that took place during the 1955–60 and 1960–65 periods.

By 1960, the racial composition of the trade area upon which the center at 14th and North Avenue depended had become predominantly Negro. At the same time, Negro entry into the trade area served by the center at 27th and North Avenue was only nominal. Through analysis it can be demonstrated that retail entrants in the former center reflected the changing racial composition of the population while the latter center has been seemingly unaffected. Assuming that the same set of processes determined the nature of retail entry during the 1960–65 interval as during the previous five-year interval, a first-order Markov Chain analysis should produce a close approximation of the retail structure of these centers in 1965 (Table 4).

In both instances a general economic decline affected the predictive power of the analysis. Overprediction of shares was common for both centers. But for the 14th Street center, the analysis seriously underpredicted the proportion of retail outlets providing personal services and eating and drinking accommodations. These two categories are those which Negro businessmen are known to have a high propensity for entry. These same two categories were overpredicted for the 27th Street center.

TABLE 4
Retail Composition of Two Neighborhood Retail Centers 1965

	N. Ave. at N. 14th St.		N. Ave. at N. 27th St.	
	Observed	Predicted	Observed	Predicted
Retail Category	Percentages			
Professional	3.3	3.2	2.5	0.0
Personal	26.6	16.6	12.8	16.1
Financial	9.9	3.2	10.2	1.2
Eating & Drinking	16.6	6.4	25.6	28.2
Groceries	10.0	17.2	0.0	2.0
Clothing	0.0	3.2	0.0	2.4
Automotive	6.6	5.6	0.0	0.0
Multifunctional	0.0	0.0	5.1	7.6
Specialty	10.0	9.6	7.6	10.0
Household	6.6	11.2	17.9	13.3
Miscellaneous·	6.6	6.4	7.6	5.1
Vacant	13.3	19.3	10.2	2.5

It is apparent that the process of economic decline continued within both centers and actually accelerated during the most recent period at the 27th Street center. It is likewise obvious that social factors influenced the decision of retail entrants, especially in the other center.

The retail mix of neighborhood centers characteristically reflects the cultural taste of the trade area's residents, and a structure once initiated affects the future use of existing retail outlets. Ethnic propensities were apparent in the retail character of the two neighborhood shopping centers during the initial time period. In 1950 the center at 14th and North Avenue still served a sizable Jewish population, a fact that was evident in the number of grocery and related activities occupying units there. Similarly, the *gemuetlichkeit* of the German neighborhood was expressed by the importance of the German-owned drinking establishments occupying space in the center at 27th and North Avenue. The Negro population, representing the most recent entrant into the area, is in effect responsible for the superimposition of a new retail structure upon the remnants of a decaying

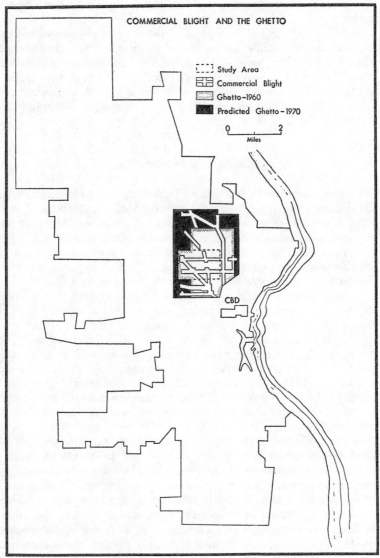

COMMERCIAL BLIGHT AND THE GHETTO

Study Area
Commercial Blight
Ghetto-1960
Predicted Ghetto-1970

0   2
Miles

CBD

Figure 1

structure. Although the social and economic factors cannot always be easily separated, while operating together they each yield outcomes which are more readily related to one than to the other.

Obviously, it is difficult to ascertain the effects of racial composition on the retention probabilities of the derived matrices, but the probability of entry is more clearly associated with the racial composition of the trade area. Thus, the land uses Pred [15] described as being more characteristic of Negro commercial development appear to be widespread, showing up in commercial developments serving a Negro population in cities throughout the nation.

SUMMARY AND CONCLUSIONS

It is apparent that competition for business space in older areas is on the decline, thereby permitting the easy entry of a multiplicity of low-order businesses. This deterioration in demand subsequently leads to the evolution of commercial blight. When one considers the relative location of commercial ribbons transecting ghetto areas one cannot be certain of the role which race plays in this situation. Yet it is apparent that race tends to serve as a catalyst which accelerates the commercial transition.

Through the use of a simplified Markov Chain analysis it was found that one could predict rather accurately the retail mix along a commercial ribbon prior to Negro entry. After Negro entry, the matrices of transition probabilities demonstrated the operation of a set of forces that were not previously discernible. The major drawback of Markov Chain analysis in this kind of study is that it does not permit one to identify precisely the roles of specific change-producing variables. Improvements in this respect might be obtained either by increasing the number of retail categories or reducing the length of the time interval upon which the matrix of transition probabilities is based, or both.

In the evolution of the Negro business street, the dropping out of goods-supplying units is frequently observed, and this permits an increase in the relative importance of suppliers of social services. The Negro business operator along the arteries is principally engaged in operating units in this latter category. With the declining relative importance of goods outlets along commercial ribbons in Negro residential areas, the neighborhood center diminishes in importance as a source of convenience goods. At the same time, the neighborhood center becomes essentially a place for obtaining social services. This phenomenon more and more draws convenience goods shoppers into the shopping goods center, a situation that is somewhat unique.

The continuous expansion of the ghetto as an urban subsystem also

means the continuous spread of commercial blight unless some stabilizing
forces are intentionally introduced. As the prospective Negro business operator is by custom forced to operate within Negro neighborhoods [11],
and has access to only limited risk capital, one could hardly expect him to
alter this condition. If the process of commercial change which was observed within a very limited area is permitted to continue unaltered, then
the problem of predicting certain kinds of commercial landscape changes,
especially the intensity of blight, is a task that can be readily conducted
within the context of predicting the spatial pattern of the Negro ghetto
(Fig. 1).

<h2 style="text-align:center">LITERATURE CITED</h2>

1. Alexis, M. "Some Negro-White Differences in Consumption," *Ameri-can Journal of Economics and Sociology,* 21 (1962), 11.

2. Bauer, R. A., S. M. Cunningham, and L. H. Wortzel. "The Marketing Dilemma of Negroes," *Journal of Marketing,* 29 (1965), 1–6.

3. Berry, B. J. L. *Commercial Structure and Commercial Blight,* Research Paper 85, Department of Geography, University of Chicago, Chicago (1963), 173–76.

4. ———. "The Retail Component of the Urban Model," *Journal of the American Institute of Planners,* 31 (1965), 151.

5. ———. "Comparative Mortality Experience of Small Business in Four Chicago Communities," Background Paper No. 4, *Small Business Relocation Study,* Center for Urban Studies, The University of Chicago (1966), 19–20.

6. Boal, F. W. and D. B. Johnson. "The Functions of Retail and Service Establishments on Commercial Ribbons," *The Canadian Geographer,* 9 (1965), 157.

7. Bucklin, L. P. "The Concept of Mass in Intra-urban Shopping," *Journal of Marketing,* 31 (1967), 41–42.

8. Bullock, H. A. "Consumer Motivations in Black and White," *Harvard Business Review,* 39 (1961), 89–124.

9. Clark, W. A. V. "Markov Chain Analysis in Geography: An Applica-tion to the Movement of Rental Housing Areas," *Annals,* the Associa-tion of American Geographers, 55 (1965), 351–59.

10. Downs, A. and J. McClean. "Many are Sick, Many are Dying . . . What Can Be Done?" *Journal of Property Management,* 28 (1963), 132–42.

11. Foley, E. P. "The Negro Businessman: In Search of a Tradition," *Daedalus,* 95 (1966), 113.

12. Galloway, L. E. "The Negro and Poverty," *The Journal of Business,* 40 (1967), 29–31.

13. Goodman, C. S. "Do the Poor Pay More?" *Journal of Marketing* (Jan. 1968), 23.
14. Marble, D. F. "A Simple Markovian Model of Trip Structures in a Metropolitan Region," *Papers, Regional Science Assoc. Western Section* (1964), 150–56.
15. Pred, A. "Business Thoroughfares as Expressions of Urban Negro Culture," *Economic Geography*, 39 (1963), 217–33.
16. Rolph, I. K. "The Population Pattern in Relation to Retail Buying," *The American Journal of Sociology*, 38 (1932), 368.
17. Sengstock, M. C. "The Corporation and the Ghetto: An Analysis of the Effects of Corporate Retail Grocery Sales on Ghetto Life," *Journal of Urban Law*, 45 (1968), 673–703.
18. *The Wall Street Journal* (July 28, 1967), 5.
19. Tien, Y. *Milwaukee Metropolitan Area Fact Book—1940, 1950 and 1960*, Madison, Wisconsin: The University of Wisconsin Press, 1962.

TRANSPORTATION PROBLEMS IN NEGRO GHETTOS

James O. Wheeler

Of the many problems confronting the American Negro, most have been rather widely described and analyzed by social scientists.[1] The considerable rural to urban Negro migration and the concomitant adjustment processes for both Negroes and whites have attracted much research interest, one major focus of which is on residential segregation.[2] The dual housing market, long existing in American cities, has largely restricted Negroes to crowded, older housing near central districts of urban areas. The problems arising from such discrimination are complex and interrelated, involving educational, employment, housing, medical, and social variables. Although one of the general results of discrimination by the white society has been the severe limits placed on Negro social mobility, a specific consequence of residential segregation has been to restrict the Negro's geographical mobility within the city.

The geographical isolation of Negro residences, a physical manifestation of discrimination, is related to the kind and variety of transportation problems confronting ghetto dwellers. Yet few studies have dealt with these problems.[3] To the Negro, inadequate transportation, though inseparable from many other difficulties of ghetto life, looms as a major barrier to several of his day-to-day activities, perpetuating his isolation. That a lack of good transportation exists in Negro areas was recently brought to general attention by the McCone Report on the 1965 Watts riot, which found that inadequate transportation "handicaps (Negroes) in seeking and holding jobs, attending schools, shopping, and in fulfilling other needs."[4] Although recognizing the general problems of transportation in Negro areas, the report's recommendations dealt only with improvements in bus transit, one part of the over-all transportation system.

The net effect of these transportation problems is to minimize social interaction with whites and to greatly restrict the economic alternatives open to the Negro. These transportation inadequacies range from lack of traffic signs and signals in many ghettos to a low rate of automobile ownership. Part of the problem is related simply to the areal clustering of Negro residences. If Negroes were evenly spread throughout the city, a much higher probability would exist for greater social and economic ties with whites. The ghetto, due to the normal drop off in interaction with increasing distance, retards connections with more distant parts of the city and, because of perceived social distance, concentrates interaction within the ghetto. Low automobile ownership greatly curtails travel flexibility, both in time and direction. The rigid and limited scheduling of transit facilities frequently results in slow, circuitous, and costly travel. Freeways, which may be built through areas of deteriorating ghetto housing rather than across districts of higher quality homes, are of little use to automobile-less Negroes, whose residences may be displaced by construction to even more inaccessible locations.

PURPOSE AND DATA

It is the purpose of this study to focus on certain features of Negro travel in Tulsa, Oklahoma. Recent data on work trips are used to illustrate differences in Negro and white travel behavior, and to outline major barriers to spatial mobility among urban Negroes. Specifically, it is hypothesized that travel differences between Negroes and whites may be explained by the concept of "forced mobility" among Negroes, i.e., Negroes, because they are limited in residential choice, may have to travel a considerable distance to find employment.

The data, collected in 1964 as part of the Tulsa Metropolitan Area Transportation Study (TMATS), consist of a 5 per cent sample of households in densely populated districts and a 10 per cent sample in sparsely

TABLE I
Percentage Distributions by Race and Sex

Groups	Percentages
Negroes	5.47
Whites	94.53
Negro Males	3.42
Negro Females	2.05
White Males	68.18
White Females	26.35

Source: Computer from 1964 TMATS data.

populated areas. The study area includes a 1964 estimated population of 363,876. Data were provided on some 4,000 IBM punch cards, each card representing a first work trip, with breakdowns by sex and race of traveler.[5] The percentage distributions of work trips by race and sex are given in Table I. Travel time was determined from departure and arrival times, and travel distance was calculated among the forty-eight metropolitan zones established by TMATS.

TRAVEL CHARACTERISTICS

A social problem of increasing importance is the large number of relatively unskilled workers chasing fewer and fewer manual jobs farther and farther into suburban areas. The apparent transportation advantage of workers living near the central business district (CBD) is being removed by suburbanization of work places, and as this suburbanization continues transportation disadvantages seem certain to intensify, particularly for Negroes residentially trapped in the inner city. Different cities are of course in various stages of this process of industrial decentralization.

Previous studies, based on cities much larger than Tulsa, have generally found that Negroes average shorter work trips than whites.[6] Some Negroes are employed in peripheral suburban locations, but, since their proportion is typically small in these larger cities, these commuters increase the over-all mean distance traveled to work only slightly. In smaller cities, a higher percentage of Negroes may be employed in the distant suburban areas, and the mean distance to work by Negroes may exceed that by whites.

Virtually all Negroes in Tulsa are confined to the ghetto immediately north of the CBD; but due to the sizable proportion of Negroes, especially

TABLE II
Mean Distance to Work in Airline Miles

Groups	All Work Trips	CBD Work Trips	Non-CBD Work Trips
Negroes	4.65	2.14	5.11
Whites	4.10	3.99	4.12
Negro Males	3.85	1.95	4.27
Negro Females	6.02	2.67	6.46
White Males	4.31	4.28	4.31
White Females	3.54	3.58	3.52

Source: Computer from 1964 TMATSdata.

females, employed in suburban areas, Negroes in Tulsa have mean work trips approximately one-half mile longer than whites, as seen in Table II. As expected, work trips which terminate in the CBD, however, are substantially longer for whites, more than one and eight-tenths miles greater than for Negroes. Clearly, it is work trips to non-CBD locations which place the mean for Negroes over that for whites.

When these data are broken down into sex and race categories, several other differences can be seen. For example, the high mean distance to work for Negroes is primarily attributable to the extremely long trips by Negro females, who average over two miles farther than Negro males. White males travel farther than Negro males, nearly one-half mile farther for all trips and well over two miles farther for CBD terminating work trips. The differential for non-CBD work trips is not as great. Negro females travel farther than white females, except to CBD work places.

Distance between home and work is only a gross index of travel differences. A somewhat more meaningful measure is travel time, shown in Table III. Some of the observations made on the basis of travel distance hold for travel time as well, but others do not. Negroes take longer to reach their work places and show greater variation than whites in time of trip. Longest trips are again by Negro females, who also have the greatest variability in travel time. There is no difference between the means for all trips by Negro and white males.

TABLE III
Work-Trip Travel Time in Minutes

Groups	Mean All Trips	Standard Deviation of All Trips	Mean of CBD Trips	Standard Deviation of CBD Trips
Negroes	21.8	12.7	21.8	8.7
Whites	19.6	9.9	20.4	8.9
Negro Males	20.0	9.8	22.8	9.4
Negro Females	24.9	15.9	19.2	6.0
White Males	20.0	9.9	20.7	8.7
White Females	18.5	9.7	19.9	9.2

Source: Computer from 1964 TMATS data.

Mean travel time to CBD work places is greater for Negroes than whites, despite the residential clustering of the Negroes near the CBD. Negro males have the longest travel time to the CBD of any group, due in part to a high proportion of walking trips. Whites working in the CBD, many of whom live in suburban areas, are able to travel a greater distance to work more rapidly than Negroes are able to traverse a shorter distance. These findings are consistent with those of Morgan: "Those who live in the central cities of the twelve largest metropolitan areas spend the longest time getting to work and back, because the closer one is to the center and the larger the urban area, the slower the travel speeds."[7] Not only does the Negro live in an area with poor transportation, but also in an area with considerable traffic congestion.

CONCLUDING REMARKS

What are the implications of these data? Since the low average income of Tulsa Negroes is associated with their low per capita automobile ownership, many Negroes must therefore travel to work by bus, or walk if the distance is not prohibitive. The system of bus routing focuses on the CBD, and Negroes from the ghetto may reach the nearby CBD with relatively little difficulty. However, the employment pattern of Negroes is much more widely spread over the metropolitan area than their residential pattern. Negroes who work neither in the CBD nor the ghetto find themselves moving counter, both morning and night, to the major commuter streams. Commuter buses are scheduled to carry workers to the CBD, and workers living downtown cannot easily commute to suburban areas. Suburban firms in Tulsa, therefore, recruit much of their labor locally and draw a smaller proportion of workers from the downtown Negro ghetto, due to the considerable travel effort involved. Of the Negroes employed in the suburbs in Tulsa, many are female domestic servants who work in the higher class white residential area southeast of the CBD.

Transit routing is determined by the major travel demands. Buses are not routed directly from one side of the city to another. Many trips add circuity by routing through the CBD, where a transfer is necessary to get to some other part of the city. In the areas of high population density, even a small departure from the shortest distance route is likely to generate more passengers and thus greater revenue. Hence, in many parts of Tulsa, the routing of buses is highly circuitous, and the time of travel is correspondingly slow. For example, travel from the CBD to the white residential area southeast of the CBD requires an average of thirty to thirty-five minutes, plus another ten to fifteen minutes to get from the ghetto to the CBD. Additional time may be consumed in walking once the last bus stop is reached, since suburban areas are very thinly serviced by bus transit.

In addition to the quality of transportation available, the question of how far and how long Negroes travel to work as compared to whites depends on the spatial arrangements of their home and work within the city. Among whites in many cities there appears to be a positive relationship between socioeconomic status and distance traveled to work. Groups with high socioeconomic status tend to reside in suburban areas and have long trips to CBD work places. Some researchers have concluded that "in Western cities the poor live at the center and the more mobile rich at the periphery . . ."[8] This generalization of relative mobility, however, does not fully apply to Negro work trips in Tulsa and may be breaking down for other cities as well.

The greater mobility of Negroes, whose median income is significantly below that of whites in Tulsa, suggests the operation of the "forced mobility" concept associated with limited residential choice. This "forced mobility," however, is mainly characteristic of Negro women, as Negro and white men show no important difference in travel to work. A study using 1938–48 data for Chicago dealt with changing home to work patterns of low-income workers, largely Negro, who initially lived in areas of inexpensive rental dwellings and who subsequently moved to a new residence. The study found that low-income workers "living in substandard housing will move to good low-rent housing even though they must travel farther to work."[9] In time, however, these workers tend to reorient themselves, if possible, to jobs closer to their new homes. These low-income workers may, at least temporarily, be forced to travel farther to work than they would prefer if inexpensive housing were widely available in the city. Likewise in Tulsa, Negroes who are employed in areas distant from the ghetto would probably live closer to work if such housing were available to them. Thus the low-income Negro who lives near the center of the city differs in mobility from the low-income white with similar downtown residence but nearby employment.

In sum, the paradox of Tulsa Negroes, confronted with numerous barriers to mobility but with mobility equal to or greater than whites, seems to be explained partially by their residential concentration and the resulting forced mobility. The greater time of travel by Negroes, particularly females, however, cannot be attributed solely to longer distance; rather, the composite of walking trips, bus transfers, automobile traffic congestion, and the directional and temporal biases of transit services are responsible. The advantage of living near the CBD has already been partially removed for Negro males in Tulsa by suburbanization of manual employment, as Negro men travel as far as white males on the average despite the much shorter trip to the CBD by Negroes. As the decentralization trend in jobs continues, it would seem that forced mobility will become a greater factor in work trips by Negro men, as it now is among Negro women.

The solutions to the transportation problems of the ghetto are, in the end, not limited to the ghetto but are an urban transportation problem cutting across racial lines, just as the transport system itself affects all parts of a metropolitan area. To achieve better interaction and an equilibrium with the urban environment, the Negro must not only be able to increase his alternatives of residential location but also his choices of employment location. Thus, permanent solutions are not to be found merely in rerouting of transit or in reducing congestion by building additional freeways, but rather in the physical disintegration of the ghetto in response to a general upward social mobility among Negroes—which in its final evaluation is dependent upon changing social attitudes. If all of this is to occur, the Negro will no longer be restricted in traveling from a ghetto to selected destinations along somewhat prescribed routes within the city; instead, his economic, social, recreational, and pleasure-driving trips would pass through and terminate in all parts of the urban area.

LITERATURE CITED

1. For excellent surveys of research on the American Negro, see John P. Davis (ed.), *The American Negro Reference Book* (Englewood Cliffs, N.J.: Prentice-Hall, 1966); Ray Murphy and Howard Elinson (eds.), *Problems and Prospects of the Negro Movement* (Belmont, Cal.: Wadsworth Co., 1966); and Talcott Parsons and Kenneth B. Clark (eds.), *The Negro American* (Boston: Houghton Mifflin Co., 1966).

2. One of the best overviews is Karl E. Taeuber and Alma F. Taeuber, *Negroes in Cities* (Chicago: Aldine Publishing Co., 1965). See also Otis Dudley Duncan and Beverly Duncan, *The Negro Population of Chicago* (Chicago: University of Chicago Press, 1957); and Karl E. Taeuber, "Negro Residential Segregation: Trends and Measurements," *Social Problems*, 12 (Summer 1964), 42–50.

3. Two recent studies provide some data on Negro travel behavior, the first drawing upon Chicago and Detroit examples and the second on Pittsburgh. "Race and the Urban Transportation Problem," in J. R. Meyer, J. F. Kain, and M. Wohl (eds.), *The Urban Transportation Problem* (Cambridge, Mass.: Harvard University Press, 1965), 144–67; and James O. Wheeler, "Work-Trip Length and the Ghetto," *Land Economics*, 44 (February, 1968), 107–12.

4. Governor's Commission on the Los Angeles Riots, *Violence in the City —An End or a Beginning*, Dec. 2, 1965, p. 65. Chairman of the commission was John A. McCone. For a critical evaluation of the so-called McCone Report and analysis of the Los Angeles riots, see Anthony Oberschall, "The Los Angeles Riot of August 1965," *Social Problems*, 15 (Winter 1968), 322–41.

5. One reason for the paucity of research on Negro travel behavior is lack of data. While occupation, sex, and even income are commonly used

variables in metropolitan transportation surveys, relatively few cities record travel data by race. Although the transportation surveys of Chicago, Detroit, and Pittsburgh, conducted during the 1950s, obtained data by race, many cities having conducted more recent surveys either cannot or will not use such a breakdown.

6. Meyer, et al., op. cit.; Wheeler, op. cit.; for a comparison of Negro and white travel in a rural area, in which Negroes travel farther than whites, see James O. Wheeler and Stanley D. Brunn, "Negro Migration into Rural Southwestern Michigan," *Geographical Review,* 58 (April 1968), 214–30.

7. James N. Morgan, "A Note on the Time Spent on the Journey to Work," *Demography,* 4 (1967), 360.

8. Brian J. L. Berry, James W. Simmons, and Robert J. Tennant, "Urban Population Densities: Structure and Change," *Geographical Review,* 53 (July 1963), 404.

9. Robert F. Whiting, "Home-to-Work Relationships of Workers Living in Public Housing Projects in Chicago," *Land Economics,* 28 (August 1952), 289.

CHAPTER V

Locational Aspects of Black Political Activity

INTRODUCTORY NOTE

Politics always have been of great consequence to black Americans. However, for too long blacks have been objects of political practices and not participants in the political scene. But recently many blacks have become involved in political processes, a participation that ranges from ballot box to urban rebellions.

Geographical implications of political activity have also been of great importance to blacks. Historically, locational restrictions, such as gerrymandering and residential segregation, have limited black political power. Today, blacks have found political strength by utilizing their isolation as a positive force in that ghettos have evolved into foci of political organization based on the power of bloc voting, unified dissent, and opposition to established political structures.

Within the last several years, political geographers have become increasingly concerned with political problems on a microscale rather than with traditional emphases on international geopolitical affairs. Such interest is manifested by articles on intracity voting behavior, local control of government functions, and urban policy making. Chapter Five concerns racial politics in ghetto social territory. Each article analyzes different facets of this new approach to political geography.

The locational focus of black political power is the ghetto, as has been demonstrated by the fact that most black rebellions and militant activities have centered in ghettos. Howard F. Salisbury has brought to light several fascinating and even alarming parallels between the black ghetto and the insurgent state. In the article, Salisbury proposes to provide an answer to questions raised concerning reasons for the territorial focus of racial violence in black ghettos by drawing areal comparisons between ghettos and guerrilla bases of insurgent states.

Salisbury marks as very important the rapid and intense development of the concept of black culture as a major manifestation of the new black *raison d'être*. Belief by blacks that they cannot operate within a white cultural system and must develop a separate distinctly black cultural system is shown to be remarkably similar to antigovernment philosophy that develops and helps sustain insurgent states.

Locational superiority of ghettos makes them ideal bases of operations for urban guerrilla war. Salisbury, however, does not advocate open rebellion but merely emphasizes the strategic importance of ghettos. The ghetto, long a center of stress, has become recently a nucleus of violent opposition to the dominant white culture. Situated near the CBD, ghettos provide access to strategic political and economic targets. The familiar terrain of the ghetto gives residents definite initial advantages in the advent of open hostilities.

Black ghettos share many important political elements with insurgent states. These similarities include: (1) a clear sense of territory; (2) clearly perceived boundaries; (3) homogeneous population; (4) core area; and (5) ability to provide the necessities of life.

Ghettos defined further as territories giving black residents feelings of unity and identity and, as such, are power bases secure from white authority. Salisbury claims that ghettos and guerrilla bases are locational analogues, in that ghettos have become areas of increasing and definite revolutionary experience and antigovernment activity.

Salisbury has demonstrated successfully locational similarities between guerrilla bases and black ghettos. The riots of the 1960s illustrate even more powerfully that these parallels exist in reality and not just in academic literature. Obviously, geographers bear great responsibilities, with other social scientists, in resolving socioeconomic discrepancies in use and allocation of territory in cities. They must eschew "scientific objectivity" for meaningful research which will be solution rather than problem orientated.

Equality of opportunity to purchase or lease a place of residence is a basic inalienable right for all citizens of the United States, as guaranteed by the Civil Rights Acts of 1866 and 1968. Unfortunately, enforcement of this right and law has varied widely, particularly as far as racial and ethnic minorities are concerned. In the past several years, the federal government, for the first time in history, in both the Congress and the Supreme Court, has expressed strong support of open housing.

Although many political geographers study locational characteristics of urban voting patterns, few are concerned with nonpartisan issues. Stanley D. Brunn and Wayne L. Hoffman utilize data from one nonpartisan urban referendum, that of Flint, Michigan, to analyze several geographical aspects related to open housing. Specifically, three objectives are pursued in the work: black and white reactions toward open housing as measured by the referendum vote; geographic variation with respect to income, education, and housing values for blacks and whites; and effect of distance from the ghetto on voting behavior of whites in Flint.

Simple and stepwise multiple regression models and various map comparisons and profiles are used to analyze and exhibit voting behavior of blacks and whites. Cartographic techniques are employed to enable the authors to "fit" wards and precincts to census blocks and tracts, a procedure that is only partially successful.

Brunn and Hoffman conclude that, although there are perceivable differences between black and white voting behavior, there are no significant areal voting patterns based on income, education, and housing by race. However, the distance factor proved statistically significant, with whites close to black areas voting against it. Analysis of voting behavior by race revealed blacks voted almost solidly for the referendum while the white vote varied considerably.

Brunn and Hoffman contribute an important work to the literature of political behavior. By studying locational patterns of a nonpartisan referendum by race, they demonstrate need for more research on areal-political significance of social variables.

Michael Jenkins and John Shepherd investigate decentralization of school administration, a problem particularly thorny due to basically conflicting ideologies of neighborhood control and racial integration. Detroit is used as a case study as Michigan Public Act Number 244 requires the city to be divided into decentralized school boards.

The authors utilize computerized grouping algorithms to generate all possible ways of amalgamating Detroit's high school districts into new regions given enrollment (25,000–50,000 students) and contiguity constraints. Thus, Jenkins and Shepherd attempt to extend the range of choice to community organizations rather than to draw up yet another "best" plan or selection of plans suitable to only one group or organization.

They conclude from the study's results that both demographic and geographic disadvantages will accrue to black communities whenever federal requirements of integration and equal representation (one man-one vote) are included in decentralization proposals. When these requirements are part of decentralization proposals virtually all purported solutions result in white-dominated situations.

Jenkins and Shepherd state that a more appropriate strategy for ghetto and civil rights organizations is to promote and support decentralization plans stressing racial homogeneity or community control of education. Such solutions will result in black children under black control and white children under white control. Actualization of such a proposal might conceivably result in such diametrically opposed organizations as Black Panthers and John Birch Society, both supporting the same decentralization scheme for different yet related reasons. Unfortunately, this fascinating situation is unlikely to develop considering the federal courts' current penchant for cross-city and school district busing to achieve integration.

THE STATE WITHIN A STATE:
SOME COMPARISONS BETWEEN THE URBAN GHETTO
AND THE INSURGENT STATE

Howard G. Salisbury

———

The American black ghetto has long been the center of disorders and riots. Recent riots have been classified by the press as a black rebellion or even the beginning of a major black revolution. Such disruptions have affected hundreds of American cities and range in scale from major riots such as Los Angeles (Watts, 1965) or Detroit (1967) to small local incidences. Along with physical violence of riots and burning there has also been a considerable increase in the frequency and intensity of activity by militant groups such as the Black Panthers.

Though violence and rhetoric have been the focus for the press and most social scientists, ghetto geography has often been ignored. While black hatred was focused on the white man and white society, violence has been concentrated in the ghetto. Why? The territorial focus of disorders has been the urban ghetto. Riots usually occur within the ghetto and most of the militant activity is also centered there. Why? The purpose of this paper is to provide one answer through a geopolitical analysis of the black ghetto and to draw some comparisons between the ghetto and the insurgent state[1] including the guerrilla base area—the most important part of the insurgent state. In addition I will point out important parallels between location factors of the guerrilla base area which are also important aspects of the ghettos' location. This is not to imply that the entire ghetto population is actively engaged in guerrilla war, but rather that there are certain similarities or geopolitical parallels between the ghetto and the insurgent state that should be considered.

GEOPOLITICAL FEATURES OF THE URBAN GHETTO

An insurgent state such as the National Liberation Front in Vietnam occurs when a totally separate or alien enclave is created within the legitimate state. It may be consciously created, as in the Vietnam and China revolutions, or it may simply evolve as in the American ghetto. In any case, the insurgent state includes "the creation of territorial units complete with all the attributes of any legitimate state, namely a *raison d'être*, control of territory and population and, particularly the creation of its core areas and administrative units as well as a power base in its guerrilla army."[2] Some of the more important elements of the insurgent state include (1) a clear sense of territory (turf) which often involves perception of your own territory, the legitimate government's territory and contested areas; (2) clearly perceived boundaries; (3) a homogeneous population; (4) a core area; and (5) ability to provide all the necessities of life, especially food and defense. Although the urban ghetto was not intentionally created to become an insurgent state it has developed many of the characteristics and therefore should be analyzed in these terms. Such analysis yields a more dynamic picture of the ghetto than the more bleak social or economic analyses.

There are many geopolitical similarities between the guerrillas' rural insurgent state of underdeveloped countries and the modern American urban black ghetto. The ghetto is developing into an enclave of antiwhite resentment and activity within the United States. Tom Wicker has described a typical urban rioter as:

> By and large the rioters were young Negroes, natives of the ghetto (not of the South), hostile to the white society surrounding and repressing them, and equally hostile to the middle class Negroes who accommodated themselves to white dominance. The rioters were mistrustful of white politics, they hated the police, they were proud of their race and acutely conscious of the discrimination they suffered.[3]

This antiwhite feeling, along with lack of faith in the government by many blacks, is similar to the type of resentment which provides the antigovernment *raison d'être* for popular revolution in insurgent areas.

The reason for existence is probably the most critical factor of the insurgent state. The careful formulation of a statement of motivation differentiates the insurgent from the bandit, and provides the rationale for his cause and his followers. The *raison d'être* of the modern black ghetto is racism.[4] The psychological and sociological development and description of racism are beyond the scope of this paper, but the existence and the serious implications of racism in black America have been clearly established.[5] In the past decade the black reaction to racism has changed from one of pacifism to one of activism.[6] This change to active resistance has taken a wide variety of forms, ranging from "soul food" to "naturals" to "Afro-dress" and riots against "whitey," yet the essence of the black motivation is a combination of antiwhite values and problack mores. The best example of this phenomenon is the growing development of a recognized black culture in America.[7]

The rapid and intense development of the concept of black culture has been a major manifestation of the new black *raison d'être* during the last decade. The rise of this culture is founded on the belief by blacks that they cannot operate in a white cultural system and therefore they must develop a separate cultural system. After a hundred years of trying to adapt black culture to white America, it now seems that most blacks believe there is an urgent need for a distinctly black cultural system. This is often referred to as "Black Pride." An example of this desire for a separate culture is the "Black Is Beautiful" movement, involving rejection of white beauty standards and adoption of standards more suited to blacks such as "naturals." The rejection of white values has been extended to black eating habits with the development of "soul food"; to dress standards by the adoption of Afro-dress or the black jacket, light blue pants and black beret of the Black Panthers; or new forms of interaction, such as referring to each other as "soul brother" or the new black handshake of interlocking thumbs, not hands. The whole concept of black power, which is symbolized by the clenched black fist, is based on the premise that only blacks should rule and control blacks. Blacks should have final say on all legislation concerning blacks, all administration, economic ownership, and all other economic and political activity dealing with blacks. These are only a few of the signs of a developing separatism. Some of the more extreme views of black culture are provided by the militant groups.

An extreme *raison d'être*, but at the same time contributing substantially to the over-all pattern is the number of militant movements. Black militants such as the Black Panthers, Black Muslims, Organization of Afro-American Unity, Blackstone Rangers, Black Liberation Front, and others demand total rejection of everything that is white. The degree of militancy varies from the Muslim demands for an independent state (probably in the southeastern United States), to the Black Panthers' demand for total overthrow of the United States. A major aspect of the militants' philosophy is based upon the belief (real or not) that white society is proceeding on a course of genocide against all black people. Their rhetoric usually refers to white America as foreign oppressors. They often refer to the ghetto as the colony or black colony of these foreign oppressors. It is common for them to use terms like "Babylon," "Americka," or

"Amerikka" to refer to the United States and speak in terms of the police as the soldiers of Babylon or use the term "pig." The combination of these feelings, both militant and nonmilitant has crystallized a definite antiwhite core in the modern United States urban ghetto that is similar to the antigovernment philosophy that develops and helps sustain the insurgent state.

An important aspect of both the insurgent state and the ghetto is its identification with identifiable territory. The insurgent state and ghetto both have a specific territory with a core area (heartland or ecumene) and clearly established and perceived boundaries. In Vietnam there are "liberated areas" (Viet Cong controlled), government controlled areas, and contested areas. In the city there are also clearly established boundaries demarcating the black, white, and fringe areas based on racial distribution, and these boundaries are clearly perceived and rigidly adhered to by both sides.[8] A good example of one of these boundaries is Alameda Avenue which forms the political and racial boundary between Watts and its neighbors to the east—Lynwood and South Gate. The "contested areas," which would correspond to the "fringe area," are not as clearly defined as they are in a war zone, but would generally coincide with any area into which the blacks are expanding, such as lower class white or other minority areas.[9] While such "fringe areas" mark the outer limits of the ghetto, the "core area" is the heart of the ghetto.

Just as guerrilla base areas provide the core area for the insurgent state, the ghetto also has its heartland or core area. The location, size, and number of core areas within a ghetto will vary from city to city but their function remains the same. The core is found where the people conduct most of their activity, have most economic dealings, look for leadership, feel most secure, and where they turn in time of need or crisis. Some well-known core areas of black ghettos include Watts (Los Angeles), Harlem (New York), Hough (Cleveland), Roxbury (Boston), The Hill (Pittsburgh), and the Central Ward (Newark). It is in or near the core area where the ghetto resident is most likely to challenge or resist authority because it is here that he feels most secure on his turf, an area furthest removed from the white power base. Most recent riots have begun in and reached the greatest intensity in the ghetto core area.[10]

The ghetto, its boundaries, core area, homogeneity of population, and *raison d'être* all combine to give the ghetto resident his feeling of identity. The ghetto is his territory. It is where he is most familiar, the area in which he is most effective and the area which he will defend. This is his "turf" and the closer he is to the core area the stronger his sense of territory and security becomes. This strong sense of territory was shown by the behavior of the ghetto residents during most urban riots in past decades. Although the riots were almost always antiwhite and anticommercial, they always remained within the ghetto territory where the participants felt safest. Logically, if the rioters were antiwhite and anticommercial they should have attacked the white suburbs, central business district, or industrial section, and spared the ghetto, but the reverse has been the case and the riots have caused maximum damage to the ghetto itself. The core area is an important focus of activity during nonriot situations.

The core area acts as the center of revolutionary activity in both the insurgent state and ghetto. Almost all of the militant groups have headquarters in or near the core area. This gives the militants maximum protection while at the same time placing them in a position of maximum contact with the community for dissemination of information. This seems to be an important aspect of the Black Panthers' choice of location for their various headquarters throughout the nation. By locating in the ghetto and defending these locations so violently, they show the ghetto resident that they are there to stay and that they intend to defend the ghetto against "the white invaders" at all costs.

THE GHETTO AND THE GUERRILLA BASE: ANALOGUES IN LOCATION

The foregoing geopolitical discussion and analysis of the black ghetto has emphasized a comparison with the insurgent state. I would now like to make a locational analysis of the ghetto in terms of some factors that determine the location of the traditional guerrilla base area, the most important power or functional part of the insurgent state. Although the ghetto is not intentionally located in certain areas as the guerrilla base area is, there are certain geographic parallels or features that are worthy of consideration. This is not to imply that the author believes that a black guerrilla war is inevitable but rather that there are some features of the possible strategic location of the ghetto that have not been considered before.

McColl has outlined several location factors or attributes that are critical in the location of a guerrilla base area. These include: (1) If possible an area should be chosen that has had previous experience in revolution or political opposition to the central government; (2) political stability at both national and local levels should be weak or actually lacking; (3) the location must provide access to important military and political objectives, such as provincial capitals, regional cities, and critical resource and transport services; (4) areas of weak or confused political authority, such as borders between provinces or between police or military areas, or even along international boundaries are ideal locations; (5) terrain should be favorable for military operations and personal security; (6) insofar as possible the area should be economically self-sufficient.[11]

An area of previous revolutionary experience or political opposition to the government is desirable because the people usually already retain strong antigovernment feelings and often an antigovernment infrastructure is already present. As shown above, the ghetto has long been a major center of disruptions and political opposition in the United States. The major difference today is the increased awareness of Black Culture and Black Power. This was one of the major negative consequences of the urban riots that have hit hundreds of urban centers in the last ten years. These riots provided a large segment of population, especially the young, with an antigovernment experience and reinforced many of the antiwhite attitudes discussed above. However, rioting as serious as it is, is only a small part of the antigovernment experience being gathered in the ghetto that reinforces the "us" versus "them" concept which is so important in an insurgent state. These range from major shootouts, such as those with Black Panthers, and bombings of San Francisco and New York, to minor daily incidents termed "police harassment" by the blacks. The total effect is that the ghetto has become an area of increasing and definite revolutionary experience and antigovernment activity.

An ideal location for a typical guerrilla base area is one that provides access to important military targets. As I mentioned, the ghetto was not intentionally located in the "inner city," yet its location is almost ideal for access to the CBD, major transportation routes and facilities, utility and communication centers, and most other vital economic sections of the city, such as the wholesale, retail, and manufacturing districts. To date most of the rioting has been limited to the ghetto, but if the new rioting or even guerrilla warfare spread into these important areas the human and economic consequences would be far greater than anything we have seen.

The ghetto is usually found near to or surrounding the CBD; this certainly would be considered an important economic target during urban rioting or urban guerrilla war. Usually at least one and often several vital transportation routes such as major freeways or highways, railroads, or water transport pass through the ghetto and might be closed, thus separating many suburbanites from their place of work. An example was the closing of the Harbor Freeway during the Watts riot. Usually many vital utilities and communications networks are vulnerable to attack from the ghetto. One reason there were so few police to help stop the early rioting in Detroit (1967) was that a large number were used to guard the vital utility and communications center that might have been threatened. The ghetto is usually strategically located in terms of access to other vital districts such as wholesale, retail, and manufacturing. McColl has drawn an idealized map showing a typical ghetto location in reference to the districts of the city, which in reality is close to the present pattern in most American cities.[12] It reveals that the location of most ghettos would be ideal locations for a guerrilla base in an urban area. Compare for example the location of the ghetto in relation to its targets with that of the ideal rural guerrilla base areas with relation to their potential targets, where the spatial pattern is different but locational factors are remarkably similar. Thus it can be seen that the ghetto has the locational potential to cripple most American cities.

The ghetto is a good example of weak or confused political authority. Because nobody wants the problems of the ghetto, most municipal, county, and special districts, such as water, sewage, rapid transit, education and others have been gerrymandered to exclude the ghetto. Many agencies such as police, fire, health, and welfare having responsibilities in the ghetto often ignore these responsibilities or "pass the buck" to other agencies. In addition, many communities incorporate separately to exclude the area of the ghetto. The end result is a confused political situation with all sorts of overlapping or insufficient jurisdiction.[13] A good example of this confusion occurred during the Watts riot of 1965 when nobody could decide whose jurisdiction the area came under or who should have administrative control.[14] The indecisiveness of action and decisions caused by this confused line of authority was one reason there was so much damage in Los Angeles. Salter and Mings point out that there was a similar confusion in the Miami riots (1968).[15] Apparently most antiriot forces are more organized now but the ghetto remains an area of confused political control.

In terms of the analogy with a terrain suitable for military operations and personal safety, there is little natural similarity between the landscape of an entire country and the urban situation, but the urban landscape often provides a favorable "terrain" for the ghetto resident. Buildings and alleys provide the same cover and concealment as jungle or forest does for the rural insurgent. The ghetto resident's knowledge of his territory gives a mobility advantage over an outsider who is unfamiliar with the "terrain."

One aspect where ghetto and guerrilla base differ is in economic self-sufficiency. As mentioned above, the latter should insofar as possible be economically self-sufficient, providing the necessities of food, munitions, medical aid, education, communication, and other needs. The black ghetto has tended to function as an independent social and economic unit in America; there is no doubt it could provide most items that it might need to be self-sufficient, but one item is missing in an urban environment: agriculture. The urban ghetto has no agriculture base and therefore can never be totally self-sufficient, which is one reason the ghetto could never be a base for a protracted war but might be an effective base in terms of limited rioting or guerrilla war.[16]

In this paper I have tried to point out some geographic and geopolitical similarities between the rural insurgent state of national revolutionary wars and the urban black ghetto. I am aware that many conditions that exist in the guerrilla-created insurgent state are intentionally planned, while most of the conditions and similarities of the ghetto are part of a greater cultural phenomenon, much of which is basically unplanned. Yet we have seen that much like the insurgent state the black ghetto has its own *raison d'être*, core area, boundaries, territory, and often tends to function as an autonomous enclave rather than an integral part of the state. In addition I have shown that there are locational similarities between the guerrilla base area and the ghetto. It is clear that the ghetto has a more strategic location than has been recognized in the past.

Literature Cited

1. McColl, R. W., "The Insurgent State: Territorial Bases of Revolution," *Annals* of the American Association of Geographers, Vol. 59, No. 4, Dec. 1969.

2. Ibid., p. 614.

3. *Report of the National Advisory Commission on Civil Disorders*, National Advisory Commission on Civil Disorders, Bantam, New York, 1968, p. x.

4. Ibid., pp. 203–35.

5. Ibid., pp. 203–35.

6. Conot, Robert, *Rivers of Blood, Years of Darkness*, Bantam, New York, 1967, pp. ix–x.

7. "Black America 1970," *Time* Magazine, Vol. 95, Part 2, April 6, 1970, p. 13.

8. Taeuber, Karl, "The Problem of Residential Segregation," in R. H. Connery (ed.), *Urban Riots*, Vintage, New York, 1969, p. 109.

9. "Journey Through Two Americas," *Time* Magazine, Vol. 95, Part 2, April 6, 1970, pp. 30–35.

10. National Advisory Commission on Civil Disorders, op. cit., pp. 109–200.

11. McColl, R. W., op. cit., pp. 617–18; "A Political Geography of Revolution: China, Viet Nam, and Thailand," *The Journal of Conflict Resolution*, Vol. 2, 1967, pp. 153–67.

12. McColl, R. W., "Vietnam, Cuba, and the Ghetto," *Kansas Alumni*, University of Kansas Alumni Association, Lawrence, Jan. 1970, p. 13.

13. Gans, Herbert, "The Ghetto Rebellions and Urban Class Conflict," in R. H. Connery (ed.), *Urban Riots*, Vintage, New York, 1969, pp. 45–54.

14. Conot, R., op. cit., especially pp. 214–38.

15. Salter, Paul, and Mings, Robert, "A Geographic Aspect of the 1968 Miami Racial Disturbance: A Preliminary Investigation," *Professional Geographer*, Vol. 21, No. 2, March 1969, pp. 79–86.
16. See Martin Oppenheimer, *The Urban Guerrilla*, Quadrangle Books, Chicago, 1969.

THE SPATIAL RESPONSE OF NEGROES AND WHITES
TOWARD OPEN HOUSING: THE FLINT REFERENDUM

Stanley D. Brunn
and
Wayne L. Hoffman

The social, economic, and political controversy surrounding the issue of open housing has been heightened in the past few years by the passage of civil rights legislation affecting minority groups, by the judicial decisions rendered by the United States Supreme Court and lower courts, and by the election to public offices of individuals with certain persuasions.[1] The responses toward open housing, other than in a legal framework, have been reflected in various ways. For example, there have been the reactions of real estate developers who have tied Negro presence and ownership to declining land values, the appearance of "block-busters," community zoning ordinances as well as the financial investment of groups into integrated housing ventures, the establishment and enforcement of "fair housing" codes, and the election of public officials with favorable stances on open housing and similar legislation. In spite of some obstacles and apparent setbacks, attitudes with respect to residential integration have been gaining increasing acceptance in the South as well as in the North.[2] The overriding importance of this residential issue is linked closely with other civil rights programs such as school desegregation, busing pupils for "neighborhood balance," desegregation of public facilities such as playgrounds, voter registration, and equal job opportunity.

Prior to the congressional passage of the open housing bill in April, and the Supreme Court's judgment in June 1968, voters in several states and cities had expressed their views about open housing.[3] The federal ruling stated that discrimination based on race in the sale or rental of housing was illegal.[4] It is worth noting from a historical perspective that from 1935 to 1950 the federal government aided residential discrimination against Negroes in various financial and construction policies. During this period the government encouraged neighborhood homogeneity, which meant the exclusion of Negroes.[5] Such programs and policies thereby helped promote white dominance in the suburbs and public housing concentrations for Negroes in the central cities. Prior to the 1968 federal ruling on open housing, this topic had been a hotly contested issue in several northern industrial cities, one of which was Flint, Michigan. This was the first city to have a referendum on open housing approved by its voters, and this was only after the city council had approved it by a narrow five to four margin.[6]

Brink and Harris stated that probably no civil rights measure other than possibly that on intermarriage has had such a profound emotional effect on white urban Americans.[7] The emotional response evoked questions of whether open housing invades the sanctity of the home, the inherent "right" to private property, and the basic freedom to make individual decisions. In addition this issue arouses a number of less subtle but evident white responses toward Negroes such as stereotyping physical characteristics, social values, economic spirit and, above all, their association with declining land values once they appear in white neighborhoods. For the Negro the equal response to purchase or rent a residence is viewed as a basic inalienable right.[8] Their frustration to achieve this goal leads to despair and may manifest itself in the form of peaceful or violent noncooperation with the white power structure.

Open housing for all citizens has become a more acute need in recent years from the civil rights point of view and from the short and long term consequences of *de facto* segregation policies in our cities. This has become a problem in the northern as well as the southern cities.[9] At the very root of the open housing question lie such issues as the survival of the commercial core in the cities, the employment and education opportunities and facilities for minority groups in the inner city, and the necessity for coordinated decisions rendered by representatives from the varying social and economic strata in the city.[10] Today there are few major cities where Negroes do not comprise a sizeable segment of the urban population and where housing for them is not a major problem. By restricting complete freedom in the sale or rental of residence many urban planners have concluded that policies of housing apartheid will lead eventually to increased ghetto expansion and a host of related social, economic, and political problems.[11] Some of the planning schemes designed to "solve" Negro housing problems, such as urban renewal, have not always been popular with Negroes. Frequently these programs have stressed commercial development in former residential areas which has meant that the residential space available for immediate Negro occupancy has been reduced. This results in increased crowding in already overcrowded facilities.[12] It is not difficult to imagine how feelings of separateness have developed among the black residents in our cities especially when urban housing problems are considered. Recent investigations by Farley and Taeuber into population increases and densities for Negroes and whites in our major cities have demonstrated that there is more residential segregation today between the inner city and the suburbs than in 1960.[13] Furthermore, they indicate the separateness is increasing.

For many central city Negroes not only has the finding of adequate and sufficient housing become a major problem but so has locating a permanent source of employment. Discrimination in housing does reduce the job opportunities for those in the middle as well as the lower stratum. For many Negroes their place of employment is not in the central city but in the suburbs. This means their journey-to-work in terms of distance, time, and cost is placing them far from their residences.[14] Some central city ghetto Negroes have solved their residence problems by leapfrogging the suburbs to settle in small rural towns beyond the white suburban ring.[15] There can be no doubt but that *de facto* segregation policies associated with housing, schooling, and employment have contributed substantially to the separation of the white and Negro populations, the former being allowed the freedom of selection and mobility and the latter being denied the same privileges.

In a consideration of an open housing issue there are a number of facets that make the issue worthy of a political and social geographic investigation, and that have some utility in city planning. For example, what is the areal extent of the white and Negro populations? What are the spatial facets important in ghetto expansion? What effect does urban renewal have on the Negro migration? Do views of whites and blacks toward open housing, as reflected in a referendum, vary over space? What social and economic characteristics are associated with the vote in the ghetto, the suburbs, and the transitional zone? And what effect does distance from the ghetto have on the voting pattern for the whites?

The February 20, 1968, referendum in Flint, Michigan, was used to test and analyze several of the above spatial aspects related to open housing. This achieved national attention because it was the first time the residents of a major city had approved an open housing referendum. The final vote was indeed very close: 20,170 for the issue and 20,140 against.[16] Flint is similar to other large northern industrial centers such as Cleveland, Detroit, Gary, and Chicago which also have large Negro populations. In Flint about 17 per cent of the city was Negro in 1960, and it was estimated to be about 20 per cent in 1968. Most Negroes reside in two main concentrations that are surrounded by the white population.[17] In using Flint as a case study the purposes of this investigation are threefold: 1) to determine the white and Negro reactions toward open housing as measured by the vote; 2) to examine the geographic variation with respect to income, education, and housing values for Negroes and whites; and 3) to investigate the effects distance from the center of the ghetto and from the ghetto periphery have on the voting behavior of the whites. The social, economic, and distance indicators and the open housing vote were incorporated into simple and stepwise multiple regression models. Separate models were used to investigate the behavior of the blacks and the whites. In addition to the statistical results various maps and tables are incorporated into the analysis.

SURVEY OF LITERATURE

There is a wealth of literature by political scientists, sociologists, psychologists, public administrators, economists, and some geographers that has bearing on this problem. For example, there are studies concerned with policy making, voting behavior, Negro-white relations, ghetto characteristics, Negro "invasion," real estate values, housing conditions, and attitudes toward issues such as open housing. However, it is not the purpose of this study to present a review and summarize all these topics but rather to concentrate on urban voting patterns and especially those related to nonpartisan referendums and on the attitudes of whites and Negroes toward open housing.

A notable trend in social and political geography in recent years has been the concern with voting behavior and patterns. Although most of the voting studies have been concerned with political parties in states or countries there have been several that have dealt with cities such as those by Clodfelter, Van Duzer, Kasperson, Lewis, Roberts and Rumage, Rowley, Simmons, and Cox.[18] To date there has been only one geographic study that has considered aspects of urban nonpartisan referendums, even though the research possibilities for future studies are great.[19] In the main the urban investigations by political scientists and sociologists have dealt with both partisan and nonpartisan issues. They have been concerned with the administering of elections, the policy-making mechanisms at various levels, the salient differences in central city and suburban behavior, the growing political power of the suburbs, and the role of religion, party, class, and race in given elections.[20]

With regard to housing there have been several studies by geographers concerned with topics related to its quality, density, and composition in different cities and parts of a city.[21] There have been no studies that have dealt with such social issues as open housing or about the variation in attitudes toward this or similar programs. The urban sociologists have done a great deal of work on such topics as varying attitudes within urban areas, social distances between groups, residential patterns for ethnic groups, Negro population changes, urban discrimination indices, and the movement of Negroes into white areas.[22] Of particular relevance to this study are those that have investigated the opinions and attitudes of both Negroes and whites prior to, during, and after Negroes have moved into predominantly all-white neighborhoods.[23] Also, the contributions of urban economists and real estate and appraisal experts demonstrate a concern for a number of facets related to open housing that may be associated with how people vote on open housing referendums. Their concern has been mainly with the changes in property values, taxation discrimination, and land use changes as a result of the invasion of Negroes into transitional areas and exclusive white residential areas.[24] The significant findings of these studies and others help form a basis from which to postulate research hypotheses that can be used to analyze the voting patterns for the open housing referendum in Flint.

HYPOTHESES

From the literature of various associated studies by geographers, sociologists, political scientists, and others several hypotheses relating to the geographic distribution of the open housing referendum are advanced. Separate hypotheses are postulated for the white and the Negro populations.

First, in relation to the white sector a positive relationship is predicted between the affirmative vote and median income, median education level, and the median value of owner occupied dwellings. The correlation between education and racial attitudes is particularly well documented by Lipset and Allport; both devote ample attention to this relationship.[25] Their findings substantiate the expected relationship. Allport, for example, stated ". . . that general education to an appreciable degree helps raise the level of tolerance."[26] Median income plays a key role according to Lipset; he concluded that for many underlying reasons the wealthier are more tolerant where issues of civil liberties and race relations are concerned.[27] This notion was corroborated further by Brink and Harris, who found in their survey research that affluent whites are much more favorably inclined toward the Negro than their low income counterpart.[28] The role of the median value of owner occupied dwellings, although not dealt with specifically in the literature on attitude formation, seems to be directly related to the above statements. It is assumed that the better educated and wealthier classes would occupy, with only slight exceptions, the homes of higher median value.

For the white population it is also hypothesized that physical proximity to Negroes will play an important role in their voting decision process.

TABLE 1

Spontaneous Expressions of Anti-Negro Sentiment: After Kramer

	Zone 1	Zone 2	Zone 3	Zone 4	Zone 5
Percent Spontaneously Expressing Anti-Negro Sentiment	64	43	27	14	4
Number Interviewed	118	115	121	123	142

Source: Allport, op. cit., footnote 25, p. 257.

Various studies have demonstrated that social distance between groups has affected whites' voting behavior for minority group leaders.[29] The elements of social distance can be related in an urban setting to physical distance between groups (ethnic, racial, social, or occupational classes) which likewise would undoubtedly affect voting patterns.[30] The result may be "block" voting by whites, blacks, or other major groups which exhibit strong feelings of unity. In Kramer's study of the southern edge of the black belt in Chicago he found that when interviewing whites the physical distance from Negroes did play a definite role in the attitude formation and in the amount of racial friction.[31] After marking off five zones, with number one being at the point of contact with the expanding Negro ghetto and number five three miles away, he interviewed white respondents for spontaneous expressions of black hostility (Table 1). A similar finding was reported by Winder; he found that low income whites in the same zone with Negroes showed more prejudice than those in an intermediate zone. The difference was attributed to competition for low income housing.[32] The concept of distance and its effect on the voting behavior is tested in this study by incorporating two spatial variables into the framework of the regression model. They are straight line distance from the center of the ghetto and straight line distance from the closest Negro precinct. It is postulated that a positive relationship exists between the favorable vote for open housing and distance from the ghetto and nearest Negro precinct.[33]

For the Negro, racial concern and pride, plus an awareness of the inherent advantages of open housing, are expected to override major internal differences. Survey research has indicated that Negroes of all income classes do desire to live in integrated neighborhoods (Table 2).[34] It has been demonstrated by Horton and Thompson, Wilson, and Wilson and

TABLE 2

Negro Attitudes Toward Desired Housing and Neighborhood: After Brink and Harris

Question: In living in a neighborhood, if you could find the housing you want and like, would you rather live in a neighborhood with Negro families, or in a neighborhood that had both whites and Negroes?

	Negroes		Whites and Negroes			Not Sure	
	1966 %	1963 %	1966 %	1963 %		1966 %	1963 %
Total all interviews	17	20	68	64		15	16
Total non-South	8	11	79	75		13	14
Non-South							
Low Income	10	19	79	75		11	6
Lower Middle Income	7	11	78	75		15	14
Middle and Upper Income	6	12	80	69		14	19
Total South	26	27	57	55		17	18
South							
Urban	22	26	58	57		20	17
Non-Urban	29	33	56	50		15	17
Middle and Upper Income	17	6	70	69		13	25
Age							
Under 35 years	12		75			13	
35-49 years	17		67			16	
50 years and over	21		63			16	
Civil rights pace too slow	13		75			12	
Negro community leaders	10		59			31	

Source: Brink and Harris, op. cit., footnote 7, p. 232.

Banfield that some of the socially and economically deprived groups vote negatively on nonpartisan issues.[35] Wilson and Banfield in their research on Negroes mention that they, as distinct from some other minority groups, have a greater "public regardingness" on certain issues and vote in a positive manner. Even though most Negroes in Flint live in relatively

TABLE 3
Predicted Direction of Relationships

	Median income	Median education	Median housing value	Distance center of ghetto	Distance nearest Negro precinct
Negroes	—	—	—	—	—
Whites	+	+	+	+	+

— = negative relationship.
+ = positive relationship.
Source: Calculated by authors.

low valued housing areas, and have lower education levels than their white counterparts, they are expected to support strongly this particular nonpartisan issue. It is postulated, therefore, that for Negroes there is a negative relationship between the favorable open housing vote and median income, median education, and median housing values. These assumptions are strengthened by recent research in Columbus, Ohio, where in another nonpartisan referendum, viz., one dealing with urban renewal, rather large negative correlation values appeared between such variables as education, income, and the vote when the Negro community was isolated for analysis.[36] The effect of distance and the vote was also tested for the black area in Flint. It is interesting to speculate here on the influence of the white proximity to the Negro. If, as Kramer contended, white hostility increases with proximity to Negroes, could it also be assumed that Negro hostility increases with proximity to whites in transitional areas? Unfortunately little work has been done in this area to formulate a sound hypothesis. A negative relationship is expected between the positive vote and distance from the center of the ghetto (Table 3).

RESEARCH DESIGN

Through the use of simple and stepwise regression models, map comparisons, and profiles the above hypotheses are tested. It is felt that through the marriage of such traditional geographic techniques as mapping and construction of profiles in conjunction with the somewhat more recent statistical manipulations of data a higher level and more meaningful analysis is obtained.

In this study there are, however, two inherent difficulties that merit brief consideration. The first is aimed at reconciling variations in the sizes of reporting units, whereas the second is concerned with justifying differences between the 1960 population characteristics from the census and the 1968 voting data. Urban voting returns are given usually on a ward and precinct basis, whereas population characteristics from the census sources are provided for blocks and census tracts. The problem, then, is to "fit" one reporting unit to the other. In this study Flint's 122 precincts were assigned, through the use of an overlay procedure, either entirely or partially to one of the city's forty-one census tracts.[37] It is worth noting at this juncture that, as aggregate data are used, the problem of ecological correlation arises. Therefore, the findings of this study are linked to areal units and cannot be attributed to the voting behavior of individual residents of Flint.[38] Had survey data been available on income, age, occupation, political orientation, participation rates, open housing views, and attitudes of the blacks toward whites and vice versa, they would have provided a basis for examining individual attitudes through the city.[39]

As noted in the formulation of the hypotheses, the white and Negro populations have been divided for purposes of examining inter- and intra-variation. This is necessary in order to insure a meaningful interpretation of the voting behavior since, for example, the Negro poor are not expected to vote in similar fashion to their white counterparts. An initial regression analysis was made with no division between the groups; however, it revealed the weight of the Negro vote adversely affected the correlations and interpretations for such variables as the vote for open housing and median income and median education. Once the division of the populations into two groups was accomplished a more realistic picture of the relationships emerged. The division of the precincts into the black or white group was based on the percentage of Negroes residing in a particular precinct according to the 1960 census. Any unit with 10 per cent or more Negro population, which in this case was thirty-nine precincts, was included in the Negro sector, whereas those with fewer than 10 per cent Negro population, eighty-three precincts, were included in the white group. The decision to use 10 per cent as a basis for dividing the two groups was based on similar usage by Morrill, and by Smith, as indicating meaningful threshold levels for Negro expansion.[40] Once any unit reaches 10 per cent Negro population, it seems to indicate a swing toward eventual complete Negro dominance. With increases in the Negro population

TABLE 4

Characteristics of Selected Precincts in Flint

Precinct number	Percent favorable vote	Median income	Median years education	Median housing value	Percent Negro	Distance center of ghetto	Distance nearest Negro precinct
2	92	$4342	9.1	$ 9,280	82	.4 mi.	0.00 mi.
18	31	$5437	9.8	$ 8,600	0	1.0 mi.	.53 mi.
43	56	$7158	12.3	$13,200	0	1.5 mi.	.82 mi.
53	98	$5167	9.3	$ 8,900	96	0.0 mi.	0.00 mi.
63	72	$6390	10.3	$11,500	0	1.1 mi.	.24 mi.
71	17	$5831	10.2	$ 9,700	0	2.1 mi.	1.00 mi.
112	48	$7005	12.1	$12,600	0	2.7 mi.	.75 mi.
117	33	$7265	11.9	$13,600	10	1.6 mi.	0.00 mi.

Sources: United States Bureau of the Census, United States Censuses of Population and Housing: 1960, Census Tracts, Final Report PHC (1)-47, Flint, Michigan (Washington, D.C.: Government Printing Office, 1962).

Distances calculated by authors. The voting data were obtained from The Flint Journal, February 21, 1968, p. 17.

since 1960, many of those precincts which had almost 10 per cent then undoubtedly had much greater percentages in 1968. This difference from the time of the census and the vote for open housing in 1968 presents difficulties in providing a meaningful interpretation of the white and Negro voting behavior, especially for those precincts in the transitional zones. It is suggested that the areas of Flint that overwhelmingly supported open housing may represent a rather accurate picture of the major Negro concentrations in 1968.[41]

ANALYSIS

A visual comparison of the voting map and the map of Negro population suggests immediately that the Negro precincts supported open housing and the white precincts did not. However, in view of the fact that only a small per cent of the population is Negro, it is evident that a considerable amount of white support was necessary for passage of this issue. A good part of this support came from such organizations as the National Association for the Advancement of Colored People, Urban League, UAW-CIO labor organization, Council of Churches, American Civil Liberties Union, League of Women Voters, and two other local organizations known as HOME (Housing Opportunities Made Equal) and the Friends of Fair Housing. The variations of the vote and the social and economic characteristics of the population are illustrated for a sample of eight precincts in Table 4.

Within the city there were entire wards, such as 4, 6, and 8, where not one precinct yielded one half or more of its vote in favor of open housing. This concentrated opposition is not surprising for Wards 4 and 8 when the voting pattern is compared with that of median income. It is observed readily that these white areas are comprised with few exceptions of the income levels in the middle or lower segments.[42] The visual correlation of the vote and median income does not materialize in Ward 6 or in parts of Ward 2. In fact in such precincts as numbers 38, 80, 81, 106, and 107, which are some of the wealthiest in Flint, there was very little support for this issue. We can only speculate at this juncture why this pattern occurred. First, it is noted that the "white precincts" that did support the referendum are located in proximity to the Negro area. As stated previously some of these transitional "white precincts" would have to be classed as "black precincts" today. When such an explanation is offered, it is easier to interpret the patterns in Ward 5 which generally supported the issue and the reaction of certain precincts in the contiguous Wards 2 and 6.

The profiles produce another view of the distribution of the vote. They were drawn from the northwest corner of the city to the southeast corner and from the northeast to the southwest corner. The profiles are very similar with only slight deviations. The outlying white dominated areas simply did not support the open housing referendum. In fact as one moves from the ghetto, where the blacks voted overwhelmingly in favor of open housing, to the city fringe, racial attitudes in the form of a positive vote for the issue appear either to harden or at best to remain constant. Therefore, empirical observation suggests that a spatial element, as hypothesized above, is not strongly present in this referendum.

By carrying the investigation of the white population a step further through the vehicle of simple correlation, measured relationships were produced which can be used to confirm or reject the empirical observations. An examination of the simple correlations shed considerable light on the voting behavior. The virtual absence of any significant correlation between the vote and median income ($-.06$), median education ($-.08$), and median value of owner occupied dwellings ($+.04$) confirms the empirical observations and, therefore, leads to a rejection of the research hypotheses for the whites. Thus, it would appear that on the basis of the categories for white and black precincts the general behavior of white residents with high as well as low incomes and those with few and many years of schooling do not fit into one homogeneous voting pattern. There are examples of some low income precincts, which are probably predominantly Negro today, and some high income precincts which supported open housing. On the other hand there are precincts of low, middle, and high median incomes that opposed the referendum. These variations in behavior are not in accord with previous research on the attitudes of white people and their support for social welfare measures. It may be that the explosive and emotional nature of this issue to many white people of differing incomes makes it different from other nonpartisan issues such as those dealing with education bonds or library construction funds. Two factors may account partially for this apparent anomalous pattern of white behavior. One is that much of the previous research on attitudes involving racial feelings has been of the survey nature.[43] In forming opinions for these surveys the white residents of the more educated and affluent areas of cities may perceive that it is "unfashionable" or unwise to exhibit their true feelings to a stranger conducting the interviews. Therefore, as a recent study on opinions about open housing has demonstrated, very few of the respondents strongly approved or opposed open housing. Most of the people were unwilling or unable to state their preferences on the open housing question frankly.[44] Abrams has stated that when a person finds his moral and property rights in conflict, as in open housing, the person will usually vote his property rights against his moral scruples.[45]

TABLE 5

Correlation Coefficients for White and Negro Sectors

Variable	White sector	Negro sector
X1 Median Income	−.06	−.49**
X2 Median Years Completed	−.08	−.53**
X3 Median Value of House	.04	−.40**
X4 Distance from Center of Ghetto	−.36**	−.56**
X5 Distance from Nearest Negro Precinct	−.30**	#

**Significant at .01 level.

#Omitted from regression analysis as all Negro precincts have at least ten percent Negro population, as defined for purposes of this study.

Source: Calculated by authors.

Therefore, once inside a voting booth where no one can hold him accountable for his attitudes, the individual may vent his true feelings and cast a vote which has little bearing on his educational achievement or philosophical commitments.

When measuring the effects of proximity of the whites to the Negro population, both relationships, straight line distance to the ghetto center (−.36), and straight line distance to the nearest black precinct (−.30), were statistically significant. This suggests that the transitional areas voted in favor of open housing and those in the fringes voted against the measure. The increases in Negro population in the transitional areas between 1960 and 1968 account in part for this deviation. It can be stated, however, that the correlation values do indicate that the spatial element as presented by Kramer in Chicago was not reflected in the attitudes of the whites in terms of this vote.

For the Negro sector a visual correlation of the maps of the vote and the Negro population demonstrates the great similarity in the two patterns. Some of the areas with a very high favorable vote for open housing reflect Negro expansion since 1960 especially in the Buick district. The vote for open housing carried heavily in all those Negro precincts except where from 10 to 29.9 per cent of the population was black. Here the support on occasion fell below 50 per cent. As might be expected there is also an excellent visual fit between the areas of low median income and the favorable vote. In northern cities such as Flint the Negro occupies the lowest rungs of the economic ladder and it is in these areas of lowest average incomes that a very high per cent of their vote was in favor of open housing.

When the hypotheses were tested statistically for the Negro sector the simple correlations support the empirical contentions (Table 4). Very high and statistically significant relationships were observed for all variables. As postulated these were negative correlations. That is, there were inverse relationships between the positive vote and median income, median education level, and median value of owner occupied dwellings. These research hypotheses were accepted. Furthermore, the negative relationships between the vote and distance from the ghetto were confirmed.

At this juncture it seems appropriate to examine the validity of the variables utilized in the regression model and to determine to what extent they together helped explain the total open housing vote. Individually some played a much more important part than others. In order to determine what per cent of the total variation was accounted for by all the variables together, the stepwise multiple regression model was used. In this model the variables are selected one by one in order of the amount they explained of the total variance. For the white sector, distance from the ghetto proved to be the most important variable in explaining the vote (Table 6). This was followed by the median value of owner occupied dwellings, median income, distance from the nearest black precinct, and median education level. When all these variables were considered together in the model, 32 per cent of the total variation was explained. Although this is a statistically significant figure it does not account for a large portion of the variance. It is suggested that additional studies on nonpartisan referendums incorporate other variables, use other sources of data, hopefully survey data, and employ more sophisticated models such as factor analysis. Some indices that might have a bearing on the voting behavior are the ethnic population, age, dominant religion, owner versus rented residences, and years residence in the same dwelling.

For the Negro area the explained variance is slightly higher, 46 per cent. The distance from the center of the ghetto proved to be the most important variable in the stepwise regression model, the same index as in the white sector. Others that were important were median education level, median value of owner occupied homes, and median income. Variables that merit inclusion in future ecological studies where Negro voting behavior is measured are indicators of unemployment, welfare coverage, household characteristics, family size, and major occupations.

An additional factor that should be considered in this analysis is the voter participation or turnout on this crucial issue. An examination of the per cent of eligible voters in each precinct reveals the turnout varied widely in the wards and precincts. The largest number of precincts with low turnouts were in Wards 4 and 9 and fewer precincts in Wards 5, 6,

TABLE 6

Coefficients of Multiple Correlation and Multiple Determination: Stepwise Regression Model

	White sector				Negro Sector		
Variable	R	R^2		Variable	R	R^2
Distance from Center of Ghetto	−.36	13%		Distance from Center of Ghetto	−.56	31%
Median Value of House	.43	19%		Median Years Completed	.67	46%
Median Income	.55	30%		Median Value of House	.68	46%
Distance from Nearest Negro Precinct	.56	32%		Median Income	.68**	46%
Median Years Completed	.56**	32%				

**Significant at .01 level.

Source: Calculated by authors.

and 7. In these particular precincts fewer than 40 per cent of the registered voters cast ballots on this referendum. In several only 34 per cent voted. By contrast the precincts in Wards 2, 3, and parts of 6, 7, and 9 were considerably above the city average of 51 per cent. A number of these had over 60 per cent of the eligible voters on the referendum. The highest turnouts were in several precincts in Ward 9 where 74 per cent of the voters voted. The highest turnouts in the city were in the very low income Negro areas and upper middle and high-income white areas. In general these areas had over 55 per cent of the eligible voters cast ballots. These two groups occasionally vote in like manner on nonpartisan issues, according to Wilson and Banfield.[46] However, on this issue a homogeneous voting pattern is not apparent. As has been mentioned the low-income black areas voted heavily in favor of open housing. The white behavior did not fit into a homogeneous pattern. The high-income precincts in Wards 2 and 6 did not support open housing although adjacent precincts with slightly lower incomes did. By contrast the high-income areas in Ward 7 did tend to favor the referendum. In general the low-income and middle-income white areas, especially in Wards 4, 6, and 8 did not support open housing nor did they have exceptionally high turnouts, generally less than 50 per cent. It seems that the slim margin of victory for this issue is attributed to the high turnout and overwhelming support in the Negro areas and the small margins of support in several upper middle and high-income white precincts. It is probably individuals in these income groupings who comprised the various civic organizations that favored passage of this issue.

SUMMARY AND CONCLUSIONS

This study has been concerned with investigating some of the reasons behind the geographic variation in the attitudes of the residents of Flint, Michigan, toward open housing. These variations in attitudes are analyzed by a consideration of the recent referendum dealing with this issue. An examination of the maps, profiles, and correlation values revealed there were measurable differences between the Negro and white behavior. In the case of the Negroes, they turned out in large numbers and voted almost solidly for this measure. The behavior of the whites was not unanimously against open housing as support from various upper middle and high-income precincts was necessary for its passage. When the whites were considered as one group, their behavior did not seem related to expected measures of income or education. It is worthy of note that the white turnout varied considerably, with the lowest turnouts in the low-income and highest in the upper middle and high-income precincts. Also the distances of whites from the center and edge of the ghettos did not affect the voting pattern noticeably on this particular issue. This study has demonstrated that there needs to be a great deal more geographic research performed on black and white voting behavior on nonpartisan issues before we can attach meaningful results to differences in income, education, race, and various spatial measures.

Whether the findings for Flint on this or similar issues are indicative of the political behavior in other cities merits further research. For example, what meaningful geographic patterns are characteristic of votes for such issues as urban renewal, school bonds, fluoridation, public works, or welfare levies? Are there similar voting patterns on these issues for the central cities, the suburbs, or the lower, middle, and upper-income areas? What effects do age groups, sex ratios, race, occupation status, and home owners *versus* renters have on voting behavior? Does affiliation with a national political party exhibit a positive or negative relationship with certain urban social referendums? Is there a national or regional voting model that can be formulated through other techniques such as factor analysis, or predicted from simulation runs? What effect do other geographic elements such as psychological barriers, stress points, territoriality, and gerrymandering have on attitude formation and expression in voting for or against particular issues? The answers to these questions are dependent on future research on urban voting behavior in which geographers include other variables and use other models or techniques, as well as keep abreast of related research in fields such as political science, sociology, and psychology. It is in this manner that the contribution of social and political geographers will not only aid in the gradual construction of significant urban models for the social sciences but likewise lead perhaps to the formulation of urban policies.

LITERATURE CITED

1. For several statements on ghetto development, open housing schemes, and related urban residential problems, see: M. Grodzins, "The New Shame of the Cities," *Confluence*, Vol. 7 (1958), pp. 29–46; F. S. Horne, "Interracial Housing in the United States," *Phylon*, Vol. 19 (1958), pp. 13–20; R. C. Weaver, "Non-White Population Movements and Urban Ghettoes," *Phylon*, Vol. 29 (1959), pp. 235–41.

2. P. S. Sheatsley, "White Attitudes Toward the Negro," *Daedalus* (Winter 1966), pp. 217–38.

3. Prior to Flint, the issue was subject to a vote by the electorate in Berkeley, California (in 1963); the state of California with its controversial Proposition 14 (in 1964); Seattle and Tacoma, Washington;

Akron and Springfield, Ohio; Jackson and Flint, Michigan; and Columbia, Missouri. "Flint Recount," *Trends in Housing*, Vol. 12 (April 1968), p. 7.

4. "Open-Housing Law Highlights 20 Year Civil Rights Effort," *Congressional Quarterly*, April 19, 1968, pp. 888–902.

5. The federal government's position and role in encouraging residential segregation is covered in: E. and G. Grier, "Equality and Beyond: Housing Segregation and the Great Society," *Daedalus* (Winter 1966), pp. 77–106.

6. *The Flint Journal*, February 21, 1968, p. 17.

7. W. Brink and L. Harris, *Black and White, A Study of U. S. Racial Attitudes Today* (New York: Simon and Schuster, 1966), pp. 40–41.

8. G. Myrdal, *The American Dilemma. Vol. 1. The Negro in a White Dilemma* (New York: McGraw-Hill, Paperback Edition, 1964; originally published in 1944), p. 4.

9. C. Abrams, "The Housing Problem and the Negro," *Daedalus* (Winter 1966), p. 68.

10. J. Meltzer and J. Whitley, "Social and Physical Planning for the Urban Slum," in B. J. L. Berry and J. Meltzer, *Goals for Urban America* (Englewood Cliffs, N.J.: Prentice-Hall, Inc., 1967), pp. 133–52.

11. Brink and Harris, op. cit., footnote 7, pp. 131–32 and 136.

12. Abrams, op. cit., footnote 9, pp. 64–76.

13. R. Farley and K. E. Taeuber, "Population Trends and Residential Segregation since 1960," *Science*, Vol. 159 (1968), pp. 953–56.

14. J. O. Wheeler, "Work-Trip Length and the Ghetto," *Land Economics*, Vol. 44 (1968), pp. 107–12.

15. J. O. Wheeler and S. D. Brunn, "Negro Migration into Rural Southwestern Michigan," *Geographical Review*, Vol. 58 (1968), pp. 214–30.

16. *The Flint Journal*, March 6, 1968, p. 1.

17. P. F. Lewis, "Impact of Negro Migration on the Electoral Geography of Flint, Michigan, 1932–1962: A Cartographic Analysis," *Annals*, Association of American Geographers, Vol. 55 (1965), pp. 1–25.

18. Examples of voting studies by geographers on partisan elections in cities include: R. E. Kasperson, "Toward a Geography of Urban Politics: Chicago, A Case Study," *Economic Geography*, Vol. 41 (1965), pp. 95–107; Lewis, op. cit., footnote 17; M. C. Roberts and K. W. Rumage, "The Spatial Variations in Urban Left Wing Voting in England and Wales in 1951," *Annals*, Association of American Geographers, Vol. 55 (1965), pp. 161–78; G. Rowley, "The Greater London Council Elections of 1964: Some Geographical Considerations," *Tijdschrift voor economische en sociale geografie*, Vol. 56 (1965), pp. 113–14; J. W. Simmons, "Voting Behavior and Socio-Economic Char-

acteristics: The Middlesex East Federal Election, 1965," *Canadian Journal of Economic and Political Science*, Vol. 33 (1967), pp. 389–400, and K. R. Cox, "Suburbia and Voting Behavior in the London Metropolitan Area," *Annals*, Association of American Geographers, Vol. 58 (1968), pp. 111–27.

19. The only example of a nonpartisan urban referendum analyzed by a geographer is: W. L. Hoffman, "A Statistical and Cartographic Analysis of the 1954 and 1964 Urban Renewal Referendums for Columbus, Ohio" (unpublished M.A. thesis, Department of Geography, Ohio State University, 1966).

20. For examples of urban voting studies by political scientists and sociologists see: C. R. Adrian, "A Typology of Nonpartisan Elections," *Western Political Quarterly*, Vol. 12 (1959), pp. 449–58; O. Gantz, "Protestant and Catholic Voting in a Metropolitan Area," *Public Opinion Quarterly*, Vol. 23 (1959), pp. 73–82; W. C. Kaufman and S. Greer, "Voting in a Metropolitan Community: An Application of Social Area Analysis," *Social Forces*, Vol. 38 (1960), pp. 196–210; J. A. Norton, "Referenda Voting in a Metropolitan Area," *Western Political Quarterly*, Vol. 16 (1963), pp. 195–214; J. Zikmund, "A Comparison of the Political Attitude and Activity Patterns in Central Cities and Suburbs," *Public Opinion Quarterly*, Vol. 31 (1967), pp. 69–75.

21. Studies by geographers on housing and the residential structure of cities include: G. W. Hartman and J. C. Hook, "Substandard Urban Housing in the United States: A Quantitative Analysis," *Economic Geography*, Vol. 32 (1956), pp. 95–114.

22. O. D. Duncan and B. Duncan, "Residential Distribution and Occupational Stratification," *American Journal of Sociology*, Vol. 60 (1955), pp. 493–503; D. O. Cowgill, "Trends in Residential Segregation of Non-Whites in American Cities, 1940–1950," *American Sociological Review*, Vol. 21 (1956), pp. 43–47 and his "Segregation Scores for Metropolitan Areas," *American Sociological Review*, Vol. 27 (1962), pp. 400–02; R. J. Fuchs, "Intraurban Variations in Residential Quality," *Economic Geography*, Vol. 36 (1960), pp. 313–25; K. E. Corey, "A Geographic Analysis of an Urban Renewal Area: A Case Study of the Avondale I-Corryville Conservation Project (Ohio R-6), Cincinnati, Ohio" (unpublished Master's thesis, Department of Geography, University of Cincinnati, 1962).

23. For example, see the following studies: A. E. Winder, "White Attitudes Toward Negro-white Integration in an Area of Changing Racial Composition," *American Psychologist*, Vol. 7 (1952), pp. 330–31; A. M. Rose, et al., "Neighborhood Reactions to Isolated Negro Residents: An Alternative to Invasion and Succession," *American Sociological Review*, Vol. 18 (1953), pp. 497–507; O. D. and B. Duncan, *The Negro Population of Chicago: A Study of Residential Succession* (Chicago: University of Chicago Press, 1957).

24. Several examples of relevant studies include: L. Rodwin, "The Theory of Residential Growth and Structure," *Appraisal Journal*, Vol. 18 (1950), pp. 295–317; L. Laurenti, *Property Values and Race. Studies in Seven Cities* (Berkeley: University of California Press, 1960); E. Palmore and J. Howe, "Residential Integration and Property Values," *Social Problems*, Vol. 10 (1962), pp. 52–55.

25. S. M. Lipset, *Political Man: The Social Bases for Politics* (New York: Doubleday and Company, Inc., 1963), pp. 101–03 and 318–22; G. W. Allport, *The Nature of Prejudice* (New York: Doubleday and Company, 1958), pp. 405–07. In addition, in Casstevens' study on the Berkeley fair housing referendum in 1963 he found that persons with a postgraduate training and in professional or semiprofessional occupations supported the measure; T. W. Casstevens, *Politics, Housing and Race Relations: The Defeat of Berkeley's Fair Housing Ordinance* (Berkeley: University of California, Institute of Governmental Studies, 1965), pp. 90–94. See also R. E. Wolfinger and F. I. Greenstein, "The Repeal of Fair Housing in California: An Analysis of Referendum Voting," *American Political Science Review*, Vol. 62 (1968), pp. 753–69. This recent study demonstrates, likewise, that the voting differences on Proposition 14 or the Rumford Act were attributed to educational and regional differences.

26. Allport, op. cit., footnote 25, p. 406.

27. Lipset, op. cit., footnote 25, p. 318.

28. Brink and Harris, op. cit., footnote 7, p. 136.

29. As an example, see A. D. Kirsch, *Social Distance in Voting Behavior Related to N Variables* (Lafayette, Indiana: Purdue University, Division of Educational Reference, Studies in Higher Education No. 86, 1967).

30. Duncan and Duncan, op. cit., footnote 22, p. 502. They stated that there is ". . . strong support for the proposition that spatial distances between occupational groups are closely related to social distances. . . ."

31. B. M. Kramer, "Residential Contact as a Determinant of Attitudes Toward Negroes" (unpublished paper, Harvard College Library, 1950).

32. Winder, op. cit., footnote 23.

33. The physical and social distances between the city and its suburbs and the effects on contrasting political behavior are mentioned by Norton, op. cit., footnote 20; and by Zikmund, op. cit., footnote 20.

34. Brink and Harris, op. cit., footnote 7, p. 10.

35. J. Q. Wilson and E. C. Banfield, "Public Regardingness as a Value Premise in Voting Behavior," *American Political Science Review*, Vol. 53 (1964), pp. 876–87.

36. Hoffman, op. cit., footnote 19.

37. For a concise and clear explanation of the use of overlays in electoral analyses, see Lewis, op. cit., footnote 17.

38. For a discussion on the limitations of the application of ecological correlations to individual attributes, see: W. S. Robinson, "Ecological Correlations and the Behavior of Individuals," *American Sociological Review*, Vol. 15 (1956), pp. 351–57.

39. For a recent exchange on the merits of survey data as opposed to ecological data in geography see: R. E. Kasperson, "On Suburbia and Voting Behavior," *Annals*, Association of American Geographers, Vol. 59 (1969), pp. 406–07, and K. R. Cox, "Comments in Reply to Kasperson and Taylor," *Annals*, Association of American Geographers, Vol. 59 (1969), p. 413.

40. Morrill, op. cit., footnote 1; and B. Smith, op. cit., footnote 23.

41. The authors acknowledge gratefully the assistance provided by Mr. Henry Horton of the Model Cities Program, Mr. Donald Johnson of the Department of Community Development, Mr. William Chase of *The Flint Journal*, and Mrs. Richard F. Beardsley for knowledge of recent changes and developments in the population of Flint as well as local accounts of the open housing referendum.

42. A further indication of the attitudes of the white population toward the various emotions and views attached to open housing is the vote of the 1968 American Independent Party candidate, George C. Wallace.

43. The recent study by H. Hahn, "Northern Referenda on Fair Housing: The Response of White Votes," *Western Political Quarterly*, Vol. 21 (1968), pp. 483–95, reveals the attitudes of a small sample of Detroit's residents for support of the 1964 Home Owners Ordinance, government activity and desegregation of schools, and neighborhood integration. Hahn finds no consistent attitude among whites of varying socio-economic status for these three measures.

44. G. H. DeFriese and W. S. Ford, Jr., "Open Occupancy—What Whites Say, What They Do," *Transaction*, Vol. 5 (April 1968), pp. 53–56.

45. Abrams, op. cit., footnote 9, p. 72.

46. Wilson and Banfield, op. cit., footnote 35.

DECENTRALIZING HIGH SCHOOL ADMINISTRATION IN DETROIT: AN EVALUATION OF ALTERNATIVE STRATEGIES OF POLITICAL CONTROL

Michael A. Jenkins and John W. Shepherd

Decentralization of school administration has become a contentious political issue in a number of metropolitan areas in the United States. The immediate objective of such proposals is to break up the unwieldy bureaucracies that have evolved with the growth of the city and its school system. Bringing the administration nearer to both teachers and parents, it is argued, will make possible a speedier adaptation to demographic and social change and provide a more receptive environment for the introduction of innovations in teaching methods and administrative practice. A first step along this path, to quote the Mayor's Advisory Panel on Decentralization of the New York City Schools, entails providing "a means of reconnecting the parties at interest so they can work in concert" [8, p. 2]. The long-term aim is nothing less than the reconstruction of the physical and social environment of inner-city education in order to "afford the children, parents, teachers, other educators and the city-at-large, a single school system that combines the advantages of big city education with the opportunities of the finest small city and suburban educational systems" [8, p. xiii].

Conflict over decentralization arises not only from administrators and teachers who are content with the status quo, but also from certain groups in the city who recognize that their aims can be promoted in such a way as to obtain a complete redistribution of policy-making power in a crucial municipal function. Thus, some academics and black community leaders consider the substantial transfer of decision making from city hall to neighborhood an important alternative means of compensating for the worst effects of long-standing poverty and social segregation on the educational attainment of inner-city children. Progress toward the ethnic integration of schools, they contend, is too slow. Indeed, research indicates that schools in cities of the northern United States, in response to both political and environmental factors, are actually becoming *increasingly* segregated despite the passage of federal civil rights legislation [5]. In all but a few small and peculiarly enlightened cities such as Berkeley, California, and Princeton, New Jersey, integration is seen as having failed. In the metropolitan areas, residential segregation has reached such a scale and positions have become so entrenched, that policies for desegregation involving the pairing of predominantly black and white schools, busing, and redrawing the boundaries of school catchment areas have all proved impossible to implement.

A solution that is being increasingly advocated as an alternative is community or neighborhood control of schools. Local control by locally elected or selected governing bodies over such critical areas as school personnel, budgets, curricula, and pupil policy could, it is argued, serve as a powerful implement for social change in deprived urban areas in two main ways. First, it would provide an education that is relevant to the needs and aspirations of children of the central city. Second, it would enhance the self-esteem not only of the children of minority groups but also of the communities from which they come.

These issues have arisen in discussions of plans to decentralize the educational system of Detroit. In common with other major U.S. cities, Detroit (population 1.53 million in 1965) has experienced over-all population decline in the last two decades. This is the main effect of the migration of white middle-income groups to suburban areas beyond the city boundary. As a result, the population of Detroit is now approximately 40 per cent black. However, the drop in total population has not led to a corresponding decrease in the number of pupils served by the city school system. In fact, between 1956 and 1966 the school population rose by 17,000 pupils, the main reason being the larger number of children of school age in the average black family. In 1970, over 60 per cent of all students in Detroit public schools were black, and five of its twenty-one high school districts had a student enrollment which was more than 90 per cent black.

Despite the fact that Detroit's record in citizen participation in education is generally better than most cities in the United States [7], previous proposals, some made by the school board itself, for more substantial reforms in this direction have always failed for lack of strong political support. The very latest attempt, however, has taken the form of an act of the State legislature, *requiring* more effective decentralization of power in education and the submission of a plan to implement it. The provisions of this act, coupled with the recent rise in the number and militancy of black and civil rights organizations in the city, have been viewed as providing the first opportunity for real community involvement and control in the educational process.

THE DETROIT DECENTRALIZATION ACT

Public Act Number 244 was approved by the Michigan legislature on August 11, 1969 [12]. It required first class school districts (the only one being the school district of Detroit) to be divided into decentralized regional school boards. The twenty-one existing high school districts of Detroit were therefore to be replaced by not less than seven, nor more than eleven new regions, each containing between twenty-five thousand and fifty thousand enrolled students. Each new high school region would be run by a regional board of nine elected members whose powers would be substantially greater than those of the districts it replaced. These powers included control over the appointment of the regional board superintendent, the employment, assignment, and promotion of teaching staff, the determination of school curricula, the use of facilities, and the allocation of the district budget.

Like the existing system, the decentralized one was to be a two-tiered structure of administration. Thus a first-class district board or "upper-tier" would still decide "city-wide" aspects of educational policy, though obviously with somewhat reduced powers. Its span of control was nevertheless impressive, ranging from central purchasing, payroll management, settlement of contracts with employees, property management, special educational programs, and the final confirmation of some of the decisions taken by regional boards. The new first-class board would be composed of seven members elected "at large" and an additional number elected one from each of the new regional boards. The final number of members of the first-class board could therefore range from fourteen to eighteen, depending upon the eventual number of regions in the proposed scheme.

THE PROBLEM AND OPERATIONAL DEFINITIONS

Late in 1969, the authors were asked by a predominantly black community group in Detroit, the West Central Organization, to assess the political effects of the decentralization act. At least eight other local organizations across the city had submitted plans in response to the school board's call for suggestions, and it had become obvious to the West Central Organization that although the objectives of the groups were similar, the implications of their separate plans could be very different, even contradictory. The rationale behind the authors' approach to the problem was to extend the range of choice before community workers, rather than to draw up yet another plan or selection of plans in an ad hoc manner. In this way, the West Central Organization or any other group would not only be in a position to choose its own strategy from a variety of plans, but any new counter proposal, either from the school board or another community group, could be evaluated immediately and placed in perspective. Such a study left the final, political, choice to those directly responsible for promoting it, yet went as far as possible toward redressing the advantages that the Detroit school board had over the community organizations in terms of consultants, staff, and resources for researching its own proposals.

The working definition of community control adopted in the analysis was that each regional board should have an electoral majority which reflected the two overwhelming ethnic proportions in high school enrollments. Data were therefore obtained on the total student population (black and white) in each of the twenty-one existing high school districts. Relative community political preferences were similarly defined. A black voter was taken as a vote cast for the only black candidate in the primary elections for city mayor held in August 1969. A white voter was defined as a vote for either of the two white candidates. Polling district data were summed to school district level and these voting figures were taken as indicating the likelihood of a high school district electing a black or white majority of representatives in polling for a new regional board.

This black-white dichotomy was adopted as the least equivocal manner in which to assess the geographical and numerical distribution of power, and children, among the various decentralization plans that might emerge. It derived directly, of course, from the West Central Organization's perception of the main issue at stake in the decentralization proposal, namely, in what way were the two main ethnic communities in Detroit to control or influence the education of their respective sets of children. Although there are a number of substantive problems with the voting data as an expression of the distribution of community power (for example, as recorded in a primary election, turnout was less than in the final poll, a fact which would tend to act differentially on the black vote; again, some white people would obviously vote for a black candidate and vice-versa; the data ignored other minority groups in Detroit), there were two reasons which indicated they could be employed with a certain validity in the analysis. First, an examination of Table 1 shows that the absolute differences between black and white voters are so great in most segregated districts that it would take an extremely large, and probably unforthcoming, increase in turnout rates to substantially shift the balance of power. Second, the *variability* among the two proportions, children and voters, is so similar ($r^2 = 0.89$), we can conclude that the voting data reasonably reflect the distribution of community preferences.

TABLE I

Black-White Enrollment and Voting at High School District

District	Students			Voters		
	Black	White	% Black	Black	White	% Black
Central	13,554	43	99.7	14,907	1,007	93.7
Chadsey	1,994	3,645	35.4	1,452	6,491	18.3
Cody	1,518	14,009	9.8	1,236	18,322	6.3
Cooley	11 119	7,211	60.7	7,104	17,866	28.5
Denby	386	9,564	3.9	1,087	19,910	5.2
Finney	7,632	6,860	52.7	4,724	12,396	27.6
Ford	965	8,201	10.5	1,079	9,564	10.1
Kettering	15,936	2,241	87.7	6,948	5,146	57.4
King	11,567	471	96.1	6,880	3,634	65.4
Mackenzie	19,419	2,275	89.5	13,052	6,975	65.2
Mumford	12,069	986	92.4	13,132	6,213	67.9
Murray Wright	7,460	2,401	75.7	2,958	2,749	51.8
Northeastern	9,980	1,211	89.2	6,765	3,776	64.2
Northern	10,510	111	99.0	9,256	1,363	87.2
Northwestern	15,274	60	99.6	13,010	877	93.7
Osborn	3,945	9,160	30.1	1,314	19,725	6.3
Pershing	7,886	5,634	57.4	7,829	9,870	44.2
Redford	545	14,370	3.7	1,461	17,693	7.6
Southeastern	11,600	3,914	74.8	4,722	5,241	47.4
Southwestern	5,380	5,255	50.6	3,537	4,559	43.7
Western	5,562	4,643	54.5	3,089	5,594	46.2

Geographic similarities and differences between the two communities are immediately clear from Tables 1 and 2. Both show the central-city and northwestern sectoral offshoot in the concentration of black students and black-voting electors, and the suburban location of the corresponding white populations. Between the core and peripheral areas are a number of districts with intermediate proportions of the two characteristics. An important point to note is that there are high proportions of black students in more districts than there are high proportions of black voters. Or, to put it another way, school districts with high proportions of black students become only intermediate or even low observations on the voting measure. One reason for these differences in turnout rates has already been mentioned. Two others are more crucial for they represent demographic and institutional disadvantages which the black community faces in a city-wide, democratic framework of community control. On the one hand, as pointed out above, black families on the average have a larger number of children of school age. On the other, a significant and growing number of white families, even in highly segregated suburban areas, send their children to private rather than public schools to escape the real and imagined privations of the city school system. As the results of this study are presented, it will become clear how the size and location of these disparities have very important consequences for the black community in terms of its propensity to control the education of its own children.

THE REGROUPING PROCEDURE

An understanding of the spatial and computational aspects of the study can be obtained if it is seen as a process of amalgamating the twenty-one existing districts into a lesser number of effective regions. These amalgamations are constrained first by the enrollment limitations set out in Act 244. In order to proceed with regrouping, it was also necessary to impose a constraint not laid down in the act, namely that amalgamations should consist only of whole, contiguous districts. This was, in fact, not an unreasonable requirement considering the intricate and established relationship a school has with its immediate neighborhood and the benefits of simplicity and efficiency in administration that accrue from having geographically contiguous regions. Given these constraints, the objective was to find all possible solutions to the amalgamation problem and assess their political significance.

The following simple approach was used to generate all the possible ways of amalgamating Detroit's high school districts into new regions. First, a set of possible new regions are chosen, i.e., groups of original districts which are connected and which in aggregate satisfy the enrollment constraints. This set of new regions is generated using a connectivity matrix and enrollment data. Of the 21 districts, there were 158 possible regions that met the constraints. A valid decentralization plan can then be found by choosing from this set of regions a subset which includes every old district just once. In other words, the problem is reduced to selecting subsets of the set of 158 regions such that the map of Detroit is completely filled without overlap. This can be accomplished by a recursive search of the 158 regions.

Before turning to the description of the results of this study, it is important to discuss the suitability of this approach. It became clear that the method of generating all possible solutions to a grouping problem and then analyzing them relative to various criteria is not computationally feasible for problems much larger than the one discussed here. An alternative approach is to examine one criterion at a time and solve the corresponding optimization problem. Nagel [9], in the context of bipartisan redistricting, gives an ALGOL program which attempts this by fixing the number of districts, choosing an initial division into regions, and then improving the division relative to the criterion by switching districts, one at a time, between regions within the plan. This approach works well provided the number of districts per region is fairly large and there is no need to compare solutions with different numbers of regions. Nagel's method would have been a less satisfactory approach for the problem discussed here due to the fact that the number of districts per region is small and the optimum solution(s) might therefore be easily missed. Nevertheless, Nagel's work should not be overlooked as it could prove to be the only practicable course.

If an amalgamation problem is small enough to make the generation of all the possible solutions computationally feasible, then there are some points worth further study. In our approach, we have divided the solution into two parts. The constraint and connectivity information is used to construct the set of valid regions, but once the set is determined, we then treat a purely combinatorial problem. This intuitive approach was appropriate considering the time limits involved in the study. However, there are reasons to believe that the connectivity information could be used to control the order in which the map is searched for possible amalgamation plans in order to avoid duplication of work. The algorithm used here for generating all possible amalgamations is quite efficient for small problems and might easily prove useful as a tool in analyzing subparts of a larger one. However, it becomes less efficient as the number of districts increases, and it is an open research question as to whether there is an optimal method of solving a geographic regrouping problem of this nature. There is a close analogy here with constrained enumeration problems in mathematical graph theory, and this relationship, we feel, deserves further investigation.

THE RESULTS

The analysis revealed that there were no less than 7,330 ways to amalgamate the existing high school districts into new regional boards using just the contiguity and enrollment constraints. The magnitude of this number is significant in that it immediately places any single plan or group of plans into the vast range of possible alternatives. Since these 7,330 solutions could meet many different political strategies of control over the education system, it was necessary to categorize this total into the basic political objectives that could be met. Statistics were produced on the breakdown of plans with varying numbers of new regions providing different black-white splits of representation at the metropolitan level

TABLE 2
Representation at the Metropolitan Level

Number of Regional Boards

7		8		9	
Black-White Split	Number of Plans	Black-White Split	Number of Plans	Black-White Split	Number of Plans
1-6	84	2-6	447	3-6	41
2-5	872	3-5	1876	4-5	45
3-4	1662	4-4	1468	5-4	38
4-3	512	5-3	268	6-3	6
5-2	24	6-2	28		
Total	3154	Total	4087	Total	130

(i.e., given one representative per regional board). In addition, we needed to know the proportion of children under the control of either community at the local or regional board level and figures were also gathered to demonstrate this.

It was first found that a number of 6-, 7-, 8-, and 9-region schemes satisfied the population and contiguity constraints. Given the terms of Act 244, this meant that the 19 six-region schemes were invalid and they were therefore dropped from the study yielding a total of 7,311 legal plans for consideration. Table 2 shows the number of plans falling into various splits of black and white representation at the metropolitan level. If, from this table, we consider all plans having a white majority split, we find there are 4,967. By contrast, there are only 876 plans with a black majority representation. The remaining 1,468 plans have 8 regions with a 4–4 black-white division. This indicates that unless a plan is chosen with consideration of representation at this level, it is much more likely that it will have a white majority. Note too, that the possible range for gerrymandering any plan is great since the split can vary from a 6–1 majority for the white community (84 solutions) to a 6–2 split for the black one (28 solutions).

The next step in the study was to analyze the effects of the numerous decentralization plans on different local political strategies. This was done in terms of the proportion of white and black children under various types of control. Four criteria of control were deemed relevant and were defined.

1. *Black Community Control.* Let B_b and B_w represent the number of black students in regions which are, respectively, black and white controlled. Then black community control is measured by

$$\frac{B_b}{B_b + B_w}$$

expressed as a percentage. This histogram of this measure illustrates the number of plans in five-percentile intervals (the number of plans being plotted on a logarithmic scale). Hence there are, for example, twenty plans in which between 15 and 20 per cent of all black children are in new regions with a black voter majority. This histogram shows that: the measure of black community control ranges from 10–15 per cent up to 90–95 per cent; the vast majority of plans fall into the range 35–75 per cent; and only a small number (194 to be exact) place more than 80 per cent of black children under black control.

2. *White Community Control.* Let W_w and W_b represent the number of white students in regions which are, respectively, white and black controlled. Then white community control is measured by

$$\frac{W_w}{W_w + W_b}$$

similarly expressed as a percentage, ranging from 55–60 per cent to 95–100 per cent, with over half the total of plans (4,386) placing more than 80 per cent of white children under white control.

3. *Homogeneity.* We define this to be a measure of the extent to which both black and white community control can be achieved simultaneously. It is expressed as

$$\frac{B_b + W_w}{B_b + B_w + W_w + W_b}$$

again in percentage form, ranging from 40–45 per cent to 80–85 per cent, and most (6,170) of the plans fall in the interval 60–75 per cent. There are 356 plans which rate highly, i.e., over 75 per cent, on the homogeneity scale.

4. *Integration.* Let R be the percentage of black students in the city at large and let R_i be the percentage of black students in the ith new region. Assuming a plan to have N regions, the degree of integration is measured by

$$\frac{\sum_{i=1}^{N} \left| R - R_i \right|}{N}$$

showing the integration measure in one-percentile intervals (plans plotted on a linear scale). Note that a high degree of integration is reflected by a small average deviation between the percentage of black students in the city at large and the percentage in each new region. Integration ranges from 8–28 per cent; the majority of plans fall between 16 and 26 per cent.

If plans below 16 per cent on this measure could be considered as adequately integrated, then we can select from 527 such plans.

What then do these measures, taken separately or interacting together, mean for the political strategies that can possibly be followed in the decentralization proposal? The first two measures are computed to explore the extent to which the black and white communities of Detroit can, in turn, control the education of their own children. Homogeneity represents an attempt to assess some "fair" solutions in the sense of achieving community control for black and white people at the same time. The integration measure was computed to determine to what extent the Detroit decentralization proposal could satisfy Supreme Court guidelines on integration in public schools.

Comparison of the histograms for the first two measures reveals a vast difference between the possibilities for the black community to control the education of its own children and the same control for the white community. This suggests that black community leaders must be highly selective when choosing a decentralization plan which satisfies their particular aims and which might also prove acceptable to other groups. The white community, however, can rarely fail to achieve a high degree of influence over its own children when nearly three fifths of all possible plans are favorable to it. The corollary to this result is that to black people almost any plan could be interpreted as being gerrymandered by the establishment in favor of white control. This is the decisive effect of the disparity between high black student enrollment and low black voter propensity.

If the maximization of either of the first two measures is pursued, it is likely to be politically unacceptable in a city as racially divided as Detroit. We therefore considered two alternatives which might gain more support: *homogeneity* because it represents a compromise between the two communities, and *integration* because it is an ultimate goal of the Supreme Court. There are numerous plans with relatively high homogeneity scores and it is important at this point to observe the relationship between high homogeneity and black community control. Because black students form a majority of the student enrollment, there will be a fairly large percentage of black children under black control if homogeneity is high. Also, the percentage of white children under white control is high on *all* plans (even those with over 80 per cent black community control). A homogeneous solution is therefore likely to be satisfactory if each community is concerned with seeing as little bias as possible in the final sharing of influence.

The integration measure indicates how far, in fact, the high schools of Detroit are from being integrated. Even the most integrated plan has an average deviation from the city's percentage of black students of 8.9 per cent and one of the districts in that plan is over 30 per cent more segregated than Detroit as a whole. Moreover, all of the plans with less than 10 per cent on the integration measure are substantially white dominated in terms of children controlled and have a 2–5, black-white split in regional boards. Any attempt to promote decentralization as a step toward integration, therefore, could be interpreted by leaders of the black community as deliberate gerrymandering by the existing power structure.

AN EVALUATION OF STRATEGIES

In May 1970, the Detroit Board of Education presented its final decentralization plan to the public. In addition to meeting the school population constraints of Act 244, the Board stated two other requirements which it felt legally obliged to satisfy. One was that the new regions must be "substantially equal in total population so that the Federal requirement of one-man, one-vote may be met," and the other that each region be "a racially integrated district in compliance with both State and Federal constitutions" [3, p. 1]. Our study was initiated in terms of Act 244 and we did not have a suitable breakdown of Detroit population estimates available to allow us to test the equality of population requirement, but in view of the ambiguity of the term "substantially equal," we were not disheartened at being unable to evaluate this criterion. The board's plan, aiming at high integration, contained one discontiguity which placed the Northern district, a heavily black area, in with suburban Pershing and Osborn although they are physically separated by the Hamtramck industrial section. It also made adjustments to district boundaries in order to meet the enrollment constraint.

The geography of the Board's plan is compared with that of three others drawn from our generated solutions and promoting different strategies of political control. Table 3 and Figure 1 present a comparison on the various measures explained above. The three additional plans represent a community control, integration, and "community compromise" solution. As our earlier discussion indicated, pursuance of a strategy of integration results in white community domination at the metropolitan level and also leaves the black community with very little potential control over the education of its own children. This is achieved geographically by creating wedge-shaped regions directed into the heart of the city, and therefore combining districts with high suburban voting power (but relatively fewer children in the school system) with districts where many black children but lower numbers of black voters are found. This is a striking example of how the unswerving pursuit of a long-standing liberal goal intended to advance the cause of black people could deny them a political base from which to build control of their own environment.

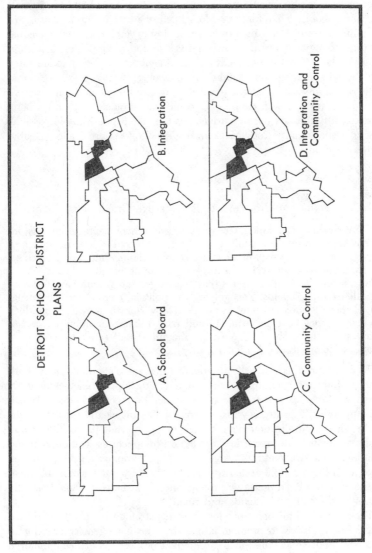

DETROIT SCHOOL DISTRICT
PLANS

A. School Board

B. Integration

C. Community Control

D. Integration and
Community Control

Figure 1

In contrast, high levels of community control can be achieved with relative fairness to both the black and white communities (Table 3). However, such a solution would probably bar any long-term hope of integrating the schools. Therefore, the fourth strategy aims for a sharing of community control and integration in a single plan. It creates an equal sharing of regional board representatives at the metropolitan level and respects the real pattern of Detroit's social geography. Yet there are three regions where integration might prove geographically possible in that some of the physical means of redistributing children among schools mentioned in the opening paragraphs could be implemented and where, perhaps, attitudes are not so hardened as to make it politically impossible. These regions are Cody-Mackenzie, Pershing-Osborn, and Denby-Kettering-Finney.

CONCLUSION

In *The Politics of Urban Education,* Marilyn Gittell has written:

> Integration has failed. In most cities, school segregation has intensified; the political conflict continues. The tremendous resistance of parent groups, as well as of many school administrators and teachers, has engulfed those trying to implement the orders of the courts. . . . As a result, civil rights groups that once urged integration have virtually tabled their demands. Recognizing the political character of the struggle, these groups are now aware that they lack the power to produce change. They have also come to understand that integration per se cannot solve the problem of reducing inequities that result from cultural and sociological deprivation [6, p. 7].

As a result of this study the authors feel that there are, in addition, both demographic and geographical disadvantages facing the black community whenever integration is coupled with democratic precepts in decentralization proposals. The strategy histograms for Detroit clearly show that virtually all decentralization plans which are purported to mix black and white pupils in high proportions are bound to appear as white dominated solutions. Also, we venture to suggest that integration as a goal could well clash with the principle of decentralization itself by forcing weak alliances at the local level and preserving the autonomy of the city school board by permitting a policy of "divide and rule."

From an electoral point of view a better strategy for ghetto and civil rights organizations to promote is one stressing homogeneity or community control of education. Since more equal proportions of black children under black control and white children under white control can be obtained in this way, then greater public participation in education could be achieved while at the same time making reform politically acceptable

TABLE 3
Characteristics of Evaluated Plans

CHARACTERISTICS → PLAN ↓	Regional Split Black-White	Black Control	White Control	Homogeneity	Integration Average Deviation	Range of Deviation
School board	2-5	36.0	75.0	50.4	9.9	39.1
Integration	2-5	38.9	82.6	55.1	9.6	41.3
Community control	5-3	84.0	74.0	80.3	25.7	86.0
Integration and Community control	4-4	59.8	71.7	64.2	14.8	49.0

to the community. Where it is still desired to promote integration, this is best done in those regions of the city where accessibility, social relationships, and politics make it practically possible. In the Detroit "community compromise" plan illustrated above, roughly 20 per cent of all school children would come under integrated control, a figure which could be increased if necessary by relaxing enrollment constraints in the regions involved. At the same time, the long-standing division of Detroit into black and white communities would be recognized by implementing schemes of community control in the suburbs and around the city center.

The basic cause of the differences in range of choice between white and black decentralization plans is the disparity between black registered electoral figures and the number of black students in the high school system. The geographic polarization of Detroit into an overwhelmingly black inner city and surrounding white suburbs reinforces this effect. Other major cities in the United States have a similar distribution and some are more segregated than Detroit. As a result, the findings reported in this paper can be regarded as having some generality.

LITERATURE CITED

1. Campbell, A. K. and P. Meranto. "The Metropolitan Education Dilemma," *Urban Affairs Quarterly*, 11 (1966).
2. Detroit Board of Education. "On Implementation of Public Act 244: Progress Report 2," Detroit (March 1970).
3. Detroit Board of Education. "Regional School District Boundaries," Detroit (May 1970).
4. Detroit Geographical Expedition and Institute. "A Report to the Parents of Detroit on Decentralization," Detroit (December 1969).
5. Dye, T. R. "Urban School Segregation: A Comparative Analysis," *Urban Affairs Quarterly*, 4 (1968).
6. Gittell, M. and A. G. Hevesi, eds. *The Politics of Urban Education.* New York: Praeger, 1969.
7. Gittell, M. and T. E. Hollander. *Six Urban School Districts.* New York: Praeger, 1968.
8. Mayor's Advisory Panel on Decentralization of the New York City Schools. *Reconnection for Learning: A Community School System for New York City.* New York: Praeger, 1969.
9. Nagel, S. S. "Simplified Bipartisan Computer Redistricting," *Stanford Law Review*, 17 (1964–1965).
10. Passow, A. H., ed. *Education in Depressed Areas.* New York: Columbia University Press, 1963.

11. Shepherd, J. W. and M. A. Jenkins. "Decentralizing High School Administration in Detroit: A Computer Evaluation of Alternate Strategies of Political Control," *Proceedings, Conference on Interdisciplinary Research in Computer Science.* Computer Science Association of Canada, Winnipeg, June 1970.

12. Michigan. "Act No. 244, Public Acts of 1969," Lansing (1969).

CHAPTER VI

Urban Black Rebellions

INTRODUCTORY NOTE

Civil disobedience, civil disturbance, riot, and rebellion are terms used to describe racial violence of the 1960s. "Rebellion" was selected for this chapter title as the editors feel that it best describes the majority of these violent situations. Rebellion implies open, organized, and often armed defiance and resistance to established authority or government. But not all urban racial violence begins as rebellion. In fact, there are strong arguments supporting the statement that most of these violent occurrences began as riots and few, if any, as rebellions. However, many observers are persuaded that whatever the initial causes and characteristics the riots quickly escalated into rebellions in which legitimacy of the established power structure was challenged. A significant part of this violence was perpetrated against visible symbols of governmental authority: policemen, firemen, and National Guardsmen. Actually, many rebellions began as single isolated incidents of black resistance to police power as enforced in the ghetto.

Use of the term "rebellion" must be qualified lest the reader misunderstand its application in this chapter. The editors do not believe that the majority of urban black rebellions can be characterized as organized armed resistance. The preponderance of available evidence has shown that the greater majority of these rebellions were spontaneous, unarmed, and loosely organized at best, a position strongly supported by the Kerner Commission.

From the end of World War II until the present day, there have been many large-scale urban disturbances which reflect black discontent and frustration with white American society. Violence in 1964, in Harlem, sparked a series of urban riots. A spirit of defiance and resistance diffused to many cities over the urban North, Midwest, and West. Violence climaxed in 1968, when blacks protested collectively the assassination of

Dr. Martin Luther King with open rebellion. These violent events were actions of people expressing frustration, anger, powerlessness, and alienation. Impoverished and overcrowded in large slum ghettos, blacks rose up in anger against affluent, indifferent white-controlled American society. Riots of the sixties—Harlem, Watts, Newark, Detroit, and others—resulted from the failure of American society to raise to equality with whites the economic, social, and political status of blacks trapped in inner-city ghettos.

Many social scientists have surveyed causes and effects of urban racial violence in the twentieth century. Sociologists, psychologists, political scientists, and historians, but few geographers have been involved in this research. The locational significance of urban disturbances is one social problem with which geographers were not concerned until after urban conflagrations in the late 1960s. Recently, several geographers have shown research interest in occurrence and distribution of black rebellions. The following articles illustrate several of many directions that geographic investigations of urban black rebellions have taken.

John S. Adams' work seeks to explain variations in occurrence of urban racial rebellions in the United States by investigating locational influences on the psychological and physical environments, and on inter- and intra-urban variation of riot behavior. Specifically, Adams analyzes why some cities have had racial disturbances while other cities were peaceful, by presenting a statistical model which illustrates these reasons.

Adams examines some causal factors of the riots by demonstrating "dysfunctional population and housing changes." These changes involve growing black populations and housing shortages of alarming proportions in the 1950–60 decade in certain parts of the black ghetto. These changes were particularly important in zones where working class and lower middle-class blacks saw their environment deteriorate at the very time their expectations were rising.

Three theories of riot origin are expounded by Adams. These theories differentiate rioters from nonrioters and describe environmental prerequisites to rioting. The most applicable explanation of riot origin seems to result from the combination of two of these theories: relative deprivation and blocked opportunity. The relative deprivation theory accounts for intense discontent among working class and lower middle-class blacks. The blocked opportunity theory posits low levels of capabilities or realizations of personal, economic, and environment rewards to be gained by blacks within the American system.

Factor analysis and multiple regression are used by Adams to provide statistical analyses of the data, with significant factor scores regressed to test validity and reliability of regression coefficients. Several manipulations of the factor analytic-regression technique support the relative deprivation-block opportunity theory, especially when the equations are applied to specific large Midwestern cities affected by riots.

Adams states solution to many social problems which resulted in urban racial violence can be found in improving the quality of life in the ghetto and in halting utilization of the ghetto as a "storage bin for the poor."

Adams concludes that, similar to other social pathologies,* evidence from urban riots of the 1960s resembles the tip of an iceberg, with the greater majority of information hidden below the surface. He states social scientists have yet to understand either areal organization of ghettos or processes and behavior which produced and maintain them today.

Although Donald I. Warren is a sociologist and not directly involved in geographic research, much of his work is location orientated. Warren is concerned with investigation of social structures in urban black ghettos. He is particularly concerned with delimitation and analysis of relationships between neighborhood structure and riot behavior. Focus of the research is not on individual rioter but on locational context—the immediate neighborhood. Warren views neighborhood as a potentially key social unit that initiates community participation and social interaction.

Importance of local environment as a social unit, and as the geographic basis for formal and informal social participation patterns, is established by Warren's use of a six-fold typology of neighborhoods that defines a community in terms of its organization and orientation to the larger urban community. The neighborhood typology is based on criteria of social organization and positive or negative reference. One central hypothesis of Warren's research is that the role of local neighborhood is more significant in a black ghetto than in white communities. This hypothesis is tested utilizing the neighborhood typology to discover relationships between neighborhoods and riot behavior.

Warren concludes by stating the research reveals relationships which suggest riot, counterriot, and riot withdrawal behaviors of individuals are correlated with particular, carefully defined, types of neighborhood environments. Warren further states the immediate neighborhood has a high potential for positive social action especially as there is relative absence of alternative mechanisms and structures in segregated urban ghetto environments.

Paul S. Salter and Robert C. Mings present a brief cartographic account of geographic aspects of Miami's racial violence in 1968. The authors propose to delimit distinctive geopolitical patterns of Miami's riots, identify areal effects of differing law enforcement approaches, and suggest

---

* The editors disagree with Adams on this point. Riots are symptomatic of the pathogenic spatial-socioeconomic conditions in the ghetto, but are not in themselves a social disease.

several needed research topics concerning geography of racial disturbances.

Although the authors state that they do not intend to describe the violence or to establish specific causes for the riot, they take up much of their article's few pages in doing just that. The authors use four maps in their description of the geographic patterns of the violence, and attempt to relate spatial flow of the riot to police-community relations. Without establishing empirical verification, Salter and Mings assert that satisfactory relationships between the Dade County Public Safety Department and the black community kept violence out of the region's unincorporated areas. Salter and Mings claim that violence moved east into Miami rather than west into Dade County because of the two police departments' different approaches to involvement with the black communities. Although this hypothesis makes some sense, it does not seem to be the main reason for describing directional flows of Miami's racial violence, especially considering the authors give little evidence in support of their views.

THE GEOGRAPHY OF RIOTS AND CIVIL DISORDERS
IN THE 1960s

John S. Adams

Alexis de Tocqueville wrote that:

> The sufferings that are endured patiently, as being inevitable, become intolerable the moment it appears there might be an escape. Reform then only serves to reveal more closely what still remains oppressive and now all the more unbearable. The suffering, it is true, has been reduced, but one's sensitivity has become more acute.

This paper explores the psychological and physical environments that surrounded the riots of the 1960s. It examines why some cities had riots while others were peaceful, and presents a model proposing why some black neighborhoods exploded while others remained tense but calm. The study concludes that during the decade, urban black Americans experienced a widening gap between sharply rising expectations and limited capabilities. This "relative deprivation" gap appears to have been greatest in neighborhoods which exploded first.

THE REVOLT OF THE GHETTOS, 1964 TO 1968:
THE PSYCHOLOGICAL SIDE

The revolt of black America did not happen overnight; it began with an unfulfilled promise. Claude Brown, in his *Manchild in the Promised Land,* began his portrayal of Harlem with this denial of the promise:

> I want to talk about the first Northern urban generation of Negroes. I want to talk about the experiences of a misplaced generation of a misplaced people in an extremely complex, confused society. . . . These migrants were told that unlimited opportunities for prosperity

existed in New York and that there was no "color problem" there. They
were told that Negroes lived in houses with bathrooms, electricity, running water, and indoor toilets. To them, this was the "promised land"
that Mammy had been singing about in the cotton fields for many
years. . . . There was a tremendous difference in the way people lived
up north. There were too many people full of hate and bitterness
crowded into a dirty, stinky, uncared-for closet-sized section of a great
city. . . .

The children of these disillusioned colored pioneers inherited the
total lot of their parents—the disappointments, the anger. To add to
their misery, they had little hope of deliverance. For where does one
run to when he's already in the promised land? [7, pp. vii–viii].

One runs to one's soul brother. Sentiment and experience fused in Harlem
and in ghettos across the country. Metropolitan areas grew, ghettos expanded, whites escaped to the suburbs, more blacks arrived, and ghetto
life deteriorated.

Any living organism thrives at only one scale according to a "law of
proper proportions," but it will collapse of its own weight if size is
doubled, tripled, or quadrupled and proportions are held constant [46,
pp. 15–22]. The same laws of allometric growth may apply to cities and
ghettos. Let us say a city's black neighborhood comprised a compact zone
covering a tenth of the city in 1920, and by 1960 the urbanized area and
its black neighborhood had both tripled in size. Even though the black
neighborhood is segregated from white neighborhoods in both cases, the
"activity space" of an average black resident intersects a proportionately
wider spectrum of the available urban experience in 1920 than in 1960.
As the metropolis and the ghetto expand, activity spaces of poor residents
remain constant or shrink somewhat as public transportation deteriorates.
In 1920, blacks and whites lived rather close to one another. By 1960, due
partly to the geometry of human behavior and unregulated urban and
ghetto expansion, the centers of gravity of each city's black and white
populations were drifting farther and farther apart.

What started out as an urban experience ended as a ghetto existence for
black newcomers to the northern city. From Harlem to Watts ghetto life
became the common denominator, with its own life style, language, and
restricted range of experience. The ghetto became a dead end for many of
its residents. It became an object of loathing, a mirror of a squalid existence. Feelings of helplessness and isolation recurred in city after city.
When asked what she would do if she had enough income one woman
declared: "The first thing I would do myself is move out of the neighborhood. I feel the entire neighborhood is more or less a trap" [49, p. 6].

Compounding these antagonisms were the intensifying anti-urban attitudes of whites, drawn to the city by economic necessity but seizing the

first opportunity to escape to the suburbs [*19*, pp. 187–89]. Meanwhile, the poorest citizens were not only poor, they were black and located in those sections of the city vacated by earlier immigrant groups who had succeeded in translating upward social and economic mobility into geographic mobility [*48, 51, 41*]. As Kenneth Clark wrote:

> The poor are always alienated from normal society, and when the poor are Negro as they increasingly are in American cities, a double trauma exists—rejection on the basis of class and race is a danger to the stability of the society as a whole [*11*, p. 21].

The inauguration of John F. Kennedy in 1961 introduced the rhetoric and promises of the New Frontier and a significant fraction of mesmerized Americans became convinced that change was not only possible, but that rapid improvement of their lot lay just around the corner. President Kennedy's death in 1963 interrupted that dream, but even more extravagant promises accompanied the unveiling of a plan for a Great Society with full civil rights for all and a war on poverty [*34*, pp. 119–21].

Gradually at first, then picking up steam, a sense of betrayal of expectations brought grievances into focus. To lower class and lower middle-class blacks, the visibility of an affluent and comfortable white middle class, exaggerated by mass media, induced dual feelings of emulation and smoldering resentment. After the riots, the Kerner Commission found the same complaints in city after city [*40*, p. 143]. The most intensely felt problems were: 1) police practices, perceived as attacks against personal dignity; 2) unemployment and underemployment, perceived as attacks against personal and family economic security; and 3) inadequate housing, perceived as an attack against the health, safety, and comfort of the family's personal environment. Such deep-seated, long-term malaise can lead to only one result in a decade of rapid change and rising expectations. Aaron Wildavsky summarized the situation in his recipe for violence:

> Promise a lot; deliver a little. Lead people to believe they will be much better off, but let there be no dramatic improvement. Try a variety of small programs, each interesting but marginal in impact and severely underfinanced. Avoid any attempted solution remotely comparable in size to the dimensions of the problem you are trying to solve. . . . Get some poor people involved in local decision-making, only to discover that there is not enough at stake to be worth bothering about. Feel guilty about what has happened to black people; tell them you are surprised that they have not revolted before; express shock and dismay when they follow your advice. Go in for a little force, just enough to anger, not to discourage. Feel guilty again; say you are surprised that worse has not happened. Alternate with a little suppression. Mix well, apply a match, and run . . . [*34*, p. ii].

DYSFUNCTIONAL POPULATION AND HOUSING CHANGES,
1950 TO 1960:
THE STAGE FOR UNREST

In most large cities the spatial organization of the housing supply resembles a series of distinct concentric zones around the downtown. Higher density, lower priced, and older housing is available in the inner rings; newer, lower density, higher priced units, mainly single family detached dwellings, are concentrated in the outer rings (Figure 1).

The demand for housing is expressed sectorally. As each household passes through the stages of the family life cycle its housing needs change and the household relocates, either *outward* to a larger more expensive unit, or *inward* to a smaller, cheaper dwelling. Most households try to satisfy changed housing requirements with a move as short as possible, so a city's aggregate migration fabric displays pronounced sectoral biases.

At the suburban edge of each sector, the addition of new housing provides upwardly mobile inner-city families with an opportunity to move outward. As they move outward they vacate older housing which then becomes available to families localized nearer to the downtown core. Within each areal sector, the invasion-succession process is the principal means by which better housing "filters down" from the prosperous to the poor [20]. In normal times housing filters smoothly, but from 1950 to the 1960s, the poor and the middle-class black neighborhoods experienced a housing squeeze of alarming proportions.

Let us examine the source of the housing squeeze. Residential structures have high durability. According to the 1960 census of housing there were 58 million housing units in the United States. Thus, 1.5 million new housing starts in one year is only about 2.5 per cent of the housing stock, a relatively small change in the total number which is also affected by housing removals, especially in core areas of cities. In the aggregate metropolitan housing market, removals generate a replacement demand which is less important than either household formations or other influences on housing demand. In certain areal submarkets, however, demolition in one neighborhood is the principal stimulus for incremental demand in adjacent neighborhoods [32].

During the 1960s demolitions due to public and private urban land redevelopment and urban highway construction proceeded at a brisk rate, but housing starts and vacancy rates varied widely, putting a serious crunch on the most active housing sectors. Despite *increasing* demands for more housing throughout the 1960s, annual new private housing starts reached a peak of 1.6 million in 1963, then dropped to 1.2 million by

Housing Change

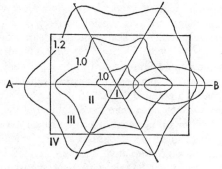

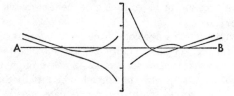

Population Change

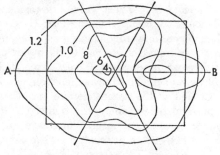

FIG. 1 A MAP OF HOUSING CHANGE RATIOS (1960 HOUSING UNITS IN A TRACT DIVIDED BY 1950 UNITS) HAS FOUR HOUSING ZONES: ZONE I HOUSING INCREASED, ZONE II HOUSING DECLINED, ZONE III WAS STABLE OR HAD A MODEST HOUSING INCREASE, ZONE IV HAD VIGOROUS SUBURBAN GROWTH. THE MAP OF POPULATION CHANGE RATIOS (1960 TRACT POPULATION DIVIDED BY 1950) REVEALS THE SHARPEST LOSSES NEXT TO THE DOWNTOWN CENTER AND SHARP INCREASES IN SUBURBAN AREAS. DYSFUNCTIONAL CHANGE OCCURS WHEN POPULATION RATIOS EXCEED HOUSING RATIOS AS THEY OFTEN DID IN THE MIDDLE ZONES (SMALL ELIPSE) OF THE BLACK NEIGHBORHOOD (LARGE ELIPSE).

1966. By 1968, with only 1.5 million private units started, the construction industry still had not recovered to its 1962 levels of production. Just when more housing was desperately needed, less was provided; meanwhile, in some neighborhoods housing was even being removed.

Vacancy rates are another indicator of the degree of pressure that demand is exerting on available supplies. The annual average rental vacancy rate for the United States rose from 5.1 per cent in 1957 to 6.4 per cent in 1959, and to 8.1 per cent in the second quarter of 1961. Then, dropping as the market tightened, the rate fell to 4.9 per cent at the end of 1968. Homeowner vacancy rates were more stable, but they too reached a peak in 1963 and fell to 1.0 per cent in 1968. From 1960 to 1968 mobile home shipments quadrupled in response to strong demand, but this particular low income housing alternative, virtually banned from core housing areas of cities, remained largely a rural or suburban option. Thus, black households account for fewer than 2 per cent of mobile home households [50, p. 92].

Racial and ethnic ghettos develop in the most vigorous residential sectors [44]. At the turn of the century diverse ethnic groups clustered around the downtowns of American cities. Some groups, usually white Anglo-Saxon Protestant or Jewish, prospered more rapidly than others and moved outward, as a group, with disproportionate speed. Because they moved in large numbers they vacated whole neighborhoods, which then stood ready for occupancy by the next wave of newcomers. This explains why black populations now occupy housing formerly used by the city's largest and most prosperous upwardly mobile groups [42, pp. 7–16].

The expansion of the Indo-Chinese war in the 1960s prompted major increases in the federal military budget. Increased spending coupled with deficit financing of the war produced severe inflation, which persisted and intensified until the end of the decade despite tax increases. Monetary controls were applied to the economy and tighter credit hit the home mortgage market. As government insured mortgage interest rates rose from 5 and 6 per cent to 9 and 10 per cent, suburban new home construction was drastically curtailed. The sectors where the black ghettos were located were hit the hardest. Filtering was sharply curtailed. Departures from middle-class black neighborhoods (in the form of migration outward, or to other cities, or death) did not keep up either with arrivals or with the pressing need for additional space (immigration from core areas, from other cities, or from the South; births; infants and young children becoming young children and adolescents). Thus, crowding or congestion radically increased without a safety valve during the 1960s *in certain parts* of black neighborhoods—not in the oldest core area, nor the upper middle class advancing edges, but in the middle zones where working class and lower middle-class blacks saw their situation deteriorate at precisely the time when they expected their lot to improve. These middle zones were precisely the places where violence erupted.

THEORIES OF RIOT ORIGIN

Some explanations of riot occurrence differentiate rioters from nonrioters. Other theories emphasize environmental circumstances, arguing that certain sets of conditions, if prevalent in a place, trigger violence. The most successful theories are psychological and emphasize the difference between what people think they have and what they feel they deserve.

The Riffraff Theory. The "riffraff theory" argues that "rioters are irresponsible deviants: criminals, unassimilated migrants, emotionally disturbed persons or members of an underclass . . . peripheral to organized society with no broad social or political concerns, and views the frustration that leads to rioting as simply part of a long history of personal failure" [9, p. 15]. By sampling populations in the Detroit and Newark census tracts where violence and damage occurred, Kerner Commission interviewers found no differences between rioters and nonrioters that would support the riffraff theory. Instead, occupational aspirations of the rioters in Newark were higher than among nonrioters. Moreover, the vast majority of the rioters were Northerners, either born in the riot city or immigrants from another Northern city.

Relative Deprivation. The "relative deprivation theory" was rejected by the Kerner Commission for the same reason as the riffraff theory: it failed to distinguish rioters from nonrioters in the census tracts which exploded. Relative deprivation is more complex than a simple "want-get" ratio suggests. The greater the deprivation a person perceives relative to what he feels are "justified expectations" the greater his discontent. Relative deprivation is not what the outside observer thinks people ought to be dissatisfied with. It is people's perception of a discrepancy between their level of expectations and the capabilities they realize. People become most intensely discontented when they fail to get what they think they justly deserve, not just what they *want* in an ideal sense, and when they feel they are making inadequate progress beyond their expectations, not whether they have actually attained them or not [22].

Progressive deprivation, the third form of relative deprivation seems to be often tied to revolutionary movements. Prolonged experience of increasing well-being generates intense expectations about continued increases. If changing circumstances mean that these expectations seem unsatisfiable, the likely consequence is intense discontent [12].

Applied to black populations and black neighborhoods, the relative deprivation theory can emphasize: 1) the economic gap between blacks and whites, which is a popular and somewhat invalid impression; 2) the gap between urban blacks and rural blacks, which is a discounted view and in any case fails to explain urban discontent [21]; and, 3) the perceived gap between upper middle-class blacks and the blacks that rioted. The Kerner Commission found substantial and unexpected support for this third type of gap; the rioters used prosperous, successful blacks as their principal reference group [9, 43].

Black Americans in the 1960s should have benefited from the most prolonged economic expansion in the nation's history, and they apparently did. Median income of nonwhite families as a per cent of white family income rose from 53 per cent in 1961 to 62 per cent in 1967. The percentage of nonwhite persons below the poverty line fell from 55 in 1961 to 35 in 1967 [33]. But just looking at income changes—the realizations or capabilities—misses half the point. Expectations changed too! As Boulding paraphrases Veblen: "We cannot assume that tastes are given in any dynamic theory . . . we cannot afford to neglect the processes by which cultures are created and by which preferences are learned" [6, p. 2].

Blocked Opportunity.   Another theory of riot origin stresses "blocked opportunities." It claims that black Americans have been systematically excluded from white society and white-controlled economic institutions. "This theory views white discrimination as a constant barrier to occupational mobility; thus, the Negroes who are most likely to react violently are those who want to better themselves . . ." [9, p. 15].

The most useful theory of riot origin seems to be a combination of the second and third theories. The relative deprivation theory accounts for the level of intense discontent among the working class and lower middle-class blacks who are neither the poorest nor the most prosperous. The blocked opportunity theory accounts for the low level of capabilities or realization of personal, economic, and environmental rewards inside the American system.

Besides overt discrimination in many places, feelings of relative deprivation and blocked opportunity were sometimes aggravated in innocent ways as well. The exclusion of blacks from many construction jobs is frequently cited as a particularly glaring form of blocked opportunity. Because such jobs are highly visible, reputed to be lucrative, and seem relatively easy to learn, "justified expectations" on the part of blacks are that a representative fraction of all construction workers should be black. Yet many of these occupations have little if any room for newcomers, black or white [1]. Journeymen tradesmen, often anxious for their own jobs in the face of automation and declining employment, jealously guard their union membership as a birthright to pass on to whomever they choose. From the black point of view, opportunities appear to be blocked just when aspirations are rising.

THE LOCATION OF RIOTS AND CIVIL DISORDERS

Rioting black Americans can be classified in socioeconomic or locational terms. In socioeconomic terms the question "Who riots?" is answered in terms of an ambitious, hard working, but intensely dissatisfied group of working class and lower middle-class blacks who feel deprived and excluded from what they feel are justified expectations. In geographical terms the question can be handled either at a macro-scale (Why did some cities explode while others were peaceful?) or at a micro-scale (Why did some black neighborhoods explode and others remain quiet?).

Intercity Analysis

In an analysis of seventy-six black-white race riots between 1913 and 1963, Lieberson and Silverman [27] found no important connection between the occurrence of violence and population growth, a city's proportion of black population, the unemployment rate, black income levels, the proportion of blacks in good housing, or other local environmental conditions.

A reanalysis of the Lieberson and Silverman data confirmed that no single factor discriminated clearly between riot and control cities, but did reveal that of the nine variables used, employment conditions discriminated better than any other single factor [4]. Reporting these results Downes agrees with Tomlinson that: "What is unacceptable about Negro life does not vary much from city to city . . . the differences in Negro life from city to city are irrelevant" [14; 47, p. 30]. Yet in his study of 239 outbursts between January 1964 and May 1968, Downes concluded that violence was somewhat more likely in cities that were densely settled, were large with little post-1950 population change, had a high and rapidly increasing fraction of black population since 1950, lower educational and income levels, higher unemployment rates, less sound housing, relatively little owner occupied housing, and high central employment. The differences turned out to be statistically significant because each municipality, whether a central city or a suburb, was treated as a "city." Thus, the conclusions merely emphasize the city-suburb distinction instead of the differences between riot metropolises and nonriot metropolises.

In a 1967 study, Maloney [28] tried to show how Standard Metropolitan Statistical Areas (SMSAs) that had riots differed from those that were peaceful in 1967. He selected eighty-five metropolitan areas on the basis of data availability and studied their differences in terms of 70 census and noncensus variables. A factor analysis of the 70 by 70 correlation matrix revealed eight principal dimensions of variation: metropolitanism or size, urban growth, a southern syndrome, sporadic employment, highway spending, Negro concentration, a suburban syndrome, and density. Each metropolitan area received a separate factor score for each of the eight independent factors. Each score's magnitude depended on the metropolitan area's alignment with the corresponding factor or basic pattern of variation. The 85 by 8 matrix of factor scores provided Maloney with a set of eight measures for each SMSA. With the factor scores as independent variables, and a binary measurement of riot activity for the dependent variable (SMSAs having a riot before August 5, 1967 received a 1; others received a 0), a regression analysis produced a model arguing that riot experience (RE) varied positively with metropolitan size (M), the presence of a black population (B), and metropolitan density (D); and varied inversely with "Southernness" (S).

Only four regression coefficients were statistically significant, but even with all eight variables included the coefficient of multiple determination was only .35. The eighty-five metropolitan areas were ranked on the basis of their "expected riot scores." Of the twenty-four highest scoring SMSAs, twenty-two had riots; of the twenty-nine lowest scoring areas, mainly southern cities or cities lacking black populations, twenty-six were peaceful. Between these extremes the regression model was a poor predictor of riot experiences of different SMSAs.

Maloney's model is consistent with the theory that the largest SMSAs are the best known and most popular migration destinations for blacks looking for economic opportunity. Migrants expect greater rewards from the system than nonmigrants. Migration out of southern cities has been selective; outmigrants have been more aggressive and better educated than others left behind. If a northern or western metropolitan area has a disproportionately high concentration of blacks, it is because the area was large and well known and perceived as a place of opportunity vis-à-vis alternative destinations. Metropolitan density is associated with riot activity because some of the largest and most attractive migration destinations in the North and Northeast are also very old cities with extensive high density central city areas.

When Maloney [29] expanded his study to include ninety-six metropolitan areas and additional variables he found little additional explanation, although by correlating individual variables with the occurrence or nonoccurrence of riots he made some surprising discoveries which support the combined relative-deprivation blocked-opportunity theory. The following SMSA variables were correlated with riot activity:

(a) per cent of adults that voted in 1964 (correlation = +.42), reflecting a basic sense of political involvement and faith in the system;

(b) per cent of adults with less than five years of schooling, and per cent of families with less than $3,000 annual income (both −.38), reflecting that when well-educated migrants enter an area in large numbers they dilute the relative concentration of the resident poor and uneducated at the destination, and intensify the concentration in source areas;

(c) per cent of sound housing, and per cent of families with incomes over $15,000 (both +.40), reflecting visible prosperity and the generation of high expectations; and,

(d) per cent of the SMSA population living in suburbs, and number of local governments (both +.35), reflecting rapid metropolitan and suburban expansion, producing further expectations about drastic change in housing environments.

The relative deprivation theory argues that a rising gap between justifiable expectations and current capabilities produces intense frustration; the blocked opportunity theory explains why capabilities rise slowly if at all. Maloney's metropolitan area model yielded patterns consistent with both constructs. A midwestern city model linking city scores with riot scores brings patterns into even sharper focus.

Riot Experiences of Midwestern Cities

Berry [3] computed city scores for 1,762 legal cities with 1960 populations exceeding 10,000, using 97 standardized and normalized census variables. A factor analysis of the 1,762 by 97 data matrix identified 14 basic urban factors or dimensions accounting for 77 per cent of the variation in the original data matrix. The dimensions included: functional size, socioeconomic status, family structure, nonwhite concentrations, foreign born concentrations, recent population growth, recent employment growth, females in the labor force, elderly males in the labor force, manufacturing activity, mining activity, college and university activity, military installations, and service centers or central places. Each city received fourteen scores, a separate score in terms of each factor. The city receiving top score on a certain factor is the most typical representative of the combination of traits that reflect the factor. For example, on the college and university factor, the highest scoring cities included State College, Pennsylvania, Chapel Hill, North Carolina, and Athens, Ohio. Cities with the highest socioeconomic status scores were Scarsdale, New York, and Winnetka, Illinois, and so forth. From Berry's 1,762 by 14 matrix of stand-

ardized factor scores this author selected the 212 rows representing all
the midwestern cities in the East North Central and the West North Central census divisions.

Riot scores were computed from 15 riot variables describing 166 major
disturbances that occurred between 1965 and July 31, 1968 [52]. The
author expected a factor analysis to reveal just one major pattern of riot
activity, but three independent dimensions of civil disorder were un-
covered, accounting for 59 per cent of the original data variation. The first
rotated factor represented the number of law officers and civilians killed
and injured, arson, arrests, and property damage. The second factor
emphasized the number of state police used to contain the disturbances,
and the occurrence of interference with firemen. The third factor, independent of the other two, was linked to the incidence of sniping, vandalism, and the use of the national guard. Three standardized factor
scores were computed for each of the 166 riots, 59 of which occurred in
37 midwestern cities. For cities having two or more riots, a mean score
was computed for each factor. For the 175 midwestern cities which had
no *major* disturbances (most of which presumably had minor unrest),
dummy factor scores were provided. The lowest Riot I score among the
166 riots was −.59; thus, the 175 nonriot cities were assigned a Riot I
score of −1.0. The lowest Riot II and Riot III scores (−2.56, −3.02)
meant assigning scores of −3.0 and −4.0, respectively, to the nonriot
cities.

The riot scores as dependent variables and city scores as independent
variables were put into a stepwise multiple regression procedure whereby
all statistically significant independent variables enter the regression equation one at a time in decreasing order of importance.

The first regression equation suggests that riot deaths and injuries,
arson, arrests, and property damage vary directly with city size, black
population concentrations, and recent employment growth. The third
equation ties sniping, vandalism, and the use of the National Guard with
the same independent variables. The second equation relates the use of
state police and interference with firemen to city size and black population.

This three-equation midwestern cities model, like the Maloney model,
is consistent with the relative-deprivation blocked-opportunity theory. Big
cities with expanding job opportunities are not only the most common
migration destinations for black migrants, but also the places where expectations are highest for local residents. Small stagnant areas of out-
migration had low riot scores, and the large thriving cities tended to have
the most serious problems. Maloney's use of SMSA data caused certain
city-suburb and large-city small-city contrasts to be diluted or overlooked.
Downes' use of city data identified city-suburb contrasts but because it

included cities from every part of the country, it failed to reveal important regional differences. The three-equation midwestern cities model does not escape the city-suburb bias, but by dealing with only one region's cities it eliminates or controls one source of data variation. Yet coefficients of determination are still low because patterns of riot occurrence are difficult to explain at the macro scale. Comparing black neighborhoods inside specific cities seems to be a much more fruitful approach.

The Experience Inside Seven Midwestern Cities

The people who live in cities also live in neighborhoods, and although cities differ substantially from one another, the range of neighborhood diversity is much greater. Two attributes which dramatize neighborhood diversity are census tract population change between 1950 and 1960, and the change in each tract's housing supply during the same decade.

The *population change ratio* for a census tract is computed by dividing the tract's 1960 population by its 1950 population. An isopleth map of the ratio for each of seven midwestern cities reveals that in every case the downtown is surrounded by a zone of sharp population decline, which gives way to stability and then growth from the city edge into the suburbs. The deepest losses are concentrated in the all-white sectors (Figure 1). The black neighborhood develops in the most active housing sector (Figure 1). Housing filters down to lower income black newcomers as the previous residents prosper and move as a group toward the suburbs. The faster the original residents prosper, the sooner they are able and anxious to abandon old housing for something better. New suburban housing is built wherever demand warrants; it is erected at the locations where builders expect effective purchasing power to be strongest. The large volume of old housing units that are vacated in a sector attracts newcomers. If more are attracted than can be comfortably housed, the tract population change ratios are stabilized instead of dropping as fast as they do in the more stagnant all-white sectors. In Cleveland, the black population is concentrated east of downtown and net population losses were highest on the west side. In Cincinnati the largest black neighborhoods lie to the northeast of downtown but the largest population decline occurred in tracts north and southeast of downtown. In St. Louis the black sector is northwest of downtown, but the tracts with the most abrupt population losses in the 1950s were in the western and southern sectors.

The *housing change ratio* equals 1960 housing units in a tract divided by the number in 1950. When mapped, each midwestern city studied revealed four distinct housing zones (Figure 1). The number of housing units increased in zone I, which is a public and private renewal area; zone II underwent net housing losses in the 1950s; zone III was an area of stability where the few demolitions were canceled out by modest growth. Zone IV represents vigorous suburban expansion. Housing problems are concentrated in zones I and II of the active sectors containing black populations. Because black neighborhoods lie in the most active housing sectors, they are exceptionally visible to a substantial fraction of community economic and political leaders. Moreover, in midwestern cities, the *center* of the downtown has migrated *from* its initial location *toward* the center of gravity of the city's purchasing power. This direction of movement approximates the location of the most active housing sector. If there are two exceptionally active sectors, the direction of displacement of the downtown center represents a resolution of forces. A consequence of all this is that today, black neighborhoods lie between the vigorous retailing and service edge of the downtown, and the mass, upper middle-class clientele that downtown tries to tap as employees and customers. Thus, downtown councils in midwestern cities have been more anxious to support public and private renewal in black neighborhoods than in poor white sectors elsewhere. Expressways also displace housing and particularly black housing for at least two reasons: black neighborhoods as we have just seen usually lie between downtown and the largest concentrations of prosperous commuters and shoppers; and, black neighborhoods, especially those close to downtown, have had practically no political punch in city politics and are unable to get roads relocated when they threaten to cut neighborhoods in two.

In Cleveland, Cincinnati, and Detroit serious riots and civil disorders occurred midway between ancient, emptying ghetto cores, and youthful, prosperous, advancing ghetto margins. Trapped in the middle zones were people with intense expectations who found the relative deprivation gap widening when it should have diminished. Housing was a major problem. In these middle zones the population ratio actually exceeded the housing ratio and crowding as measured by persons per dwelling unit thereby increased. The squeeze was especially grim in Cleveland's Hough neighborhood. This "middle zone" in Cincinnati was only about 40 per cent black, but the crowding got worse nevertheless. In the neighborhood at the center of the 1967 Detroit riot, population rose from 22,000 in 1956 to 38,000 in 1967 while the available housing supply was stable to declining [53, vol. 5, p. 1276]. At the ghetto margins and in white suburbs outside the city, young nuclear families live in single family dwellings. In these circumstances when the population ratio exceeds the housing ratio it is due to childbirth.

In Kansas City and Milwaukee the black neighborhood's expanding edge and its crowded midsection overlap. Yet when violence flared in the middle zone it was at locations analogous to those in Cleveland, Detroit, and Cincinnati.

St. Louis and Minneapolis avoided serious disturbances between 1965 and 1968 (low Riot I, II, and III scores), but were included in the analysis to see how housing and population ratios in middle zones differed from patterns in riot cities. Census data for St. Louis reveals no increased crowding problems in the middle zones, but only the evidence of typical family growth on the ghetto margins. Housing appears to have been filtering smoothly up through 1960. In the Minneapolis case, the black population was so small in 1960 that in no census tract did black population reach 75 per cent of the total. Black neighborhoods west and south of downtown reflect vigorous urban expansion mainly in these directions, but in no "black" tract did the population ratio exceed the housing ratio.

REFLECTIONS ON ENVIRONMENTAL STIMULATION AND THE
NEED FOR PERSONAL SPACE

As with many social pathologies, our evidence about the riots of the 1960s resembles the tip of an iceberg—it gives only a hint of the structure that lurks below. We have barely scratched the surface in our understanding of the spatial organization of black neighborhoods, of the processes and behavior that produced them, or of the ways in which they influence learning as young people grow toward adulthood. It seems likely however that ghetto neighborhoods are a trap reinforced not only from without but from within as well. Yet, according to Dubos, in every kind of neighborhood:

> Man makes himself in the very act of responding to his environment through an uninterrupted series of feedback processes. . . . Early influences are of particular importance because man's body and brain are incompletely developed at the time of birth. It is well known that various forms of deprivation impair learning ability. By acting on a child during formative years, the environment shapes him physically and mentally and influences how he will function as an adult [17, p. 153].

If children are denied the opportunity to experience early in life the kind of stimuli needed for mental development, if they fail to acquire needed mental resources, their range of free choices as adults shrinks to zero. As Dubos continues:

> It is not right to say that lack of culture is responsible for the behavior of slum children or for their failure to be successful in our society. The more painful truth is that these children acquire early in life a slum culture from which escape is almost impossible. Their early surroundings and ways of life at a critical period in their development limit the range of manifestations of their innate endowment and thus destroy much of their potential freedom [17, p. 153].

Cities are created by man's need and ability to move, to interact, and to exchange. Yet, after it reaches a certain size a city unfortunately becomes a collection of functionally and spatially segregated districts. Sheer size reduces the city to an administrative abstraction. Interaction is thwarted as the number of "contact choices" (different persons, goods, services) offered to the average citizen within an hour's round trip declines. In the ideal city, each resident's activity space should produce an optimum level of stimulation and opportunity. Visual monotony has adverse psychological consequences, especially for children who need a degree of diversity in their surroundings and in the orbit of their daily wanderings [13, 16, 25, 39].

In addition to the psychological consequences of excessive residential segregation, the social and physiological consequences of increased crowding (number of persons per dwelling unit) and high density (number of persons per unit area) are only dimly understood [45]. Calhoun's [8] crowding experiments with rats and Christian's [10] studies of animal crowding revealed pathologies that may be relevant to the problem of crowding and density in cities.

Hall [24] in his work on proxemics (the perception and use of space) observes that man shares with lower life forms certain basic needs for territory. Each man has around him an invisible series of space bubbles that expand and contract, depending on his emotional state, culture, activities, and social status [15]. People from different ethnic origins need spaces of different kinds. There are those who like to touch and those who do not. There are those who like to be auditorially involved with everyone else and those who depend on architectural barriers to screen them from the world [23].

Besides ethnic differences in spatial requirements, there are variations from person to person in each culture. When Hall studied urban renewal's effects on slum dwellers he found evidence indicating "that poor uneducated people have a much lower tolerance for being displaced than people of the middle class. Even a move across the street can be traumatic because it alters the pattern of social relationships" [24, p. 182]. Nowhere does he find evidence that public housing or urban renewal plans recognize the existence of different needs for different ethnic groups.

CONCLUSIONS

If it can be shown that uncoordinated programs of tight money, urban renewal, and highway construction can have a disastrous aggregate impact on certain parts of the city, what should be done? The President's

Committee on Urban Housing argued that federally assisted and public housing should be built where people want to live and where production costs are low. But it recognized that "the removal of existing constraints on freedom of location, such as racial discrimination and zoning abuses, is essential to the achievement of decent housing for all" [1, pp. 69–70]. On the subject of quality and location of government assisted housing, care must be taken that it does not become an additional "storage bin for the poor" [1, pp. 12, 71]. Instead of exclusive reliance on public housing programs around the downtown core, additional sound housing could be supplied to the inner city poor and working classes by speeding up the filtering process. Abundant new housing at the suburban margins of each residential sector stimulates outmigration from the central city portions of the sector. Vacated housing is thereby released to the poor, who can afford sound housing only when they are subsidized or when prices are stabilized or depressed by rapid expansion in the amount of new housing supplied [35, 36, 37].

Yet solving the housing quality problem is more than a supply and demand situation. The isolation of ghetto children must be dealt with. The spatial arrangement of human settlements may be the most basic item in preparing children to live and participate in diverse groups, to travel, to profit from their experiences, and to be at home in strange environments. As the metropolis and its black neighborhoods expand, ghetto youngsters become progressively more cut off from a diverse, instructive, and racially integrated urban experience [31]. Integrated schools become segregated, then segregated schools near the ghetto core start deteriorating. The busing of young school children attempts to equalize educational opportunities that have been rendered unequal by economic and racial segregation. If busing is to succeed in overcoming ghetto isolation, care must be taken to avoid journeys which *seem* long to the child, whether they are or not, thereby affecting his perception of his accessibility to his home and mother [26, pp. 111–12].

Because of its full range of problems and promises, the metropolis is a useful model for tomorrow's world. For example, the urbanized-industrialized Northeast has been settled since the eighteenth century, and has spread since then into the Florida, Gulf, and West Coast areas. A map of net migration shows that the edges gain at the expense of the older settled interior. The metropolis with its old-style core of high density residential and business activities is adjusting in a parallel way. Concentrations at the downtown center are dropping and residential, commercial, and industrial efforts on the edges are spreading aggressively into the former agricultural countryside.

At a still more detailed scale we can consider the racial-ethnic ghetto as a metropolis in miniature. High densities at the core of the ghetto have been dropping sharply as jobs and houses have fallen into decay and ruin. The bright, the young, the successful, and the enterprising have pushed outward from the old ghetto core and have invaded adjacent residential territories on the outer edges of the ghetto territory. Looked at in this way we see the ghetto as a small expanding world, located within the metropolis, which itself comprises a larger and expanding spatial unit. As these changes occur, society must either regulate them, or society will be regulated by their consequences. Our recent national experiences with violence reflect a vacillation between an anachronistic culture of violence that surrounds us, and the perplexing culture of constant change that makes impossible demands on the ill-equipped. Violent aggression was once a useful form of coping behavior, but in today's urban and technological age it produces maladaptive and destructive results [18].

LITERATURE CITED

1. A Decent Home: The Report of the President's Committee on Urban Housing. Washington, D.C.: Government Printing Office, 1968.

2. Altman, I., "Ecological Aspects of Interpersonal Functioning." Paper presented at the annual meeting of the American Association for the Advancement of Science, Dallas, Texas, December 31, 1968. (Mimeographed.)

3. Berry, B. J. L., American Urban Dimensions: 1960. Chicago: Center for Urban Studies, University of Chicago. (Mimeographed.)

4. Bloombaum, M., "The Conditions Underlying Race Riots as Portrayed by Multidimensional Scalogram Analysis: A Reanalysis of the Lieberson and Silverman Data," American Sociological Review, 33 (February 1968), pp. 76–91.

5. Boskin, J., "The Revolt of the Urban Ghettos," Annals of the American Academy of Political and Social Science, 382 (March 1969), pp. 1–14.

6. Boulding, K., "Economics as a Moral Science," American Economic Review, 59 (March 1969), pp. 151–54.

7. Brown, C., Manchild in the Promised Land. New York: New American Library, 1965.

8. Calhoun, J. B., "Population Density and Social Pathology," Scientific American, 206 (February 1962), pp. 139–48.

9. Caplan, N. S. and J. M. Paige, "A Study of Ghetto Rioters," Scientific American, 219 (August 1968), pp. 15–21.

10. Christian, J., "The Pathology of Overpopulation," Military Medicine, 7 (July 1963), pp. 571–603.

11. Clark, K., Dark Ghetto. New York: Harper and Row, 1964.

12. Davies, J. C., "The J-Curve of Rising and Declining Satisfactions as a Cause of Some Great Revolutions and a Contained Rebellion." *The History of Violence in America.* Edited by H. D. Graham and T. R. Gurr. New York: Bantam Books, 1969.

13. Deutsch, K., "On Social Communication and the Metropolis," *Daedalus*, 90 (Winter 1961), pp. 99–110.

14. Downes, B. T., "The Social Characteristics of Riot Cities: A Comparative Study," *Social Science Quarterly*, 49 (December 1968), pp. 504–20.

15. Doxiadis, C. A., "A City for Human Development," *Ekistics*, 25 (June 1968), pp. 374–94.

16. ——, "Man's Movement and His City," *Science*, 162 (October 1968), pp. 326–34.

17. Dubos, R., "The Crisis of Man in His Environment," *Ekistics*, 27 (March 1969), pp. 151–54.

18. Gilula, M. F. and D. N. Daniels, "Violence and Man's Struggle to Adapt," *Science*, 164 (April 25, 1969), pp. 396–405.

19. Glazer, N. and D. P. Moynihan, *Beyond the Melting Pot.* Cambridge: MIT Press, 1963.

20. Grigsby, W. G., *Housing Markets and Public Policy.* Philadelphia: University of Pennsylvania Press, 1963.

21. Grindstaff, C. G., "The Negro, Urbanization, and Relative Deprivation in the Deep South," *Social Problems*, 15 (Winter 1968), pp. 342–52.

22. Gurr, T. R., "A Comparative Study of Civil Strife," *The History of Violence in America.* Edited by H. D. Graham and T. R. Gurr. New York: Bantam Books, 1969.

23. Hall, E. T., *The Hidden Dimension.* Garden City: Doubleday, 1966.

24. ——, "Human Needs and Inhuman Cities," *Ekistics*, 160 (March 1969), pp. 181–84.

25. Hobsbawn, E., "Cities and Insurrections," *Architectural Design*, 38 (December 1968), pp. 581–88.

26. Lee, T., "On the Relation Between the School Journey and Social and Emotional Adjustment in Rural Infant Children," *The British Journal of Educational Psychology*, 27 (June 1957), pp. 110–14.

27. Lieberson, E. and A. R. Silverman, "The Precipitants and Underlying Conditions of Race Riots," *American Sociological Review*, 30 (December 1965), pp. 887–98.

28. Maloney, J. C., "Metropolitan Area Characteristics and Problems." Memorandum to: A.P.M.E. Conference Participants. Evanston: Medill School of Journalism, Northwestern University, October 19, 1967. (Mimeographed.)

29. ——, *Statistical Analysis of 1967 Disturbance Data.* (Letter to

Anthony Downs.) Evanston: Medill School of Journalism, Northwestern University, December 14, 1967. (Mimeographed.)

30. Marx, G. T., *Protest and Prejudice: A Study of Belief in the Black Community.* New York: Harper and Row, 1967.

31. Mead, M., "Preparedness for Participation in a Highly Differentiated Society," *Ekistics,* 167 (October 1969), p. 243.

32. Miller, G. H., Jr., "Housing in the 60s: A Survey of Some Non-Financial Factors," *Monthly Review,* Federal Reserve Bank of Kansas City (May 1969), pp. 3–10.

33. Mooney, J. D., "Urban Poverty and Labor Force Participation: Reply," *American Economic Review,* 59 (March 1969), pp. 194–98.

34. Moynihan, D. P., *Maximum Feasible Misunderstanding.* New York: Free Press, 1969.

35. National Commission on Urban Problems. *Housing America's Low and Moderate Income Families.* Research Report No. 7. Washington, D.C.: Government Printing Office, 1968.

36. National Commission on Urban Problems. *Housing Conditions in Urban Poverty Areas.* Research Report No. 9. Washington, D.C.: Government Printing Office, 1968.

37. National Commission on Urban Problems. *Urban Housing Needs Through the 1980s.* Research Report No. 10. Washington, D.C.: Government Printing Office, 1968.

38. Oberschall, A., "The Los Angeles Riot of August, 1966," *Social Problems,* 15 (Winter 1968), pp. 322–41.

39. Parr, A. E., "Psychological Aspects of Urbanology," *Journal of Social Issues,* 22 (October 1966), pp. 29–38.

40. *Report of the National Advisory Commission on Civil Disorders.* New York: Bantam Books, 1968.

41. Rodman, H., "Family and Social Pathology in the Ghetto," *Science,* 161 (August 23, 1968), pp. 756–62.

42. Rose, H. M., *Social Processes in the City: Race and Urban Residential Choice.* Resource Paper No. 9. Washington, D.C.: Association of American Geographers, 1969.

43. Sommers, M. S. and G. D. Bruce, "Blacks, Whites, and Products: Relative Deprivation and Reference Group Theory," *Social Science Quarterly,* 49 (December 1968), pp. 631–42.

44. Taeuber, K. and A. Taeuber, *Negroes in Cities.* Chicago: Aldine Publishing Company, 1965.

45. Taylor, D. A., L. Wheeler, and I. Altman, "Stress Relations in Socially Isolated Groups," *Journal of Personality and Social Psychology,* 9 (August 1968), pp. 369–76.

46. Thompson, D. W., *On Growth and Form.* Cambridge: Cambridge University Press, 1966.

47. Tomlinson, T. M., "Development of a Riot Ideology Among Urban Negroes," *The American Behavioral Scientist,* 2 (March-April 1968), pp. 27–31.

48. U.S. Bureau of the Census. *Poverty Areas in the 100 Largest Metropolitan Areas.* Report PC (51)–54. Washington, D.C.: Government Printing Office, 1968.

49. U.S. Commission on Civil Rights. *A Time to Listen . . . A Time to Act.* Washington, D.C.: Government Printing Office, 1967.

50. U.S. Department of Housing and Urban Development. "Mobile Homes and the Housing Supply." Part 2, *Housing Surveys.* Washington, D.C.: Government Printing Office, 1968.

51. U.S. Office of Economic Opportunity. *Maps of Major Concentrations of Poverty in Standard Metropolitan Statistical Areas of 250,000 or More Population.* 3 vols. Washington, D.C.: Government Printing Office, 1967.

52. U.S. Senate. Permanent Subcommittee on Investigations of the Committee on Government Operations. *Staff Study of Major Riots and Civil Disorders—1965 Through July 31, 1968.* Washington, D.C.: Government Printing Office, 1968.

53. U.S. Senate. Permanent Subcommittee on Investigations of the Committee on Government Operations. *Riots, Civil and Criminal Disorders.* Hearings. Washington, D.C.: Government Printing Office, 1967–1969. 23 volumes.

54. Wohlwill, J. F., "The Physical Environment: A Problem for a Psychology of Stimulation," *Journal of Social Issues,* 22 (October 1966), pp. 29–38.

NEIGHBORHOOD STRUCTURE AND RIOT BEHAVIOR IN DETROIT: SOME EXPLORATORY FINDINGS

Donald I. Warren

The recent spate of studies and surveys[1] in cities which have experienced major civil disorders have stressed either the individual attributes of rioters[2] or the process of collective behavior in rioting.[3] These studies show a lack of concern with the social structure of urban ghettos.[4]

Moreover, the preoccupation of such research has been with delineating the level of riot participation. In contrast, the Kerner report points out: "In all but six of the 24 disorders [studied by the Kerner Commission], Negro private citizens were active on the streets attempting to restore order primarily by means of persuasion."[5] Furthermore:

> In a Detroit survey of riot-area residents over the age of 15, some 14 per cent stated that they had been active as counter-rioters. . . . The typical counter-rioter . . . was an active supporter of existing social institutions. . . . As the riot alternately waxed and waned, one area of the ghetto remained insulated. . . . When the riot broke out, the residents, through the block clubs, were able to organize quickly. Youngsters, agreeing to stay in the neighborhood, participated in detouring traffic. . . . In some areas residents organized rifle squads to protect firefighters.

These patterns of behavior suggest a need to examine in greater detail the social organization of the black ghetto. Such an opportunity is present in Detroit because of extensive data collected prior to the July 1967 disorder and by a post-riot survey done in August 1967. Our focus in the present paper, therefore, is less on the individual rioter than on his social milieu—in particular, his immediate neighborhood.[6] Ecological correlations[7] provide a convenient method for discovering the forms of social control which promote or restrain riot activity.

THE SIGNIFICANCE OF THE LOCAL NEIGHBORHOOD

Evidence of the important role played by the area of residence reveals the neighborhood to be a potentially key social unit[8]—a cohesive center for social interaction. The influence of neighborhoods involves the "structural effects" of selection and socialization of residential clusterings[9] as well as the formal and informal social participation patterns organized on a geographic basis.[10] Neighborhoods as reference groups[11] or integrating mechanisms[12] for social mobility represent small units roughly corresponding to a "walking distance" social milieu.

Aside from defining the proper size or the exclusiveness of a "neighborhood effect,"[13] it is important to focus on the concept of social control and examine the structural elements of neighborhoods which are conducive to given social processes. Neighborhoods may (or may not) support the values and goals of other social institutions such as the family, and the economic and political structures of society as a whole. Two kinds of influences may be distinguished: those directly related to the individual's attitude toward social interaction with neighbors, and those related to the institutional structure of a neighborhood. An individual may be willing to alter his behavior or to engage in joint social action with his neighbors, but may find no available means to do so. For purposes of the present discussion, we are giving priority to this latter problem in order to move toward understanding alienation and civil disorder in urban ghettos.

TYPES OF NEIGHBORHOODS AND CONSEQUENCES OF PARTICULAR SETTINGS

In Table 1 we have suggested a typology of neighborhoods using criteria of social organization and reference orientation.[14] It is possible to attribute to each of the six varieties some potential for the effective or ineffective enforcement of prevailing values, or the creation of new values or social goals. Those neighborhoods in which there is a positive attitude and identification reflect reference orientations that may be sources of both integration and alienation.

The Integrated neighborhood individuals are bound to one another by frequent face-to-face contacts and/or extensive membership in formal organizations. The norms and attitudes of these persons support the values of the larger community and there are behavioral indicators of such support, such as voting in elections and initiating contact with the political members of the community.

TABLE 1

A Typology of Neighborhoods Based on Social Organization and Reference Orientation

	Typology	Informal and Formal Organization	Orientation to Larger Community
Neighborhood is a positive reference group	INTEGRATED	+	+
	PAROCHIAL	+	−
	DIFFUSE	−	−
Neighborhood is not a positive reference group	STEPPING-STONE	+	+
	TRANSITORY	−	+
	ANOMIC	−	−

The Parochial neighborhood is characterized by an extensive amount of face-to-face contact with neighbors but an absence of values or behavioral ties to the larger community. A typical example of such areas is the public housing project which is both physically and organizationally separated from the rest of the black or white community. In the settings where a positive identification with the neighborhood exists, structural weaknesses may occur as a result of deviant values or ineffective social control for conforming values. In the Parochial neighborhood this problem is likely to be a serious one. For example, a lack of ties to the larger community may cause "definitions of the situation" to emerge which do not take into account events impinging from the larger community. Neighborhood organizations which define problems in localized ways may be unable to link up with other groups to carry out social goals sought by large portions of a community. Moreover, the separate and isolated subculture of the neighborhood may exacerbate conflicts with the values and goals of the larger society. This may produce greater estrangement from such values as well as withdrawal from participation in voting or other areas of the larger community's functioning.

In the Diffuse neighborhood social participation is not extensive. Even a person's activity in formal organizations may not substitute for face-to-face "neighboring." Because of the lack of flexibility in social communication, the Diffuse neighborhood may develop both an active elite and an active formal organizational network which do not necessarily reflect the values of persons in the area. Such a situation might produce intra-neighborhood conflict or result in the inability of new social goals or values to be effectively carried out by the existing network of organizations in the area.[15] The Diffuse neighborhood may face the danger of developing a common set of values without the means to implement them. Thus, even if a program of neighborhood improvement could be accomplished without the aid of larger social institutions, it may fail due to lack of communication and organization. Common values and local identity act as sources for social alienation by reinforcing a sense of powerlessness and potential withdrawal from efforts at social change.

The Stepping-stone neighborhood as defined by Litwak and Fellin[16] is one in which individuals have learned ways to become involved rapidly or in which the neighborhood has the social institutions to involve newcomers quickly. Their value orientation and ultimate identity may lie with a future status or neighborhood, or they may be willing to give up their current locale if job or other commitments necessitate a move. The Stepping-stone neighborhood provides for effective operation of socialization mechanisms and the possible resources of higher status leaders. What is likely to occur, however, is that conflicts may arise in given areas of goal striving between the needs of the local neighborhood and the values of the larger society. In addition, when value conflicts exist in an area, contact in organizations may aggravate them and hasten the movement out of local organizations of persons already oriented to such a transition.[17] Such conflicts may cause high personnel turnover in organizations. However, if effective mechanisms exist for speeding the integration of newcomers, this problem may not be a serious one.

Residents of the Transitory neighborhood fail to participate and identify with the local community. Any neighborhood structure is absent except as persons may deliberately avoid participation or involvements which might interfere with other values or status destinations. Anticipatory socialization and other processes often prevent neighborhood integration from becoming effective or extensive. The Transitory neighborhood has potential for social deviance because of the absence of social control mechanisms. As Litwak et al. have pointed out,[18] this might be particularly desirable for upwardly mobile families who do not want their values undermined by contact with those neighbors who do not share their outlook. Thus the Transitory neighborhood, viewed as a temporary way station by upwardly mobile persons, may deprive the remaining population of the benefit of elite leadership to carry out social goals.

The Anomic neighborhood, which is a more generally defined situation of urban disorganization, represents the absence of both social organization and social identity with a neighborhood. In this setting individuals are atomized. Attributes of the "mass society" concept are evident. Estrangement from the values of a larger community manifests itself in nonvoting and indifference to the goals of a larger community, be they racial, class, or societal. The Anomic neighborhood would be unlikely to influence or change its residents' values or enforce existing values. The very absence of social organization might itself suggest the emergence of values defined as deviant by the larger community. However, the more reasonable hypothesis is that residents of the Anomic neighborhood engage in passive behavior and cannot identify a cause of their alienation.

PERTINENCE OF NEIGHBORHOOD TYPOLOGY FOR THE BLACK GHETTO

One of our central theses is that the role of the local neighborhood is more significant in a black ghetto than in white communities. This argument rests on the following assumptions and empirical generalizations:

1. Ghettoization compresses the arena of social interaction of blacks.

a. This leads to heightened status conflicts between ghetto inhabitants.

b. This limits institutional alternatives (which are available to whites) to achieve social goals and enforce social values.

2. Ghettoization enforces isolation from the larger society and community.

a. This heightens the role of the neighborhood as an arena for value definition and social control.

b. Where socioeconomic status is homogeneous, neighborhoods will become particularly isolated from the values and structures of the ghetto as a whole and the outer community. Deviant subcultures and social withdrawal may be alternative consequences.

c. Where neighborhoods are heterogeneous in status, neighborhood interaction may heighten conflict and lead to withdrawal of some elements and alienation from outer community values by others.

As starting points for considering the role of neighborhoods in black ghettos, these assumptions and generalizations suggest that the typology we have constructed may show a statistical distribution in the ghetto that is different from that in the white community. While we cannot validate such a hypothesis, we can strongly suggest, from what we know of ghettoization, that particular kinds of neighborhoods may be prevalent in the ghetto. These would be the Parochial, the Stepping-stone, and the Transitory. The attributes of these neighborhoods seem to reflect processes that are more pronounced in the ghetto than elsewhere. Socioeconomic status may determine neighborhood setting to some extent—but ghettoization gives rise to additional consequences and determinants.

DATA UTILIZATION AND METHODOLOGY

Our concern here is to discover relationships between neighborhood types and riot behavior. Pre-riot data were available from two studies done in 1963 and 1964 in a number of Detroit neighborhoods where rioting later occurred or where a high proportion of persons surveyed later indicated riot participation. These early studies permitted an *ex post facto* test of propositions about neighborhoods.

The major portion of analysis, however, is based on a post-riot survey conducted in August 1967 in the two zones in Detroit where major riot activity took place in July 1967. This study was carried out using a block sample and personal interviews of blacks. The post-riot survey yielded 417 respondents and contained questions which provided indicators analogous or identical to questions in the two earlier studies.

The pre-riot basis for definition of neighborhood was the elementary school district. Its relatively small size, high degree of physical homogeneity, and built-in provision for shared interests in the given school met most of the criteria considered in defining neighborhood. In the 1963 study, directed by Litwak and Meyer, mothers of fifth and sixth grade children from eighteen elementary school districts were interviewed. A sample of 593 Negroes in eight (of the eighteen) districts was obtained by analyzing only all-Negro neighborhoods. Of these eight, four proved to be centers of riot activity, and four experienced virtually no riot activity. The same eight elementary school neighborhoods in the 1964 study yielded a sample of 260 respondents.

In order to match the concept of neighborhood employed in the pre-riot studies, the post-riot survey sample population was grouped according to their location in nineteen elementary school districts. Six of these nineteen neighborhoods overlapped with the 1963–64 areas studied. Although the sampling procedures differed somewhat, the use of the elementary school neighborhood as a basis permitted reasonable and valid comparisons over time.

DATA ANALYSIS: INDICES OF RIOT BEHAVIOR

In the post-riot survey respondents were asked questions about their own participation in the disorders as well as their attitudes concerning its origins and consequences. Specific indicators of riot involvement were based on the accumulated percentages for five activities:

1. Entering into broken stores
2. Picking up goods and taking them home
3. Breaking windows
4. Making fire bombs
5. Throwing fire bombs

Individual neighborhoods varied considerably on this index, from zero per cent to 42 per cent participation reported.

The second index concerns counter-riot activity. Measures included the following items:

1. Trying to stop the riot
2. Painting "soul brother" signs on buildings
3. Helping to put out fires
4. Giving help to people hurt or homeless
5. Calling the fire department
6. Giving sandwiches and coffee to soldiers

The third index of neighborhood patterns concerns the extent of behavior which reflects a withdrawal from either supportive or subverting activities in regard to the riot. The following two interview items provided a measure of nonparticipation:

1. Leaving the neighborhood during the disturbance
2. Staying at home and not going out during the disturbance

Based on Spearman rank-order correlations for the nineteen neighborhoods, Table 2 shows the intercorrelations of the three indices of neighborhood riot behavior. Of particular note is the significant negative relationship between counter-riot activity and withdrawal. This suggests several consequences for neighborhood social organization that are explored in subsequent tables. Table 2 undermines the common sense concept that riot behavior and counter-riot behavior are antithetical. In-

TABLE 2
Neighborhood Riot Participation Index Intercorrelations

	Riot Index	Counter-riot Index	Withdrawal Index
Riot Index	—	+.102	+.110
Counter-riot Index		—	−.404*
Withdrawal Index			—

*In this and subsequent tables an asterisk indicates Spearman rank-order correlations significant at the ±.05 level.

stead, we have a slight positive correlation between the two, with riot behavior similarly related to withdrawal. Consequently, neighborhoods where riot support or opposition occurred may be more similar to one another than areas where no involvement took place.

In Table 3 the nineteen surveyed neighborhoods are shown in regard to the number of structures damaged or destroyed during the riot. One of the assumptions underlying our analysis is that the riot was an event located

TABLE 3
Number of Destroyed Structures in Relation to Elementary School Neighborhoods

Neighborhood[1]	Destroyed and damaged structures[2]
Hw	54
Cn	52
On	41
Br	29
Hl	22
Ns	20
Mb	15
Fs	14
Cs	12
Lg	10
As	9
Pr	9
Mc	8
Ni	6
Gl	5
Cu	4
Sc	4
Pb	2
Ja	1
Total[3]	317

Correlation with riot index is +.182

[1]Alphabetic abbreviations refer to names of elementary schools forming the neighborhood units. These are also employed in subsequent tables.

[2]Source: Detroit City Planning Commission, Preliminary Estimate of Riot Damage, August 9, 1967.

[3]Total structures destroyed in riot was given in the above source as 604.

within the ghetto community having a localized basis of support. This argument implies that rioters were persons living near the areas where they burned or looted buildings. In the nineteen elementary school neighborhood units, correlations with the riot index offer limited support for this premise. A correlation between the number of structures affected by rioting and the reported riot activity in a neighborhood is +.182.

Because our conceptual model of neighborhoods focuses on neighborhood structure (social integration), the factor of residential mobility becomes particularly salient as a determinant of social organization. In Table 4 the relationship between the three riot indices and the persons of recent arrival in their neighborhood or in Detroit is shown. A large positive correlation obtains between the riot activity index and the percentage of persons less than one year in the neighborhood. A small negative correlation occurs for the counter-riot index. These same relationships contrast with the percentage of native Detroit respondents. Here riot and counter-riot indices have similar modestly high positive correlations. In effect, this suggests that riot-active neighborhoods include many persons who have moved recently from other Detroit neighborhoods, whereas counter-riot areas imply long-term residence in the present neighborhood. The withdrawal index is negatively related to Detroit birth but positively related to recent household residence. This pattern suggests neighborhoods of southern-born, recent urban immigrants. The important finding in Table 4 is the strong relationship between high neighborhood turnover and riot participation. Given this finding the efficacy of social integration mechanisms in the neighborhood takes on greater significance.

TABLE 4

Correlations of Mobility and Neighborhood Riot Participation.

	Percent of respondents less than one year in household	Percent of respondents born in Detroit
Riot Index	+.738*	+.270*
Counter-riot Index	−.093	+.311*
Withdrawal Index	+.162	−.121

INFORMAL SOCIAL CONTACT IN THE NEIGHBORHOOD

The typology of neighborhoods defined in Table 1 stresses forms of social participation and identification with the local neighborhood. Data obtained in both the pre-riot studies and the post-riot survey bear on these issues. One way to define neighborhood social patterns is to ask about contacts between persons living in the area. This is examined in Table 5. In the post-riot survey the respondents were asked, "How often do you visit with your neighbors?" The counter-riot index shows a strong positive correlation with the percentage of persons indicating contact at least once a week.

A second indicator of informal neighboring is based on responses given to the question "Which of these things describes your neighborhood best?" One choice was "most people just keep to themselves about important issues." A significant negative correlation occurs between this response and the counter-riot index—this suggests high neighbor contact. The withdrawal neighborhoods show the least evidence of neighbor con-

TABLE 5

Neighborhood Informal Social Interaction Using Pre- and Post-Riot Indices

	Post-Riot	
	Percent or respondents in neighborhood who see neighbors at least once a week	Percent saying "most people just keep to themselves about important issues"
Riot Index	−.043	−.151
Counter-riot Index	+.441*	−.414*
Withdrawal Index	−.073	+.226

	Pre-Riot			
	Frequency of visiting		Volume of contact	
	1963	1964	1963	1964
Riot:				
Cn	Low	Low	Low	Low
HI	Low	Low	Low	Low
Lg	High	Low	Low	Low
Sc	Low	Low	Low	Low
Non-riot:				
Cu	High	High	High	High
Fo	High	High	High	High
Ma	Low	Low	High	High
On	Low	High	Low	Low

tact. Riot neighborhoods are neither extensive in social contacts nor particularly oriented to "people keeping to themselves."

Pre-riot analysis of neighborhoods is based on the surveys of 1963 and 1964 in which inner-city black neighborhoods were included. In all, six of these areas were also found in the post-riot survey zone. Of these six neighborhoods, four had a high level of riot activity when using this index as a dichotomy, and two were low. Two all-Negro neighborhoods which are adjacent to the riot zones in Detroit were combined with two neighborhoods having low riot activity. Note that the distinction between "riot" and "non-riot" as indicated in Table 5 is not comparable to the three indices based on post-riot data—i.e., the "non-riot" neighborhoods are not equivalent to counter-riot or withdrawal neighborhoods. The pre-riot data only provide comparisons of neighborhoods where the riot activity was high versus low or absent.

The two measures of social interaction found in the pre-riot studies were based on responses to the following questions:

1. "How often do you visit with your neighbors—to go out or just to get together at your home or theirs?"

2. "How many of your neighbors on this block do you know well enough that you are likely to spend half an hour with them now and then?"

The first measure is directly equivalent to the post-riot indicator on visiting. Using the percentage of visiting once a week or more (and dichotomizing at the mean), we find all four riot neighborhoods with low ratings in 1964 and only one low for non-riot neighborhoods. The 1963 ratings are similar in pattern, with three lows for riot areas and two highs and two lows for the non-riot areas. The volume of contact measure of neighboring is based on the percentage of respondents in each neighborhood who know two or more neighbors. In this measure riot areas are, for both 1963 and 1964, consistently low in volume of contact, but non-riot areas are high.

Table 5, as we have observed, provides a post-riot view of counter-riot behavior associated with a high level of informal neighboring. Withdrawal behavior shows an opposite pattern. Riot behavior is associated with a lack of extensive neighboring. Pre-riot data indicate that informal social contact patterns were weak in neighborhoods that later became riot areas. Neighborhoods where the rioting was limited or where it did not occur showed a high level of informal social participation. Given this pattern, the typology shown in Table 1 would suggest that riot behavior might be more likely to occur in the Diffuse, Transitory, or Anomic neighborhoods than in the Integrated, Parochial, or Stepping-stone settings. The same would tend to be true for withdrawal behavior. Pre-riot data imply that Integrated, Parochial, or Diffuse neighborhoods could expect low riot activity. Counter-riot behavior appears to take place in neighborhoods which are of the Integrated, Parochial, or Stepping-stone types.

Further analysis of neighborhood informal structure is provided by Table 6, which presents pre-riot measures of opinion leadership patterns and face-to-face social organization. If we examine each of these measures, we find that neighborhoods with high riot activity were generally low in patterns of informal leadership. The only exception is in the measure of social-emotional leader—both riot and non-riot areas are equal. The differences shown in Table 6 further underscore the patterns found in Table 5. They imply in particular that *task* leadership may be least structured in the riot-prone neighborhood.

TABLE 6
Neighborhood Indices of Social Organization Using Pre-Riot Indices

	Someone in area you respect[1] 1963	1964	Task Leader[2] 1964	Social-Emotional Leader[3] 1964	Integration of newcomers[4] 1964	Someone active on millage[5] 1964
Riot:						
Cn*	Low	Low	Low	High	Low	Low
HI	Low	Low	Low	High	Low	Low
Lg	High	High	High	Low	High	Low
Sc*	Low	High	High	High	Low	Low
Non-riot:						
Cu	High	High	High	High	High	High
Fo	High	High	High	High	High	High
Ma	Low	High	High	High	High	High
On	High	Low	High	Low	High	Low

[1] "Are there people in your neighborhood ... you really respect with whom you might discuss some problem?"

[2] "Would you say that this block has someone on it who usually takes the lead in getting things done?"

[3] "Is there someone on this block that people turn to when they feel especially sad or depressed, and want to get cheered up?"

[4] "In general which of these attitudes do your neighbors take when new families move in?" Percent indicating "Go over to their house after they move in and offer help" or "Go over to their house and introduce themselves, but do not offer to help unless they are asked for it."

[5] "Thinking about the millage election, was there someone on this block or nearby who was very active in organizing people for that campaign?"

Neighborhood As Reference Group

The reference-group orientation of a neighborhood involves the identification of people with the area in which they live and a sense of common purpose with their neighbors. Three indicators from the post-riot survey were used as a measure of neighborhood reference-group orientation. The first sought to find out if respondents felt similar to their neighbors and had common interests with them—that "most people in the neighborhood agree on important things." This measure is a form of projective identification. If a person is attached to his neighborhood, he may well overestimate value homophily in his area. Therefore this indicator of agreement was not meant to define the *objective* fact of value or behavioral similarity but to measure the *perception* of it as an expression of reference-group commitment. Table 7 includes measures of both pre-riot and post-riot responses to this indicator.

The second indicator of reference-group orientation was based on replies to the question "Suppose a bill collector came around asking where a former neighbor has moved. If you knew would you tell him?" This item seems to pose a dilemma of commitment. When respondents said they would not tell, these responses were taken to indicate positive neighborhood reference orientation.

The third measure, less direct, considered the neighborhood commitment of a black respondent who rejects integrated housing. The question asked in the post-riot survey was "Would you rather live in a neighborhood with only Negro families, or in a neighborhood that had both Negro and white families?" Since the areas surveyed were overwhelmingly Negro, persons who chose the latter response were in effect rejecting their current neighborhood setting. The response of preferring "only Negro families" was taken as an indicator of positive neighborhood reference orientation.

Table 7 indicates that these three post-riot reference measures show no consistent pattern. The exception is the riot index. Here, negative correlations (one is statistically significant) occur for all three measures of neighborhood reference-group orientation. The counter-riot index shows one positive relationship, as does the withdrawal index. Since two of the questions were also employed in the pre-riot studies, the lower portion of Table 7 offers further comparisons. According to these indicators, riot neighborhoods are just as likely to have a positive reference orientation as non-riot neighborhoods. The exception is the 1964 response to the bill-collector question. A third pre-riot indicator was the response to the question, "How much do you like this neighborhood, that is, the area within

TABLE 7

Reference-Group Orientation of Neighborhoods Using Pre- and Post-Riot Indicators

Post-Riot

	"Most people in the neighborhood agree on important things"	Would not tell bill collector where neighbor has moved	Prefer to live in neighborhood with only Negro families
Riot Index	−.388*	−.091	−.166
Counter-riot Index	+.311*	−.186	−.221
Withdrawal Index	−.115	−.111	+.361*

Pre-Riot

	Most people agree 1964	Not tell bill collector 1963	Not tell bill collector 1964	Like neighborhood "very much" 1964
Riot:				
Cn	High	Low	High	Low
Hl	High	Low	High	High
Lg	Low	High	High	Low
Sc	Low	Low	Low	Low
Non-riot:				
Cu	High	Low	High	Low
Fo	High	Low	High	Low
Ma	Low	High	High	High
On	Low	Low	High	Low

walking distance of your home?" Both riot and non-riot areas are low in three out of four instances.

Thus, the findings in Table 7 provide no clear picture of neighborhood reference orientation, but they do offer some insight into our perception of attitudes. Factors other than neighborhood reference-group orientation may have entered into the respondents' choices, thus shading to some degree the validity of the indicators. When post-riot findings are emphasized, riot behavior fits the Transitory or Anomic types of neighborhood, according to the findings of Tables 5 through 7. Counter-riot behavior, if we stress the correlation in Table 7 for "most people agree," would narrow to the Integrated or Parochial neighborhoods. If we follow the trends for the other two reference-group indicators, counter-riot areas fit the Stepping-stone type of neighborhood. The findings in Table 7 suggest that riot areas are not positive in reference-group orientation, but no consistent relationships were found using the measures available.

Although participation in voluntary associations is itself an indicator of social organization in a neighborhood, there may be high participation but without a focus on the local geographic unit. In Table 8 we examine pre-riot data on associational involvement. If we view only the *volume* of participation, we find more active persons in riot that in non-riot neighborhoods. Including responses to the question, "In how many of the organizations that you belong to will you see other people from your neighborhood?" the pattern is altered. Using the percentage for *non-neighbor* organizational involvement, Table 8 indicates that five out of eight times this level is high for riot neighborhoods; low designations are consistently found in the non-riot areas.

The pattern in Table 8 implies that the weak reference-group attachment associated with riot areas may occur because persons leave their area to find salient associational ties. Not only does this further reflect a negative reference orientation, but it weakens neighborhood leadership structure. Without full participation from the persons who form the organizational elite, i.e., the joiners and other active members of a community, the effectiveness of existing groups in a neighborhood is likely to be undermined. Moreover, the tendency for residents to find associational ties elsewhere provides a basis for potential intra-neighborhood conflict and lack of effective social action. These patterns suggest that a Stepping-stone neighborhood could deteriorate to the Transitory type.

TIES TO THE LARGER COMMUNITY

Data from both pre- and post-riot studies provide some basis for defining both the attitudinal and behavioral linkage of neighborhoods to

TABLE 8

*Voluntary Association Membership and its Linkage to the
Neighborhood Using Pre-Riot Studies*

	Percent of respondents belonging to one or more organizations		Percent of respondents belonging to organizations where they do not see their neighbors	
	1963	1964	1963	1964
Riot:				
Cn	High	High	High	High
HI	High	High	Low	Low
Lg	High	High	High	High
Sc	Low	High	Low	High
Non-riot:				
Cu	Low	Low	Low	Low
Fo	Low	High	Low	Low
Ma	High	Low	Low	Low
On	Low	Low	Low	Low

the other society. The term "alienation" could be interchanged with "ties to the larger community," but specification of this concept involves issues which are not approachable within the context of the data here analyzed. Therefore a more general term of "tied in" is used as a better description of what we are in fact measuring.

In the post-riot survey several questions were employed to measure attitudinal ties to the social structure outside the neighborhood. Responses to the following questions were used as indicators:

1. "If the United States got into a big world war today, would you personally feel this country is worth fighting for?"
2. "If Negroes would try harder, they could solve their problems without any help from whites—true or false?"
3. "Which of the following things do you think were responsible for causing the riot?"
   a. "Lack of strong Negro leaders"
   b. "Failure of parents to control their children"

The first two questions measure both alienation from society and a sense that the Negro community is dependent in some way on a larger structure. Answers to the question of riot causes reflect, in the first choice, the attitude that the *larger* Negro community was a source of breakdown in social

TABLE 9

Attitudinal Indices of "Local" Versus "Larger Community" Orientation in Post-Riot Survey

Post-Riot

	Percent saying country is worth fighting for	Percent saying Negroes cannot solve problems without white help	Riot cause: lack of strong Negro leaders	Riot cause: failure to control children
Riot Index	−.232	−.214	−.355*	−.428*
Counter-riot Index	+.323*	+.173	+.152	+.271
Withdrawal Index	−.364*	−.217	−.143	−.058

Pre-Riot

	Police doing "excellent" or "good" job		Churches		Banks		Schools doing "as much as they should" for Negro children	
	1963	1964	1963	1964	1963	1964	1963	1964
Riot:								
Cn*	High	Low	Low	Low	Low	Low	Low	Low
Hl	High	Low	Low	Low	Low	Low	Low	High
Lg	High	High	High	High	High	High	High	High
Sc	Low	High	Low	Low	High	High	Low	Low
Non-riot:								
Cu	High	Low	High	High	Low	Low	High	Low
Fo	Low	High	High	High	Low	Low	Low	Low
Ma	Low	Low	High	Low	Low	High	High	Low
On	Low	Low	High	High	Low	Low	Low	Low

functioning which led to or justified the rioting, and in the second choice, the attitude that a breakdown in *local* social control processes was to blame.

Table 9 shows that the riot index is negatively related to linkage to the white society, but positively related to the Negro community. In the counter-riot index the opposite is true. The withdrawal index closely resembles the riot index: negative to the outer white society, and not critical of the role of Negro leaders or families. The differences between counter-riot and riot perceptions of parent control are particularly striking. The same is so for the "country is worth fighting for" attitudes. Counter-riot areas are critical of Negro leadership; riot areas are not.

Pre-riot measures of attitudinal ties lacked any directly comparable indicators with the post-riot survey questions. Both the 1963 and 1964 studies contained ratings of the performance of important community institutions: "Are they doing an excellent job, a good job, a fair job, or a poor job of serving the public?" Ratings shown in Table 9 were based on percentages for "excellent" and "good" responses. If we look at what are mainly white institutions (the police and banks), we find that riot areas gave more favorable ratings than non-riot areas. The ratings of churches are somewhat ambiguous, but may be presumed to reflect a more Negro-based institution at the local level. Here evaluations for riot areas were more negative in 1963 than non-riot areas but equally low in 1964. Ratings of the schools' job in teaching Negro children ("schools are doing as much as they should") directly focused on the local neighborhood. Riot areas are somewhat more positive in their view than non-riot areas.

Over-all the pre-riot findings suggest that a shift in judgment may be characteristic of riot neighborhoods in their assessment of community institutions. In the post-riot data withdrawal and riot behavior show greater estrangement from the white world; pre-riot data (in the neighborhoods where comparisons are possible) indicate *less* estrangement than where little or no subsequent riot activity took place. The interim of three years included important changes in the progress of the civil rights movement. The promise of 1963 was particularly evident in Detroit, where a march of several hundred thousand Negroes served to demonstrate a sense of hope and determination. The explanation for the differences we find in Table 9 may well reflect the difference between a high point of promise in the access and sense of linkage to the larger society and the subsequent period of perceived stagnation and disappointment.

One way to sense optimism toward institutional problem-solving (which in turn implies the tie to the larger community) is to use measures of "activism." By "activism" we mean attitudes that reflect the view that problems *can be solved* versus a sense that it is *futile to try*. In the post-riot survey two questions seemed most to reflect "active" versus "passive" views of civil rights:

1. "Negroes who get ahead do it by fighting for their rights—true, false, or don't know?"

2. "Do you feel that Negroes have more to gain or more to lose by resorting to violence in the civil rights movement?"

Table 10 presents the correlations with indices of riot behavior. The riot index is positively correlated both to Negroes fighting for their rights and to feeling that violence helps to gain rights. At the same time, the counter-riot index shows, respectively, a small positive correlation and no correla-

TABLE 10
Active-Passive Orientation to Problem-Solving

| | Post-Riot | |
	Percent saying Negroes get ahead by fighting for their rights	Percent saying violence is way to gain rights
Riot Index	+.416*	+.266
Counter-riot Index	+.132	+.008
Withdrawal Index	−.102	−.362*

| | Pre-Riot | | | |
| | Percent who agree that people can do little to change their lives | | Percent agreeing that "public officials don't care much about what people like me think" | |
	1963	1964	1963	1964
Riot:				
Cn	High	Low	Low	Low
Hl	Low	Low	Low	Low
Lg	Low	Low	Low	Low
Sc	Low	Low	Low	Low
Non-riot:				
Cu	High	High	Low	Low
Fo	High	High	High	High
Ma	High	High	High	High
On	High	High	High	High

tion with these same two items. By contrast the withdrawal index is negatively correlated with both measures—significantly in the "violence" correlation. These findings reveal that riot areas and, to some degree, counter-riot areas share an "active" orientation toward problems. Withdrawal areas do not.

Examining pre-riot measures of active versus passive attitudes we find riot areas sharply different from non-riot areas. In the non-riot neighborhoods a passive orientation prevails. For riot neighborhoods these attitudes are noticeably absent. Consequently, both the pre- and post-riot studies show a clear pattern of active orientation toward problem-solving for riot areas. This is coupled with a sense of estrangement from the outer

TABLE 11

Behavioral Measures of Orientation to Larger Community

	Post-Riot	
	Voted in 1964 Presidential Election	Percent Registered To Vote
Riot Index	−.081	+.065
Counter-riot Index	+.553*	+.433*
Withdrawal Index	−.261	−.083

	Pre-Riot			
	Ever got in touch with city hall[1]		Voting in most recent election	
	1963	1964	1963[2]	1964[3]
Riot:				
Cn	High	Low	Low	High
Hl	Low	High	High	High
Lg	High	High	High	High
Sc	High	High	High	High
Non-riot:				
Cu	Low	Low	Low	High
Fo	Low	Low	High	High
Ma	Low	High	High	High
On	Low	Low	Low	Low

[1] "Have you ever called or gotten in touch with city agencies about things like street cleaning, street repair, garbage collection, parks and recreational facilities, or other matters of that kind?"

[2] Refers to gubernatorial election of fall, 1962.

[3] Refers to school millage election of fall, 1963.

white society which was not present at an earlier point in time. What appears to separate riot and counter-riot areas is not so much their acceptance or rejection of the status quo but the place where they locate the source of their difficulties—for the riot behavior areas this is the white community; for the counter-riot areas it is the black community. If we relate this concept to the typology of neighborhoods, we receive further confirmation that the counter-riot areas are Stepping-stone or Integrated more than they are Parochial. Riot areas are Anomic or Diffuse more than Transitory. Withdrawal areas appear to be Parochial (if we apply pre-riot findings) more than Diffuse or Anomic.

In Table 11 we examine several behavioral measures of ties to the larger community. The two voting measures in the post-riot survey data show that counter-riot behavior is strongly positively correlated to voting. Riot behavior shows a moderate to weak negative correlation with voting. The pre-riot studies contained measures of contacts with local government agencies and voting behavior. What emerges from the pre-riot data is that riot neighborhoods are more active than non-riot areas on both measures. This conforms with the attitudinal measures discussed from Table 10. We again find a basis for an apparent shift in the riot neighborhoods. Where formerly these areas might have been called Stepping-stone or Transitory neighborhoods, they appear in 1967 to resemble more the Anomic neighborhood. Because reference-group orientation is positive and informal social participation high, the positive linkage to the outer community found for counter-riot behavior suggests the Integrated neighborhood. Where reference orientation is low, the Stepping-stone type is suggested. Withdrawal is associated with little linkage, behaviorally *or* attitudinally, to the larger white or black community. The one positive reference orientation makes such areas approximate the Diffuse neighborhood type.

SUMMARY AND CONCLUSIONS

Reviewing our over-all findings, the following relationships are implied by the data:

1. *Integrated neighborhood*—associated with counter-riot behavior, particularly when using white institutional ties.

2. *Parochial neighborhood*—characterizes the non-riot areas using the 1963–64 studies.

3. *Diffuse neighborhood*—characterizes the riot neighborhoods when 1963–64 data are used; the withdrawal areas when using the post-riot correlations.

4. *Stepping-stone neighborhood*—associated with the non-riot neigh-

borhoods in 1963–64, some support for this type defining counter-riot areas using the post-riot data.

5. *Transitory neighborhood*—characterizes the riot areas using post-riot data, particularly if measures of linkage to the larger Negro, not white, community are employed.

6. *Anomic neighborhood*—characterizes the withdrawal and riot neighborhoods using post-riot data.

In a study done immediately after the 1967 Detroit riot, we have analyzed data from nineteen neighborhoods in Detroit using the elementary school district as the unit of analysis. We also employed data from studies which were done three and four years prior to the July 1967 riot. Although both the sampling procedures and the limited overlap in operational measures restricted the validity of our implied longitudinal analysis, our primary purpose was to relate our findings to our typology of six neighborhoods. With a degree of success we found relationships which suggest that riot, counter-riot, and withdrawal behaviors of individuals correlated with particular, carefully defined, types of neighborhood settings.

The essential inquiry was: "Given certain criteria of social participation and value orientations in a neighborhood, what forms of behavior are likely to emerge from these varied milieus?" The answers, in terms of the black ghetto, have important implications for social organization at middle levels of power—i.e., individual effort can become effective through informal and formal neighborhood-based activities.

We found that neighborhoods that experienced high riot activity were lacking in extensive informal social interaction. Moreover, while there was no strong reference orientation to the neighborhood where riot behavior was extensive, there was fairly extensive involvement with the larger community.

Where counter-riot activity took place, neighboring was extensive and linkage to the larger community was present, but more in terms of white than black centers of power. Here the Stepping-stone neighborhood type, where weak local reference-group ties exist, was suggested—particularly when the estrangement from Negro leaders and parents was taken into account.

The withdrawal from riot behavior was much more appropriate to the model of the alienated urban dweller. In neighborhoods with a high degree of withdrawal from the riot, informal social ties and both attitudinal and behavioral linkage to the larger white and black communities were lacking.

The data appear to imply further that estrangement from white institutions increased in the relatively short interval spanned in this analysis. The period between the 1963–64 and the 1967 studies reflects important shifts, particularly in riot neighborhoods. However, the immediate post-riot setting may have exaggerated these differences.

Whatever attitudinal shifts have occurred, the basic questions addressed in our analysis concern the structural underpinnings for enforcing values. We have suggested that neighborhoods vary greatly in this capacity. The mobilization of both riot and counter-riot activism required forms of social organization. In the majority of instances, riot and counter-riot areas more closely match one another than they do the withdrawal areas, despite the low correlation between riot and counter-riot indices themselves. We may conclude that neighborhood units are useful starting points for defining social organization in the black ghetto.

Given the relative absence of alternative mechanisms and structures in an essentially segregated urban environment, it is particularly important to note the potential for social action found in the immediate residential area. Were this unit to be employed as a focus of amelioration by both indigenous groups and external agencies, a more effective basis for implementing and evaluating programs would be provided. The neighborhood offers a visible yardstick of progress in social welfare and social change. Too often the ghetto is viewed monolithically when it is frequently as alienating and amorphous a concept to its inhabitants as is the "White Power Structure."

Certainly the data we have analyzed are more suggestive than definitive, since weaknesses exist in some of the measures used. However, the failure of social scientists, particularly sociologists, to attend to the varieties and functions of *middle-level* social structures in urban settings is a more salient criticism, for this failing ought to be redressed. Studies of the family, on the one hand, and community-wide power structures on the other may well overlook the linkage between the bottom and the top in community organization.

The present effort to draw a social-structural analysis of riot behavior has been useful if it stimulates further efforts to define the context of the ghetto dwellers' existence. Analysis and social action related to the black ghetto must go beyond the concern with the ghetto's sporadic, albeit dramatic, outbursts.

LITERATURE CITED

1. Among the most pertinent studies are those of the 1965 Watts riot, by Raymond J. Murphy and James M. Watson, "The Structure of Discontent," Institute of Government and Public Affairs, UCLA, 1967; and a survey conducted by Nathan Caplan for the Detroit Urban

League and discussed in the Report of the National Advisory Commission on Civil Disorders, 1968.

2. See Report of the National Advisory Commission . . . , op. cit., chap. 2, footnotes 111–43, pp. 171–78.

3. Stanley Lieberson and Arnold R. Silverman, "The Precipitants and Underlying Conditions of Race Riots," *American Sociological Review*, 30 (Dec., 1965), pp. 887–98; Allen D. Grimshaw, "Urban Racial Violence in the United States: Changing Ecological Consideration," *American Journal of Sociology*, 66 (1960), pp. 109–19; Milton Bloombaum, "The Conditions Underlying Race Riots as Portrayed by Multi-dimensional Scalogram Analysis: A Reanalysis of Lieberson and Silverman's Data," *American Sociological Review*, 33 (Feb. 1968), pp. 76–91.

4. Aside from considering social structure in terms of socioeconomic position of individuals, no analysis of the recent riots has treated social structure as an independent variable.

5. All quotations here are from the Report of the National Advisory Commission . . . , op. cit., pp. 127, 129, 96, and 92 respectively.

6. The significance of local neighborhood in riot behavior is indirectly suggested in several riot studies.

7. See the classic article by W. S. Robinson, "Ecological Correlations and the Behavior of Individuals," *American Sociological Review*, 15 (June 1950), pp. 351–57.

8. See for example W. Bell and M. D. Boat, "Urban Neighborhoods and Informal Social Relations," *American Journal of Sociology*, 42 (Jan. 1957), pp. 391–98.

9. Peter Blau, "Structural Effects," *American Sociological Review*, 25 (April 1960), pp. 178–99.

10. M. Axelrod, "Urban Structure and Social Participation," *American Sociological Review*, 21 (Feb. 1956), pp. 13–18.

11. Eugene Litwak, "Reference Group Theory, Bureaucratic Careers, and Neighborhood Cohesion," *Sociometry*, 23 (March 1960), pp. 72–84.

12. ———, "Voluntary Associations and Neighborhood Cohesion," *American Sociological Review*, 26 (April 1961), pp. 258–71.

13. E. Litwak, H. Meyer, and D. Warner, "Relationship Between School-Community Coordinating Procedures and Reading Achievement," *Final Report*, Project No. 5-0355, U.S. Department of Health, Education and Welfare, Office of Education, 1960, p. 124.

14. There are two logical possibilities for neighborhoods not included in Table 1. There is a situation where there is a plus-plus with a positive reference group, and a plus-minus where the orientation is negative. In the first situation we would have to imagine persons living in an area, being attached to it, but remaining totally uninvolved and hav-

ing no social interaction with neighbors. Only temporarily could such a situation prevail, since either a lack of attachment to the neighborhood would develop or the continuation of a positive orientation would lead to social interaction. In the second situation we would have to conjure up a setting in which no positive orientation prevails, yet extensive informal and/or formal social interaction and participation occurs. In other words, social interaction would occur focused on neighborhood values and goals but still the orientation to the neighborhood would be negative. Both situations seem improbable.

15. This is analogous to the distinctions made by Litwak between the advantages of bureaucratic forms of organization versus primary groups. E. Litwak, "Bureaucratic Structures and Primary Groups," *American Journal of Sociology*, 73 (Jan. 1968), pp. 468–81.

16. Fellin and Litwak, "Neighborhood Cohesion Under Conditions of Mobility," op. cit.

17. In discussing the role of voluntary associations Litwak states that "where individuals are negatively oriented toward their neighbors, the longer their residence, the more likely they are to realize the differences and the more likely they are to seek to dissociate from their neighbors."

18. See Litwak, Meyer, and Warren, "Relationship Between School-Community . . . ," *Final Report*, op. cit., Part II, pp. 79–181.

A GEOGRAPHIC ASPECT OF THE 1968
MIAMI RACIAL DISTURBANCE:
A PRELIMINARY INVESTIGATION

Paul S. Salter and Robert C. Mings

On the afternoon of August 7, 1968, the first outbreak of racial violence occurred in the northwest section of the city of Miami in the predominantly Negro area known as Liberty City, whose territory lies partly within the city of Miami but extends across the county boundary into an unincorporated area. Approximately 150 teen-agers had gathered on the corners of NW 17th Avenue and NW 62nd Street, following a "Black Power" meeting, and began hurling stones at passing motorists.[1] There ensued, for three days and nights, further and more destructive occurrences, eventually culminating in three deaths, numerous injuries, arrests, and the destruction of several hundred thousands of dollars worth of property.

The purposes of this paper are to delimit the distinctive geopolitical pattern of the disturbance, to identify the spatial pattern of differing approaches to police-community relations programs, and to suggest some needed research topics. It is not our intent to describe the violence, nor to attempt to establish a single or particular set of causes for the outbreak. The authors do feel, however, that the geographic pattern of the violence raises many questions and presents fertile areas for expanded social science research. We believe that the Miami experience has considerable relevance to other cities. In addition, the unique political organization of Dade County presents a further advantage for geographical analysis.

It should be recalled that during the week of August 5–9 Miami Beach was the scene of the Republican National Convention and that Negro leaders had made several prior attempts to focus national attention on the Miami area. On Monday, August 5, the first day of the convention, a meeting was held in Liberty City featuring several prominent Negro leaders. The next day, Tuesday, Reverend Ralph Abernathy and approximately fifty persons from the Poor Peoples March had demonstrated in front of the Republican convention hall.

Within a three-hour period following the Wednesday afternoon rock throwing incident, the Miami police department had stationed two hundred men along the central business street of Liberty City, NW 62nd Street. Rock throwing continued and cars were stopped and burned and drivers beaten. The police, with the help of tear gas, managed to confine the outbreak to the 62nd Street area between NW 7th and 17th Avenue, but trouble flared up in small outbreaks in other areas as far away as the central Negro district and Coconut Grove. The Miami police considered the disorder under control by 4:30 A.M. Thursday and that property damage had been light.[2] During this first night, Sheriff E. Wilson Purdy, director of the Dade County Public Safety Department, had mustered a large force of deputies into the county portion of Liberty City. The force remained in this position from 7:00 P.M. Wednesday until 7:00 A.M. Thursday.

The disturbance erupted again during the morning hours of Thursday, August 8, still along the main artery of Liberty City, but this time further east in the vicinity of NW 13th Avenue. The Miami police closed 62nd Street from NW 7th Avenue to NW 17th Avenue at approximately 9:45 A.M. The county portion of Liberty City remained quiet throughout this period.

Violence continued to escalate throughout the remainder of Thursday morning and into the afternoon. Miami police had requested help by this time, both from county forces and the Florida Highway Patrol and had put their prepared riot operations plan into effect. The situation worsened, however, with shooting outbreaks in the downtown central Negro district. At about 3:30 P.M. Thursday, with the incidents continuing to multiply and spread, the Miami city manager requested that the Florida governor call out the Florida National Guard. On the governor's orders, the 124th Infantry Regiment of the Guard was placed under the command of Dade County Sheriff E. Wilson Purdy. Also, the governor ordered the Miami police to withdraw from the Liberty City area. The Miami police pulled back to the perimeter of Liberty City after the arrival of eight hundred National Guardsmen and two hundred Dade County sheriff deputies. The enlarged force swept the troublesome core area of 62nd Street.

A curfew was then placed by the city manager over Liberty City and the central Negro district. Later that same night the curfew was extended to include the Negro area of Coconut Grove, a southern section of the city, as limited looting and violence had erupted.

Heavy rains early Friday morning August 9, coupled with the enlarged curfew restrictions and the show of force by the National Guard, are credited with finally quieting the disturbances. The riot areas were declared secure by 2:30 A.M., Saturday, August 10, but curfew restrictions were not withdrawn until Monday, August 12.[3]

In reflecting on the geographic flow of events, several questions assert themselves: questions that cannot be answered in a preliminary investigation, but questions that certainly warrant further inquiry by geographers and others.

The geographic relationship of the city of Miami within the larger political framework of Dade County is unique. The city of Miami is one of twenty-seven municipalities that, with the unincorporated area of the county, comprise Metropolitan Dade County. The city of Miami and most other municipalities, while participating in Dade County metropolitan government[4] have maintained complete local autonomy over their respective law enforcement agencies. This political arrangement is germane to the 1968 racial disturbances because the Negro community of Liberty City is located within both the unincorporated county and the city of Miami. Consequently, Liberty City is subjected to the law enforcement policies of two separate police departments. Perhaps of greatest significance are the different approaches to community relations employed by the respective law enforcement agencies.

The city of Miami police department, directed by Chief of Police Walter Headley, is the largest municipal law enforcement agency in Dade County. Metro law enforcement is under the jurisdiction of the Dade County Public Safety Department and is directed by Sheriff E. Wilson Purdy. This department is responsible principally for law enforcement in the county unincorporated areas. Both Police Chief Headley and Sheriff Purdy are well-known professional law enforcement leaders and are so recognized nationally.

Approaches to certain aspects of law enforcement, particularly police-community relations, vary markedly between these two men and their respective departments. Chief Headley has taken a "hard line" stance toward crime in Miami and has received considerable notoriety concerning this position.[5] Sheriff Purdy, on the other hand, has not taken such a public view and has received considerably less attention in his approach to crime prevention.[6]

The two departments differ also in their approaches to involvement in community relations. The city police are represented on various private and public sponsored community relations organizations, but the Miami police have sponsored no such agency of their own. Activity of this type was conducted under the broader auspices of the Public Information Division, but since the August rioting a police officer has been assigned to a newly created, city-sponsored community relations program. The Dade County Public Safety Department has established a rather elaborate subagency for this specific purpose. Beginning in January of 1967, with the avowed purpose of producing a dialogue, the county established the Police Community Council. With the assistance of five policemen doing "grass roots" observing and contacting, frequent meetings were arranged between police administrators and Negro leaders—in Negro areas. In February of 1968, the federal government awarded the county police $10,000 for in-service training of fifty-one officers and 211 sergeants in the theory and application of community relations. The very fact that the public is aware of these differences,[7] coupled with the unique areal pattern of the ensuing racial disturbance provided the initial impetus for the writing of this paper.

The geographic delimitation of the disturbance indicates that it was confined almost exclusively within the political boundaries of the city of Miami. Field investigation indicates that the political boundaries separating the unincorporated county portion of Liberty City from the city of Miami portion of the Liberty City area are purely artificial. No physical barriers separate the two areas. Homogeneous house types, both single and multiple type dwellings, extend well beyond both sides of the city line. Linear-type business establishments also extend on either side of the city line along NW 62nd Street. In short, a low-income Negro neighborhood has been divided, quite arbitrarily, between two local governing authorities, the county and the city of Miami, yet the violence, while originating on the 17th Avenue division, spread eastward and southward, deeper into the city of Miami.

The fact that violence did not spread into the unincorporated area poses a significant question. Why did the disturbance move in this direction? Why did the violence move into the Coconut Grove area and not further southward into the county? There are large Negro neighborhoods in the southern and NW portions of the unincorporated county. To be sure, some of these Negro areas represent a higher income group (e.g., Richmond Heights), but other areas (e.g., Perrine and vicinity) are less fortunate and can be compared with the Coconut Grove area or the central Negro district in the Center City.

The Miami incident raises an important question concerning the relationship between rioting and police-community relations programs. Is it necessary to formalize community relations departments within police administrations? To what extent did the fact that the Dade County Safety Department had an active, formally organized and larger program account for the lack of violence in the county area? Of additional significance is the whole question of community relations programs. Do they have the beneficial effect most authorities attribute to them? The 1968 racial disturbance in Miami seems to bear out this contention, but other metropolitan areas with more comprehensive programs than Miami have experienced much more racial unrest. Clearly, this aspect of violence merits further research.[8]

Also, an analysis of the disturbance raises other important urban-racial questions. Is there a relationship between rioting and income? What effect does distance have upon violence participation within a quasi homogeneous neighborhood? What is the effect of distance from slums on racial bigotry? How does distance affect human perception of danger? Can stress points be established prior to such outbreaks? How refined are these relationships and can a quantitative measurement be established?

These are but some of the questions that merit further investigation in Miami and elsewhere, both by geographers and other social scientists. Finally, we re-emphasize that we are fully aware of and appreciate the extreme complexities of these questions and this total area of research. No single answer or set of answers exists, but we are convinced that unless these and other questions are asked and answered, the consequences will be severe for our urban areas and, eventually, our entire nation.

LITERATURE CITED

1. The *Miami News*, August 8, 1968.
2. Memo to City Manager Reese from City of Miami Police, the *Miami News*, August 8, 1968.
3. For a thorough rundown of the events, see the special Metro "white paper" or either the *Miami Herald* or the *Miami News*.
4. In this paper Metropolitan Dade County refers to the Metropolitan Dade County Government. This includes the twenty-seven municipalities and the unincorporated area of the county. For an excellent account of Metro, see Edward Sofen, *Miami Metropolitan Experience*, Indiana University Press, 1963.
5. Chief Headley received national attention in December of 1967 with his announced policy of using police dogs, issuing shotguns to patrolmen, and employing "stop and frisk" measures in the high crime rate areas of Miami. See: Editorial, New York *Times*, December 28, 1967. Since this paper was written, Police Chief Headley died on November 16, 1968.
6. Editorial, the *Miami News*, October 11, 1968.
7. This is especially true of the Negro public. Note the editorial of Miami's leading Negro newspaper, the *Miami Times*, August 16, 1968.
8. Stanley Lieberson and Arnold R. Silverman, "The Precipitants and Underlying Conditions of Race Riots," *American Sociological Review*, Vol. 30, No. 6, December 1965, pp. 887–98.

CHAPTER VII

Changing Black Settlement Patterns

INTRODUCTORY NOTE

Geographic bases of human settlement have been studied intensely through physical, cultural, economic, political, and demographic factors in world-wide patterns. Within specific countries, basic structures of human settlement patterns have been considered. Patterns and types of housing, population distribution, and urban and rural components of human settlement have been thoroughly researched. However, certain variations of human settlement within countries only recently have been objects of geographical investigation. Differences in migration and settlement patterns of racial groups in the United States are aspects of geography that must be augmented by further research. Several geographers and other social scientists have investigated and sought to explain differences in black and white migration and settlement patterns across the nation.

Recent studies have demonstrated black migrants can no longer be characterized as emanating from the rural South and settling the urban North and West. Intercity migration and movements from central cities to suburban and rural locations have become increasingly documented in social science literature. In fact, Karl and Alma Taeuber and others have asserted migration patterns and demographic characteristics of black migrants are remarkably similar to those exhibited by the white population. In this chapter, Reynolds Farley views recent trends of black population distribution that are moving toward and creating new suburbs; origin, evolution, and function of the all-black town are discussed by Harold M. Rose; Robert T. Ernst examines the socioeconomic and physical isolation of an all-black city; and James O. Wheeler and Stanley D. Brunn examine black migrational flows into rural southwestern Michigan.

One recent research theme in urban studies of geographic interest involves extended debate over homogeneity or heterogeneity of suburban residents' social characteristics. Reynolds Farley investigates one facet of this problem. He hypothesizes that cities and suburbs possess racially dissimilar populations. Cities contain principally black populations while outlying suburbs are primarily white. This situation pertains even though there are now, and historically have been, suburban communities consisting mainly of black residents. Farley supports his contention by reviewing historical trends in racial composition; studying rapidity of black suburban growth; examining socioeconomic characteristics of suburban black residents and migrants; and describing types of suburbs experiencing black migration.

Farley illustrates that, in recent years, general suburban black population growth has accelerated. There are three locational foci which appear to be receiving the majority of black migration: older suburbs which are undergoing population succession; new tracts specifically built for black occupancy; and previously established, impoverished black enclaves. The author postulates that future expansion of black suburban population depends on rates of improvement of black economic status, rates of new housing construction, and rapidity with which suburban housing becomes available to blacks—a situation that depends on enforcement of open housing laws and reduction of racial discrimination.

In his conclusion, Farley relates consequences of black suburbanization. He shows, despite increase in black suburban population, there has been no significant decline in suburban residential segregation since World War II. Instead of integration, there has appeared in suburbs persistent patterns of residential segregation characteristic of central cities. Farley demonstrates that suburbanization of blacks does not necessarily denote changes in patterns of racial segregation within urban areas. However, blacks are becoming more decentralized throughout metropolitan areas, and black suburbanization may someday hasten residential integration. At the present time, black suburban growth merely reinforces residential segregation.

Investigation of the universe of all-black towns is the subject of Harold Rose's article. Rose attempts to construct a valid definition of all-black towns, identify all such towns in the United States, establish these racial communities as a unique population, and, finally, discover valid generalizations applying to these communities as a unit and not individual cases.

According to Rose, all-black towns are defined as all places of over one thousand population, 95 per cent of whom are classified as nonwhite. Using this definition, Rose identifies nineteen places as all-black. Of this number, seven are eliminated as "pseudo towns" that are not separate places but are nonpolitical appendages of larger places. Thus, the remaining twelve communities are the basis for research.

One important and interesting development in the article is Rose's attempt to assess the relationship of all-black towns to the "suburbs" concept. The black towns' occupational structures are examined to ascertain whether they are independent satellites, dependent dormitory suburbs, or some other phenomenon. In addition, analysis of variance is utilized to determine whether all-black towns and their nearest neighbor (which Rose assumes to be suburban) could have been drawn from the same population on the basis of housing substandardness. But data used are not randomly sampled, not normally distributed, and no transformations (normalization or standardization techniques) are made to correct deficiencies of this single variable approach. According to Rose, both tests establish that of all twelve towns, only one (Richmond Heights, Florida) may be classified as suburban. All the other towns are rejected as suburban, but no additional information as to the nature of these eleven towns is provided.

Rose's last major theme is devoted to present and future prospects of all-black towns. Suburbanization of the communities is projected as potentially one of the most attractive and advantageous elements in their continuing evolution. Rose, however, concludes his work realistically by stating that "the future of the towns is subject to the operation of a complex set of variables whose behavior is difficult to predict."

In research partially inspired by Rose's work, Robert T. Ernst investigates Kinloch, Missouri, an all-black city. He is concerned with providing detailed geographic information on the growth, development, and present situation of the black city.

Kinloch is shown to be characterized by old, dilapidated housing, poorly maintained roads, and deep-seated poverty. In addition, the city is surrounded by all-white suburban communities that have successfully isolated Kinloch from most contacts with the larger metropolitan area. Ernst identifies three types of barriers (physical, transportation-communication, and social) that isolate Kinloch and describes each in detail.

The main conclusion of the research is that social, economic, and locational factors indicate continuance of the isolation and poverty of Kinloch. The future appears bleak as there is no evidence present conditions will be abated.

The general problem with which Wheeler and Brunn deal concerns recent black migration into southwestern Michigan. They suggest a section of black population is not following main black migration streams. Instead, another dimension is being added to migration patterns. In this dimension, blacks bypass suburban environments completely by moving into small, previously agricultural communities, purchasing homes from out-migrating whites. Thus, by omitting the suburban stage, some blacks are striving to obtain certain benefits of the suburban way of life.

They minimize risks inherent to existence in ghettos and to settlement in potentially hostile all-white suburbs.

Wheeler and Brunn state their purpose in performing this research is to examine conditions and characteristics behind distributions of blacks in southwestern Michigan. Specifically, they trace migration of blacks into the area, analyze the demographic composition, and compare black social and economic ties with those of the native white population.

Research results prove to be significant. The greater majority (80 per cent) of black adults living in rural southwestern Michigan were born and raised in the rural South. Only 6 per cent of the blacks migrated directly to the area from the South. Most had first migrated to northern urban centers. Black migration to the study area is not primarily a response to economic opportunities, as evidenced by longer journey-to-work trips for blacks. The great majority of blacks moved to the area to escape northern urban ghettos. These conclusions are important as Wheeler and Brunn corroborated earlier studies by the Taeubers. The authors show blacks increasingly exhibit demographic patterns similar to the white population although at a slower pace and later time in history.

THE CHANGING DISTRIBUTION OF NEGROES
WITHIN METROPOLITAN AREAS:
THE EMERGENCE OF BLACK SUBURBS

Reynolds Farley

INTRODUCTION

After World War II, many studies claimed that new life-styles were developing within suburbia. These life-styles demanded that suburbanites be very friendly to their neighbors, spend much time on child-rearing activities, and participate in many community endeavors. Some sociologists argued that the major reason for the development of these new social patterns was that suburbs contained a young, middle-class, native American population which shared common values, unlike central cities which contained a heterogeneous population (Fava, 1956; Martin, 1956; Riesman, 1957; Whyte, 1957).

Long ago some authors had shown there was a variety of types of communities in the suburban territory surrounding central cities (Douglas, 1925; Harris, 1943), but further research was required to challenge the myth of suburban homogeneity. Schnore (1957, 1965) pointed out the differences in ethnic composition and socioeconomic status which could be found within the nation's suburbs. Further study found that suburban living did not completely change working-class life-styles and that middle- and working-class residents could be found within the same suburb (Dobriner, 1963). The similarity of cities and suburbs was demonstrated by another investigation which showed that patterns of residential segregation common to central cities were also found in suburbs (Lieberson, 1962).

Recently much publicity has been given the idea that central cities are coming to contain a principally black population while the surrounding suburbs are residential areas for whites. President Johnson's Commission on Civil Disorders stated succinctly in warning that if present trends continue there will be "a white society principally located in suburbs, in smaller central cities and in the peripheral parts of large cities and a Negro society largely concentrated within large cities" (U.S. National Advisory Commission on Civil Disorders, 1968, p. 407).

This paper examines the hypothesis that cities and suburbs are coming to have racially dissimilar populations. First, historical trends in racial composition are reviewed. Second, data are examined to study the rapidity of black population growth in suburbia in recent years. Third, the socioeconomic characteristics of blacks in suburbia and those moving into suburbia are analyzed. Finally, the types of suburbs which have experienced Negro population growth are described.

HISTORICAL TRENDS

Changes since 1900 in the racial composition of central cities and the suburban area that surrounds them can be determined from census data. Figure 1 shows the proportion of the total population which was Negro in central cities and suburban rings for dates between 1900 and 1968. These figures are based on information for all the 212 Standard Metropolitan Statistical Areas (SMSA) defined in 1960. The suburban ring includes, at each date, the area which was outside the central city but within the counties comprising the SMSA in 1960. Data are shown separately for SMSAs in the North and West and for those in the South.

Central cities outside the South contained relatively few blacks prior to World War I; thereafter a cessation of European immigration combined with an influx of blacks gradually changed the racial composition of these cities. As recently as 1940, however, the proportion black was no greater than 6 per cent. During and after World War II, the in-migration of Negroes continued, and, in many cities, the white population decreased. As a consequence, the proportion black in these cities went up and by the late 1960s reached 18 per cent.

Very different trends characterize southern central cities. Prior to the Civil War the number of blacks in many southern cities actually decreased (Wade, 1964, pp. 325–30), but after Emancipation freedmen left their plantations and between 1860 and 1870 the proportion black in southern cities rose (Farley, 1968, p. 247). However, there was little change in the racial composition of these cities after 1870. While their black populations grew the cities annexed outlying territory, and their white populations have grown at about the same rate, effecting no substantial change in their color composition. Since 1950 there has been a slight rise in the proportion black in the southern cities. If these cities, in the future, find it

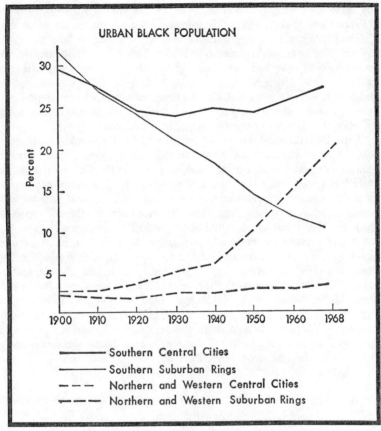

URBAN BLACK POPULATION

——————— Southern Central Cities
——————— Southern Suburban Rings
— — —   Northern and Western Central Cities
— — —   Northern and Western Suburban Rings

Figure 1

difficult to annex outlying areas which have rapidly growing white population, their color composition will change.

There have always been some blacks in the suburban rings which surround northern and western cities. The proportion black in these areas remained approximately 3 per cent for many decades. As white suburban communities were growing, Negro suburban communities were expanding at a correspondingly rapid rate. Some of these black suburbs date from the early years of this century and have histories similar to those of white suburbs. For instance, just before 1900, a tract west of St. Louis, Missouri, was subdivided, and lots were sold to Negroes. This suburb, called Kinloch, grew slowly for some decades but was incorporated in 1939, and by 1960 it had a population of 6,500, all but two of whom were black (Kramer and Walter, 1967; U.S. Bureau of the Census, 1961a, table 25). In the Chicago area, a Negro realtor secured land west of the city prior to World War I and sold homesites to blacks. This suburb, Robbins, was incorporated in 1917 and has continued to grow, reaching a population of 7,500 in 1960 (Rose, 1965, p. 369; U.S. Bureau of the Census, 1961b, table 25). Near Cincinnati, Ohio, the black suburb of Lincoln Heights developed during the 1920s and by 1960 had 7,800 residents (Rose, 1965, p. 369; U.S. Bureau of the Census, 1961g, table 22).

Suburban rings surrounding southern cities have undergone great change in racial composition. Early in this century, when these suburban rings contained extensive rural areas, at least one third of the population was black. Gradually but consistently this proportion decreased, for, as southern cities grew, suburbs developed and whites moved into outlying areas. In some suburban rings whites displaced blacks (Heberle, 1948, p. 34); in other suburban rings the black population continued to grow but at a slower rate than the white population. Nevertheless, black suburbs have sprung up near some major cities. For example, after World War II a suburban development for Negroes was built near Miami, Florida, and by 1960 this suburb, Richmond Heights, contained some of the nicer homes available to Miami blacks (U.S. Bureau of the Census, 1962a, tables 37–40; Rose, 1965, p. 370). In the 1950s, after an expressway cut through the black ghetto of Shreveport, Louisiana, many inexpensive homes were put up in an area to the north of the city. In 1960 North Shreveport had a black population of 8,000 (U.S. Bureau of the Census, 1961c, table 22; 1961f, table 37).

RECENT TRENDS

It has been almost a decade since the last national census was conducted, so it is difficult to know exactly what population changes have occurred since 1960. However, the Census Bureau's monthly Current Population Survey, which now involves a national sample of 50,000 housing units, provides increasingly detailed information about blacks. Table 1 indicates the Negro and white populations of central cities and suburban rings in 1960 and 1968 and growth rates for the intervening period. It must be remembered that these data were obtained by sampling the population and that between 1968 and 1970 many central cities may annex outlying territory. Hence, growth rates for the 1960–70 period may differ from those for the 1960–68 span contained in Table 1.

Since 1960 there has been continued growth of the black population in the nation's central cities both within and outside the South, although growth rates for the 1960s are lower than those of the 1950s (U.S. Bureau of the Census, 1963a, table 1; 1969a, pp. 2–6). The white population of central cities, with the exception of western cities, has decreased, and this too continues a trend which developed in the World War II era.

The black population in suburban rings has grown quite rapidly. In the suburban rings of the North and West, the black population has increased since 1960, not only more rapidly than it did during the 1950s but more rapidly than the white population. This has produced a slight change in the racial composition of these suburban rings as indicated by Figure 1. Within southern suburban rings, the white population increased at a higher rate than the black, but the Negro population has grown more rapidly during this decade than during the last.

Despite the suburbanization of blacks, the data in both Figure 1 and Table 1 show that central cities are becoming more racially differentiated from their suburban rings. The proportion of population which is black is rising more rapidly in central cities than in suburban rings. This finding

TABLE 1

Change of Negro and White Populations in Central Cities and Suburban Areas, 1960-68*

	Negro Population			White Population		
	1960	1968	Average Annual Change (%)	1960	1968	Average Annual Change (%)
	(in Millions)			(in Millions)		
Total population of United States	18.4	22.0	+2.2	158.7	174.0	+1.2
Northeast and North Central:						
Central cities	5.0	6.8	+3.8	28.6	26.4	−1.0
Suburban rings	0.9	1.2	+3.6	31.5	37.7	+2.2
South:						
Central cities	3.7	4.1	+1.3	11.1	10.8	−0.3
Suburban rings	1.4	1.6	+1.7	10.1	14.2	+4.3
West:						
Central cities	0.7	0.9	+3.2	8.0	8.2	+0.3
Suburban rings	0.3	0.5	+6.4	10.3	14.0	+3.8

Source: U.S., Bureau of the Census 1969a, pp. 2 and 6.

*Standard metropolitan statistical areas as defined in 1960 were used in this analysis. The suburban ring includes that area outside the central city but within the standard metropolitan statistical area.

lends credence to the view of the Commission on Civil Disorders, but two facts should not be overlooked.

First, at present blacks are a minority in most central cities. In 1965, only one of the nation's thirty largest cities, Washington, D.C., had a black majority; and in only four others (Atlanta, Georgia; Memphis, Tennessee; New Orleans, Louisiana; and Newark, New Jersey) did blacks comprise as much as 40 per cent of the population (U.S. Bureau of the Census, 1967a, p. 11). In the future some large cities in both the North and the South will have black majorities, but these cities will be the exceptions rather than the rule. If the growth rates from central cities which obtained between 1960 and 1966 continue to 1980, the proportion of population in central cities which is nonwhite will rise from 22 per cent in 1966 to 32 per cent in 1980. (This projection is based on figures from U.S. Bureau of the Census, 1967b, table A. For a more elaborate set of projections, see Hodge and Hauser, 1968, p. 26.) Since 1960 the rate of natural increase among blacks has decreased for fertility rates have fallen (U.S. Bureau of the Census, 1969d, tables 2 and 3), and by 1967 only a little more than one million blacks remained on the nation's farms (U.S. Bureau of the Census, 1969e, table 3). The black population is simply not growing rapidly enough, nor are there sufficient numbers of rural Negroes to radically change the racial composition of most central cities even if whites continue to move away.

Second, suburban rings do contain Negroes, and some suburban black communities, both in the North and the South, have grown in the recent past. A Census Bureau study indicates that within suburban rings the black population increased much more rapidly between 1966 and 1968 than between 1960 and 1966, although sampling variability may affect this finding (U.S. Bureau of the Census, 1969a, p. 3).

Aggregate figures obtained from national samples of the population give no indication of which specific suburban communities have growing black populations. In both Illinois and New York, however, a number of communities have requested the Census Bureau to conduct special enumerations since 1960 because certain state appropriations are based upon the population of local areas as officially enumerated. This provides an incentive for growing suburbs to request special censuses, and in both the Chicago and New York metropolitan areas many of these have been conducted. This permits us to investigate racial change in the suburbs near the nation's two largest cities, New York and Chicago.

Negroes in the Chicago Suburban Area

A total of seventy-six places within Cook County but outside the city of Chicago, that is, suburban cities, towns, and villages, were covered by special census enumerations between 1964 and 1968. These places, in 1960, contained about five eighths of the suburban population of Cook County (U.S. Bureau of the Census, 1961*d*, table 7).

Chicago's suburban population increased rapidly after 1960. Among the places covered by special censuses, the total population went up from about one million in 1960 to one and one-third million at the special census dates (U.S. Bureau of the Census, 1968*a*, table A-1; 1968*b*, table 1; 1968*c*, table 1; 1969*b*, table 1; 1969*c*, table 1). The nonwhite population increased at a higher rate than the white, affecting a small change in the proportion nonwhite in these suburbs, a rise from 2.2 per cent in 1960 to 2.6 per cent when the special enumerations were carried out (U.S. Bureau of the Census, 1961*b*, tables 21 and 22; 1965, table 1; 1966*a*, table 1; 1967*c*, table 1; 1968*a*, table 1; 1968*b*, table 1; 1968*c*, table 1; 1969*b*, table 1; 1969*c*, table 1).

A closer examination of these data reveals that little integration has occurred. Rather than being distributed throughout the suburbs, the growth of black population has concentrated in three areas; one in Maywood, one in and around Harvey, and a third area of Chicago Heights and East Chicago Heights.

Between 1960 and 1965 the black population of Maywood doubled, increasing from 5,000 to 10,000. This is an older suburb which was settled after the Civil War and grew rapidly when rail lines linked it to Chicago (Kitagawa and Taeuber, 1963, p. 194). Maywood did not participate in the post-World War II boom; in fact, its peak growth followed World War I. It is a suburb of older, relatively less expensive homes (U.S. Bureau of the Census, 1962*b*, tables 17 and 21). Maywood has experienced population replacement since 1950, for as its white population declined, its Negro population grew, while its total population has remained about constant.

The black population of Harvey, another old suburb, and the nearby but newer suburb of Markham increased. Harvey was founded in the 1890s but has continued to grow, and in recent years manufacturing firms have located in this area (U.S. Bureau of the Census, 1966*b*, table 4). In 1960 the majority of blacks in Harvey lived in older homes, but one third lived in houses which had been erected after World War II (U.S. Bureau of the Census, 1962*b*, table 37). Since 1960 there has been a modest building boom in this suburb, and new construction as well as the conversion of older homes from white to Negro occupancy account for the growth of black population. Markham is a post-World War II suburb. In recent years many new single-family homes have been built, and both the white and Negro populations have increased (U.S. Bureau of the Census, 1966*c*, table B-6; 1965, table 1).

The third suburban area which had a growing black population included a section of Chicago Heights and the village of East Chicago Heights. Steel and chemical plants have been in this area since the 1890s. During World War I blacks began moving into Chicago Heights, and their members rose during World War II (Kitagawa and Taeuber, 1963, p. 176). A pattern of intracommunity segregation emerged; and an area separated from the rest of the suburb by a major rail line contained the black population (U.S. Bureau of the Census, 1962c, table P-1). Bordering Chicago Heights is an area of older, low-quality homes. In 1960, 60 per cent of them lacked indoor toilets and half were in deteriorating or dilapidated condition (U.S. Bureau of the Census, 1962b, table 37). This is the suburb of East Chicago Heights. During 1964 a public housing project was started, and this along with other new construction explains the rise of black population.

Negroes in the New York Suburban Area

New York City's suburban ring, in 1960, included four counties. Those closer to the city are Nassau, which lies immediately east of New York on Long Island, and Westchester, which is located just north of the city. The outer counties are Suffolk on Long Island and Rockland, which is northwest of the city and across the Hudson River. Between 1965 and 1968 the population of this entire area was enumerated by special census except for some small enclaves. These special census data make it possible to determine the number and age of recent migrants to the suburban ring. Data are shown for two sections of Suffolk County, for an area nearer the central city which was enumerated in 1967, and for an area further from the city which was counted one year later.

The figures indicate, first, that the Negro population of the suburban ring has grown since 1960; by the mid-1960s there were at least 175,000 blacks in these suburbs. In each suburban area, except the outer towns of Suffolk County, the Negro population increased more rapidly than the white, producing a small rise in the proportion black within the New York suburban ring.

Second, Negro population growth has occurred not only because of natural increase but also because blacks are migrating into these suburbs. Examination of the migration rates reveals that the highest rates were for the age groups 20–34 and 0–4 in 1960. This indicates that black families headed by young adults along with their young children are moving into the suburban ring.

Third, there are racial differences in growth rates and migration patterns. Population growth has been very slow in the suburban counties closer to New York. These counties attracted whites who were in the early stages of family formation but lost about an equal number of teen-agers and older whites, so their net migration rates for whites were near zero. The outer counties, Suffolk and Rockland, have grown rapidly and attracted whites of all ages. Black population growth has occurred in all counties, but the largest increases in numbers occurred within the suburban areas nearer New York City.

Long Island will be considered first in investigating which suburbs have growing black populations. Although there are few incorporated cities on Long Island, census tracts—that is, geographical areas containing about 5,000 people—were defined for the entire area in 1960, and special census tabulations have been presented for these same areas. Twenty-two census tracts on Long Island had increases of 250 or more blacks between 1960 and the special census date. They can be divided into two groups.

One group, located principally within the county near New York, gained Negroes and lost whites while the total population remained about constant. The homes in these census tracts were older than was typical for Long Island (U.S. Bureau of the Census, 1962d, table H-1). Population replacement occurred in these suburbs. The second group of tracts, most of them within Suffolk County, gained large numbers of both Negroes and whites. Many new homes must have been built to accommodate these population increases, although it is impossible to determine from special census data the number of new homes or the race of their occupants. The Census of 1970 will reveal more about these suburban areas which gained both whites and Negroes and will indicate whether blacks have occupied new homes or have replaced whites in older homes.

Most of the recent growth of black population within Westchester County has taken place within four suburbs. Mount Vernon, New Rochelle, White Plains, and Yonkers are large and older suburbs. World War I interrupted their period of most rapid growth. While the number of blacks in each of these suburbs increased, their patterns of demographic change were quite different. These same patterns of change undoubtedly are occurring in central cities and suburbs throughout the nation.

Mount Vernon exemplifies a common pattern of change. This suburb lost whites and gained Negroes while its total population slowly declined. By 1965, one quarter of the population was black. The tracks of the New York, New Haven and Hartford Railroad bisect Mount Vernon. In 1960 the area south of the railroad was racially mixed, but since then whites have moved away and Negroes moved in. If the patterns of racial change observed in large cities in the 1940s and 1950s (Duncan and Duncan, 1957, chap. 6; Taeuber and Taeuber, 1965a, chap. 5) are duplicated in Mount Vernon, whites will continue to leave and the southern half will soon be a black ghetto of 30,000. North of the rail line there has been little population change. The area was 98 per cent white in 1960 and 97 per cent white in 1965 (U.S. Bureau of the Census, 1962d, table P-1; 1966d, table 2).

Yonkers illustrates a second pattern of change. This suburb attracted relatively many blacks, but among whites in-migration has been matched by out-migration. An area of older homes near the center of Yonkers has lost white and gained black population. In the northern extremities of this suburb, new construction has taken place, and the increase in white population in one area offsets a loss in another area. If no vacant land for new construction remains, the color composition of this suburb will change as more blacks move into older residential areas.

Other types of change, reflecting urban renewal activities, occurred within New Rochelle and White Plains. New Rochelle's population and racial composition remained stable after 1960. An urban renewal project was begun in New Rochelle which led to an out-migration of both blacks and whites sufficient in size to offset the effects of natural increase (U.S. Department of Housing and Urban Development, 1967, p. 44).

Since 1960, the white population of White Plains decreased while its black population grew slowly. This suburb has many of the same characteristics as Mount Vernon and Yonkers, and one might expect its black population to increase rapidly. However, an urban renewal project was started which will raze the homes of 400 whites and 400 Negro families (U.S. Department of Housing and Urban Development, 1967, p. 44). This involves only about 3 per cent of the white but 21 per cent of the Negro population (U.S. Bureau of the Census, 1961e, table 21). If the displaced black families relocate outside this suburb, the process of racial succession will be slowed.

Rockland County had a sparse population in 1960, so census tracts in this county included very extensive land areas. The black population in a number of tracts went up, but more detailed information is needed to ascertain which particular areas have attracted black residents.

THE CHARACTERISTICS OF SUBURBAN IN-MIGRANTS

Data from the special censuses conducted in the New York and Chicago suburban rings indicate there is a growing black suburban population and suggest that young black families are moving into suburbia. However, the socioeconomic selectivity of these suburban in-migrants or the status of blacks in suburbia, compared to that of blacks in central cities, is not revealed by these special censuses.

Whites who live in suburbs, particularly suburbs near the large central cities, are typically better educated, hold more prestigious jobs, and have larger incomes than central city whites (Duncan and Reiss, 1956, pp.

	Whites (%)		Nonwhites (%)	
	Cities	Suburban Rings	Cities	Suburban Rings
Proportion of adults with some college education	18	21	10	9
Proportion of families with incomes of $10,000 or more	19	23	6	7
Proportion of employed men with white-collar jobs	31	30	14	11

Figure 1

127–33; Schnore, 1965, p. 245; U.S. Bureau of the Census, 1963a, tables 3, 6a and 8). One of the reasons for this is the selectivity of migrants who move into suburbs. The Taeubers investigated metropolitan migration patterns for whites for the period 1955–60 and discovered that suburban rings attracted large streams of high-status migrants from their central cities. In addition, there was a sizable stream of intermetropolitan migrants, many of whom moved directly into suburbs when they came into a new area (Taeuber and Taeuber, 1964a, pp. 718–29).

The most recent data showing the socioeconomic characteristics of suburban blacks pertain to 1960, and the latest period for which figures are available about the characteristics of migrants is 1955–60. To describe the Negro suburban population, the ten metropolitan areas whose suburban rings had the largest black populations in 1960 were selected.

Central city blacks rather than suburban blacks had the higher socioeconomic status. Both in the South and in the North, men in the cities held proportionally more of the prestigious jobs than did men in suburbia. Only in Newark was there a reversal of this pattern. A comparison of differences in educational attainment (data not shown) revealed a similar finding. In each of these areas, save Newark, the proportion of blacks who were high school graduates was higher in the central city than in the suburban ring.

This finding—that unlike whites suburban blacks in 1960 were often lower in social status than those in the city—is further substantiated by the figures below which refer to all SMSAs which had populations of 250,000 or more in 1960 (U.S. Bureau of the Census, 1963a, tables 3, 6a, and 8).

The causes of this unusual pattern of city-suburban differentiation are difficult to specify. In the South, suburban rings still contain some blacks who are farmers, and this tends to lower average socioeconomic status in southern suburban rings. Within the North it was thought that city-suburban differences in age composition might account for this finding. However, after age differences were taken into account by a standardization procedure, suburban blacks still did not match central city blacks in social status. (For further discussion, see Schnore, 1965, pp. 242–52.)

Metropolitan migration patterns among blacks are similar to those of whites, even though there are important differences in the volume of migration. In eight of the ten metropolitan areas for which data are presented, the largest stream of blacks moving into suburban rings were people leaving the central city. In each area except Birmingham, these city-to-suburb movers were higher in socioeconomic status than either the blacks who remained in the central city or the other blacks who lived in the suburban ring.

The suburbs attracted two other, but typically smaller, streams of migrants. Among Negroes, as among whites, there was a stream of higher status intermetropolitan migrants who moved directly into the suburban ring between 1955 and 1960. (For further description of these higher status intermetropolitan nonwhite migrants, see Taeuber and Taeuber, 1965b, pp. 429–41.) There was also a stream of young migrants from nonmetropolitan areas who were low in socioeconomic status. Many of these migrants may have left southern rural areas or small towns for the economic opportunities of large metropolitan areas.

These central cities attracted two streams of migrants which were of approximately equal size. One stream came from other metropolitan areas and was high in socioeconomic status. The second stream came from nonmetropolitan areas, and few of the men held white collar or craftsmen jobs. In addition, the central cities attracted migrants from suburbia, and these ring-to-city movers were generally high in socioeconomic status. This is similar to the Taeubers' finding that, between 1955 and 1960, cities and their suburbs exchanged relatively high-status white population (Taeuber and Taeuber, 1964a). Unlike the situation for whites, however, among Negroes the number of city-to-ring movers did not always greatly exceed the number of ring-to-city movers. In some areas, New York and Miami, for instance, the number moving from the city to the ring exceeded the number moving in the other direction, but in other areas, such as Detroit, Michigan, ring-to-city movers were more numerous.

The data presented in this paper clearly indicate that between 1955 and 1960 suburban rings attracted higher status black residents from their central cities and also attracted a sizable share of the higher status intermetropolitan migrants. The growth of the Negro suburban population has increased since 1960, and the migrants to suburbia during this decade are probably of higher status as were the migrants during the last decade. This migration may already be of sufficient size to establish a pattern of city-suburban socioeconomic differences among blacks, similar to that observed among whites. For instance, in 1959 median family income among blacks in the suburban rings was far below that of blacks in central cities, but by 1967 it was higher in the suburban rings (U.S. Bureau of the Census, 1969a, p. 37). Among young adult blacks, educational attainment levels in 1960 were lower in the suburban rings than in the cities, but by 1968 this was reversed, probably reflecting the migration to the suburbs of well-educated young Negroes (U.S. Bureau of the Census, 1969a, p. 23). It is likely that the Census of 1970 will find that suburban blacks are higher in socioeconomic status than those in central cities.

THE PROCESS OF SUBURBANIZATION

The demographic data indicate that suburban rings are attracting black migrants and that, while all economic levels are represented, the migrants to suburbia tend to be higher in socioeconomic status. It appears that three types of suburban areas have gained black population. First, particularly in the North, there are older, densely settled suburbs often containing or near employment centers. Such places as Maywood, Yonkers, and East Cleveland, Ohio, have experienced population replacement—that is, decreases in white population but growth of black—and in the future more suburbs will undergo similar change. Studies of residential change have found that the first Negroes to move into a white neighborhood are those who are financially able to purchase better housing than that which is generally available to blacks (Taeuber and Taeuber, 1965a, pp. 154–66; Duncan and Duncan, 1957, pp. 215–36). Such older suburbs contain housing units which are better than those blacks can occupy in the ghettos. On the other hand, because of the age of the homes and the small lots on which they were built, homes in these suburbs may not appeal to whites who move out from the central city. The causes of racial change in any particular older suburb may be idiosyncratic, but proximity to employment is probably an important factor.

The second type of area with growing black population is the new suburban development. Some are built exclusively for Negroes. Richmond Heights, Florida, which was described previously, is one example; in recent years Hollydale has been built near Cincinnati (Rose, 1965, p. 380), and new homes have gone up in Inkster, a Detroit suburb with a large black population (U.S. Bureau of the Census, 1966c, table B-6). In addition, it is possible that a small number of blacks are moving into new and integrated suburban developments.

A third type of area with a growing Negro population is to be found in the suburban rings of many large cities. Areas lacking adequate sewer and water facilities, containing dilapidated homes of low value, and having exclusively black populations could be located in 1960 in suburban areas. They have grown partly because of natural increase, partly because some public housing has been erected (between 1959 and 1966, seventy-five public housing units were authorized in Robbins, 216 in East Chicago Heights, and 150 in Kinloch [U.S. Bureau of the Census, 1966c, table B-7; 1968d, table 8]), and partly because low-income blacks may find inexpensive housing close to their jobs in these suburbs.

Expansion of the black suburban population will depend upon many factors; three of the most important are discussed here. First is the rate at which the economic status of blacks improves. In recent years the income of Negroes has gone up much faster than have prices. For instance, median family income of blacks increased about 6 per cent each year from 1960 to 1967 while the cost of living went up by less than 2 per cent annually (U.S. Bureau of the Census, 1967d, table G; 1968e, table 3; 1968g, table 505). Negroes now have more money to spend for shelter and consumer goods. The migration of blacks to suburbia reflects such economic gains, and if incomes continue to go up more rapidly than the cost of living, more blacks will be able to afford better housing.

The second factor is the rate at which new housing is constructed and the housing policies which will be favored by the federal government. At present, a little over 1.5 million housing units are built annually (U.S. Bureau of the Census, 1969f, table 1). The President's Committee on Urban Housing estimated that 2.7 million new housing units were needed each year to provide for the growing population and to replace substandard housing (U.S. President's Committee on Urban Housing, 1967, p. 7). The Kerner Commission Report recommended numerous programs to encourage building new homes for low- and moderate-income families outside central city ghettos (U.S. National Advisory Commission on Civil Disorders, 1968, pp. 467–82). If there is a great volume of new construction, and if clusters of low and moderately priced homes are spread throughout suburbia and are open to Negro occupancy, there may be a rise in the black suburban population.

The third factor is the rapidity with which suburban housing becomes available to blacks. Since 1960 the incomes of Negroes have increased more rapidly than those of whites (U.S. Bureau of the Census, 1968f, p. 6). If this continues, more Negroes will be able to compete with whites for suburban housing. Perhaps when the federal open occupancy law becomes fully effective, discrimination will be reduced, and more suburbs will include blacks in their population. This is an optimistic view. Racial policies in the new suburb of Levittown, New Jersey, were described by Gans (1967, pp. 22, 371–78). Despite a state open occupancy law, the developers announced plans to sell only to whites and turned away black customers. Negroes were eventually accepted after a suit proceeded through the courts for two years. Even after this, special policies were instituted to screen Negro buyers and place them in isolated areas. If this is duplicated in other suburbs, blacks who desire to move into the suburbs will still face immense difficulties regardless of their financial means.

THE CONSEQUENCES OF SUBURBANIZATION

The suburbanization of blacks does not herald a basic change in the patterns of racial segregation within metropolitan areas. Cities and their suburban rings are becoming more dissimilar in racial composition, and the out-migration of some blacks from the city will not alter this process. It will do no more than slow the growth of the black population of some cities while adding still greater diversity to the already heterogeneous population of suburbia.

It does indicate that Negroes, similar to European ethnic groups, are

becoming more decentralized throughout the metropolitan area after they
have been in the city for some time and improved their economic status
(Cressey, 1938, pp. 59–69; Taeuber and Taeuber, 1966, pp. 130–36;
Schnore, 1965, pp. 126–33). However, improvements in economic status
brought about not only the residential decentralization of European immigrant groups but also reductions in their residential segregation
(Lieberson, 1963, chaps. 3 and 4). Negroes have deviated widely from
this pattern for, despite economic gains and some decentralization of predominately black residential areas, the residential segregation of Negroes
has persisted (Taeuber and Taeuber, 1964b, pp. 374–82). Even during
the prosperous period from the end of World War II to the present, there
is no evidence that the residential segregation of blacks decreased
(Taeuber and Taeuber, 1965a, chap. 3; Clemence, 1967, pp. 562–68;
Farley and Taeuber, 1968, p. 983). It is possible that the suburbanization
of blacks will alter this pattern, and a future census may reveal integrated
suburban neighborhoods. In the meantime, we can be certain that the residential segregation patterns of central cities are reappearing within the
suburbs.

Literature Cited

Clemence, Theodore G. 1967. "Residential Segregation in the Mid-
    Sixties." Demography 4:562–68.
Cressey, Paul Frederick. 1938. "Population Succession in Chicago:
    1898–1930." American Journal of Sociology 44 (July): 59–69.
Dobriner, William. 1963. Class in Suburbia. Englewood Cliffs, N.J.:
    Prentice-Hall.
Douglas, Harlan Paul. 1925. The Suburban Trend. New York: Century.
Duncan, Otis Dudley, and Beverly Duncan. 1957. The Negro Population
    of Chicago. Chicago: University of Chicago Press.
Duncan, Otis Dudley, and Albert J. Reiss, Jr. 1956. Social Characteristics
    of Urban and Rural Communities, 1950. New York: Wiley.
Farley, Reynolds. 1968. "The Urbanization of Negroes in the United
    States." Journal of Social History 2 (Spring): 241–58.
Farley, Reynolds, and Karl E. Taeuber. 1968. "Population Trends and
    Residential Segregation Since 1960." Science 156 (March 1):
    953–56.
Fava, Sylvia. 1956. "Suburbanization as a Way of Life." American
    Sociological Review 21 (February): 34–43.
Gans, Herbert J. 1967. The Levittowners. New York: Pantheon.
Harris, Chauncy D. 1943. "Suburbs." American Journal of Sociology 47
    (May): 1–13.
Heberle, Rudolph. 1948. "Social Consequences of the Industrialization of
    Southern Cities." Social Forces 27 (October): 29–37.

Hodge, Patricia Leavy, and Philip M. Hauser. 1968. *The Challenge of America's Metropolitan Population Outlook, 1960–1985*. New York: Praeger.

Kitagawa, Evelyn M., and Karl E. Taeuber. 1963. *Local Community Fact Book, Chicago Metropolitan Area: 1960*. Chicago: Chicago Community Inventory.

Kramer, John, and Ingo Walter. 1967. "An Analysis of the Social Structure of an All Negro City." Mimeographed. St. Louis: University of Missouri.

Lieberson, Stanley. 1962. "Suburbs and Ethnic Residential Patterns." *American Journal of Sociology* 67 (May): 673–81.

——. 1963. *Ethnic Patterns in American Cities*. New York: Free Press.

Martin, Walter. 1956. "The Structuring of Social Relationships Engendered by Suburban Residence." *American Sociological Review* 21 (August): 446–53.

Riesman, David. 1957. "The Suburban Dislocation." *Annals of the American Academy of Political and Social Science* 312 (November): 123–47.

Rose, Harold M. 1965. "The All Negro Town: Its Evolution and Function." *Geographical Review* 55 (July): 362–81.

Schnore, Leo. 1957. "Satellites and Suburbs." *Social Forces* 36 (December): 121–27.

——. 1965. *The Urban Scene*. New York: Free Press.

Taeuber, Karl E., and Alma F. Taeuber. 1964a. "White Migration and Socio-Economic Differences between Cities and Suburbs." *American Sociological Review* 29 (October): 718–29.

——. 1964b. "The Negro as an Immigrant Group: Recent Trends in Racial and Ethnic Segregation in Chicago." *American Journal of Sociology* 69 (January): 374–82.

——. 1965a. *Negroes in Cities*. Chicago: Aldine.

——. 1965b. "The Changing Character of Negro Migration." *American Journal of Sociology* 70 (January): 429–41.

——. 1966. "The Negro Population in the United States." In *The American Negro Reference Book*, edited by John P. Davis. Englewood Cliffs, N.J.: Prentice-Hall.

U.S. Bureau of the Census. 1961a. *Census of Population: 1960*. PC(1)-27B.

——. 1961b. *Census of Population: 1960*, PC(1)-15B.

——. 1961c. *Census of Population: 1960*, PC(1)-20B.

——. 1961d. *Census of Population: 1960*, PC(1)-15A.

——. 1961e. *Census of Population: 1960*, PC(1)-34B.

——. 1961f. *Census of Housing: 1960*, HC(1)-20.

——. 1961g. *Census of Population: 1960*, PC(1)-37B.

——. 1962a. *Census of Housing: 1960*, HC(1)-11.

——. 1962b. *Census of Housing: 1960*, HC(1)-15.

——. 1962c. *Censuses of Population and Housing: 1960*, PHC(1)-26.

———. 1962d. *Censuses of Population and Housing: 1960*, PHC(1)-104, pt. 2.

———. 1963a. *Census of Population: 1960*, PC(3)-1D.

———. 1963b. *Census of Population: 1960*, PC(2)-2C.

———. 1965. "Summary of Special Censuses Conducted by the Bureau of the Census between Jan. 1 and Dec. 31, 1964." *Current Population Reports*, ser. P-28, no. 1388.

———. 1966a. "Summary of Special Censuses Conducted by the Bureau of the Census between Jan. 1 and Dec. 31, 1965." *Current Population Reports*, ser. P-28, no. 1420.

———. 1966b. *Census of Manufacturers: 1960*, MC63(3)-14.

———. 1966c. *Housing Construction Statistics: 1889–1964.*

———. 1966d. "Special Census of Westchester County, New York: April 6, 1965." *Current Population Reports*, ser. P-28, no. 1394.

———. 1966e. "Special Census of Oyster Bay Town, New York: April 26, 1965." *Current Population Reports*, ser. P-28, no. 1395.

———. 1966f. "Special Census of Hempstead Town, New York: March 15, 1965." *Current Population Reports*, ser. P-28, no. 1396.

———. 1966g. "Special Census of Rockland County, New York: April 28, 1966." *Current Population Reports*, ser. P-28, no. 1428.

———. 1967a. "Social and Economic Conditions of Negroes in the United States." *Current Population Reports*, ser. P-23, no. 24.

———. 1967b. "Population of the United States by Metropolitan and Non-Metropolitan Residence: April 1966 and 1960." *Current Population Reports*, ser. P-20, no. 167.

———. 1967c. "Summary of Special Censuses Conducted by the Bureau of the Census between January 1 and December 31, 1966." *Current Population Reports*, ser. P-28, no. 1447.

———. 1967d. "Income in 1966 of Families and Persons in the United States." *Current Population Reports*, ser. P-60, no. 53.

———. 1967e. "Special Census of Huntington Town, New York: May 13, 1967." *Current Population Reports*, ser. P-28, no. 1454.

———. 1967f. "Special Census of Babylon Town, New York: May 6, 1967." *Current Population Reports*, ser. P-28, no. 1456.

———. 1968a. "Summary of Special Censuses Conducted by the Bureau of the Census between January 1 and December 31, 1967." *Current Population Reports*, ser. P-28, no. 1466.

———. 1968b. "Summary of Special Censuses Conducted by the Bureau of the Census between January 1 and March 31, 1968." *Current Population Reports*, ser. P-28, no. 1468.

———. 1968c. "Summary of Special Censuses Conducted by the Bureau of the Census between April 1 and June 30, 1968." *Current Population Reports*, ser. P-28, no. 1474.

———. 1968d. "Housing Authorized by Building Permits and Public Contracts: 1967." *Construction Reports*, C40/C42-67-13.

———. 1968e. "Family Income Advances, Poverty Reduced in 1967." *Current Population Reports*, ser. P-60, no. 55.

——. 1968*f*. "Recent Trends in Social and Economic Conditions of Negroes in the United States." *Current Population Reports,* ser. P-23, no. 26.

——. 1968*g*. *Statistical Abstract of the United States: 1968.*

——. 1968*h*. "Special Census of Brookhaven Town, New York: May 6, 1968." *Current Population Reports,* ser. P-38, no. 1471.

——. 1968*i*. "Special Census of Smithtown Town, New York: May 6, 1968." *Current Population Reports,* ser. P-28, no. 1473.

——. 1969*a*. "Trends in Social and Economic Conditions in Metropolitan Areas." *Current Population Reports,* ser. P-23, no. 27.

——. 1969*b*. "Summary of Special Censuses Conducted by the Bureau of the Census between July 1 and September 30, 1968." *Current Population Reports,* ser. P-28, no. 1480.

——. 1969*c*. "Summary of Special Censuses Conducted by the Bureau of the Census between October 1 and December 31, 1968." *Current Population Reports,* ser. P-28, no. 1484.

——. 1969*d*. "Estimates of the Population of the United States and Components of Change: 1940 to 1969." *Current Population Reports,* ser. P-25, no. 418.

——. 1969*e*. "Farm Population of the United States: 1967." *Current Population Reports,* ser. P-27, no. 39.

——. 1969*f*. "Housing Authorized by Building Permits and Public Contracts." *Construction Reports,* C42-69-4.

U.S. Department of Housing and Urban Development. 1967. *Urban Renewal Project Characteristics: June 30, 1966.*

U.S. National Advisory Commission on Civil Disorders. 1968. *Report of the National Advisory Commission on Civil Disorders.*

U.S. President's Committee on Urban Housing. 1967. *The Report of the President's Committee on Urban Housing: Technical Studies,* vol. 1.

Wade, Richard C. 1964. *Slavery in Cities.* New York: Oxford University Press.

Whyte, William. 1957. *The Organization Man.* Garden City, N.Y.: Doubleday.

THE ALL-NEGRO TOWN:
ITS EVOLUTION AND FUNCTION

Harold M. Rose

A phenomenon that appears to have eluded urban geographers, urban sociologists, and others concerned with community development is the all-Negro town in the United States.[1] The existence of such towns has seldom come to the attention of persons who are not living near them, and the few previous works on the subject have generally focused attention on a single place. One of the objectives of the present study is to identify the universe of all-Negro towns on an operational basis; another is to detect the effects of socioeconomic development on their form and structure.

The term "all-Negro town" as it is here used applies to all places with a population of 1,000 or more of whom more than 95 per cent are classified as nonwhite. This percentage was thought to be a rational cutoff level, for the presence of whites at 5 per cent or less might be thought to represent a random occurrence. Within the limits of this definition nineteen places were identified as all-Negro towns (Fig. 1). On closer investigation of the data it was found that seven of them were statistical illusions. They are not separate places physically or politically but are nonpolitical appendages of larger places. However, instead of being completely ignored, they are retained and identified as "pseudo towns." The remaining twelve places, which are physically or politically separated from their nearest neighbors, constitute the primary focus of this study. In most of them the white population is less than 1 per cent, and in none of them are whites in positions of dominance.[2]

THE ALL-NEGRO TOWN AS A POLITICAL ENTITY

Of the twelve separate communities ten are politically independent, having been incorporated as villages or towns (Table I). Two are unincor-

ALL-NEGRO TOWNS

Robbins

Urbancrest   Glenarden   Lawnside
Brooklyn   Lincoln   Fairmount
Kinloch   Heights   Heights
                           Pleasant Hill
                      Lloyd Place Saratoga
                                   Place

Mound
Bayou   Bennetsville
N.   Grambling
Shreveport   Independent
         Greenwood   Dependent
Samtown   Pseudo
                                    POPULATION
                                    ○ 1000-2499
                                    ○ 2500-4999
                                    ○ 5000 & Over

                        Gifford

0   200   400
      Miles
                        Richmond
                        Heights

Figure 1

porated but are physically separate from the nearest neighbor; they are
therefore designated as dependent towns. The lack of a formal political
structure in these two towns probably reflects the recency of their having
attained the necessary threshold population to promote political identification. The incorporated all-Negro town invariably possesses a mayor-
council form of governmental organization. Although this is the form most
prevalent among the nation's municipalities,[3] it is generally considered to
predominate among working-class communities.

The pseudo towns are communities which are identified in the 1960
census as separate places but which are, in fact, economic appendages of

larger parent communities. The pseudo town, by lying beyond the political margin of the parent community, is politically disfranchised. It is difficult to account for the occurrence of such towns, but they are generally related to one or a combination of several factors: the historical development of the Negro community on the fringe of the parent;[4] the rapid expansion of the parent community, which frequently eliminates the open space that separated the two communities; and the deliberate manipulation of political boundaries to exclude the Negro community from access to the vote. Only one clear-cut example of the last was identified.[5]

All the pseudo towns are in the South; therefore the pattern of social and economic development in this section may do much to explain their occurrence. Pseudo towns, almost without exception, are situated in predominantly rural counties in which agriculture or agricultural processing industries are the major employers. The seven towns and their parent communities are Samtown, Louisiana (Alexandria, Louisiana); Greenwood, Alabama (Tuskegee, Alabama); Gifford, Florida (Vero Beach, Florida); Pleasant Hill, Saratoga Place, and Lloyd Place, Virginia (Suffolk, Virginia); and Bennettsville Southwest, South Carolina (Bennettsville, South Carolina).

TABLE I
Political Status of All-Negro Towns

Place	Incorporation		Place	Incorporation	
	Date	Form		Date	Form
Brooklyn, Ill.	1874	Village	Lincoln Heights, Ohio	1946	City
Mound Bayou, Miss.	1898	Village	Urbancrest, Ohio	1947	Village
	1912	Town	Kinloch, Mo.	1948	Town
Robbins, Ill.	1917	Village	Grambling, La.	1953	Town
Lawnside, N. J.	1926	Borough	North Shreveport, La.	Uninc.	
Fairmount Heights, Md.	1927	Town	Richmond Heights, Fla.	Uninc.	
Glenarden, Md.	1939	Town			

Sources: The Columbia Lippincott Gazetteer and personal communications with mayors of respective communities.

There appears to be little direct relationship between political status and size of population in the all-Negro towns. The smallest, a pseudo town, has only 22 persons more than the number established here as critical; the largest has some 7,800 residents. The second largest is a dependent town, with 7,700. None of the pseudo towns has more than 5,000 residents, though the largest has more than 4,000. The form and density of the all-Negro towns differ greatly, but the highest densities characterize those which are surrounded by other "suburban" communities. Density is generally lower in the older towns, as a result of the availability of larger tracts for development during the early period of growth. For example, North Shreveport, Louisiana, which displayed the most rapid growth during the fifties, encompasses the largest land area.

EMERGENCE OF THE ALL-NEGRO TOWN

The date of the emergence of the all-Negro town as a distinct entity is difficult to pinpoint, presumably because several of the towns did not originate as uniracial communities. However, sufficient general information is available to permit the towns to be placed in a temporal continuum. There appear to be four distinct periods of evolution: the pre-Civil War period; the post-Civil War period; the period of the "Great Migration" during and after World War I; and the post-World War II period.

Pre-Civil War Communities

It is rather paradoxical that the first all-Negro towns were of non-southern origin, but viewed within a historical-geographical framework the situation appears less strange. By 1840, the abolition movement had reached unprecedented heights, and a small band of dedicated individuals were lending their support to the organization of the Underground Railroad. The evidence suggests that the early all-Negro towns were related to the abolition movement and to the hostility of northerners and their fear that the North would soon be plagued by large numbers of fugitive slaves.[6] The first of these towns to evolve was Brooklyn, Illinois, on the American Bottoms across the river from St. Louis. Brooklyn did not originate as an all-Negro community but soon came to have a Negro majority, which assumed political control in 1910. The community was originally incorporated as Lovejoy, in honor of Elijah P. Lovejoy, the area's most vocal abolitionist.[7]

Following closely on the heels of Brooklyn came Lawnside, New Jersey, known originally as Free Haven and later as Snow Hill, across the Delaware from Philadelphia. The Philadelphia area was likewise the scene of extensive abolitionist activity. The Quaker population, deeply concerned with man's relations with his fellow man, became active in the operation of the Underground Railroad.[8] The site of Lawnside was purchased for Negroes by Quaker abolitionists in 1840, and the town began as a station on the Underground. It was incorporated in 1926.

Post-Civil War Communities

Four of the present all-Negro towns came into being after the Civil War: Mound Bayou, Mississippi; Kinloch, Missouri; Urbancrest, Ohio; and Grambling, Louisiana. Several other towns that came into existence at this time are now nothing more than remnants of once viable communities.[9]

The oldest and youngest of the four towns are Mound Bayou and Grambling respectively. Mound Bayou, unlike its contemporaries, had a specific *raison d'être*, based on a philosophic principle. Isaiah T. Montgomery, a former slave and body servant of Jefferson Davis, thought the way to escape from the abuse that had been heaped on the Negro during slavery was to develop an all-Negro community, and he did something about it. The original site of Montgomery's community was Davis Bend, on the Mississippi south of Vicksburg. Because of its lowland site, Davis Bend was plagued by frequent floods, and after eight years a new site was developed farther north in a part of the delta that was little more than wilderness. This site, cleared in 1887 by Montgomery and a relative, Benjamin T. Green, was called Mound Bayou.[10] Most of the original residents of Davis Bend willingly moved north and became residents of Montgomery's new town.[11]

Grambling, a few miles west of Ruston, grew up at the turn of the century around a sawmill. A local parish clerk assigned to the evolving community the name Grambling, in honor of the millowner.[12] Since 1905, the town has been the site of a Negro institution of higher education.

The two northern communities of Kinloch, Missouri, and Urbancrest, Ohio, are known to have originated in the late nineteenth century (about 1890). Although there is little information relating to the specifics of their development, it is known that during this period voluntary northward movement of Negroes, with or without assistance, was common. Many businessmen and politicians imported Negroes into northern communities for the purpose of altering the labor market,[13] breaking strikes or—allegedly—casting illegal ballots.[14] Both Kinloch and Urbancrest developed in rural areas, though they were less than fifteen miles from the urban centers of St. Louis and Columbus respectively. Thus both communities probably emerged as agricultural villages on the fringes of urban complexes.

Communities of the Great Migration

The advent of war in Europe in 1914 slowed down European emigration to the United States and thereby opened new opportunities in the northern job market for southern Negroes. Their South-to-North migration was intensified by the boll-weevil panic of 1910–20[15] and extended into the twenties as Congress passed a national immigration act restricting the number of aliens allowed to enter the country. This fact, coupled with the fact that cotton prices did not regain their former levels until 1922, increased the outward movement of agricultural workers from the South.

During the first thirty years after emancipation Negro migration was directed to the West.[16] But by the turn of the century the course had altered; Deep South residents moved up the Mississippi Valley, and residents of the Piedmont followed the Atlantic seaboard. Four all-Negro towns emerged: Robbins, Illinois; Lincoln Heights, Ohio; Fairmount Heights, Maryland; and Glenarden, Maryland. The evidence suggests that these communities, like Mound Bayou, have been all-Negro since their inception. Each was developed on the fringe of a major metropolitan complex—Chicago, Cincinnati, and Washington, D.C. Of the four communities, only the rise of Robbins is well documented.

Robbins, southwest of Chicago, was incorporated as a village in 1917, before the first large wave of southern Negro migrants reached the central city. It was one of several communities to evolve during Chicago's "railroad era,"[17] which saw the radial extension of rail nets from a central hub into various sectors of the city. Robbins about 1921 was "not attractive physically. It is not on a car line and there is no pretense of paved streets, or even sidewalks. The houses are homemade . . . Tar paper, roofing paper, homemade tiles, hardly seem sufficient to shut out the weather."[18] Robbins was the brainchild of Eugene S. Robbins, a Negro realtor, who developed a site on the poorly drained flats just southwest of Blue Island for an independent community made up of Negro occupants only.[19] Thus out of the interest of a single individual, but undoubtedly a strong personality, a community sprang that has essentially maintained the characteristics desired by its founder. Industrialization of the Calumet region during this period also promoted the growth of Negro settlement in the communities of Blue Island and Harvey.

Lincoln Heights, north of Cincinnati and long a place of Negro abode, was organized in 1926. Its development was promoted by a lumber company, which sold tracts of land to Negroes only.[20] By 1960, this community had attained the status of the largest all-Negro town in the country and probably one of the more stable.

The two Maryland communities, on the margin of the nation's capital, evolved after World War I. The reason for their evolution is not clear but is thought to be associated with conditions of an earlier period.[21]

Post-World War II Communities

Only two all-Negro towns have evolved in what might be called the modern period. Both are in the South and are in metropolitan areas. Their locations were largely determined by housing developers producing for a Negro market, a common phenomenon in the South.

North Shreveport, Louisiana, the larger of the two, is a few miles northwest of the regional metropolis of Shreveport. The town was created almost by default. In 1950 a population smaller than the minimum employed here in identifying all-Negro towns was living on the site of the present North Shreveport. The construction of an expressway through a section of Shreveport occupied by Negroes resulted in a demand for alternative housing. Housing developers took advantage of the existence of the incipient Negro settlement on a large tract near the edge of town to relocate Negroes displaced by the expressway. This node, then, served as the central organism around which North Shreveport developed. In 1960, the town had more than 7,700 residents, making it the second-ranking all-Negro town in the country.

Richmond Heights, Florida, the southernmost all-Negro town, had its inception in the late forties.[22] Unlike North Shreveport, whose rapid growth was associated with the forced dislocation of central-city residents, Richmond Heights evolved out of a recognized need for the expansion of Negro housing. It offers the best housing currently occupied by Negroes in the Miami Standard Metropolitan Statistical Area.

The foregoing comments have been made in an attempt to place the all-Negro communities in proper perspective. The very fact that the older ones have survived does much to support a recent statement by Killian and Grigg:[23]

> For over two hundred years the Negro American has not been a stranger in the land. He has nonetheless found himself isolated economically and socially, in the land of his birth. Whether on the plantations of the Old South, in the Smoky Hollows of southern towns, or in the Black Belts of the cities, Negroes have created and sustained Negro communities which are enduring, not evanescent realities.

Although the authors are referring to Negro islands within larger communities, their remarks appear to be equally valid for all-Negro towns. Their evolution is likewise considered a normal process by Gist, who notes that the tendency for racial or ethnic groups to form separate communities, "either voluntarily or involuntarily, is apparently a universal characteristic of human beings."[24] The fact should be acknowledged that some of the all-Negro towns have evolved as a result of both voluntary and involuntary actions. Let us now take a closer look at the present status and function of these towns.

THE ALL-NEGRO TOWN AND THE SUBURB CONCEPT

All but two of the twelve all-Negro towns are situated along the outer fringes of standard metropolitan statistical areas, a factor that should allow us to observe how well the all-Negro town fits the "suburb" concept. The two exceptions lie in rural farm environments. One of them, Grambling, has exceeded the upper population limit of places designated as rural, but because its urban designation rests on inclusion of its college population in the censuses of 1950 and 1960,[25] it seems fair to regard the town as essentially rural.

The predominance of all-Negro towns in metropolitan rings is often a reflection of the occupational advantages associated with such locations before the establishment of efficient transportation systems. Of course the rise of the newer communities, such as Richmond Heights and North Shreveport, must be otherwise accounted for.

Ten all-Negro towns are situated within metropolitan rings of central cities. Both Brooklyn and Lawnside, the oldest of these towns, are economically dependent on central cities other than the principal central city of the metropolitan complex. The spatial arrangement of the ten communities permits their evaluation within a suburban framework.[26]

The suburb concept, although employed extensively in the social-science literature, is still without a universally accepted definition.[27] But it is generally assumed that residence in a suburban community represents the middle-class ideal, the American dream. Thus, we are here concerned with determination of the status of the all-Negro town on a metropolitan fringe as suburban or nonsuburban. The age of most of the all-Negro towns precludes the possibility of their having originated as suburban communities. In view of the factors responsible for their evolution, it is clear that suburbanization, if it exists, has been superimposed on an already existing community type.

Recent studies of suburban communities have been limited to places of more than 10,000 population. It appears reasonable that any of the all-Negro towns situated within a metropolitan complex can be analyzed within this frame of reference, since the minimum limiting population of 1,000 employed here is to the 10,000 figure as the Negro population of the country is to the national total.[28]

Two basic types of suburban communities exist in the United States: those in which most of the population are employed in the town itself, referred to as satellites[29] or industrial suburbs;[30] and those in which most

TABLE II

Variations in the Extent of Substandard Housing in All-Negro Towns, Nearest Neighbors, and Central-City Samples*

All-Negro Towns	Substandardness Percentage	Nearest Neighbor	Substandardness Percentage	Central-City Sample	Substandardness Percentage
Brooklyn	81	Venice	39	East St. Louis	69
Kinloch	62	Berkeley	30	St. Louis	41
Glenarden	53	Carrollton	7	Washington	6
Urbancrest	52	Grove City	5	Columbus	29
North Shreveport	49	North Highlands	9	Shreveport	33
Fairmount Heights	44	Seat Pleasant	6	Washington	6
Robbins	43	Midlothian	9	Chicago	40
Lawnside	34	Magnolia	2	Camden	69
Lincoln Heights	27	Woodlawn	6	Cincinnati	81
Richmond Heights	1	Perrine	38	Miami	20

*Compiled from United States census reports.

of the population commute to work, commonly called dormitory towns. It is this second category to which the term "suburb" is most frequently applied; in 1960 it comprised about 60 per cent of the nation's suburban units.[31] All the metropolitan all-Negro towns fall into the category of dormitory towns. Generally their employment potential is restricted by the small volume of retail trade. Robbins, Illinois, provides a more extensive variety of retail services, and of better quality, than any of the other communities. The local availability of basic services and convenience goods appears to reflect the distance and efficiency of transportation between the all-Negro town and the major or secondary central city.

The occupational structure of the ten metropolitan-ring communities makes it unlikely that they would be characterized by the way of life usually attributed to suburban developments, though it has been reported that a phenomenon known as the "working class" suburb is on the increase. Dobriner describes the "working class" as "those of the work force who do manual labor, who join unions, who earn a 'wage' rather than a 'salary,' and whose characteristic is the blue rather than the white collar."[32] Each of the all-Negro towns is characterized by a predominance of blue-collar workers. The highest percentage of white-collar workers, 26, is found in Fairmount Heights, Maryland, a community on the fringe of the nation's capital. The lowest percentage, 10, is found in North Shreveport, Louisiana. Low percentages are characteristic of most of the South; for as Hart[33] pointed out nearly a decade ago, a high percentage of the labor force is employed in service industries in areas having a high Negro ratio. The Shreveport Standard Metropolitan Statistical Area was 34 per cent Negro in 1960.

Because a multiplicity of variables have frequently been employed in the description of suburban communities, a single variable, the amount of substandard housing, has been selected as an index of suburbanization. As people tend to have physical images of what constitutes suburbia, this seems a feasible solution. But the role of other variables such as median family income, age of housing, extent of home ownership, and economic stability as factors influencing the extent of substandardness should be kept in mind.[34] The city image is not fixed; for "the city is a living organism, . . . it has a history, and the form of the city at any moment is both a description of its present life form and a record of its past."[35]

Analysis of variance was employed to determine whether the all-Negro towns and their nearest neighbors could have been drawn from the same universe on the basis of substandardness in housing. The nearest neighbor is the community closest to the individual all-Negro town. These communities, with few exceptions, might be singled out as "all-white" towns, by use of the same criteria that were employed in establishing the identity of the Negro community. It was found that the variations of the means of the two groups were too high for them to have been drawn from the same universe, at the 0.05, 0.01, and 0.001 levels of significance. We may therefore conclude that these communities, though separated by less intervening area than other places, do not reflect similarity of image based on substandardness of housing.

The failure of the first test to establish support for the existence of two fairly homogeneous groups of communities led to the selection of another set of data for analysis. A random sample was drawn from census tracts in each of the central cities of the standard metropolitan statistical areas in which the all-Negro towns are located. The sampling characteristics were based on similarity, in terms of size and racial mix, to the outlying Negro communities. The purpose of the analysis was to determine if the all-Negro towns, in terms of their projected image, were more like their nearest neighbor or the central-city sample. The variance ratio proved to be smaller than in the earlier analysis. But even in this case the null hypothesis would be rejected at the 0.05 and 0.01 levels of significance. Employing the substandardness index, the similarity between the all-Negro town and the central-city sample was greater than in the earlier example. This close similarity, then, leads us to reject the thesis that all-Negro towns as a group represent suburban communities.

Hartman and Hook,[36] using 1950 housing data, found that "dependent" urban places within the large urbanized areas of the country were characterized by substandardness of less than 13 per cent. If we employ this index, which is nonfunctional, we find that only Richmond Heights, Florida, of the all-Negro towns, can be strictly classified as a suburban community, and even it must be categorized as a "working class" suburb. Richmond Heights likewise fits the functional definition of a suburban community, as opposed to a satellite community.

THE ALL-NEGRO TOWN IN A RURAL SETTING

Two all-Negro towns are situated in a rural farm environment and have not yet come under metropolitan dominance. These two "Deep South" communities differ in evolution and modern role from their northern counterparts.

The older of the two, Mound Bayou, Mississippi, lies in the productive cotton lands of Bolivar County, the South's largest cotton-producing county. Mound Bayou fits well into the central-place scheme, as a provider of goods and services associated with a second-order town. It has several service stations, a restaurant and hotel, two hospitals, a post office, a school, a cotton gin, and a cotton broker. Negro farmers own 37,000 acres of farmland in the vicinity and are moving from monoculture to a diversified farm economy.[37] Most of the farmers currently developing holdings contiguous or near to Mound Bayou are owner-operators. In recent years the farm population, especially the sharecropper element, has declined.[38]

Grambling, Louisiana, represents a special case. It is an educational center. Educational attainment, median family income, and number of white-collar workers are higher here than in any of the other communities. None of the other all-Negro towns are so totally dependent on the performance of a single function. Without the presence of Grambling College, this would in all probability be just another small north Louisiana village.

PRESENT AND FUTURE DEVELOPMENTS

Changes since 1960 in several of the all-Negro towns may eventually result in a change of status. Robbins, Illinois, for example, is currently witnessing a rapid expansion of its housing. Only in Robbins is the increase in housing in an all-Negro town comparable with that in the nearest neighbor community. The new housing on the western and southern margins includes split-levels and other characteristic suburban forms, ranging in price from about $13,000 to $32,000. The situation is, of course, transforming the Robbins image. But for Robbins to become a truly suburban community the older housing, reminiscent of the Negro section in many small southern communities, would have to be eliminated. As the Negro population in the central city becomes more middle class in its orientation, segments of it will seek the comforts of suburbia. The present group of blue-collar workers will probably look for communities such as Robbins, where no social obstacles bar entry.

Lincoln Heights, Ohio, with an already low level of substandardness among all-Negro towns, has reached its physical limits of expansion. But several former residents have been responsible for the establishment of a new all-Negro community, Hollydale, a typical suburban tract development of some one hundred units a few miles west of the original community on Hamilton County's rural-urban fringe. Glenarden, Maryland, in rapidly suburbanizing Prince Georges County northeast of Washington, is likewise undergoing a face-lifting as new tract developments are being completed. The expansion of the federal highway system in this area will probably increase Glenarden's attractiveness as a place of residence. Lawnside, New Jersey, one of the older and more stable of the all-Negro towns, appears to be slow-growing, and considering the age of its housing it is likely to deteriorate. However, the median family income of $4,917 is the highest among all the Negro communities in the metropolitan fringe.

Suburbanization of the remaining communities might be more difficult, for several reasons: the economic plight of their residents; the high density of housing; the economic instability of the central-city residents; the failure of developers to recognize a potential market; and, finally, the opposition to further promotion and maintenance of all-Negro communities.

Kinloch, Missouri, probably has the greatest potential for suburbanization, though in the past it has not tended to attract central-city residents. Kinloch has recently been described as a low-status fringe community that is "more familistic than the average central city Negro population."[39] There appears to be little prospect that Brooklyn, Illinois, a second community in the St. Louis Standard Metropolitan Statistical Area, can easily alter its status. It is currently the most depressed town in the group, a fact that can be attributed partly to its age and partly to the current economic situation in the East St. Louis area. "The city is not attracting new industry. Of its eighteen manufacturing establishments employing over 125 employees, all but two originated before 1930 . . . East St. Louis has been losing industry."[40] Since Brooklyn is virtually dependent on East St. Louis and the adjacent Granite City as sources of employment, its fortune is tied to the prevailing economic situation in these and other nearby employment centers.

A final factor that does much to deny suburban identity to several of the all-Negro towns is the prevalence of multiple-dwelling units. These units frequently represent the result of the community's participation in urban renewal programs as a means of eliminating zones of substandard housing. Only Kinloch of the metropolitan-ring communities in St. Louis County possesses a public-housing authority.[41] Slum clearance and suburbanization can hardly be thought of as compatible forces.

The future of the all-Negro town as a distinct entity will be specifically related to the degree of community attachment or identification, to the presence or absence of barriers to Negro settlement in suburbia, to the changing economic status of a segment of the central-city Negro population and the prevailing philosophy of militant groups relative to the maintenance of such communities, and to the absence of a substantial tax base to provide expanded domestic services. In short, the future of the towns is subject to the operation of a complex set of variables whose behavior is difficult to predict.

LITERATURE CITED

1. In a 1962 article describing a single all-Negro town, Livy T. Wilson stated that "in the United States there are three incorporated towns which are predominantly Negro" (Housing Developments in

Grambling, Louisiana, A Southern Negro Town, 1940 to 1960, *Negro History Bull.*, Vol. 26, 1962, pp. 99–102; reference on p. 99). In the same year another writer indicated that there were only two Negro towns in the country (Louis E. Lomax: The Negro Revolt [New York, 1962], p. 174).

2. The lower limit of 1,000 was selected for two reasons: such places can be easily identified in United States census reports; and communities of this size or larger containing the indicated nonwhite percentage are likely to be viable.

3. Herbert Kaufman: Politics and Policies in State and Local Governments (Englewood Cliffs, N.J., 1963), p. 49.

4. Rudolf Heberle: Social Consequences of the Industrialization of Southern Cities, *Social Forces*, Vol. 27, 1948–49, pp. 29–37; reference on p. 34.

5. In 1957 eligible Negro voters in Tuskegee, Alabama, outnumbered whites about three to one, yet only a small number had ever been registered. Increasing demands by the Negro majority for enfranchisement led to the gerrymandering of the larger segment of the Negro community out of the political limits of the city of Tuskegee. In November 1960, the Supreme Court of the United States overruled this action (Bernard Taper: Gomillion versus Lightfoot: The Tuskegee Gerrymander Case [New York, 1962]) and thereby eliminated the pseudo town of Greenwood.

6. Louis Filler: The Crusade against Slavery, 1830–1860 (New York, 1960), pp. 78–81; Jacque Voegeli: The Northwest and the Race Issue, 1861–1862, *Mississippi Valley Hist. Rev.*, Vol. 50, 1963–64, pp. 235–51.

7. "Illinois: A Descriptive and Historical Guide" (Federal Writers' Project, American Guide Series; revised edit.; Chicago, 1947), pp. 490–91. The local school and post office still bear the name Lovejoy.

8. "New Jersey: A Guide to Its Present and Past" (Federal Writers' Project, American Guide Series; New York, 1939), pp. 123 and 600.

9. One such community is Nicodemus, Kansas.

10. Maurice E. Jackson: Mound Bayou—A Study in Social Development (unpublished Master's thesis, University of Alabama, 1937), pp. 27–28 and 30.

11. Vernon L. Wharton: The Negro in Mississippi, 1865–1890 (Chapel Hill, North Carolina, 1947), p. 42.

12. Wilson, op. cit. [see footnote 1 above], p. 99.

13. Herman G. Gutman: Reconstruction in Ohio: Negroes in the Hocking Valley Coal Mines in 1873 and 1874, *Labor History*, Vol. 3, 1962, pp. 243–64; Irving Dilliard: Civil Liberties of Negroes in Illinois since 1865, *Journ. Illinois State Hist. Soc.*, Vol. 46, 1963, pp. 592–624.

14. Elliot Rudwick: East St. Louis and the "Colonization Conspiracy" of 1916, *Journ. of Negro Education*, Vol. 33, 1964, pp. 35–42.

15. Oscar Handlin: The American People in the Twentieth Century (revised edit.; Boston, 1963), p. 111.

16. Oscar Handlin: The Newcomers (Garden City, N.Y., 1962), p. 48.

17. "A Social Geography of Metropolitan Chicago" (Chicago, 1960), pp. 13–14.

18. "The Negro in Chicago" (Chicago Commission on Race Relations, Chicago, 1922), pp. 138–39.

19. "Illinois: A . . . Guide" [see footnote 7 above], p. 398.

20. Personal interview, April 12, 1963, with an original purchaser of a tract in Lincoln Heights. The original seller of the tracts was the Lewin Lumber Company.

21. Although these communities have evolved during the twentieth century, Eunice Grier has stated that the presence of Negroes in what is now suburban Washington is not a recent phenomenon; "they have been there since before the Civil War, for the most part" (Housing in Washington: Hearings before the United States Commission on Civil Rights [Washington, D.C., 1962], p. 322).

22. Land was cleared for development in 1949, but the first houses were not constructed until 1951 (personal communication, March 23, 1964, from Mrs. Elizabeth Virrick, Director Coconut Grove Slum Clearance Committee, Miami, Florida).

23. Lewis M. Killian and Charles M. Grigg: Racial Crisis in America (Englewood Cliffs, N.J., 1964), p. 124.

24. Noel P. Gist: Urbanism at Mid-Century, *Population Rev.*, Vol. 3, No. 1, 1959, pp. 33–42; reference on p. 37.

25. Student enrollment at Grambling College in 1960 was 2,724.

26. The mere presence of an all-Negro town within a metropolitan ring does not make it a suburban community. Schnore in a recent study employed metropolitan-ring community synonomously with suburb, but he recognized the shortcomings of the usage (Leo F. Schnore: City-Suburban Income Differentials in Metropolitan Areas, *Amer. Sociol. Rev.*, Vol. 27, 1962, pp. 252–55; reference on p. 255).

27. Leo F. Schnore: Satellites and Suburbs, *Social Forces*, Vol. 36, 1957–58, pp. 121–27; reference on p. 121.

28. The term "Negro suburb" has been used in association with metropolitan-ring communities with a population of more than 10,000 whose nonwhite ratio is more than 20 per cent. Such terminology is misleading by its very nature, and even more so when a strict definition is assigned to the concept, utilizing variables generally thought to characterize suburban communities. See Leo F. Schnore and Harry P. Sharp: Racial Changes in Metropolitan Areas, 1950–60, *Social Forces*, Vol. 41, 1962–63, pp. 247–53; reference on p. 252.

29. Schnore, Satellites and Suburbs [see footnote 27 above].

30. Chauncy D. Harris: Suburbs, *Amer. Journ. of Sociology*, Vol. 49, 1943-44, pp. 1-13; reference on p. 8.

31. Victor Jones, Richard L. Forstall, and Andrew Collver: Economic and Social Classification of Cities, *Public Management*, Vol. 45, 1963, pp. 98-101; reference on p. 100.

32. William M. Dobriner: Class in Suburbia (Englewood Cliffs, N.J., 1963), p. 49.

33. John Fraser Hart: Functions and Occupational Structures of Cities of the American South, *Annals Assn. of Amer. Geogrs.*, Vol. 45, 1955, pp. 269-86; reference on pp. 279-80.

34. Geographers have not been consistent in the selection of variables to measure substandardness. Hartman and Hook used the Census Bureau's 1950 concept of substandardness (George W. Hartman and John C. Hook: Substandard Urban Housing in United States: A Quantitative Analysis, *Econ. Geogr.*, Vol. 32, 1956, pp. 95-114), and in a more recent study Fuchs used contract monthly rent as a measure of housing quality (Roland J. Fuchs: Intraurban Variation of Residential Quality, ibid., Vol. 36, 1960, pp. 313-25).

35. Joseph R. Passomoreau: The Emergence of City Form, *in* Urban Life and Form (edited by Werner Z. Hirsch; New York and London, 1963), p. 18.

36. Op. cit. [see footnote 34 above], p. 99. The term "'dependent' urban places" is interpreted to mean suburban places.

37. "Mound Bayou, Mississippi, 75th Anniversary, July 12-15, 1962" [brochure], pp. 43-45.

38. The Mississippi State University recently received a federal Area Redevelopment grant to study the feasibility of expanding industrial employment opportunities for Mound Bayou residents.

39. Scott A. Greer: Governing the Metropolis (New York, 1962), p. 86.

40. Theodore V. Purcell: Blue Collar Man (Cambridge, Mass., 1960), pp. 44-47.

41. "Background for Action" (University City, Mo., 1957), p. 48.

GROWTH, DEVELOPMENT, AND ISOLATION OF AN
ALL-BLACK CITY: KINLOCH, MISSOURI

Robert T. Ernst

The social geography of ethnic and racial minorities in the United States has become, in recent decades, a topic of much interest and research specialization among American geographers.[1] There is a growing body of literature concerning the locational behavior and characteristics of such minority groups.[2] Much of the current geographic research on minority groups is focused on black Americans, as is evidenced in articles by Hart,[3] Calef and Nelson,[4] Pred,[5] Lowry,[6] Morrill,[7] Rose,[8] Deskins,[9] and others. The majority of these articles concentrate on three major facets of black geographic experience: rural to urban migration, inner-city ghettos and slums, and central city versus suburban residence.

However, patterns of black settlement are much more complex than to be constrained by the limited description "urban." Hart,[10] Wheeler and Brunn,[11] and Hesslink,[12] have studied urban to rural black migration in the Great Lakes area; Hill,[13] Rose,[14] and many others[15] have been concerned with all-black towns; Karl and Alma Taeuber,[16] Farley and Taeuber,[17] and Farley[18] have published research on black suburbs. Documentation of the emergence of these settlement patterns illustrates the necessity of more and detailed areal research into the origin, development, and potential of these patterns as distinct from the prototypical black urban experience.

The principal purpose of this paper involves continuation of geographic research into the universe of all-black towns and cities as a distinct urban entity separate from biracial communities and central city ghettos. However, only an extremely limited amount of geographic research has been gathered relating to all-black towns and cities. In fact, one of the few geographic articles concerning this subject is the previously mentioned work by Harold M. Rose.[19] Other than Rose's contribution, very little geographic research dealing with these communities is available. Almost all of the research which has been performed is nongeographic and involves examination of social, political, and economic factors of all-black communities, while areal characteristics of all-black towns and cities either have been ignored, or at best, neglected.

To be able to form valid generalizations concerning all-black settlements as they now exist, and to be able to predict the future of such settlements specific information must be available concerning such communities. The lack of detailed observations dealing with geographic realities of individual all-black towns and cities prevents construction of valid generalizations concerning the present and future of the universe of such settlements.

This paper is a case study specifically concerned with the geographic significance of the development and present situation of one community identified by Rose as an all-black city—Kinloch, Missouri. The research is related directly to several of the conclusions of Rose's work.

"The future of all-Negro towns as a distinct entity will be specifically related . . . to the presence or absence of barriers to Negro settlement in suburbia . . . and to the absence of a substantial tax base to provide expanded domestic services."[20]

Accordingly, this paper documents the precise nature and degree of such barriers in Kinloch and present socioeconomic characteristics of the residents in an attempt to further understanding of all-black towns and cities in general.

DEFINITION OF ALL-BLACK TOWN AND CITY

Harold Rose, in his seminal study of 1965, identified the universe of all-black towns.[21] However, Rose neglected to differentiate between towns and cities and somewhat arbitrarily classified all-black settlements as towns and pseudo-towns with little justification for such separation. In addition, in the several years since his research, many changes have occurred in the number and distribution of racial settlements. These factors, coupled with a new enthusiasm among American geographers for racial research, are sufficient to warrant a detailed redefinition and reexamination of the universe of all-black towns and cities in the United States.[22]

The term "all-black town" is defined operationally as all places, incorporated and unincorporated, with populations ranging from 1,000 to 2,499, of whom 90 per cent or more are nonwhite.[23] "All-black city" includes all places of 2,500 or more of whom 90 per cent or more are nonwhite.

Threshold values of 1,000 and 2,500 are used for two reasons: communities of these minimum sizes are enumerated separately in the United States Census reports,[24] and, as such, data are readily available. In addition, towns and cities of these sizes have the capacity of developing economic, social, and political characteristics commonly associated with urban places.

The second part of the definition, "90 per cent or more are nonwhite," is used as data do not exist in any other form. The United States Census reports urban places having a population of 1,000 or more by per cent nonwhite rather than black. Consequently, great care must be exercised to determine if there are large numbers of other racial groups (Indians, Orientals, etc.) present that might bias the information. The limit of 90 per cent is utilized as 10 per cent or less white population is thought to result from chance occurrence and does not restrict or prevent the appropriate use of the term "all-black."

There are several difficulties in operationalizing "all-black town and city" in the above manner. First, threshold populations of 1,000 and 2,500 are arbitrary figures justified only partially by citing ease in identification and data limitations. A second problem, related to the first, involves using legal limits of incorporated towns or cities to determine minimum population thresholds. These arbitrary limits may have the effect of excluding communities with a small population within the city limits but a sizable rural population which may be well integrated areally and socioeconomically with the urban center.

The nature and availability of data in the United States Census reports made these problems unavoidable; furthermore, the information is simply not available in any other source. Consequently, these problems, although difficult to resolve, are not so overwhelming as to prevent utilization of the data, if some limitations are placed on the generalizations derived from them.

DELIMITING THE UNIVERSE OF ALL-BLACK TOWNS AND CITIES

When all-black towns and cities are defined as places having 1,000 persons or more in the United States, a total of thirty-seven such centers are identified. In terms of population size, these communities range from 1,100 to over 23,000 persons (Table 1), with the percentage black varying from the definitional minimum 90.0 per cent to 99.9 per cent.

Table 1 also shows that twenty-four (65 per cent) all-black towns and cities are contained within boundaries of Standard Metropolitan Statistical Areas. The remaining thirteen towns and cities are not associated with other SMSAs or urbanized areas, though eight of these communities

TABLE 1
All-Black Towns and Cities by State

State	Towns and Cities	Population	Part of an SMSA	Percent Black
Alabama (1)				
	Hobson City	1,123	No	99.8
California (1)				
	West Compton (u)[a]	5,748	Yes	90.0
Florida (13)				
	Browns Village (u)	23,442	Yes	91.8
	Browardale (u)	17,444	Yes	90.5
	Bunche Park (u)	5,773	Yes	97.9
	Fort Myers Southeast (u)	3,150	No	96.4
	Goulds (u)	5,772	Yes	90.7
	Memphis (u)	3,207	No	96.0
	Richmond Heights	6,663	Yes	99.9
	Belle Glade Camp (u)	1,892	Yes	92.0
	Dade City East (u)	1,163	Yes	99.0
	Eatonville	2,024	Yes	99.9
	Harlem	2,006	No	99.0
	Midway Canaan	2,060	Yes	92.0
	South Apopka (u)	2,293	Yes	91.0
Georgia (1)				
	Phillipsburg (u)	2,335	No	99.0
Illinois (3)				
	East Chicago Heights	5,000	Yes	98.2
	Robbins	9,641	Yes	98.1
	Brooklyn	1,702	Yes	99.9
Louisiana (4)				
	Grambling	4,407	No	99.2
	Samtown (u)	4,210	No	99.5
	Scotlandville (u)	22,557	Yes	91.8
	Plaquemine Southwest (u)	1,224	No	97.0
Maryland (2)				
	Chapel Oaks-Cedar Heights (u)	6,049	Yes	99.6
	Fairmont Heights	1,972	Yes	97.0

[a]The symbol (u) indicates an unincorporated town or city.

TABLE 1 (continued)

State	Towns and Cities	Population	Part of an SMSA	Percent Black
Mississippi (3)				
	West Gulfport (u)	6,996	Yes	91.8
	Mound Bayou	2,008	No	98.5
	Tunica North (u)	1,325	No	92.0
Missouri (1)				
	Kinloch	5,629	Yes	99.1
New Jersey (1)				
	Lawnside	2,757	Yes	99.0
Ohio (1)				
	Lincoln Heights	6,099	Yes	99.1
Texas (3)				
	Prairie View (u)	3,589	Yes	98.7
	McNair (u)	2,339	Yes	96.0
	Sunrise (u)	1,213	Yes	93.0
Virginia (3)				
	Lloyd Place (u)	2,368	No	99.0
	Pleasant Hill (u)	2,277	No	99.0
	Saratoga Place (u)	1,245	No	99.0

Source: Census of Population, United States Bureau of the Census, General Population Characteristics (PC(1)), 1970.

(Samtown, Louisiana; Lloyd Place, Pleasant Hill, and Saratoga Place, Virginia; Hobson City, Alabama; Fort Myers Southeast, and Memphis, Florida; and Phillipsburg, Georgia) are located within ten miles of a city with a population exceeding 10,000. Thus, all-black settlements are as urban oriented as the total population of blacks living within the United States.

The universe of all-black towns and cities is characterized more by the small towns, with eighteen, or about half of the total, in the 1,000–2,499 category, and only three (8 per cent) with more than 10,000 inhabitants (Table 1). Almost two thirds of the towns and cities are unincorporated, and twelve, or 50 per cent, of these unincorporated places are in the 1,000–2,499 category (Table 1).

The distribution of all-black towns and cities is quite uneven in that thirty or 81 per cent of the towns and cities are located in the South.[25] Florida alone accounts for thirteen (43 per cent) of these places, many of which can be explained as a result of the widespread use of migratory black laborers.

The Study Area

Kinloch, Missouri, is located in the St. Louis Standard Metropolitan Statistical Area (Figure 1), approximately fifteen miles north-northwest of downtown St. Louis. The population, according to the 1970 Census,[26] is 5,578, of which only one permanent resident, a Catholic priest, is white;

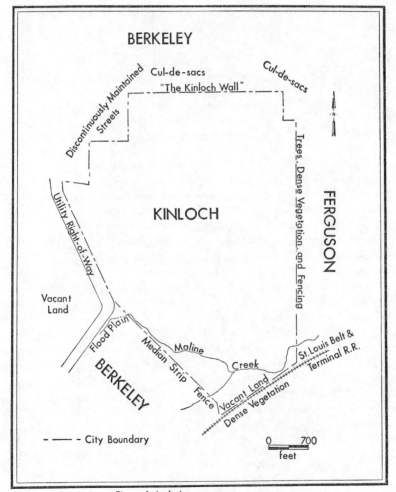

Figure 1: Isolation

all other residents are black.[27] Included in St. Louis County (Figure 2), Kinloch is a separate legal entity, having been granted a charter as city by the state of Missouri in 1948.[28]

Kinloch is surrounded completely by two suburbs (Berkeley and Ferguson), which are almost all-white (Figure 2). In addition, and more important, Kinloch is isolated from these communities by high fences, cul-de-sacs and dead-end streets, green belts, and lack of proper road maintenance at the city limits of the white communities. Kinloch also, for all

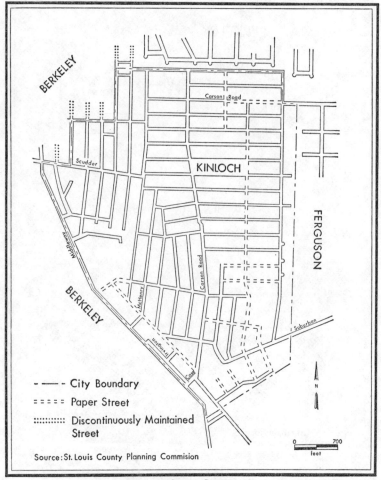

Figure 2: Street Patterns

practical purposes, totally lacks an economic resource base, having few service centers, only two small light manufacturing plants, and no heavy industry. Thus, residents of Kinloch are forced to go outside their community into the surrounding St. Louis SMSA for employment and for most consumer activities.

Therefore, the specific problem area is Kinloch, Missouri, an all-black city, isolated physically and socially from surrounding white communities, with little employment and consumer-oriented opportunities available for the inhabitants within the black community.

GENERAL SETTING

To anyone unfamiliar with the physical reality of Kinloch, the best introduction is a description of the landscape bordering the main thoroughfare to Kinloch, Carson Road, from Berkeley into Kinloch. Carson Road is not only the principal traffic artery servicing Kinloch, but it is the only major road that penetrates the all-black community. Theoretically, it extends completely through Kinloch. Actually, it is incomplete with almost two blocks of unpaved and totally impassible right-of-way in the black community. However, at the Berkeley city limits, Carson Road again is fully maintained.

Basically, Carson Road is north-south oriented and extends many miles through numerous municipalities of St. Louis County south of Kinloch. The section of road to be examined, however, begins at Interstate Highway 70 and continues north into Kinloch. Near the Interstate Highway, the area traversed by the street is typical of many older suburbs of the county, with a mixture of brick and frame single-family residences and several newer apartment complexes. The houses and lawns are neat and well kept and are within the $18,000 to $25,000 price range.[29]

The approach to the city limits of Kinloch indicates no appreciable change in the character of the streets, which are asphaltic concrete and in good repair, or of the residences. Immediately at the city limits, however, an abrupt change in the landscape is startlingly obvious. The road becomes bumpy and poorly maintained. The houses are old and many are very poorly kept. There are many vacant lots with a profusion of vegetation.

This scene, more typical of an area of rural poverty, is found in a community located in the St. Louis suburban ring. At this point, a more detailed description of Kinloch is necessary to portray this remarkable transition from a suburban environment to a ghetto slum that is miles removed from the inner city.

The roads in any community are one obvious manifestation of the amount of money allocated to city services in general. In the surrounding white cities of Berkeley and Ferguson, roads are in good condition, well maintained, with few potholes, lined with curbs and sidewalks. In Kinloch, almost all roads are in need of repair. In 1963, the St. Louis County Health Department found 92 per cent of the black community's streets to be inadequate.[30] The condition of these roads had not changed appreciably by the early 1970s. Street maintenance is all but nonexistent, with more than one third of all streets unpaved; curbs and sidewalks are almost totally absent.[31] Street lights are limited to the few "major" streets of the city, a situation that was brought about when the municipal government, after learning it could finance installation of lighting only on selected street corners, petitioned property owners to form "light clubs" that apportioned the cost of lighting the streets between the corners to property owners based on the amount of street frontage owned by each individual.[32]

There are no arterial streets running completely through Kinloch into the surrounding white communities. All major streets in the area either are at the periphery of the city, at some greater distance, or, in the case of Carson Road (in Kinloch, renamed the Martin Luther King Boulevard), come to a dead end in the community. The general pattern and the condition of streets in the city resemble rural farm lanes. The streets meander about, with a grid structure imposed by the main routes. There are also a large number of unsurfaced dirt and gravel roads, further contributing to the rural atmosphere. Many streets marked as permanent thoroughfares on maps of Kinloch are nonexistent "paper roads" consisting only of unmarked rights-of-way which are often built up with residences and used as lawns and gardens.

Another major problem affecting the street transportation system is the physical barriers restricting smooth circulation and communication of people and goods from Kinloch out into surrounding areas. Kinloch is all but totally isolated from its white neighbors by fences, cul-de-sacs, public utility rights-of-way, streams, vegetation barriers, and streets which are unrepaired at the city limits of the surrounding white communities.

The character of the residences is another principal factor in differentiating the black from the white communities. Much of the substandard quality of Kinloch's housing is readily apparent even to a casual observer. Exterior damage and disrepair such as cracked foundations, broken windows, porches and railings, sagging and crumbling brick and block walls, roofs with more shingles missing than not, and dangerously tilting chimneys are the rule rather than the exception. Also found in Kinloch are many abandoned and partially or totally destroyed residences, many of which are either vandalized or gutted by fire.

A factor associated with the quality of the maintenance of the black city's streets and houses is that of the yards and numerous vacant lots adjacent to the dwelling units. Houses with wide expanses of neat, well-trimmed, attractive lawns can be found easily in Kinloch, but they are in the minority. More generally, the yards surrounding most of the houses consist of dirt with little or no grass, weeds, and dirt halfway to the houses, and immediately surrounding the houses, vegetation runs rampant with trees, bushes, and tall weeds seemingly competing with the houses for survival.

Thus, the picture painted of the all-black city is not one of a typical suburban community, but rather a strange mixture both of the poverty and blight of inner-city ghettos and parts of the rural South. A detailed examination is necessary to illustrate mechanisms which have contributed to these seemingly disparate and incongruent trends in Kinloch.

ORIGIN AND DEVELOPMENT OF KINLOCH

In the 1860s and 1870s, the area today known as Kinloch was devoted largely to agricultural pursuits, leading to the supply of some of the produce needed in the City of St. Louis nearby. Among the farmers and farm laborers were blacks, a few of whom owned property, but most simply were hired hands. Over the years, the number of blacks living in the area slowly increased. In the late 1880s, several enterprising St. Louis real estate firms, taking advantage of the earlier history of black settlement, purchased several large tracts of land in the area,[33] subdivided the land into lots of 25 by 100 feet and 20 by 80 feet, and offered them for sale to blacks living in the St. Louis ghetto at approximately $50 and $40, respectively.[34] Although these blacks lacked the financial security and resources necessary to construct typical suburban homes of the time, they built small shanties on their property and laid out unpaved roads to provide access to their homes. The area continued to be predominantly rural, and residents had the advantage of raising some of their own food. Another benefit was that the area was wooded and hilly, with several small streams, reminding many of the residents of their former homes in the South.[35]

The black population grew steadily, expanding as additional tracts were subdivided and advertised in St. Louis. Shortly after 1930, the black population numbered over 4,000 and continued growing at nearly the same rate as the surrounding areas inhabited by white population.[36] The rapid growth of both populations necessitated establishment of a common school district with "separate but equal" facilities for blacks and whites governed by an all-white school board.[37]

During the middle and late 1930s, Kinloch and the surrounding area of white farmers were united only by the common school district. By that time, the black population outnumbered the white by almost two thousand people; however, the white electorate heavily outnumbered the black as a result of discriminatory Missouri election laws.[38] Although Missouri laws provided for segregated school systems, blacks were allowed to vote in the school board elections. With a rapidly expanding black electorate, Reverend Reuben Matthewson, a resident of Kinloch, was elected to the three-member school board. Reverend Matthewson bitterly complained about used and abused books relegated to the black schools, wide differentials in pay scales, and the school district's refusal to construct a black high school.[39]

In 1938, when the black electorate openly began to make plans to elect another black to the board, the whites responded by withdrawing from the district, and incorporating themselves as the towns of Berkeley and Ferguson with separate school systems.[40]

Between 1938 and 1948, the black population continued to grow, but at a slower rate than before.[41] The residents continued to run their school district, but without financial support previously provided by the white population's taxes, the system was operating under very stringent financial constraints, even though a local high school was eventually built in 1939 with Works Progress Administration funds.[42] The St. Louis County government, which legally was responsible for providing services to unincorporated areas, largely ignored the black community.

In 1948, hoping to improve their situation through self-determination, the black residents sought and were granted a charter of incorporation as the City of Kinloch.[43] Satisfaction with the new charter was short-lived, however, as in March 1949, approximately 2,000 residents petitioned for disincorporation, alleging insufficient taxable property within the city's 554 acres.[44] The city's principal political leaders waged a bitterly contested campaign against the move to disincorporate; the petition was ultimately overturned on a technicality by the Missouri Supreme Court.[45] Thus, the stage was set for the continuation and intensifying of two significant elements which were to shape Kinloch's future—poverty and isolation.

PRESENT SOCIOECONOMIC CONDITIONS

Kinloch today, with a population of almost 6,000 inhabitants, is an area of remarkable deep-seated poverty both in terms of absolute numbers of families earning less than a living wage and percentage of inhabitants affected by poverty. The 1970 United States Census reveals that median family income in Kinloch is only $5,202, while in Berkeley and Ferguson median family incomes are $11,001 and $12,788, respectively,[46] and $12,393, $11,868, and $10,236 in St. Louis County, the Standard Metropolitan Statistical Area, and Missouri, respectively.[47] In addition, the 1970 United States Census reports that 34 per cent, or almost 400 families in Kinloch, received some form of public assistance, particularly aid to dependent children and old age assistance;[48] the mean family income of this group is only $1,765, with a mean income deficit of $2,255 below federal poverty criteria,[49] indicating that families in Kinloch receiving public assistance had an average family income that was approximately 56 per cent below the federal poverty standard.

Accompanying these family economic statistics is another trend which characteristically indicates hard-core poverty: predominately substandard housing. The St. Louis County Planning Department, in a 1968 survey, determined that of some 1,800 dwelling units in Kinloch about 63 per cent were substandard.[50] The 1970 Census additionally reveals that over 34 per cent of all occupied housing units in Kinloch are without public sewers, 35 per cent without central or built-in heating systems, and almost 60 per cent of occupied dwelling units in 1970 were owned by their residents.[51] The 1970 Census also reveals that over 58 per cent of the dwellings in the black community were constructed before 1949 and approximately 71 per cent are valued at less than $10,000, with a mean value of only $6,700.[52]

Low incomes, welfare-dependent families, and inferior housing are not the only social and economic disadvantages of Kinloch. The tax base, partially reflecting low incomes and condition of housing, is almost totally inadequate to provide the population with necessary municipal services.[53] In 1969, the St. Louis County Department of Revenue reported that the assessed valuation of real property in Kinloch was $3,124,609, with a tax rate of $5.87 per $100 assessed valuation.[54] This tax rate is the highest in the St. Louis SMSA, but yields Kinloch only $242,298 in tax revenue.[55] The tax situation is even more serious in view of the fact that a state tax program, initiated in 1965, transferred utility and railroad property taxes to municipalities, and actually prevented a decrease in Kinloch's assessed valuation.[56]

A second serious tax problem in the black community involves an extremely high rate of tax delinquency, averaging yearly between 16 per cent and 30 per cent of the personal property and real estate tax change.[57] This failure to pay owed taxes has been increasing substantially during the past several years, resulting in additional burdens on the community.

Limitations of the educational system of Kinloch is a reflection of the financial instability of the city and school district. The school system is so antiquated that the state refused to accredit it until 1964, when it was given the lowest possible accreditation rating.[58] Specific problems of the educational system include: substandard buildings, high student-teacher ratios, and inadequate salary scale.

Unemployment and underemployment are problems endemic to Kinloch. Although figures on underemployment are very difficult to obtain, unemployment rates are available from the Department of Labor and the Office of Economic Opportunity. In 1968, approximately 9 per cent of Kinloch's adult labor force was unemployed, a figure then almost twice the national average.[59] Compounding this high official rate of unemployment is a concentration of individuals who are never enumerated as actively seeking employment, some of these are employed only part-time, or are underemployed, or simply have never registered as looking for a job. The Department of Labor has estimated that the actual rate of unemployment in black areas is often more than three to four times higher than the official rate, indicating that the actual unemployment in Kinloch is a much more serious problem than the Labor Department's figure of 9 per cent indicates.[60]

Basic to the problems of unemployment and underemployment in Kinloch are the numbers of occupational opportunities available in the black community. According to the United States Census of Business, in 1963 Kinloch had a total of fifteen retail service establishments, employing only twenty-one paid workers.[61] These establishments were: a general merchandise store, four small food stores, two restaurants, two drugstores, and two mortuaries. In 1970, a reconnaissance of the community's dilapidated business section revealed that added to the above businesses are a record-dance parlor, a beauty shop, and two gasoline service stations. The only manufacturing entity in Kinloch is a small wrought-iron firm at the town's southern boundary. Consequently, employment opportunities within the community are restricted and the greater majority of those seeking jobs must leave Kinloch to find work.

THE ISOLATION OF KINLOCH

The locational characteristics of Kinloch seem, at first, to be quite advantageous to the community. Situated in north St. Louis County and in the St. Louis SMSA, the black city is located near several of the area's foremost employers (McDonnell-Douglas, Emerson Electric, and the Universal Match Corporation), a factor primarily responsible for much of the area's rapid growth. In addition, Interstate 70 is near Kinloch's southern boundary providing transportation to the St. Louis CBD and to the airport, which is only two miles away. Other important facilities adjacent to the black community are the University of Missouri (St. Louis) and several regional shopping centers.

However, one of the most important, if not the most important, locational characteristics of Kinloch is its isolation from the surrounding white suburban communities of Berkeley and Ferguson, an isolation that is readily perceived from maps, air photographs, or field observations. This isolation is a complex reality for the black residents and can be subdivided and categorized into three forms: physical, transportation-communication, and social.

Physical barriers between Berkeley-Ferguson and Kinloch are almost completely continuous in isolating the black community and can best be understood referring to maps of the area. Classified as physical barriers are such features as: high fences (both chain link and wooden); vision and sound obstructing green belts of high, dense bushes and trees at property lines dividing white from black residential areas; wide, inviolate public utility right-of-way; and railroad tracks. All of these barriers effectively mark the limits of black settlement.

Specific instances of the presence of these physical barriers are illustrated to demonstrate the isolation of Kinloch. The Union Electric right-of-way, carrying high-tension electrical power lines, extends from the intersection of Scudder and Middleway Avenues on Kinloch's west side, paralleling Middleway, and turns in a south-southwest direction north of the intersection of McHenry and Middleway on Kinloch's southwest border.

Between the point where the right-of-way turns toward the south and McHenry is the flood plain of a small stream, Maline Creek, where the St. Louis County Planning and Zoning departments have prohibited the construction of buildings.[62] Immediately southeast of the Maline Creek flood plain is a road median, a 20–30 yard-wide grassy divider strip on the west side of Middleway, extending southeast to the intersection of Middleway and Case avenues. Providing a continuation of barriers where the median ends is a high chain-link fence beginning at Case and Middleway, following Middleway and ending at Kinloch's political boundary. Thus, it is apparent that the all-black town's west-southwest border is veritably sealed against any communication-circulation between black and white communities, essentially containing the black population from areal expansion.

On the southeast boundary of Kinloch, the situation is much the same as on the southwest side. Physical barriers in this area are vacant land that is heavily vegetated, the Maline Creek flood plain, and the St. Louis Belt and Terminal Railway right-of-way. Of these isolating factors, the railway right-of-way is the most significant, extending along the entire length of the black town's southeastern limit. The right-of-way is flanked on both sides by vacant lots which are so densely overgrown with vegetation as to be virtually impenetrable visually so that anyone on either side of the tracks is unable to see or even hear activity on the opposite side.

The situation is somewhat different along the eastern boundary of Kinloch, marking the separation of the black city and Ferguson. Along this border there are no rights-of-way; all the land on both sides of the city limits is privately owned, although, the City of Ferguson maintains a one-foot strip of easement along the entire eastern boundary of Kinloch.[63] This one-foot easement is marked by a wire fence that is overgrown with trees and bushes. All roads through Ferguson and Kinloch end short of the easement.

Along the northern section of the city's eastern limits, north of Carson Road, Ferguson's easement extends to Kinloch's northern boundary. This northern portion is similar to the central portion of the east border, with private fences and densely overgrown with vegetation.

Kinloch's northern legal limits, marking the separation of the black community from Berkeley, are delimited in part, by what is known locally as the "Kinloch Wall."[64] This barrier consists of a series of fences that Berkeley residents have erected to protect their back yards from the black community. Varying in height from four to six feet, and even topped along one section by three strands of barbed wire, the fence is cloaked by vines and an assortment of weeds and bushes shielding the white community from even visual contact with their black neighbors (Figure 1). It is in this section of Berkeley that the streets end in cul-de-sacs.

The only section of Kinloch's boundary not enclosed by physical barriers is the northwestern section between Kinloch and Berkeley. It is not surprising therefore that it is only in this section that blacks have penetrated either of the two surrounding white communities. It is into this area that the black population is slowly invading and it is only a matter of time before the whites are succeeded completely by blacks.

In the northwest area, barriers other than physical long have been in operation, especially the transportation-communication type of obstacle. Improper street construction and repair on the Berkeley side of Kinloch's northwestern political boundary in the recent past have effectively restricted the movement of vehicular traffic along the seven roads in the area.

The transportation-communication barrier can be shown to operate in areas around Kinloch other than in the city's northwest section. Leading into the city of Kinloch are only ten through streets. Of these, five in the northwest section are virtually impassible; Scudder, running east-west, abruptly changes from asphalt to an unpaved lane; Carson Road is discontinued for two blocks at Kinloch's northeastern section; Suburban Avenue has in the recent past (up to the summer of 1970) been barricaded with a large steel chain across a small bridge on the Ferguson-Kinloch border; and the other two streets are limited in length (one is only a single block long) and carry little traffic.

At the southwestern edge of Kinloch, less than one fourth of a mile from the city limits, is Interstate 70. Carson Road does not have a full or even a partial clover leaf connecting it to the Interstate Highway. Access to the Interstate is limited since one can only enter the eastward or St. Louis bound lanes. Additionally, there is only one exit and that is westward or from the direction of downtown St. Louis.

At the present time, a limited-access, six-lane divided highway, locally called the Inner Belt, is scheduled to be completed by 1975. The construction of this highway has aroused deep resentment among Kinloch residents, for the highway, which is a major artery connecting north and south St. Louis County, will pass through the southern edge of the city, yet will have neither entrance nor exit ramps servicing Kinloch. As of the late summer of 1973, public hearings and petitions have done nothing to change these plans of the Missouri Highway Commission.

In addition to the almost total absence of proper street maintenance at the mutually shared city limits of the black and white communities, transportation-communication barriers are evidenced by the presence of many cul-de-sacs and dead-end streets at Kinloch's boundaries. Along the northern and eastern borders of the black city all of the streets, with the exception of Carson Road and Suburban Avenue, in Berkeley and Ferguson are either not through or end in the cul-de-sac pattern so popular in suburban developments.

The last factor in the isolation of Kinloch is much more subtle than either physical or transportation barriers. In a real sense this factor can be said to be the cause of the other barriers. The existence of fear, lack of understanding, hatred, prejudice, and indifference on the part of white America is the ultimate cause of racial conflict in the United States and the isolation of Kinloch. These attitudes have built a plural society in which white and black relationships have been master-slave, superior-inferior for so many years that they are all but an ineradicable part of life in the United States. These factors are considered together by the author as a social barrier, responsible for the separation and isolation of Kinloch from its white neighbors.

An example of this social barrier was demonstrated to the author when he was interviewing white property owners whose property directly abutted Kinloch. Many of these people denied the presence of the black community by claiming that it was some distance away rather than at their back yard.[65] Another instance of the existence of this barrier was the initial acceptance of the children of Kinloch's only Catholic grade school by the pastor of a neighboring all-white Catholic parish into that grade school. When the white parishioners were informed of the pastor's decision, a furor erupted in which many of the parishioners withheld their

Sunday donations until the pastor was forced to cancel the arrangement with the school in Kinloch.[66]

Most social, economic, and spatial factors point to the continuance of the isolation and poverty of Kinloch, not their gradual dissolution and disappearance. Whites in the surrounding areas are steadfast in their attitudes against the black city and its residents. There is no evidence of any removal or modification of the barriers isolating Kinloch. The economic situation in Kinloch seems unlikely to improve perceptively in the near future. The community has little to offer industrial or commercial enterprises, especially in light of its isolation and deterioration. In addition, as the principal industrial employers in the area are engaged to a large extent in the production of war material, the gradual de-emphasis on United States military involvement overseas would seem to indicate fewer employment opportunities for Kinloch's labor force. It is also probable that the eventual layoffs produced in such a situation would be a severe blow to blacks employed in these industries as the jobs they most often hold are entry-level and these workers seldom are protected by seniority, consequently they frequently are the first to be fired during economic recessions.

Plans of the Missouri Highway Commission reveal that although a local four-lane divided highway, known as the Inner Belt is to be constructed in the near future through the southern section of Kinloch, there will be no entrance or exit ramps servicing the community. Thus, instead of abating the isolation of Kinloch, the highway will increase it.

The situation in the all-black city is grim as future prospects for Kinloch appear to be continuations and reflections of present conditions. It is impossible to project significant changes in any of the social, economic, or areal patterns that envelop Kinloch. Only time and further study will reveal whether Kinloch will evolve past its present situation into a community more representative of suburban America or will continue as an isolated racial community.

LITERATURE CITED

1. John A. Jakle, "The Literature of Social Geography: A Selected Bibliography," Department of Geography, University of Illinois, 1968 (Mimeographed).

2. ——, "Geographical Literature on Ethnically and Racially Defined Minority Groups in the United States and Canada: A Selected Bibliography," Department of Geography, University of Illinois, 1968 (Mimeographed).

3. John Fraser Hart, "The Changing Distribution of the American

Negro," *Annals of the Association of American Geographers*, L (September 1960), 242–66.

4. Wesley C. Calef and Howard J. Nelson, "Distribution of Negro Population in the United States," *The Geographical Review*, XXXVI (January 1956), 82–97.

5. Allan Pred, "Business Thoroughfares as Expressions of Urban Negro Culture," *Economic Geography*, IL (July 1963), 217–33.

6. Mark Lowry II, "Race and Socio-economic Well-being: A Geographical Analysis of the Mississippi Case," *The Geographical Review*, LX (October 1970), 511–28; ——, "Population and Race in Mississippi, 1940–1960," *Annals of the Association of American Geographers*, LXI (September 1971), 576–88.

7. Richard L. Morrill, "The Negro Ghetto," *The Geographical Review*, LV (July 1965), 339–61; ——, "The Persistence of the Black Ghetto as Spatial Separation," *The Southeastern Geographer*, XI (November 1971), 149–56.

8. Harold M. Rose, "The All-Negro Town: Its Evolution and Function," *The Geographical Review*, LV (July 1965), 362–81; ——, "The Origins and Patterns of Development of Urban Black Social Areas," *Journal of Geography*, LXVII (September 1969), 326–32.

9. Donald R. Deskins, Jr., "Race as an Element in the Intra-City Regionalization of Atlanta's Population," *The Southeastern Geographer*, XI (November 1971), 157–68.

10. John Fraser Hart, "A Rural Retreat for Northern Negroes," *The Geographical Review*, L (April 1960), 147–68.

11. James O. Wheeler and Stanley D. Brunn, "Negro Migration into Rural Southwestern Michigan," *The Geographical Review*, LVIII (April 1968), 214–30; ——, "An Agricultural Ghetto: Negroes in Cass County, Michigan, 1845–1968," *The Geographical Review*, LIX (July 1969), 317–29.

12. George K. Hesslink, *Black Neighbors: Negroes in a Northern Rural Community* (Indianapolis, Indiana: Bobbs-Merrill Company, Inc., 1968).

13. For a discussion of the many contributions of Mozell C. Hill to all-black settlements, see Robert T. Ernst, *Factors of Isolation and Interaction in an All-Black City: Kinloch, Missouri*, Doctoral Dissertation, Department of Geography, University of Florida, 1973; especially Chapter II, 23–32.

14. Rose, "The All-Negro Town."

15. For a review of the contributions of social scientists to all-black towns and cities, see Ernst, *Factors of Isolation*, 23–32.

16. Karl E. Taeuber and Alma F. Taeuber, "The Changing Character of Negro Migration," *American Journal of Sociology*, LXX (January 1965), 429–41.

17. Reynolds Farley and Karl E. Taeuber, "Population Trends and Residential Segregation Since 1960," *Science*, CLVI (March 1968), 953–56.

18. Reynolds Farley, "The Changing Distribution of Negroes Within Metropolitan Areas: The Emergence of Black Suburbs," *American Journal of Sociology*, LXXX (January 1970), 512–29.

19. Rose, "The All-Negro Town."

20. Ibid., 381.

21. Ibid., 362.

22. Note the establishment of the Commission on Minority Groups and Afro-Americans and the NSF-AAG All-Black Town Project.

23. This definition is after that given by Rose, "The All-Negro Town," 362. However, two major differences exist between the two definitions. First, the definition proposed by this writer differentiates between towns and cities in order to be more precise in the following analysis. Secondly, 10 per cent white population is allowed in all-black municipalities instead of Rose's 5 per cent, as the author believes that historically many well-known racial communities have existed with the higher per cent white and have remained viable and black controlled. Thus, the 10 per cent white is regarded as a chance occurrence which does not denigrate use of the term "all-black."

24. United States Department of Commerce, Bureau of the Census, *General Population Characteristics: 1970 United States*. Final Report PC (1), Table 16, Summary Data for Areas, Places, and Counties; Table 32, Data for Places of 1,000 to 2,500.

25. A chi-square test revealed weak relationship between the distribution of all-black communities and the proportion of blacks in major census regions.

26. The census estimate has been hotly disputed by city officials who claim a population of approximately 8,000.

27. John E. Kramer and Ingo Walter, "Politics in an All-Negro City," *Urban Affairs Quarterly*, IV (September 1968), 85.

28. Human Development Corporation of Metropolitan St. Louis, "Neighborhood Handbook," St. Louis, 1968, 1.

29. Interview with Charles Franklin of Lott-Hunt Realty Company; Ferguson, Missouri, June 7, 1970.

30. St. Louis County Health Department, "Sanitary Survey Report, City of Kinloch," Clayton, Missouri, 1963, 9.

31. Ibid.

32. Ingo Walter and John E. Kramer, "Political Autonomy and Economic Dependence in an All-Negro Municipality," *The American Journal of Economics and Sociology*, XXVII (July 1969), 232.

33. Kramer and Walter, "All-Negro City," 69; and interviews with Kinloch residents Elmira Wilhams, Mary Stewart, and Fred Whitted; Kinloch, Missouri, June 29, 1970.

34. Kramer and Walter, "All-Negro City," 69.

35. Interviews with Kinloch residents Samuel Anderson, William Howard, John O'Quinn, and Roosevelt Gordon; Kinloch, Missouri, July 2, 1970.

36. Walter and Kramer, "All-Negro Municipality," 227.

37. Ibid.

38. Ibid.

39. Kramer and Walter, "All-Negro City," 69.

40. Ibid.

41. Walter and Kramer, "All-Negro Municipality," 227.

42. Kramer and Walter, "All-Negro City," 69.

43. Human Development Corporation, "Neighborhood Handbook," 1.

44. Walter and Kramer, "All-Negro Municipality," 227.

45. Ibid.

46. United States Department of Commerce, Bureau of the Census, Census of Population and Housing: 1970, Census Tracts. Final Report PHC (1)-181, St. Louis Missouri-Illinois Standard Metropolitan Statistical Area; Table P-4. Income Characteristics of the Population, P-128 and P-122.

47. Ibid., 115–16.

48. Ibid., Table P-6, Economic Characteristics of the Negro Population, P-169.

49. Ibid.

50. St. Louis County, Planning Department, "Current Land Use Inventory and Structural Conditions," Clayton, Missouri, 1968, 18.

51. Bureau of the Census, Census Tracts, Table H-4, Structural Equipment, and Financial Characteristics of Housing Units with Negro Head of Household, H-85.

52. Bureau of the Census, Table H-3, Occupancy, Utilization, and Financial Characteristics of Housing Units with Negro Head of Household, H-79.

53. St. Louis County, Department of Revenue, "Tax Data—Incorporated Areas," Clayton, Missouri, 1969, 37.

54. Ibid.

55. Ibid.

56. Ibid.

57. Ibid.

58. Walter and Kramer, "All-Negro Municipality," 231.

59. Ibid., 236.

60. David Matza, "Poverty and Disrepute," in *Contemporary Social Problems*, ed. by Robert K. Merton and Robert A. Nisbet (New York: Harcourt, Brace Jovanovich, Inc., 1971), 385.
61. United States Department of Commerce, Bureau of the Census, Census of Business: 1963.
62. Interview with Gerald Stack, Planner, St. Louis County Planning Department; Clayton, Missouri, May 23, 1970.
63. John Kramer, "The Other Mayor Lee," *Focus-Midwest*, V (Spring 1967), 19.
64. Ibid.
65. Interviews with Berkeley residents James Morgan, Edward Koch, Louis Wells, and William Novak; Berkeley, Missouri, August 5, 1970.
66. Interview with Father Rudolf Beckman, Ferguson, Missouri, August 18, 1970.

NEGRO MIGRATION INTO RURAL
SOUTHWESTERN MICHIGAN

James O. Wheeler and Stanley D. Brunn

One of the dominant migration streams of the twentieth century in the United States is the flood of rural Negroes from the South to metropolitan areas in the North and, to a smaller extent, in the West.[1] But despite the magnitude of the urbanward flow, there has been almost no Negro migration to rural areas of the North. The lack of rural settlement by Negroes is attributable partly to the decreasing number of persons engaged in agriculture, especially small-scale operators, to the growing expense of entering farming, and to differences in agricultural practices.[2] In addition, industrial employment is limited in most rural areas, which have had a labor surplus since the rise of urbanization; and even when employment opportunities existed, the dominance of the whites in the rural North has kept Negroes from settling there.[3]

Recent Negro migration into rural southwestern Michigan suggests the beginning of a trend that may become increasingly common in the North. The general pattern of Negro migration from rural South to urban North seems to be taking on an added dimension. A segment of the Negro population, which is to a large extent blocked from city to suburbs migration, is skipping the suburban stage.[4] Instead, some Negroes are moving into small, formerly agricultural, communities and are buying homes from the whites who are leaving. Apparently only the difficulty of gaining a foothold and finding employment is preventing an even greater number of Negroes from settling in small rural villages and towns. Although some retired Negroes have migrated into rural southwestern Michigan, the majority there consists of Negro families who are attempting to escape the problems of ghetto living and enjoy the attractions of a comparatively quiet and peaceful rural community.

The migration patterns and distribution of the American Negro have been examined by geographers as well as by sociologists, demographers, and others.[5] A study by Hartshorne in 1938 examined the proportional distribution of Negroes in the United States.[6] His map (1930) revealed that no county in the North Central States had more than 10 per cent Negro population. Later, Calef and Nelson, using 1940 and 1950 census data, published several maps of Negro population distribution.[7] Commenting on the distribution of rural Negroes, they noted that "Western Michigan . . . shows the unusual pattern of a widely scattered rural Negro population in a northern state."[8] More recently, Hart has traced the historical changes in Negro population.[9] The Negro concentration in rural southwestern Michigan appears on several of his maps, and other maps reveal the recency of the in-migration. In another study Hart examined an area in Lake County, Michigan, used by northern Negroes as a rural retreat, a retirement and summer-resort center.[10] Most recently, Rose, in describing the development of several all-Negro towns in the United States, was able to enumerate only eight such towns of more than 1,000 population in the North, all of which are near a metropolitan area.[11]

Purpose and Method

The present study examines the conditions and characteristics underlying the spatial distribution of Negroes in southwestern Michigan. Specifically, it traces the migration of Negroes into the area, analyzes their demographic composition, and compares their social and economic ties with those of the white population. Such questions as the following are explored: What has been the basis for the recent migration? Where are the migrants from? How do their shopping and work trips compare with those of whites living in the same community?

In addition to basic census data, a sample of four communities is used: Parkville (population, 100), Vandalia (357), Covert (600), and Dowagiac (7,208).[12] These communities were selected because of differences in population size, observed Negro concentrations, and scattered location. Household interviews were conducted with both whites and Negroes during the summer and fall of 1966. Interviews were attempted at each residence in all the communities except Dowagiac, where the Negroes are segregated in the southwestern part. The sample of white interviews obtained in Dowagiac cannot be considered representative, since the houses were in or near the Negro section of the town. More than 350 interviews were obtained, of which 228 were with Negroes. Nearly 200 interviews were conducted in Dowagiac, about 70 each in Vandalia and Covert, and 26 in Parkville.

TABLE I
Negroes in North Central States Leading in Negro Population, 1910-1960

State	1910	1920	1930	1940	1950	1960	% Negro 1960
Illinois	109,049	182,274	328,972	387,446	645,980	1,037,470	10.3
Michigan	17,115	60,082	169,453	208,345	442,296	717,581	9.2
Ohio	111,452	186,187	309,304	339,461	513,072	786,097	8.1
Indiana	60,320	80,810	111,982	121,916	174,168	269,275	5.8

Source: United States Census of Population: 1960, Vol. 1, Parts 15, 16, 24, and 37 (U. S. Bureau of the Census, Washington, D. C., 1963).

NORTHWARD MOVEMENT OF NEGROES

The Negro population in the United States in 1960 was about nineteen million, or about 10.5 per cent of the total population. Some 60 per cent of the Negroes lived in the South, 40 per cent in the North and West. If the rapid out-migration to northern and western states continues, these percentages may be reversed by 1980 or 1990, and by 2000 most large cities may have a Negro majority.[13] In 1910, about 27 per cent of the Negro population was considered urban; by 1960 the same percentage was classified as rural. The spatial distribution of Negroes in the South today is largely a result of natural increase, whereas the patterns in the North and West are attributable primarily to in-migration.

Negro migration from the South did not really accelerate until the 1920s. It slowed somewhat during the depression of the 1930s, but since then it has been increasing rapidly. In Michigan, the number of Negroes jumped from 17,000 in 1910 to 717,581 in 1960 (Table I). The increments in other North Central States, though smaller, are also remarkable.

The leading North Central States in Negro population are Illinois, Ohio, Michigan, and Indiana, but there is considerable variation among and within these states. The areal pattern of Negro population by nonmetropolitan counties reveals particularly strong concentrations in southwestern Michigan, in the area south of Chicago, in southern Illinois, and in southern Ohio. The concentration in southern Illinois represents a northward extension of southern Negro populations.[14] Concentrations similar to those in southwestern Michigan and Kankakee County, Illinois, are found around the suburban areas of Cleveland and Detroit. In Wisconsin, Minnesota, and Iowa no nonmetropolitan county has more than 1 per cent of its population classed as Negro.[15]

Before the mass out-migration, most of the Negroes that left the South had been engaged in agriculture; few lived, or were employed, in urban areas. The switch from the plight of a poor rural tenant in the South to the anticipated "better life" of an urban-industrial laborer in the North has meant a marked change during the past half century in the residence and occupation patterns of the American Negro. The northern urban Negro, as well as the southern Negro (who is rapidly becoming urbanized in the South also), has lost much of the rural identity of his forefathers. Most of the Negroes in Illinois, Michigan, Ohio, and Indiana are classed as urban residents and live in the central city or in Negro settlements on its periphery[16] (Table II). Few Negroes have succeeded in becoming integrated into the suburbs, owing to the social, economic, and legal barriers established by the middle-class white community.[17]

NEGROES IN SOUTHWESTERN MICHIGAN

Southwestern Michigan has a tradition of Negro settlement dating from the Underground Railroad in the early 1840s. One line, operated by early Quaker settlers, moved runaway slaves out of Kentucky into Cass County, Michigan. Another, called the Illinois Line, helped slaves escape into Michigan from as far away as Mississippi. Initially they simply passed through Cass County on their way to Canada. But

> as time passed, the slaves enjoyed greater immunity from the dangers of pursuit and recapture, and many of them finding occupation . . . remained here with friends, thinking that they would be nearly as safe as in Canada. Some of the fugitives who had settled down in Cass County owned small tracts of ground, for which they were about equally indebted to their own industry, and the generosity of their white friends.

TABLE II
Negro Population by Rural-Urban Classes, 1960

State	Urban	Rural: Places of 1000 to 2500	Other Rural	% Rural
Illinois	1,013,199	3,668	20,603	2.3
Michigan	686,591	1,879	29,111	4.3
Ohio	751,479	2,578	32,040	4.4
Indiana	260,864	727	7,684	3.1

Source: See footnote to Table I.

By 1847 there were about fifty runaway slaves residing in Penn and Calvin Townships in Cass County.[18] The initial Negro settlement, about five miles south of Vandalia in and around the hamlet of Calvin Center, now consists of only a dozen houses.[19] This settlement formed the nucleus of a Negro colony that has survived to the present.

The wave of southern Negroes into the urban-industrial market of the North at the beginning of the century brought some Negroes into Benton Harbor (population, 19,136) and South Haven (6,149). As the influx continued, especially after World War II, Negro settlement focused on the village of Covert and the nearby rural areas, both in Van Buren County and in adjacent townships of Allegan County. Covert itself, an unincorporated settlement eight miles south of South Haven, is presently 80 per cent Negro and has some of the characteristics of a rural slum. Although the commercial businesses appear relatively viable, in most of the residential areas the houses are run-down and the streets unpaved.

Negro settlement also increased gradually in Cass County before World War II, and after the war a noticeable Negro population appeared in Vandalia, in Dowagiac, and, to a smaller extent, in Cassopolis. The community with the largest proportion of Negroes is Vandalia, shown by the interviews to be 75 per cent Negro. Two groups of Negroes reside here: those who have lived in and around Vandalia for most of their lives; and those who have recently migrated from larger places. Despite the increasing Negro population in Vandalia, the total population—about 360—has not changed much in the past generation. The rather constant population total and the lack of recently constructed houses indicate that the Negro influx has been roughly proportionate to the white exodus.

In contrast with Covert, most of the houses in Vandalia are reasonably sound, though there are some abandoned, dilapidated structures. The number of commercial establishments has decreased noticeably during the past several years. The main street (Highway 60) and adjacent side streets show abandoned businesses, such as service stations, groceries, restaurants, and apparel shops, that were once the backbone of this agricultural trade center. About a mile south of Vandalia, a Negro resort community has developed around Paradise Lake, which brings the area into greater contact with the Chicago Negroes who frequent it.

A dispersed Negro settlement developed in a rural area a mile north of Parkville immediately before World War II. A Chicago land company bought farmland cheaply, platted it into five- to twenty-acre plots, and sold it to Negroes.[20] Most of the houses, hastily constructed at the time, are abandoned. A growing Negro minority is now found in Three Rivers, and also in the hamlet of Parkville, where interviews indicated that nearly 40 per cent of the residents are Negro.

More than a dozen townships in a largely rural five-county area of southwestern Michigan now have a Negro population greater than 10 per cent. Two townships, Calvin and Covert, have 66 and 52 per cent respectively. A total of twenty-eight townships and other minor civil divisions have more than 5 per cent Negro. The largest absolute concentrations are in Benton Township and the cities of Benton Harbor, Niles, and Dowagiac. Several formerly all-white hamlets and villages have acquired Negro families in the last few years, an indication of a continuing spread of Negro settlement in rural southwestern Michigan. No other part of Michigan outside the metropolitan areas has so large a Negro component except Lake County, studied by Hart,[21] and adjoining Newaygo County.

MIGRATION PATTERNS

The great majority of Negro adults living in the rural communities of southwestern Michigan were born and grew up in the South; only about 20 per cent were raised in southwestern Michigan. In the four communities examined, the proportion of Negro adults raised in the South ranges from one half (Vandalia) to two thirds (Dowagiac). One third of the Negroes raised in the South are from Mississippi, and nearly one fifth are from Tennessee. Others came largely from Alabama, Arkansas, Missouri, and Georgia. These migration patterns are somewhat similar to those of other northern Negroes[22] in the North Central States.[23] Of the communities studied, Vandalia has the highest percentage (30) of adult Negroes who were raised in southwestern Michigan, and Covert has the lowest (10). The percentages decrease with distance from the area of initial Negro settlement in Cass County.

Only about 6 per cent of the Negro families have moved into southwestern Michigan directly from the South. Rather, they were attracted at first to the larger northern cities, principally Chicago; but becoming dissatisfied with ghetto living, especially when raising a family, they turned to the small communities near Chicago where housing opportunities existed. About half of the Negro families moved directly from Chicago into one of the four Michigan communities studied. Others moved into one of these villages from the southwestern Michigan community in which they had initially settled. There is also a considerable amount of intracommunity migration.

Negro migration into southwestern Michigan from Chicago and other urban centers of the Middle West began primarily after World War II and has continued at a slowly increasing rate. The flow of migrants is restricted by the availability of existing housing, since the Negroes move into houses that were formerly (and in some cases are still) owned by whites. One measure of the recency of migration is the average number of years Negro families have lived in their present houses. In the communities examined, the mean is less for Negroes than for whites—just over ten years in Dowagiac and eight years in Covert. In Vandalia some 37 per cent of the Negroes have lived there for more than ten years, as compared with more than 50 per cent of the whites; 46 per cent of the Negroes have lived there for five years or less, as compared with about 25 per cent of the whites. For Covert and Dowagiac the percentages are about the same, for both Negroes and whites. In Vandalia 9 per cent, and in Dowagiac 7 per cent of the Negro families have occupied the same houses for thirty years or more, but no Negro family in Covert has lived in its present house as long as that. Thus in these communities there has been a relatively long tradition of a Negro minority, which recently has been considerably enlarged.

More whites than Negroes own their houses, a larger number of Negroes than of whites are buying houses, and a slightly higher percentage of whites than of Negroes are renting. Whites who own their houses have generally lived in the community for some time and have not left simply because they do own their property, have lived most of their lives there, and either are planning to retire or have already done so. A much smaller number of whites are renters, many of whom would like to move elsewhere. The vacant and abandoned houses, especially in Vandalia, are largely the former homes of whites. Some whites cannot afford even the moderate cost of houses in these small communities. About one third of the Negro families are buying, versus less than a fifth of the whites, a reflection of the shorter period of residence of the Negroes and the realization of many whites of the lack of any future for the community.

The same contrasts are noticeable in length of time in the present job. Whites have worked in their present jobs for an average of about nine years, as compared with six years for Negroes. The lower mean for Negroes is attributable to their more recent arrival in the communities, to their relatively lower job skills and the accompanying instability of employment, and to the fact that only the most entrenched whites have remained in Vandalia and Covert as the Negroes have become a more dominant segment of the population.

Among the reasons given by Negroes for moving to the small communities of southwestern Michigan were greater personal freedom, dislike of large cities, an improved environment for raising a family, a quiet and peaceful "country life," nearness to friends and relatives, cheaper housing, less crowded schools, larger house and yard, advantages for retirement, and the opportunities for fishing and gardening. Disadvantages mentioned were the great distance to work and the lack of jobs, public transit, and city services, of recreational facilities, and of suitable activities for teen-agers.

TABLE III
Percentages Reporting Community Growing, Declining, or Stable

Community	Growing	Declining	Stable
Dowagiac			
Negro	78.8	5.9	15.2
White[a]	66.6	8.6	24.6
Covert			
Negro	78.2	2.1	19.5
White	31.2	31.2	37.6
Vandalia			
Negro	46.9	21.9	31.3
White	5.9	35.3	58.8
Parkville[b]			
Negro	80.0	10.0	10.0
White	35.7	7.1	57.2

[a]White population sampled in Dowagiac is not representative of white population of town.

[b]Based on a small number of households.

Many whites perceived a different set of problems associated with living in the small communities. Some did not like the changing character of the town, the noise and the fast automobiles, the uncooperative community attitude of certain residents, the "ghost town" environment, and, as some frankly stated, "the colored people." Other whites, however, spoke of the friendliness of the town and listed complaints similar to those of the Negroes.

The question whether the community is growing, declining, or stable also brought contrasting replies from Negroes and whites (Table III). About three quarters of the Negroes interviewed felt that their community was growing; the proportion of whites, however, was much smaller—as low as 6 per cent in Vandalia. Few Negroes viewed their community as declining, but in Vandalia, where there is a larger proportion of "established" Negro families, the response exceeded 20 per cent. In addition to the greater tendency for whites to view the community as declining, a higher percentage of whites than of Negroes seemed uncertain about their community's future, perceiving no recent trend of growth or decline.

Most Negroes reported having heard about housing availability in the community through friends and relatives. The great majority of Negro

TABLE IV
Age Structure of Population Interviewed (In percentages)

Community	Born Before 1900	1900-1920	1920-1940	1940-1950	1950-1960	After 1960
Dowagiac						
Negro	4.0	17.7	18.8	15.7	30.9	12.9
White[a]	12.3	17.2	23.1	13.5	21.2	12.7
Covert						
Negro	10.9	15.6	17.5	7.6	31.3	17.1
White	16.6	21.7	20.0	6.6	31.7	3.4
Vandalia						
Negro	11.9	13.8	24.4	9.4	21.1	19.4
White	29.4	13.7	19.6	3.9	23.5	9.8
Parkville[b]						
Negro	14.3	34.3	20.0	2.8	20.0	8.6
White	11.1	9.3	33.3	5.6	25.9	14.8

[a]White population sampled in Dowagiac is not representative of white population of town.

[b]Based on small population totals.

households have relatives living in the same community or nearby. More-over, except in Dowagiac, a larger proportion of Negro than of white households have more than 60 per cent of their friends residing in the same community.

DEMOGRAPHIC STRUCTURE

Other Negro-white contrasts are revealed by age structure (Table IV). For example, in both Vandalia and Covert there are more retired whites than retired Negroes. Nevertheless, a surprisingly large proportion of the Negroes of the four communities are also retired, one quarter of the Negro households in Covert and Vandalia having at least one member retired. Although nearly 11 per cent of the Negroes in Covert, and 12 per cent in Vandalia, are of retirement age, the percentages for whites are about 17 and 29 respectively. However, many of the elderly Negroes are recent migrants who have sought out a peaceful retirement commu-nity. In Vandalia they are not only those who have moved away from Chicago but also Negro families from the nearby countryside. A few

Negro families were encountered who, though not yet having any member at retirement age, had migrated to establish a base for their retirement. They live in the community either permanently or for only part of the year (summer vacations and weekends). The larger proportion of retired whites, by contrast, have lived in the community for many years and feel that they have no other place to go.

There is a noticeable lack of younger white children and young white adults in Covert and Vandalia, but white and Negro teen-agers are about equally represented. Some of the white families with teen-age children were established before the greatest Negro influx took place and have adjusted to their changing community. Some white families with children are very poor and seem to be economically below the general Negro level. Adults over twenty-six years of age constitute 63 and 58 per cent of the whites in Vandalia and Covert respectively; the corresponding figures for Negroes are 50 and 44 per cent. The age structure of the Negro population of Dowagiac differs somewhat from that of Covert and Vandalia, notably in having fewer adults of retirement age and more children of preschool age. Nearly 60 per cent of the Dowagiac Negro population is less than twenty-six years of age.

There is a definite contrast in the sex ratios for the whites and Negroes sampled. Although there is generally an almost even balance between men and women among the whites, there are many more Negro women than men. The proportion of Negro females is 53 per cent in Dowagiac, 55 per cent in Covert, 58 per cent in Vandalia, and 63 per cent in the small Parkville sample. However, such an imbalance in favor of the female is not unusual in Negro neighborhoods.[24]

ECONOMIC TIES

Negroes and whites living in the same community, and within the same lower ranks of the urban hierarchy, show different patterns of travel to work and to shop. The most noticeable contrasts are in trips to work: Negroes have to travel farther than whites. Although there is less difference in the use of the urban hierarchy for shopping, Negroes are again somewhat more mobile than whites, both for lower-order goods such as gasoline and groceries and for higher-order goods such as clothing. Part of the greater shopping mobility of Negroes is related to their combining shopping and work trips. In communities where Negroes own businesses, a strong local Negro clientele is served. However, few Negroes seem to travel long distances merely to patronize Negro-owned establishments, partly because these generally provide only lower-order goods and services.

In Covert there is relatively little difference in Negro and white travel for groceries, despite the fact that the two grocery stores in Covert are Negro owned. About one quarter of the households purchase some groceries in Covert, and nearly half go to South Haven. In Vandalia, on the other hand, the white-owned grocery attracts 22 per cent of the whites interviewed but only 7 per cent of the Negroes. Dowagiac is a larger community, with greater shopping opportunities. All the whites who responded to the questionnaire reported shopping for groceries in Dowagiac alone, but nearly 10 per cent of the Negroes go elsewhere.

The purchase of clothing shows an even greater contrast in Negro-white shopping behavior. In Dowagiac more than three quarters of the white households interviewed indicated that they bought their clothes in the town, but more than half of the Negroes reported buying clothes in some other community, a quarter of the households mentioning South Bend. A much larger proportion of Negroes than of whites shop for clothing in Chicago, during vacations and visits with friends and relatives.

Newspaper subscriptions by city of publication also reveal differences in Negro-white preferences. Metropolitan newspapers enable Negroes to maintain closer contact with events in Chicago, with which they are often more concerned than with the local news in the community newspapers. The Cassopolis newspaper, the chief community paper serving Vandalia, is taken by more than 30 per cent of the Vandalia whites who subscribe to a newspaper, but by only 11 per cent of Negro subscribers; however, the most popular paper in Vandalia among both whites and Negroes is the *South Bend Tribune*. In Dowagiac, among those subscribing to some newspaper, the local paper is somewhat more popular with whites than with Negroes. In Covert the Benton Harbor and South Haven newspapers account for 95 per cent of the subscriptions by whites but for only 70 per cent of Negro subscriptions. About one quarter of Covert's Negro families take a Chicago paper. In sum, the Negro families of southwestern Michigan are less likely to subscribe to a local newspaper, preferring to obtain news from a paper published in a large city.

Negro migration to the small communities of southwestern Michigan is not principally a response to job opportunities. Place of residence is determined by availability of housing—an availability more selective for Negroes than for whites. Since the small communities to which the Negro has moved cannot normally provide many additional jobs, he is often forced to travel a considerable distance to reach his place of work. Although some Negro migration within the region reflects an attempt to reside closer to work, most Negroes prefer to live in a community with friends and relatives where they can own their houses, even though this means greater effort to get to work. Some Negro breadwinners, in fact, live in Chicago during the week and return to their families on weekends.

Whether measured by distance or by travel time, Negroes average a longer work trip than whites (Table V). The differences are greatest for the smallest communities, which are lacking in employment opportunities. For example, a survey of twenty workers in the hamlet of Parkville showed that Negroes drive an average of twenty miles (twenty-eight minutes) to work, whites less than six miles (thirteen minutes).

TABLE V
Employment Characteristics of White-Negro Work Force

Community	Mean Miles Traveled to Work	Mean Minutes Traveled to Work	Mean Years At Present Job
Dowagiac			
Negro	8.9	18.2	5.2
White[a]	7.1	17.1	8.8
Covert			
Negro	10.2	21.2	7.6
White	6.2	10.6	10.6
Vandalia			
Negro	19.8	32.7	4.4
White	9.8	17.3	8.2
Parkville[b]			
Negro	20.6	28.0	1.5
White	5.7	12.5	13.6

[a]White population sampled in Dowagiac is not representative of white population of town.

[b]Based on small work-force totals.

Negroes in Vandalia travel an average of ten miles farther than whites, and the trips require an average of fifteen minutes more. In Covert, which has slightly more employment, the Negro-white contrast is smaller —four highway miles and ten minutes. Since most whites and Negroes interviewed in Dowagiac also work in that town, Negro and white work-trip averages are more nearly the same.

Although more Negroes than whites interviewed were unemployed, the percentages for unemployment were relatively low. Of the whites interviewed, most work in the town in which they live. Two thirds of the whites living in Dowagiac and Covert and about half of the white workers in Vandalia and Parkville work in their respective communities (though in the last two the number of white workers is not large). The proportions for Negroes are smaller in Covert (less than a fifth) and

Vandalia (less than a tenth); Dowagiac has just over a half, and no Parkville Negroes work within the hamlet.

Certain communities draw a disproportionate share of Negro workers, largely to factory jobs. When factory employment is not available in the community of residence, Negroes are willing to travel relatively long distances to factories in other towns. For example, 16 per cent of the Negro workers interviewed in Dowagiac travel the twenty miles to Buchanan (1960 population, 5,341), but only 4 per cent of the whites. More than 40 per cent of Covert's Negro workers work in South Haven, as compared with 13 per cent of the white workers. The Indiana towns of Mishawaka, Elkhart, and South Bend provide nearly 40 per cent of the employment for Negro workers living in Vandalia, but just over 20 per cent for whites.

URBAN-RURAL MIGRATION AS AN ALTERNATIVE TO GHETTO LIFE

Negro migration into southwestern Michigan may be an indicator of a future trend associated with metropolitan environments. As the population of central cities becomes increasingly Negro, and the growing suburbs remain predominantly white, Negroes may move from the ghettos into a third zone, beyond the suburbs. This phenomenon could become common before the end of the century. If metropolitan decentralization of industry continues, job opportunities may increase in this quasi-urban zone; and with urban renewal and the return of some whites to the central city, some Negroes may be displaced to smaller centers on the urban periphery.

Although not a satisfactory long-run solution to the problems of ghetto life, a metropolitan spatial structure with a mixture of Negroes and whites in the rural-urban fringe may represent some improvement in the short run. A recent Gallup Poll[25] indicated that seven out of ten whites in the North believed Negro families have a better life in smaller cities and towns, but only one out of three Negroes agreed.

Experiments have been carried out in the past to create new Negro settlements.[26] Several Negro communities were established in southern Ontario about the time of the Civil War, and some in Nova Scotia after the War of 1812. Recently there have been organized moves to settle Negroes in new communities in the South. Negroes in Mississippi, backed by the Delta Ministry, a civil-rights arm of the National Council of Churches, have bought a tract of land south of Greenville, where it is planned to build houses for thirty families and to coax some industry into the community.[27] Whether or not new Negro communities in the North are at present a realistic short-term alternative to ghetto living is a complex question; and the example of southwestern Michigan does not provide an unambiguous answer. The answer seems to depend, in its final evaluation, on the degree to which such migration would allow the American Negro to participate in the social mobility available to white citizens.

LITERATURE CITED

1. In spite of the slowly falling legal barriers and a rise in socioeconomic status for some Negroes, it is often as difficult for southern Negroes to "escape" rural poverty as for northern Negroes to "escape" the urban ghettos. For recent studies of the urban ghetto see Karl E. Taeuber and Alma F. Taeuber: Negroes in Cities (Chicago, 1965); and Richard L. Morrill: The Negro Ghetto: Problems and Alternatives, *Geogr. Rev.*, Vol. 55, 1965, pp. 339–61.

2. In a chapter entitled "The Negro in American Agriculture" in "The American Negro Reference Book" (edited by John P. Davis; Englewood Cliffs, N.J., 1966; pp. 161–204 [Chap. 3]), Calvin L. Beale makes no mention of rural Negroes outside the South.

3. An interesting case was reported on the NBC Huntley-Brinkley Report on December 22, 1966. An Armour meat-packing plant was recently built in Worthington, Minnesota, a community of 9,000 people, and forty-four Negro families in which there were Armour workers transferred to Worthington. Their integration into the community has been notably peaceful.

4. The same trend is currently observable in the white population. The Taeubers have concluded that "Negro migration should increasingly manifest patterns similar to those found among the white population" (Karl E. Taeuber and Alma F. Taeuber: The Changing Character of Negro Migration, *Amer. Journ. of Sociol.*, Vol. 70, 1964–65, pp. 429–41; reference on p. 440). By leapfrogging the suburbs some Negroes are attempting to obtain the benefits of suburban living and minimize the doom of ghetto life.

5. An excellent survey of research on the American Negro is Davis, op. cit. [see footnote 2 above].

6. Richard Hartshorne: Racial Maps of the United States, *Geogr. Rev.*, Vol. 28, 1938, pp. 276–88. See Figure 1 (p. 277).

7. Wesley C. Calef and Howard J. Nelson: Distribution of Negro Population in the United States, *Geogr. Rev.*, Vol. 46, 1956, pp. 82–97.

8. Ibid., p. 85.

9. John Fraser Hart: The Changing Distribution of the American Negro, *Annals Assn. of Amer. Geogrs.*, Vol. 50, 1960, pp. 242–66.

10. John Fraser Hart: A Rural Retreat for Northern Negroes, *Geogr. Rev.*, Vol. 50, 1960, pp. 147–68.

11. Harold M. Rose: The All-Negro Town: Its Evolution and Function, *Geogr. Rev.*, Vol. 55, 1965, pp. 362–81.

12. Figures for Vandalia and Dowagiac are from the United States Census of Population: 1960, Vol. 1, Part A (U. S. Bureau of the Census, Washington, D.C., 1961), pp. 16–24. The population of Parkville is an estimate based on interviews, and the Covert population is an estimate from the "Rand McNally Commercial Atlas and Marketing Guide" (98th edit.; Chicago, New York, San Francisco, 1967), p. 244.

13. "Negroes Nearing a Majority in Major Northern Cities," *Congressional Quart. Weekly Rept.*, Vol. 24, 1966, pp. 1860–63.

14. Hart, A Rural Retreat for Northern Negroes [see footnote 10 above], p. 147, footnote 1.

15. However, certain counties in northern Minnesota and northern Wisconsin have higher nonwhite percentages, due to Indian population.

16. Rose, op. cit. [see footnote 11 above].

17. Leo F. Schnore: Social Class Segregation among Nonwhites in Metropolitan Centers, *Demography*, Vol. 2, 1965, pp. 126–33; and Karl E. Taeuber: Negro Residential Segregation: Trends and Measurements, *Social Problems*, Vol. 12, 1964, pp. 42–50.

18. "History of Cass County" (Chicago, 1882), pp. 109–10. See also John C. Dancy: The Negro People in Michigan, *Michigan Hist. Mag.*, Vol. 24, 1940, pp. 221–40.

19. Another preponderantly Negro settlement in Cass County is the hamlet of Brownsville, consisting of only about a dozen houses. Possibly the most hidden hamlet in southwestern Michigan, Brownsville is tucked away between Vandalia and Calvin Center just off Route 326 on Crooked Creek Road.

20. Interview with Mrs. Joseph H. Garman, Wateredge Centennial Farm, just south of Parkville.

21. Hart, A Rural Retreat for Northern Negroes [see footnote 10 above]. In Ionia County two townships, Berlin and Easton, are listed in the census with 16.4 and 15.6 per cent Negro respectively, but the Negro population in Berlin consists of patients at the Ionia State Hospital and in Easton of inmates of the Ionia State Prison and Reformatory.

22. The use of the phrase "other Northern Negroes" is meant to indicate that the adult Negroes of southwestern Michigan who had been raised in the South had already been living in the North as urban Negroes before they migrated to this rural part of Michigan. Other Negroes grew up in the area, as a result of in-migration either by parents in the 1940s or by ancestors as early as the nineteenth century.

23. Hart, The Changing Distribution of the American Negro [see footnote 9 above], p. 265.

24. See Jeanne L. Noble: The American Negro Women, *in* The American

Negro Reference Book [see footnote 2 above], pp. 522–47 (Chap. 13).

25. Press release Aug. 17, 1966.
26. William H. Pease and Jane H. Pease: Organized Negro Communities: A North American Experiment, *Journ. of Negro History*, Vol. 47, 1962, pp. 19–34.
27. "Hardship and Heartbreak in Freedom City," *National Observer*, Dec. 26, 1966, p. 6.

The Geographical Literature of Black America; 1949-1972:
A Selected Bibliography of Journal Articles, Serial Publications, Theses, and Dissertations

Robert T. Ernst

For many years, geographers have been interested in studying human behavior as structured along three major themes of research—economic, political, and cultural. Recently, several geographers have suggested an alternate level of locational analysis of human behavior—social. Using locational analysis, geographers are capable of studying different aspects of man as a political-economic being existing within a cultural context, man as an integrated part of an organized society.

The value of studying society from the areal perspective long has been obvious to many demographers, human ecologists, urban sociologists, anthropologists, and psychologists. Nevertheless, geographers have tended to neglect social research while emphasizing the study of a particular culture and its unique manifestations rather than its interrelations within a larger societal framework.

However, there is recent evidence that social geography is becoming a major research specialization, as demonstrated by an ever-growing body of literature concerning the spatial aspects of society. A second factor indicative of growth is that particularization of research interest in social geography has caused the field to be subdivided into narrower topics of research. Geographers are now specializing in research concerning the areal aspects of such varied subjects as ethnic communities, black America, poverty, and the social pathology of crime and disease.

In the late 1960s and early 1970s, the social geography of black America has become one of the fastest growing specializations within the field of geography. Geographers have realized that they can make contributions to solving the myriad of racial-ethnic problems which are the result of a plural society in which the whites are dominant and the blacks, Indians, Latinos, and other groups are subdominant.

However, before geographers can offer significant contributions to the solution of racial problems in the United States, it is necessary to determine first what geographic research on race has been performed in the past. Only then can one separate what needs to be accomplished from what already has been achieved. The bibliography which follows provides only a partial solution to the problem in that primarily the concern is on the trends in racial research, leaving the question of future research priorities to be answered elsewhere.

Although several bibliographic surveys of geographic research on black Americans and racial themes have appeared recently, these bibliographies are limited in extent and do not survey adequately United States geographic journals or geographic theses and dissertations on the topic. Therefore, to rectify the present condition of a lack of bibliographic material on the social geography of black Americans, such material is presented to assist social scientists in relating the geographic study of black Americans to the larger body of literature.

This bibliography of journal articles and serials concentrates on the 1949–72 time period chiefly because of the paucity of racial research prior to this period. Only a few specific references to black Americans appear in the geographic literature before 1949, and those few that do either are not involved directly in racial research or are separated widely in time. The main sources for this literature review are the principal geographic journals of the United States, the *Research Catalog of the American Geographical Society, Geographical Abstracts, Dissertation Abstracts, Master's Abstracts,* and *The Professional Geographer,* which lists those theses and dissertations in geography reported completed at American universities.

The criteria used to select the articles as belonging to the geographical literature on race essentially are subjective. First, not all the works concentrate exclusively on blacks, but in all of the articles blacks, or racial issues at least, are given a major emphasis. Secondly, the author acknowledges the practical impossibility of collecting all works dealing with blacks as much of the literature is reported by title only, and often titles, especially of dissertations and theses, are poor reflections of the contents of such studies. However, the author has made every effort to verify the specific racial considerations of each study by reviewing it or by using the abstracts available through university microfilms. Thirdly, the geographic literature suffers from a lack of comprehensive indexing and abstraction, making a reviewer's task an arduous and frustrating one. Lastly, geographers publish in many professional journals peripheral to or altogether outside the realm of geography. Searching all possible periodicals and serials was impossible. Consequently, although the bibliography is reasonably complete and accurate, it is not absolutely comprehensive.

From 1949 to 1972, a total of 283 works dealing with geographic aspects of race was published. In 1949, only two articles on race appeared in the geographic literature, while in 1972, forty-three were published. However, the intervening years show that there has been no steady or gradual increment in numbers of publications, but rather a series of increases and decreases occurred that may be said to be analogous to the crests and troughs of ocean waves, which culminated in the emergence of a tremendous surge of racial articles in 1968 that has yet to peak.

Although the three major United States journals (*Annals of the Association of American Geographers, Economic Geography,* and *The Geographical Review*) have been fairly consistent with only an occasional gap in the publication record, the largest contribution to the geography of race has come from graduate student research: master's theses and doctoral dissertations. A total of 184 articles was published between 1968–72, or 65 per cent of the total 283 works from 1949–72. Of these 184 articles, 44, or almost 35 per cent, are theses and dissertations. Thus, research in the geography of blacks is strongly concentrated at the graduate level, indicating that many young geographers are developing a research interest in the spatial aspects of race. This interest, if sustained, should result in the continuation of the current trend of numerous racial geographic publications of significance to all geographers.

The bibliography is divided into several categories reflecting each article's research orientation. The eight categories selected are: 1) GENERAL STUDIES; 2) RACIAL RESEARCH IN PLACES OTHER THAN THE UNITED STATES; 3) ECONOMIC GEOGRAPHY OF RACE; 4) AREAL PATTERNS OF RACE AND EDUCATION; 5) URBAN RACIAL PATTERNS; 6) POLITICAL-ELECTORAL GEOGRAPHY OF RACE; 7) BLACK POPULATION-MIGRATION TRENDS; and 8) RURAL BLACK GEOGRAPHIC ENVIRONMENTS.

Use of asterisks in bibliography refers to abstracts only.

ABBREVIATIONS USED IN BIBLIOGRAPHY

Annals—Annals of the Association of American Geographers
Antipode—Antipode: A Radical Journal of Geography
Proceedings—Proceedings of the Association of American Geographers

Bibliography

GENERAL STUDIES

Berry, Brian J. L., et al. "Down from the Summit." Mimeographed paper, Center for Urban Studies, University of Chicago, 1969.

Birdsall, Stephen S. "Introduction to Research on Black America: Prospects and Preview." *Southeastern Geographer*, XI (November 1971), 85–89.

Blum, Harold F. "Is Sunlight a Factor in the Geographical Distribution of Human Skin Color?" *The Geographical Review*, LIX (October 1969), 557–81.

Carlson, Alvar W. "A Bibliography of the Geographical Literature on the American Negro, 1920–1971." *The Virginia Geographer*, VII (Spring-Summer 1972), 12–18.

Deskins, Donald R., Jr. "Geographical Literature on the American Negro, 1949–1968: A Bibliography." *The Professional Geographer*, XXI (May 1969), 245–49.

Donaldson, Fred. "Geography and the Black American: The White Papers and the Invisible Man." *Antipode*, I (August 1969), 17–33.

———. "Geography and the Black Man: The White Papers and the Invisible Man." *Journal of Geography*, LXX (March 1971), 138–49.

Horton, F. E. and Reynolds, D. R. "An Investigation of Individual Action Spaces: A Progress Report." *Proceedings*, I (1969), 70–75.

McCutcheon, Murry K. "Racial Geography in the Twentieth Century." Master's thesis, University of Toronto, 1951.

Meyer, David R. "Geographical Population Data: Statistical Description Not Statistical Inference." *The Professional Geographer*, XXIV (February 1972), 26–28.

Morrill, Richard L., and Donaldson, O. Fred. "Geographical Perspectives on the History of Black America." *Economic Geography*, XXXXVIII (January 1972), 1–23.

Peet, Richard. "Bibliography on American Poverty." *Antipode*, II (December 1970), 84–106.

Tatum, Charles E. "The Christian Methodist Episcopal Church, With Emphasis on Negroes in Texas, 1870 to 1970: A Study in Historical-

Cultural Geography." Ph.D. dissertation, Michigan State University, 1971.

Wilson, Bobby M., and Jenkins, Herman. "Symposium: Black Perspectives on Geography." *Antipode*, IV (July 1972), 42–44.

RACIAL RESEARCH IN PLACES OTHER THAN THE UNITED STATES

Augelli, John P. "Racial and Cultural Complexity of West Indian Population: The Case of Trinidad." *Annals*, XLIX (June 1959), 168.*

Brookfield, H. C., and Tatham, M. A. "The Distribution of Racial Groups in Durham." *The Geographical Review*, XLVII (January 1957), 44–65.

Buchanan, Keith, and Hurwitz, N. "The Coloured Community in the Union of South Africa." *The Geographical Review*, XL (July 1950), 397–414.

Clarke, Colin G. "Residential Segregation and Intermarriage in San Fernando, Trinidad." *The Geographical Review*, LXI (April 1971), 198–218.

De Blij, Harm J. "Apartheid: Conflict Resolution and the Peace in Southern Africa." *Annals*, LVII (March 1967), 171.*

De Laubenfels, David J. "Australoids, Negroids, and Negroes: A Suggested Explanation for their Disjunct Distributions." *Annals*, LVIII (March 1968), 42–50.

Fair, T. J. D., and Shaffer, Manfred. "Population Patterns, and Policies in South Africa, 1951–1960." *Economic Geography*, XL (July 1964), 261–74.

Floyd, Barry N. "Land Apportionment in Southern Rhodesia." *The Geographical Review*, LII (October 1962), 566–82.

Hunter, John M., and De Blij, Harm J. "Concept as a Teaching Device: The Example of Buffer Zones in Africa." *Journal of Geography*, LXXI (December 1972), 549–62.

Lowenthal, David. "Black Power in the Caribbean Context." *Economic Geography*, XXXXVIII (January 1972), 116–34.

Peattie, Roderick. "The Racial Problem of South Africa." *Journal of Geography*, XLIX (February 1950), 57–62.

Prescott, J. R. V. "Population Distribution in Southern Rhodesia." *The Geographical Review*, LII (October 1962), 559–65.

Roder, Wolf. "The Division of Land Resources in Southern Rhodesia." *Annals*, XLIX (March 1964), 41–52.

Sabbagh, M. Ernest. "Some Geographical Characteristics of a Plural Society: Apartheid in South Africa." *The Geographical Review*, LVIII (January 1968), 1–28.

Wilgress, Oliver J. "Spatial Organization of a Plural Society: The Effects of Land Apportionment in Rhodesia." Master's thesis, Western Washington State College, 1969.

ECONOMIC GEOGRAPHY OF RACE

Berry, Brian J. L. *Commercial Structure and Commercial Blight.* Department of Geography, University of Chicago, Research Paper No. 85 (1963).
——. "Comparative Mortality Experience of Small Business in Four Chicago Communities." Background Paper No. 4, *Small Business Relocation Study,* Center for Urban Studies, University of Chicago (1966).
Beville, William, Jr. "Money Flows in the Dexter Area: A Progress Report." *Field Notes,* Discussion Paper No. 3 (1971), 45–46.
Broude, Jeffrey E. "A Survey of 1960 Negro Occupational Patterns in Standard Metropolitan Statistical Area by Region, Total Population, and Percentage Negro." Master's thesis, University of California, Los Angeles, 1971.
Craig, William. "Recreational Activity Patterns in a Small Negro Urban Community: The Role of the Cultural Base." *Economic Geography,* XXXXVIII (January 1972), 107–15.
——. "Weekend and Vacation Recreational Behavior of a Negro Community in Louisiana: A Spatial Study." Ph.D. dissertation, University of Michigan, 1968.
Davies, Christopher S. "The Effect of Transportation on the Employment Distribution of Negro Residents Within the Indianapolis Standard Metropolitan Statistical Area." Ph.D. dissertation, Indiana University, 1970.
Davies, Shane, and Huff, David L. "Impact of Ghettoization on Black Employment." *Economic Geography,* XXXXVII (October 1972), 421–27.
Deskins, Donald R., Jr. "Residential Mobility of Negro Occupational Groups in Detroit." Ph.D. dissertation, University of Michigan, 1971.
Earickson, Robert. "Poverty and Race: The Bane of Access to Essential Public Services." *Antipode,* III (November 1971), 1–8.
Galt, John E. "The Residential Distribution of the Employees of Argonne National Laboratory: Patterns and Implications." Master's thesis, University of Chicago, 1968.
Harries, Keith D. "An Analysis of Inter-Ethnic Variations in Commercial Land-Use in Los Angeles." Ph.D. dissertation, University of California, Los Angeles, 1969.
——. "An Inter-Ethnic Analysis of Retail and Service Functions in Los Angeles County, California." *Proceedings,* II (1970), 62–67.
——. "Ethnic Variations in Los Angeles Business Patterns." *Annals,* LXI (December 1971), 736–43.
Hart, John F. "Functions and Occupational Structures of Cities of the American South." *Annals,* XLV (September 1955), 269–86.

Katzman, Martin T. "Ethnic Geography and Regional Economics." *Economic Geography*, XLV (January 1969), 45–52.

Lewis, G. M. "Levels of Living in the Northeastern United States: A New Approach to Regional Geography." *Transactions of the Institute of British Geographers*, LV (1968), 11–37.

Marge, Gail B. "A Functional Analysis of Land Use Patterns in the Negro Shopping Areas of Raleigh and Charlotte, North Carolina." Master's thesis, University of North Carolina, 1969.

Maxwell, Lawrence E. "Residential Distribution of Occupations in Los Angeles," 1966.

Morrill, Richard L., et al. "Factors Influencing Distances Traveled to Hospitals." *Economic Geography*, XLVI (April 1970), 161–71.

Nelson, Irene J. "Opportunities for Geographical Research on the Rise of the Negro in the Southern Economy." *Southeastern Geographer*, XI (November 1971), 145–48.

Peet, Richard. "Outline for a Second-Year Course on the Socioeconomic Geography of Human Poverty." *Antipode*, II (December 1970), 1–34.

Pettyjohn, Leonard. "Changing Structure of Selected Retail Activities in a Racially Changing Neighborhood." Master's thesis, University of Wisconsin, 1967.

Pred, Allan. "Business Thoroughfares as Expressions of Urban Negro Culture." *Economic Geography*, XXXIX (July 1963), 364–71.

Rose, Harold M. "The Structure of Retail Trade in a Racially Changing Trade Area." *Geographical Analysis*, II (April 1970), 135–48.

Stiffer, Larry W. "Negro Participation in Manufacturing: A Geographical Appraisal of North Carolina." Master's thesis, University of North Carolina, 1966.

Wheeler, James O. "Some Effects of Occupational Status on Work-Trips." *Journal of Regional Science*, IX (April 1969), 69–77.

——. "Transportation Problems in Negro Ghettos." *Sociology and Social Research*, LII (January 1969), 171–79.

——. "Work-Trip Length and the Ghetto." *Land Economics*, XLIV (March 1968), 107–12.

Areal Patterns of Race and Education

Black, Blanton, E. "The Impact of Extension Education Program on Rural Negroes in Georgia, 1914–1964." Master's thesis, University of Georgia, 1971.

Donaldson, Fred. "The Geography of Black America: Three Approaches." *Journal of Geography*, LXXI (October 1972), 414–21.

Deskins, Donald R., Jr., and Speil, Linda J. "The Status of Blacks in American Geography: 1970." *The Professional Geographer*, XXIII (October 1971), 283–89.

Evans, Jeanette. "An Analysis of Relevance of Education in Geography to Blacks." Master's thesis, University of Washington, 1972.

Florin, John W. "The Diffusion of the Decision to Integrate: Southern School Desegregation, 1954–1964." *Southeastern Geographer*, XI (November 1971), 139–44.

Henderson, Janet St. Cyr, and Hart, John F. "The Development and Spatial Patterns of Black Colleges." *Southeastern Geographer*, XI (November 1971), 133–38.

Horvath, Ronald J.; Deskins, Donald R., Jr.; and Larimore, Ann E. "Activity Concerning Black America in University Departments Granting M.A. and Ph.D. Degrees in Geography." *The Professional Geographer*, XXI (May 1969), 137–39.

Hunter, John M. "Teaching to Eliminate Black-White Racism: An Educational Systems Approach." *Journal of Geography*, LXXI (February 1972), 87–95.

Jenkins, Michael A., and Shepherd, John W. "Decentralizing High School Administration in Detroit: An Evaluation of Alternative Strategies of Political Control." *Economic Geography*, XXXXVIII (January 1972), 95–106.

Jones, Mary Somerville. "The Racial Factor in School Districting: The Chapel Hill, North Carolina Case." Master's thesis, University of North Carolina, 1971.

Larimore, Ann E.; Scott, Earl P.; and Deskins, Donald R., Jr. "Geographic Activity at Predominantly Negro Colleges and Universities: A Survey." *The Professional Geographer*, XXI (May 1969), 140–44.

Larson, Robert C. "An Analysis of the Distribution of Education Levels Within the City." Master's thesis, University of Cincinnati, 1970.

Sadezky, Hannelore. "The Geographical Patterns of School Desegregation in the South." Master's thesis, Michigan State University, 1965.

Shannon, Gary W. "Residential Distribution and Travel Patterns: A Case Study of Detroit Elementary School Teachers." Master's thesis, University of Michigan, 1965.

Spatta, Carolyn L. "Regionalization: One Adjustment to Racial Imbalance in the Ann Arbor Schools." Master's thesis, University of Michigan, 1968.

Speigner, Theodore R. "Critical Shortage of Black Geography Teachers." *Journal of Geography*, LXVIII (October 1969), 388–89.

Steinbrink, John E. "The Effectiveness of Advance Organizers for Teaching Geography to Disadvantaged Rural Black Elementary Students." Ed.D. dissertation, University of Georgia, 1970.

URBAN RACIAL PATTERNS

Adams, John S. "The Geography of Riots and Civil Disorders in the 1960's." *Economic Geography*, XXXXVIII (January 1972), 24–42.

——, and Sanders, Ralph S. "Urban Residential Structure and the Location of Stress in Ghettos." *Earth and Mineral Science*, XXXVIII (January 1968), 29–32.

Adamson, John C. "The Relationship Between the Commuting Problems and Job Opportunities for the Negroes in the City of Terre Haute, Indiana." Master's thesis, Indiana University, 1972.

Adjei-Barwuah, Barfour. "Socio-Economic Regions in the Louisville Ghetto." Ph.D. dissertation, Indiana University, 1972.

——, and Rose, Harold M. "Some Comparative Aspects of the West African Zongo and the Black American Ghetto." *Geography of the Ghetto*. Perspectives in Geography, Vol. II. Edited by Harold M. Rose. Dekalb, Illinois: Northern Illinois University Press, 1972.

Anderson, Marc B. "Racial Discrimination in Detroit: A Spatial Analysis of Racism." Master's thesis, Wayne State University, 1969.

Brown, William H., Jr. "Access to Housing: The Role of the Real Estate Industry." *Economic Geography*, XXXXVIII (January 1972), 66–78.

——. "Class Aspects of Residential Development and Choice in the Oakland Black Community." Ph.D. dissertation, University of California, Berkeley, 1970.

Bunge, William. "Discussion Paper # 1." *Field Notes*, Detroit Geographical Expedition (1968).

Bush, Gordan. "An Analysis of the First Year Action Program of the East St. Louis Model City Program." Master's thesis, Southern Illinois University, Edwardsville, 1971.

Clark, W. A. V. "Patterns of Black Intra-Urban Mobility and Restricted Relocation Opportunities." *Geography of the Ghetto*. Perspectives in Geography, Vol. II. Edited by Harold M. Rose. Dekalb, Illinois: Northern Illinois University Press, 1972.

Colenutt, Robert J. "Do Alternatives Exist for Central Cities?" *Geography of the Ghetto*. Perspectives in Geography, Vol. II. Edited by Harold M. Rose. Dekalb, Illinois: Northern Illinois University Press, 1972.

Cozzens, Susan. "The Children of Cass Corridor." *Field Notes*, Discussion Paper No. 3 (1971), 22–24.

Creveling, Harold F. "Mapping Cultural Groups in an American Industrial City." *Annals*, XLIII (June 1953), 162–63.*

——. "Mapping Cultural Groups in an American Industrial City." *Economic Geography*, XL (July 1964), 221–38.

Darden, Joe T. "The Spatial Dynamics of Residential Segregation of Afro-Americans in Pittsburgh." Ph.D. dissertation, University of Pittsburgh, 1972.

Davies, Shane. "The Reverse Commuter Transit Problem in Indianapolis." *Geography of the Ghetto*. Perspectives in Geography, Vol. II. Edited by Harold M. Rose. Dekalb, Illinois: Northern Illinois University Press, 1972.

——, and Fowler, Gary L. "The Disadvantaged Urban Migrant in Indianapolis." *Economic Geography*, XXXXVIII (April 1972), 153–67.

Davis, J. T. "Sources of Variation in Housing Values in Washington, D.C." *Geographical Analysis,* III (January 1971), 63–76.

Deskins, Donald R., Jr. "Negro Settlement in Ann Arbor." Master's thesis, University of Michigan, 1963.

———. "Race as an Element in the Intra-City Regionalization of Atlanta's Population." *Southeastern Geographer,* XI (November 1971), 90–100.

———. "Race, Recreation, and Region in the United States." *Geography of the Ghetto.* Perspectives in Geography, Vol. II. Edited by Harold M. Rose. Dekalb, Illinois: Northern Illinois University Press, 1972.

———; Ward, David; and Rose, Harold M. "Interaction Patterns and the Spatial Form of the Ghetto." Northwestern University, Department of Geography, *Special Publication No. 3* (1970).

Dever, Alan G. "Intra-Urban Variation of Leukemia Occurrences." Ph.D. dissertation, University of Michigan, 1971.

———. "Leukemia in Atlanta, Georgia." *Southeastern Geographer,* XII (November 1972), 91–100.

Dickinson, Joshua C., III; Gray, Robert L.; and Smith, David M. "The 'Quality of Life' in Gainesville, Florida: An Application of Territorial Indicators." *Southeastern Geographer,* XII (November 1972), 121–32.

Dobbratz, Joan. "An Analysis of the Southwest Urban Renewal Project Area in Terre Haute, Indiana." Master's thesis, Indiana State University, 1967.

Dudas, John J., and Lonbrake, David B. "Problems and Future Directions of Residential Integration: The Local Application of Federally Funded Programs in Dade County, Florida." *Southeastern Geographer,* XI (November 1971), 157–68.

Earickson, Robert J. "The Case for Decentralizing Cook County Hospital." *Hospital Planning Council for Metropolitan Chicago,* Working Paper, Vol. III, No. 4 (1968).

———. "Spatial Interaction of Patients, Physician and Hospitals—A Behavioristic Approach." Ph.D. dissertation, University of Washington, 1968.

———. *The Spatial Behavior of Hospital Patients.* Department of Geography, University of Chicago, Research Paper No. 124 (1970).

Edwards, O. L. "Patterns of Residential Segregation Within a Metropolitan Ghetto." *Demography,* VII (May 1970).

Elgie, Robert. "Rural Immigration, Urban Ghettoization, and Their Consequences." *Antipode,* II (December 1970), 35–54.

Evans, Bruce. "Elwood Park and Urban Renewal." *Field Notes,* Discussion Paper No. 3 (1971), 50–53.

Frueh, Linda K. "A Factor Analytic Investigation of the Internal Structure of the Black Community in Detroit." Master's thesis, Western Illinois University, 1971.

Fuchs, Roland J. "Intraurban Variation of Residential Quality." Ph.D. dissertation, Clark University, 1971.

Gale, Stephen, and Katzman, David M. "Black Communities: A Program for Inter-disciplinary Research." *Geography of the Ghetto.* Perspectives in Geography, Vol. II. Edited by Harold M. Rose. Dekalb, Illinois: Northern Illinois University Press, 1972.

Geale, Paul E. "Suburbanization Process in a Black Community: Pecoima, a Case Study." Master's thesis, California State University, Los Angeles, 1971.

Hansell, C. E. and Clark, W. A. V. "The Expansion of the Negro Ghetto in Milwaukee." *Tijdschrift voor Economicsche en Sociale Geografie,* LXI (March 1970), 267–77.

Hartshorn, Turman, A. "Inner City Residential Structure and Decline." *Annals,* LXI (March 1971), 72–96.

Harvey, David. "Revolutionary and Counter-Revolutionary Theory in Geography and the Problem of Ghetto Formation." *Geography of the Ghetto.* Perspectives in Geography, Vol. II. Edited by Harold M. Rose. Dekalb, Illinois: Northern Illinois University Press, 1972.

Heiges, Harvey E. "Intra-Urban Residential Movement in Seattle; 1962–1967." Ph.D. dissertation, University of Washington, 1968.

Hodgart, Robert L. "The Process of Expansion of the Negro Ghetto in Cities of the Northern United States: A Case Study of Cleveland, Ohio." Master's thesis, Pennsylvania State University, 1969.

Holdemaker, Sally B. "The Spatial Patterns of Negroes and White Middle Class: St. Louis, Missouri, 1960." Master's thesis, Southern Illinois University, Edwardsville, 1971.

Horvath, Ronald J. "The 'Detroit' Geographical Expedition and Institute Experience." *Antipode,* III (November 1971), 73–85.

Johnson, Lawrence E. "The Negro Community in Oroville, California." Master's thesis, Chico State College, 1970.

Kendall, Paul L. "Westwood, Dayton, Ohio: An Urban Geographic Study of Racial Transition." Master's thesis, Miami University, 1960.

Knos, Duane S. "The Distribution of Substandard Housing, Kansas City, Missouri." Ph.D. dissertation, University of Iowa, 1956.

Korsok, Albert J. "Residential Structure of East St. Louis, Illinois." Ph.D. dissertation, University of Illinois, 1959.

Ley, David Frederick. "The Black Inner City as Frontier Outpost: Images and Behavior of a Philadelphia Neighborhood." Ph.D. dissertation, Pennsylvania State University, 1972.

Lowry, Mark, II. "Racial Segregation: A Geographical Adaptation and Analysis." *Journal of Geography,* LXXI (January 1972), 28–40.

Maxwell, Lawrence. "Segregation by Income in Residential Areas of Large United States Cities." Ph.D. dissertation, University of California, Los Angeles, 1972.

McColl, Robert W. "Creating Ghettos: Manipulating Social Space in the Real World and the Classroom." *Journal of Geography,* LXXI (November 1972), 496–502.

Mercer, John. "Housing Quality and the Ghetto." *Geography of the*

Ghetto. Perspectives in Geography, Vol. II. Edited by Harold M. Rose. Dekalb, Illinois: Northern Illinois University Press, 1972.

Meyer, David R. "Classification of SMSA's Based upon Characteristics of Their Nonwhite Populations." *Classification of Cities: New Methods and Evolving Uses.* Edited by Brian J. L. Berry. New York: International City Managers Association and Resources for the Future, 1971.

——. "Implications of Some Recommended Alternative Urban Strategies for Black Residential Choice." *Geography of the Ghetto.* Perspectives in Geography, Vol. II. Edited by Harold M. Rose. Dekalb, Illinois: Northern Illinois University Press, 1972.

——. "Spatial Variation of Black Households in Cities Within a Residential Choice Framework." Ph.D. dissertation, University of Chicago, 1970, published as Department of Geography, Research Paper No. 129.

Meyer, Douglas K. "The Changing Negro Residential Patterns in Lansing, Michigan, 1850–1969." Ph.D. dissertation, Michigan State University, 1970.

Morrill, Richard. "A Geographical Perspective of the Black Ghetto." *Geography of the Ghetto.* Perspectives in Geography, Vol. II. Edited by Harold M. Rose. Dekalb, Illinois: Northern Illinois University Press, 1972.

——. "The Negro Ghetto: Problems and Alternatives." *The Geographical Review,* LV (July 1965), 339–61.

——. "The Persistence of the Black Ghetto as Spatial Separation." *Southeastern Geographer,* XI (November 1971), 149–56.

——, and Earickson, R. J. "Hospital Variation and Patient Travel Distance." *Inquiry,* V (January 1968), 26–34.

——. "Location Efficiency of Chicago Hospitals: An Experimental Model." *Health Services Research,* IV (March 1969), 128–41.

Price, Thomas A. "Negro Store-Front Churches in San Francisco: A Study of their Distribution in Selected Neighborhoods." Master's thesis, San Francisco State College, 1968.

Pyle, Gerald. "Heart Disease, Cancer and Stroke in Chicago: A Geographical Analysis with Facilities Plans for 1980." Ph.D. dissertation, University of Chicago, 1970, published as Department of Geography, Research Paper No. 134.

Rees, Phillip H. "The Factorial Ecology of Metropolitan Chicago, 1960." Master's thesis, University of Chicago, 1968.

Ritter, Frederic A. "Toward a Geography of the Negro in the City." *Journal of Geography,* LXX (March 1971), 150–56.

Rose, Harold M. "The All-Negro Town: Its Evolution and Function." *The Geographical Review,* LV (July 1965), 362–81.

——. "The Development of an Urban Subsystem: The Case of the Negro Ghetto." *Annals,* LX (March 1970), 1–17.

——, ed. *Geography of the Ghetto.* Perspectives in Geography, Vol. II. Dekalb, Illinois: Northern Illinois University, 1972.

——. "The Origins and Patterns of Development of Urban Black Social Areas." *Journal of Geography*, LXVIII (September 1969), 326–32.

——. *Social Process in the City: Race and Urban Residential Choice.* Commission on College Geography, Resource Paper Number 6, Association of American Geographers, 1969.

——. "The Spatial Development of Black Residential Subsystems." *Economic Geography*, XXXXVIII (January 1972), 43–65.

Roseman, Curtis C., and Bullamore, Henry W. "Factorial Ecologies of Urban Black Communities." *Geography of the Ghetto.* Perspectives in Geography, Vol. II. Edited by Harold M. Rose. Dekalb, Illinois: Northern Illinois University Press, 1972.

Salisbury, Howard. "The Demilitarized Zones." Ph.D. dissertation, University of California, Los Angeles, 1971.

——. "The State Within a State: Some Comparisons Between the Urban Ghetto and the Insurgent State." *The Professional Geographer*, XXIII (April 1971), 105–12.

Salter, Paul S., and Mings, Robert C. "A Geographical Aspect of the 1968 Miami Racial Disturbances: A Preliminary Investigation." *The Professional Geographer*, XXI (May 1969), 79–86.

Sanders, Ralph S. "Spatial Trends in Age Structure Changes within the Cleveland Ghetto: 1940–1965." Master's thesis, Pennsylvania State University, 1968.

——, and Adams, John S. "Age Structure in Expanding Ghetto-Space; Cleveland, Ohio, 1940–1965." *Southeastern Geographer*, XI (November 1971), 121–32.

Seig, Louis. "Concepts of 'Ghetto', A Geography of Minority Groups." *The Professional Geographer*, XXIII (January 1971), 1–4.

Setlow, Marcie L. "Metropolitan Open Housing Ordinance in Illinois: Their Effectiveness as a Deterrent to Segregated Housing." Master's thesis, University of Chicago, 1968.

Simmons, James W. "Changing Residence in the City: A Review of Intra-urban Mobility." *The Geographical Review*, LVIII (October 1968), 622–51.

Snyder, Roger. "An Analysis of Travel Patterns from Selected Neighborhoods in Detroit." Master's thesis, Wayne State University, 1970.

Sylvester, Robert. "Grand River-Oakman Boulevard Region." *Field Notes*, Discussion Paper No. 3 (1971), 47–49.

Taylor, Martin, et al. "Mack Avenue and Bloomfield Hills." *Field Notes*, Discussion Paper No. 3 (1971), 19–21.

Todd, William J. "Factor-Analytic Black-White Polarization in Milwaukee, 1950–1970." Master's thesis, Indiana State University, 1972.

Truesdale, Frank, et al. "Everybody Was Eating Back Then." *Field Notes*, Discussion Paper No. 3 (1971), 39–42.

Venning, Robert S. "Urban Renewal and the Social Geography of Hyde Park." Master's thesis, University of Chicago, 1966.

Walker, Earl. "The Impact of Urban Renewal on the Los Angeles Sub-community of Sawtelle." Master's thesis, University of California, Los Angeles, 1968.

Ward, Robert, Jr. "The Death of 12th Street." *Field Notes*, Discussion Paper No. 3 (1971), 36–38.

Warren, Gwendolyn. "About the Work in Detroit." *Field Notes*, Discussion Paper No. 3 (1971), 10–16.

———. "No Rat Walls on Bewick." *Field Notes*, Discussion Paper No. 3 (1971), 25–35.

Wheeler, James O. "The Spatial Interaction of Blacks in Metropolitan Areas." *Southeastern Geographer*, XI (November 1971), 101–12.

Wolfe, Jacqueline. "The Changing Pattern of Residence of the Negro in Pittsburgh, Pennsylvania, 1930–1960." Master's thesis, University of Pittsburgh, 1964.

Zentefis, Demetrios A. "Uptown Chicago—A Community in Transition, 1929–1970." Master's thesis, Western Illinois University, 1971.

POLITICAL-ELECTORAL GEOGRAPHY OF BLACK AMERICA

Balmer, Gary L. "A Spatial Analysis of Racially Mixed Voting Behavior." Master's thesis, University of Pennsylvania, 1970.

Bean, F. "Political Regionalism in an Urban Setting: Pittsburgh, Pennsylvania, 1948–1964." Master's thesis, University of Pittsburgh, 1966.

Brunn, Stanley; Hoffman, Wayne; and Romsa, Gerald. "Some Spatial Considerations of the Flint Open Housing Referendum." *Proceedings* (1969), 26–31.

———. "The Spatial Response of Negroes and Whites Toward Open Housing: The Flint Referendum." *Annals*, LX (March 1970), 18–36.

Buntzman, Gabriel F. "Negro Voting in the Electoral Geography of Raleigh, North Carolina." Master's thesis, University of North Carolina, 1970.

Bushman, Donald O., and Stanley, William R. "State Senate Reapportionment in the Southeast." *Annals*, LXI (December 1971), 654–70.

Clodfelter, C. "Political Regions of the City: An Analysis of Voting in Cincinnati." Master's thesis, Clark University, 1961.

Dakan, A. Williams. "Electoral and Population Geography of South-Central Los Angeles." *Yearbook of the Association of Pacific Coast Geographers*, XXXI (1969), 135–43.

———. "Population and Electoral Geography of Central Los Angeles." Master's thesis, University of California, Los Angeles, 1970.

Ford, Lawrence L. "The Areal Variation in Negro Registration Levels and Changes in Those Levels During the 1956–1967 Time Period in Louisiana." Master's thesis, Ohio State University, 1967.

Fuller, Ross. "Negro Voting Patterns in Akron, Ohio." Master's thesis, Kent State University, 1968.

Graham, Todd P. "Ethnic Concentrations and Socio-Political Patterns of Syracuse and Rochester, New York, 1946–1962." Master's thesis, Syracuse University, 1965.

Hoffman, Wayne L. "A Comparative Analysis of Urban Non-Partisan Voting Referendums: A Factor Analysis Solution." Ph.D. dissertation, University of Florida, 1970.

———. "A Statistical and Cartographic Analysis of the 1954 and 1964 Urban Renewal Referendums for Columbus, Ohio." Master's thesis, Ohio State University, 1966.

Jones, Jean. "The Political Redistricting of Detroit." *Field Notes*, Discussion Paper No. 3 (1971), 43–44.

Kasperson, Roger E. "Toward a Geography of Urban Politics: Chicago, A Case Study." *Economic Geography*, XLI (April 1965), 95–107.

Kory, William B. "Political Significance of Population Homogeneity: A Pittsburgh Example." *The Professional Geographer*, XXIV (May 1972), 118–22.

Lewis, Peirce F. "Geography in the Politics of Flint." Ph.D. dissertation, University of Michigan, 1957.

———. "Impact of Negro Migration on Electoral Geography in the Northern City." *Annals*, LIII (December 1963), 604.*

———. "Impact of Negro Migration on the Electoral Geography of Flint, Michigan, 1932–1962: A Cartographic Analysis." *Annals*, LV (March 1965), 1–25.

Marr, Paul D. "Functional and Spatial Innovation in the Delivery of Governmental Social Services." *Geography of the Ghetto*. Perspectives in Geography, Vol. II. Edited by Harold M. Rose. Dekalb, Illinois: Northern Illinois University Press, 1972.

McPhail, I. R. "The Vote for Mayor of Los Angeles in 1969." *Annals*, LXI (December 1971), 744–58.

Proudfoot, Malcolm J. "Chicago's Fragmented Political Structure." *The Geographical Review*, XLVII (January 1957), 106–17.

Towle, Jerry. "The Area Base of Southern Democratic Strength 1920–1960." Master's thesis, Southern Illinois University, Carbondale, 1965.

Van Duzer, E. F. "An Analysis of the Difference in Republican Presidential Vote in Cities and Their Suburbs." Ph.D. dissertation, University of Iowa, 1962.

BLACK POPULATION-MIGRATION TRENDS

Bennett, David G. "Population of North Carolina: A Study of Selected Characteristics." Master's thesis, Michigan State University, 1964.

Bogue, Donald J. "The Geography of Recent Population Trends in the United States." *Annals*, XLIII (June 1953), 162–63.*
——. "The Geography of Recent Population Trends in the United States." *Annals*, XLIV (March 1954), 124–34.
Brandon, Donald G. "Migration of Negroes in the United States, 1910–1947." Ph.D. dissertation, Columbia University, 1949.
Brown, Lawrence A., and Moore, Eric G. "The Intra-Urban Migration Process: A Perspective." *Geografiska Annaler*, Series B, LII (January 1970), 1–13.
Bryant, Nathaniel H. "Black Migration and the Settlement of the Puget Sound Country." Master's thesis, University of Washington, 1972.
Buford, Carolyn B. "The Distribution of Negroes in Maryland, 1850–1860." Master's thesis, Catholic University of America, 1956.
Calef, Wesley C., and Nelson, Howard J. "Distribution of Negro Population in the United States." *The Geographical Review*, XLVI (January 1956), 82–97.
Carter, Bernard. "An Investigation of the Black Population Concentration in the Ohio-Mississippi River Confluence Area of Illinois." Master's thesis, Southern Illinois University, Carbondale, 1969.
Cary, George W. "The Regional Interpretation of Manhattan Population and Housing Patterns Through Factor Analysis." *The Geographical Review*, LVI (October 1966), 351–69.
——; Macomber, L.; and Greenberg, M. "Educational and Demographic Factors in the Urban Geography of Washington, D.C." *The Geographical Review*, LVIII (October 1968), 515–37.
Coulson, Michael R. C. "The Distribution of Population Age Structures in Kansas City." *Annals*, LVIII (March 1968), 155–76.
Daview, C. Shane, and Fowler, Gary L. "The Disadvantaged Black Female Household Head: Migrants to Indianapolis." *Southeastern Geographer*, XI (November 1971), 113–20.
Dyer, Donald R. "The Place of Origin of Florida's Population." *Annals*, XLII (December 1952), 283–94.
Ernst, Robert T. "Negro Migration: A Review of the Literature." Master's thesis, St. Louis University, 1969.
Garver, John B., Jr. "Selected Aspects of the Geography of Poverty." Master's thesis, Syracuse University, 1966.
Hart, John F. "Censal Year of Maximum Negro Population in the Eastern United States." *Annals*, LI (June 1959), 183–84.*
——. "The Changing Distribution of the American Negro." *Annals*, L (September 1960), 242–66.
——. "Negro Migration in the United States." *Annals*, XLVIII (September 1958), 268.*
Hiltner, John. "Negro Migration in a Section of Toledo, Ohio." *Annals*, LVIII (March 1967), 177.*
Innis, Donald Q. "Human Ecology in Jamaica." Ph.D. dissertation, University of California, Berkeley, 1958.

Jordan, Terry G. "Population Origins in Texas, 1850." *The Geographical Review*, LIX (January 1969), 83–103.

Kantrowitz, Nathan. "Negro and Puerto Rican Populations of New York City in the Twentieth Century." *Studies in Urban Geography*, I (1969).

Klove, Robert C. "Urban and Metropolitan Population Trends in the United States." *Annals*, XLIV (March 1954), 222.*

Lewis, G. M. "The Distribution of the Negro in the Coterminous United States." *Geography*, LIV (November 1969), 411–16.

Lewis, Lawrence T. "Some Migration Models: Their Applicability to Negro Urban Migration." Ph.D. dissertation, Clark University, 1971.

Lowry, Mark, II. "Population and Race in Mississippi, 1940–1960." *Annals*, LXI (September 1971), 576–88.

——. "Population and Socioeconomic Well-Being in Mississippi." Master's thesis, Syracuse University, 1968.

——. "Race and Socioeconomic Well-Being: A Geographical Analysis of the Mississippi Case." *The Geographical Review*, LX (October 1970), 511–28.

Luna, Telesforo W. "Changes in the Distribution Pattern of Negro Population in the United States." Master's thesis, Clark University, 1956.

Marsh, Robert E. "Negro-White Differences in Geographic Mobility." *United States Social Security Bulletin*, XXX (May 1967), 8–19.

Mathews, Diller G., Jr. "The Distribution of the Negro Population of the District of Columbia, 1800–1960." Master's thesis, Catholic University of America, 1967.

McDonald, Patrick. "Migration Patterns to Val Verde Park." *Yearbook of the Association of Pacific Coast Geographers*, XXXII (1970), 183.*

Mikel, Linda L. "Group Membership and Migration: A Comparison of Negro and White Migration from Mississippi." Master's thesis, Indiana University, 1970.

Pathak, Chittaranjan. "Growth Patterns of Raleigh, North Carolina." Ph.D. dissertation, University of North Carolina, 1963.

——. "A Spatial Analysis of Urban Population Distribution in Raleigh, North Carolina." *Southeastern Geographer*, IV (1964), 41–50.

Peet, Richard. "Poor, Hungry America." *The Professional Geographer*, XXIII (April 1971), 99–104.

Phillips, Coy T. "Population Distribution and Trends in North Carolina." *Journal of Geography*, LV (April 1956), 182–93.

Price, Edward R., Jr. "The East Tennessee Melungeons: A Mixed-Blood Strain." *Annals*, XXXIX (March 1949), 68.*

——. "A Geographic Analysis of White-Negro Indian Racial Mixtures in Eastern United States." *Annals*, XLIII (June 1953), 138–55.

——. "The Melungeons: A Mixed-Blood Strain of the Southern Appalachians." *The Geographical Review*, XLI (April 1951), 256–71.

——. "Mixed-Blood Populations of the Eastern United States." *Annals,* XL (June 1950), 143.*
——. "Mixed-Blood Populations of the Eastern United States." *Annals,* XLI (June 1951), 175.*
——. "Mixed-Blood Populations of Eastern United States as to Origins, Localizations, and Persistence." Ph.D. dissertation, University of California, Berkeley, 1950.
Ramjoue, George. "The Negro in Utah: A Geographical Study in Population." Master's thesis, University of Utah, 1968.
Rauch, Sister Delores. "Impact of Population Changes in the Central Area of Milwaukee upon Catholic Parochial Schools, 1940–1970." Master's thesis, University of Wisconsin, Milwaukee, 1968.
Reckford, Gordon. "The Geography of Poverty in the United States." *Problems and Trends in American Geography.* Edited by Saul B. Cohen (New York: Basic Books, Inc., 1967).
Rose, Harold M. "Metropolitan Miami's Changing Negro Population, 1950–1960." *Economic Geography,* XL (July 1964), 221–38.
——. "Migration and the Changing Status of Black Americans." *The Geographical Review,* LXI (April 1971), 297–99.
Tower, J. Allen. "The Negro Exodus from the South." *Annals,* XLV (September 1955), 301–02.*
Van Duzer, E. F. "An Analysis of the Difference in Republican Presidential Vote in Cities and Their Suburbs." Ph.D. dissertation, University of Iowa, 1962.
Vaneselow, Glenn W. "Infant Mortality and Socioeconomic Conditions in the United States." Master's thesis, Oregon State University, 1970.
Vent, Herbert. "Some Population Trends in Mississippi." *Journal of Geography,* LIII (April 1954), 141–43.
Wacker, Peter O. "The Changing Geography of Black Population of New Jersey, 1810–1860: A Preliminary View." *Proceedings,* III (1971), 174–78.
Wohlenberg, Ernst H. "The Geography of Poverty in the United States: A Spatial Study of the Nation's Poor." Ph.D. dissertation, University of Washington, 1970.
Woodruff, James F. "Some Characteristics of the Distribution and Composition of the Slave Population in 1850." *Annals,* LII (September 1962), 370.*
Zelinsky, Wilbur. "The Population Geography of the Free Negro in Ante-Bellum America." *Population Studies,* III (March 1950), 386–401.
——. "Population Patterns in Georgia." Ph.D. dissertation, University of California, Berkeley, 1953.

RURAL BLACK GEOGRAPHIC ENVIRONMENT

Aiken, Charles S. "Transitional Plantation Occupance in Tate County, Mississippi." Master's thesis, University of Georgia, 1962.

Bohland, James R. "A Geographical Analysis of Single Dwelling Settlement in Northwest Georgia." Ph.D. dissertation, University of Georgia, 1970.

Carter, Bernard. "An Investigation of the Black Population Concentration in the Ohio-Mississippi River Confluence Area of Illinois." Master's thesis, Southern Illinois University, Carbondale, 1969.

Christensen, David E. "Rural Occupance in Transition: Lee and Sumpter Counties, Georgia." Ph.D. dissertation, University of Chicago, 1956, published as Department of Geography, Research Paper No. 43.

Cooper, Sherwin H. "The Rural Settlement of the Lower Savannah River Basin in Georgia." Ph.D. dissertation, University of Michigan, 1959.

Crisler, Robert M. "An Experiment in Regional Delimitation: The Little Dixie Region of Missouri." Ph.D. dissertation, Northwestern University, 1949.

——. "The Regional Status of Little Dixie in Missouri and Little Egypt in Illinois." *Journal of Geography,* XLIX (November 1950), 337–43.

Dambaugh, Luella N. "The Role of Migratory Agricultural Labor in South Florida." *Annals,* LII (September 1958), 258.*

Hart, John F. "A Rural Retreat for Northern Negroes." *The Geographical Review,* L (April 1960), 147–68.

Hazel, Joseph A. "The Geography of Negro Agricultural Slavery in Alabama, Florida and Mississippi, circa 1860." Ph.D. dissertation, Columbia University, 1972.

Jones, Dennis Eugene, "Spatial Patterns of Racial Participation at Previously Black State Parks in North Carolina." Master's thesis, University of North Carolina, 1972.

Jordan, Terry B. "The Imprint of the Upper and Lower South on Mid-Nineteenth Century Texas." *Annals,* LVII (December 1967), 667–90.

Kelley, Arthell. "Some Aspects of the Geography of the Yazzo Basin, Mississippi." Ph.D. dissertation, University of Nebraska, 1954.

Klungness, Paul H. "Negro Population Density and Agricultural Changes: The Case of North Carolina." Master's thesis, Syracuse University, 1970.

Knuth, Clarence P. "Early Immigration and Current Residential Patterns of Negroes in Southwestern Michigan." Ph.D. dissertation, University of Michigan, 1969.

Lamb, Robert B. "The Mule in Southern Agriculture." Ph.D. dissertation, University of California, Los Angeles, 1959.

Nobel, William A. "Sequent Occupance of Hopeton-Altama, 1816–1956." Master's thesis, University of Georgia, 1956.

Padgett, Herbert R. "Florida's Migratory Workers." Master's thesis, Florida State University, 1951.

Pardue, Edwin G. "A Geographic Study of Choctaw County, Oklahoma." Master's thesis, Oklahoma Agricultural and Mechanical College, 1949.

Prunty, Merle, Jr. "The Renaissance of the Southern Plantation." *The Geographical Review*, XLV (October 1955), 459–91.

Salter, Paul S. "Changing Economic Patterns of the South Carolina Sea Islands." Ph.D. dissertation, University of North Carolina, 1964.

Smith, Peter Craig. "Negro Hamlets and Gentlemen Farms: A Dichotomous Rural Settlement Pattern in Kentucky's Bluegrass Region." Ph.D. dissertation, University of Kentucky, 1972.

Stiffler, Larry W. "Negro Participation in Manufacturing: A Geographical Appraisal of North Carolina." Master's thesis, University of North Carolina, 1965.

Thompson, Alton C. "Spatial Variations in the Non-Agricultural Employment of North Carolina's Rural-Farm Population, 1960." Master's thesis, University of North Carolina, 1965.

Tower, J. Allen. "Cotton Change in Alabama, 1879–1946." *Economic Geography*, XXVI (January 1950), 6–28.

Wheeler, James O., and Brunn, Stanley D. "An Agricultural Ghetto: Negroes in Cass County, Michigan, 1845–1968." *The Geographical Review*, LIX (July 1969), 317–29.

——. "Negro Migration into Rural Southwestern Michigan." *The Geographical Review*, LVIII (April 1968), 214–30.

Winsor, Roger A. "The Geography of Poverty in Maricopa County, Arizona." Master's thesis, Arizona State University, 1966.

Woodruff, James F. "Some Characteristics of the Alabama Slave Population in 1850." *The Geographical Review*, LII (July 1962), 379–88.

——. "A Study of the Characteristics of the Alabama Slave Population in 1850." *Annals*, LI (December 1961), 427.*

Index